EUROPEAN HISTORY IN PERSPECTIVE

General Editor: Jeremy Black

By the mid-seventeenth century, several major European monarchies
were collapsing. Battered by incessant war and religious rebellion, rulers
clashed with landowners and clergy on whom they relied for territorial and
spiritual support. Nicholas Henshall argues that from this crisis emerged
a new deal. Monarchs reasserted traditional values and resolved to work
with, rather than against, their nobles and churches.

*The Zenith of European Monarchy and its Elites: The Politics of Culture,
1650–1750:*

- focuses on a previously neglected key elite bonding strategy
- explains how a common identity was forged by erecting cultural defences
  against outsiders
- demonstrates how the power and prestige of the ruling classes rose to
  unprecedented heights.

Essential reading for students and scholars of early modern European
history, this fascinating new study shows how the period 1650–1750 gains a
new coherence – as the pinnacle of Europe's monarchies and their elites.

**Nicholas Henshall** was formerly Head of History at Stockport Grammar
School and a tutor at the University of Manchester, as well as Editor of
*History Review* magazine. His previous publications include *the Myth of
Absolutism* (1992).

---

**European History in Perspective
Series Standing Order
ISBN 0–333–71694–9 hardcover
ISBN 0–333–69336–1 paperback**
(*outside North America only*)

# The Zenith of European Monarchy and its Elites

## The Politics of Culture, 1650–1750

NICHOLAS HENSHALL

palgrave
macmillan

First published 2010 by
PALGRAVE MACMILLAN

Palgrave Macmillan in the UK is an imprint of Macmillan Publishers Limited, registered in England, company number 785998, of Houndmills, Basingstoke, Hampshire RG21 6XS.

Palgrave Macmillan in the US is a division of St Martin's Press LLC, 175 Fifth Avenue, New York, NY 10010.

Palgrave Macmillan is the global academic imprint of the above companies and has companies and representatives throughout the world.

Palgrave® and Macmillan® are registered trademarks in the United States, the United Kingdom, Europe and other countries.

ISBN-13: 978–0–333–61390–0   hardback
ISBN-13: 978-0-333-61391-7   paperback

This book is printed on paper suitable for recycling and made from fully managed and sustained forest sources. Logging, pulping and manufacturing processes are expected to conform to the environmental regulations of the country of origin.

A catalogue record for this book is available from the British Library.

A catalog record for this book is available from the Library of Congress.

10  9  8  7  6  5  4  3  2  1
19  18  17  16  15  14  13  12  11  10

Transferred to Digital Printing in 2011

In memory of my parents

# Contents

# Acknowledgements

My greatest debt is to Jeremy Black, who paid me the compliment of commissioning this book. He also guided and encouraged me, as well as reading several drafts. Above all, during the long years of my inexplicable failure to finish the task, he resisted the temptation to complain. David Armitage supplied or recommended vital books and made himself available for several discussions. Colin Armstrong alerted me to the latest writing relevant to my project, posted me dozens of book reviews and queried some of my more far-fetched ideas. John Derry read the typescript at a late stage and generously gave me the benefit of his extensive experience. Tim Blanning and Derek Beales of Cambridge University influenced me without knowing it. Their twin mastery of cultural and political history is conspicuous by its rarity: the extent to which I have plundered their work is obvious throughout the text. Another such is David Starkey and I thank him for his lasting friendship and inspiration. I must also mention the influence of Theodore Rabb's *The Struggle for Stability in Early Modern Europe* (1975). We share the same starting point but end in totally different places. I am grateful to the staff of Cambridge University Library for finding and photocopying what I needed and to the Inter-Library Loan Service for its ability to meet my requirements swiftly and efficiently.

My family and friends learned to live with a book which apparently had no end. As a list would be rather long, I thank all of them collectively for their remarkably patient encouragement. Two years ago my old colleagues Jackson Towers and Stephen Cross suggested a period of social abstinence until my mission was accomplished. The former supervised what I can only call my confinement, as well as reading an early draft and correcting mistakes about seventeenth- and eighteenth-century music. Robin Taylor examined the final typescript with exceptional thoroughness and commented imaginatively and incisively. At a difficult time for himself William Hartley inspired me to keep going when I was flagging. Richard Griffiths helped me with German literature and waited patiently for the resumption of our regular visits to Italian restaurants. Graham Oxendale assisted expertly with technical aspects of the production of the final typescript. Stephen Lamley took over copy-editing and proof-reading when I became ill. I am deeply grateful to him.

To all these I am heavily indebted for whatever merits the result may possess. For what prove to be its defects I alone am responsible.

# Preface

It has been said that one does not write a book to state what one thinks but to *discover* what one thinks. This is certainly true in my case. I began with the intention of updating my views on absolute monarchy in the light of historiographical developments in the last two decades. I soon found that the cultural section of the intended book was outgrowing its allotted space. But the more I tested my cultural hypothesis the more it seemed to fit the facts. So I allowed it to expand.

The book is now intended to sit alongside my first volume, *The Myth of Absolutism* (1992). This dealt with the theory and practice of absolute monarchy as experienced in early-modern Europe. The present book deals with its cultural context and argues that absolute monarchy rested as much upon mentalities as on institutions. It also suggests that absolute monarchy and its agents had a major role in creating those mentalities – hence the book's sub-title, *The Politics of Culture.*

It is mainly addressed to students and scholars. I apologize to the former, who will have to get to grips with a book focused on culture. History students expect to activate their cultural antennae only when they tackle the Renaissance and the Enlightenment – and to a lesser extent when they study Louis XIV. I invite them to consider whether he was the only monarch to erect cultural props around his regime.

The structure of the book is simple. The Introduction sets the context, summarizes the historiography of the last two decades and adds something that I missed in my first book. In the early 1990s what is now familiar as the non-unified 'composite state' was a recent arrival on the historiographical scene. I mentioned it but its significance escaped me. It now seems clear to me that the fragility of early-modern composite states explains two things – the continuing and crucial role of elites as monarchs' partners in government, and the need for a strong cultural buttress supporting the whole structure. The latter arguably resulted in the creation of a coherent cultural identity for ruling elites. That is the hypothesis which is fleshed out and tested in the rest of the book.

Some areas of Europe have proved a problem. William St Clair's indispensable *The Reading Nation in the Romantic Period* (2004) deals mainly with Great Britain. There is no equivalent for the rest of the Continent. Nor are my Hungarian, Czech and Polish of the same standard as my English and French. In the 1650–1750 period few literary works were written in eastern European languages: those few are not translated. Readers should therefore not be alarmed if they hear more about western than eastern Europe. Most of the cultural developments considered here originated in western Europe anyway. And if the scope is geographically narrower than implied by the title, chronologically it is slightly wider. I have adhered fairly strictly to the 1650–1750 period and attempted to establish its integrity and coherence. But it has been necessary to stray slightly at both ends of the period in order to contrast it with what came before and afterwards. Establishing the character of an era can be a mainly static activity: establishing its uniqueness requires a shift of perspective.

I make no apology for frequently citing, alongside monographs and articles, several textbooks. These are all works in which distinguished editors or authors distil the historical wisdom of a lifetime. Some of them, especially the *Short Oxford History of Europe* series, consist of essays by different experts. As well as having validity in their own right, they can be of assistance in addressing the kind of regional problems mentioned above.

As a recent self-appointment to the ranks of cultural historian, I apologize for my lack of technical expertise. I have nothing to say about hermeneutics or the history of discourses. Nor am I expert in quantitative methods. Peter Burke's *Tradition and Innovation in Renaissance Italy* (1974) listed and analysed the background of 600 artists and writers. If anything on this scale exists for the 1650–1750 period, I have missed it. Nor do I possess the skills to compile such a database myself.

Instead I rely on the familiar rules of the historian's discipline. I have tried to avoid forcing the evidence and been struck by how well the hypothesis fitted most of the facts. Where it did not, I have said so. It must be admitted that there are distressingly few explicit statements of intent by contemporaries – whether about creating a cultural identity for elites, or adapting older art forms and value systems to new uses. Some of my conclusions should be regarded as tentative. Doubtless they will be.

# Introduction

On 30 January 1649 King Charles I of England and Scotland was beheaded with one blow of an axe wielded by an executioner in a mask and heavy disguise. In the following March, the monarchy was formally abolished and a republic declared. The House of Lords was abolished as 'useless and dangerous'. The Anglican Church and its prelates had already been abolished. They were replaced by a Presbyterian church without bishops. If ever there was an English Revolution, this was it.[1] France simultaneously produced a slightly less alarming sequence of events by omitting the drastic surgery. But on both sides of the Channel the bedrock alliance of king, lords and clergy was shaken, in one case to the ground.

No such calamity was to recur until the 1750s. Even then the explosion was not immediate, though signs of trouble were multiplying. The next revolution came in America in the 1770s, and finally in France in the 1780s. But between the mid-seventeenth and mid-eighteenth centuries Europe was initially in shock and then in recovery: certainly in western Europe, stability was preserved. This intervening period is the subject of all that follows.

Does history ever package itself so neatly into 100-year periods? Or is this merely a fantasy of a publishing industry which needs to chop it up in an orderly way? The reader must judge. It is argued here that in the 1650–1750 period absolute monarchy and its stately retinue of princes, prelates and aristocrats triumphed as never before or since. After the dust of the French Revolution and Napoleon had settled, dynastic monarchs and aristocrats were to retrieve some of their former power and glory. But, as lords of the earth and all they surveyed, the century between 1650 and 1750 was their last hurrah. It was the final age in which the masses were dominated by the largely unchallenged rule of priests and kings. So it had been for the previous 5,000 years.

1

A coherent epoch of roughly 100 years straddling two centuries is perhaps slightly less suspicious than alleged periods spanning exactly the seventeenth or eighteenth centuries. Here is an early statement of the artificiality of century divisions and of the pointlessness of studying them as if the lines they gouge across the historical process were anything other than arbitrary:

> To the art historian centuries rarely are neat and tidy units, which can be filed away under one simple heading. This is particularly true of the 18th century. The first half, even if we call it Rococo, is a continuation of the Baroque. ... Until about 1750 the arts stood in the service of architecture. Painters and sculptors did their most spectacular work in the decoration of churches and palaces. Their chief patrons were the church, kings, princes and nobles.[2]

Ettlinger's remarks, written forty years ago, were impressively prophetic. In the 1960s, while 1648 had long been seen as the end of one period and the start of another, few had proposed the mid-eighteenth century as a significant turning point. It has now acquired its champions.[3] The mid-seventeenth century has acquired even more.[4] Yet, as far as the present author is aware, no history has yet been written of the 1650–1750 period in Europe, framed by the so-called General Crisis of the 1640s and 1650s at one extremity and the era of Enlightenment and Revolution at the other.

## Problems and Crises

The Reformation of the sixteenth century had meant that monarchs could find themselves professing a different religion from that of some of their nobles and clergy. This was dangerous in an age when religion was not only the key to eternal salvation but also the cement which bonded government and society. The Reformation had ruptured relations between monarchs and their traditional aristocratic and ecclesiastical allies, and in France a religiously motivated nobility nearly brought down the state. The post-Reformation wars of religion stretched from the mid-sixteenth to the mid-seventeenth century, the international Thirty Years War (1618–48) being in some respects the last and greatest of them. The potential for conflict within ruling elites was thus fairly permanent in the early-modern period. The balance of forces between them and the crown was also precarious.[5]

In the 1640s and 1650s many European states simultaneously subsided into varying degrees of chaos. Contemporaries noticed this disturbing coincidence of crises. In 1643 Jeremiah Whittaker announced in his sermon to the English House of Commons that 'These days are days of shaking ... and this shaking is universal: the Palatinate, Bohemia, Germania, Catalonia, Portugal, Ireland, England.'[6] Though this perception was missed by subsequent historians until 1938,[7] these episodes are now collectively known as the 'General Crisis' of the seventeenth century. In France the ruler lost his capital for a year; in Spain he lost two mighty provinces, Catalonia and Portugal; in Denmark–Norway he lost his right to make unilateral decisions; in Poland he lost the Ukraine; in England he lost his head.

Charles I was supposedly the divinely appointed monarch of England, Scotland and Ireland. His beheading by his own subjects was perceived throughout Europe to fracture the seventeenth century's political, social, religious and cultural certainties. The keystone which held in place the edifice of church, state and society was demolished with one blow of the axe. The shock effect was immediate. Advance copies of *Eikon Basilike*, a commemorative volume celebrating his life and martyrdom, appeared on the day of his execution and the first print-run of the final version was available within the week. By the close of 1649 it had appeared in 35 editions in England and eight on the Continent.[8] Among other European hot spots, England was by far the most spectacular specimen of a world turned upside down. Once King Charles had been defeated in 1646 and the breakdown of press censorship had become total, blueprints had multiplied for establishing the kingdom of heaven on earth. Their creators regarded England as God's appointed location for the reign of King Jesus. A miscellany of self-appointed messiahs, millenarian fantasists, embryonic democrats, primitive communists and gentle anarchists jostled to instal their personal version of paradise. The values of the old hierarchical society were rejected and anything seemed possible.[9] The climax, the public execution of a divinely appointed monarch, was for early-modern Europe the equivalent of the destruction of New York's Twin Towers in 2001.

What had happened to wreck relations between monarchs and their subjects in so calamitous a manner? The loss of religious unity and subsequent religious wars were the most obvious cause. The restoration of religious consensus was therefore a high priority of most rulers during the 1650–1750 period. As for the revolts of the 1640s and 1650s, common to most of them was a provocative tax hike. This was targeted by rulers (bankrupted in the Thirty Years War) against the customary rights of nobles and provinces – and without the consent of their assemblies.[10] There was also a tendency, in the French monarchy especially, for royal officials picked from lower social groups to push aside established governing classes in order to bypass obstruction to royal initiatives. The opinions of people who mattered were ignored. Relations between monarchs and their elites therefore required fixing.

## Definitions

'Elites' is a useful word for historians. The *Who's Who* list of the seventeenth and eighteenth centuries, they were relied on by monarchs to manage their government, lead their armies and police their peasantry. Yet their study has only become academically respectable in the last thirty years. Before that, Marxist concerns were dominant. As recently as 1980 a historian of aristocratic politics was informed by a professor of Edinburgh University that the material condition of the masses was the only thing that mattered.[11]

Elites can be defined as substantial possessors of land and the unique wealth, power and status which it conferred.[12] Its unique allure is easy to explain. First, land in pre-industrial society was the most permanent of economic assets. Most elites recovered in the 1650–1750 period from preceding economic decline, and consolidated their estates on an unparalleled scale. Without this economic revival, funding of the arts by both aristocratic and ecclesiastical landowners would have dried up. This development was boosted by the growing popularity of the legal device of entail, enabling noble members of the elite to leave their property to eldest sons rather than dividing it between all their children and diluting aristocratic power. Second, land bestowed power. Authority everywhere was a function of landed property, though somewhat less at the governmental centre than in the localities. Third, ownership of land conferred unrivalled prestige and was the summit of social ambition. Awareness of status was heightened by tighter entry qualifications to the upper ranks of the elite, which emerged strengthened and consolidated. Sharper distinctions between the ranks of the social hierarchy made some people superior and most inferior. Stratification was already deeply etched into the face of society in the sixteenth century: in the seventeenth and eighteenth this procedure was intensified. Elites were more clearly distinguished from commoners, and defence of rank and status became an obsession.[13]

Most European elites consisted of nobles and lesser nobles (known in Britain as 'nobles' and 'gentry'). 'Aristocracy' signifies much the same as 'nobles', 'gentry' and 'elites', but has the ambiguity of *also* being used to indicate an elite within an elite – the tiny minority with immense wealth and power at the apex of the nobility.[14] In this book it will be used mainly in the former sense. Nobility was hereditary and, except in Russia, was endowed with political, judicial, fiscal and social privileges which differentiated elites from the common people. They were consulted by their monarch in representative assemblies, supervised local justice in their own courts, usually paid less tax than non-nobles and had a right to trial by their peers. Finally, alone among the population, they carried swords in civilian life – one of the greatest visual divides between gentlemen and commoners.[15] These entitlements were barely diminished by the monarchs of the 1650–1750 period, who were formerly supposed to have deployed their sovereign powers against noble privilege. Significant moves of this kind were actually initiated by the Enlightened despots who came after them and with whom they have probably been confused. Enlightened despots claimed far more sweeping autocratic powers than the monarchs of 1650–1750. Joseph II of Austria–Hungary consistently imposed reform from above, without consultation and on the basis of his own legislative authority.[16] And only an epic drive for centralization and uniformity after 1800, when most of western and central Europe fell within the Napoleonic Empire, succeeded in crippling (though not terminating) the nobility's feudal powers and privileges.[17]

Some historians throw the elite net more widely to include certain groups without land.[18] Their justification is that landless *nouveaux riches* could possess more wealth and power than many landowners. They are a variegated lot. On the Continent certain municipal, judicial and fiscal offices automatically conferred noble titles and could be purchased. In France their possessors were known as the new 'robe' nobility, as opposed to the old military nobility. In practice this distinction was often blurred, since more than half the ennobling offices sold in France between 1700 and 1788 fell into hands that were already noble.[19] Titles were also attached to higher service ranks in the army or bureaucracy and could be earned. Another eligible group was created by the rapid expansion of trade and finance in the 1650–1750 period. This produced a glut of new money among mercantile and banking communities, many of whom married into landed families: the English banker Hoare, who became a knight of the realm, was born the son of a horse-dealer. Further candidates for inclusion in the elite are the self-perpetuating civic oligarchs who ruled Europe's towns, some of whom were noble rather than mercantile by origin and many of whom were ennobled by their offices. The higher clergy must certainly be classified among the ruling elite: all monarchs regarded them as key allies and most of them were of noble birth. The nobility accounted for more than 78 per cent of all French bishops appointed by Louis XIV.[20]

Yet most of these originally landless groups were thought at the time to lack a vital ingredient. Many of them were nobles' younger sons, who had inherited no land. Increasingly in this period, elites subscribed to a corporate ethos which firmly differentiated between noble and commoner, and on this criterion a true noble was distinguished by ownership of a tenanted estate. Other hangers-on, though in practice members of the elite, were deemed substandard.[21] They might satisfy the power and wealth criteria but they failed the status test. Alternatively, some elites might pass on status and fail on cash count. This was underlined in 1789. Many obscure provincial nobles emerged to claim their right to sit alongside the aristocracy in the French Estates General. Some of them were dressed like scarecrows and their embarrassed colleagues had a whip-round to equip them with a decent suit of clothes.[22]

Working with elites were absolute monarchs. Absolute monarchy is hard to define precisely, since there was disagreement about its nature at the time and much debate among historians subsequently.[23] Its key characteristic was that the decisions of an absolute ruler could not be legitimately challenged: they were final. Absolute power was less about monarchs coercing their subjects than their subjects not coercing them. But in most monarchies that was not the end of the story. The notion of absolute power usually related only to a limited sphere of royal activities – mainly the royal prerogatives of appointing ministers and making war and peace, issues where someone had to have the last word.[24] That is why absolute power was paradoxically referred to as 'limited'. When the rights of nobles or provinces were at stake, an absolute monarch was expected to consult. Otherwise he was a despot – and in this period the 'd-word' was never a compliment.[25]

Unless deliberately confusing the two for reasons of propaganda, early-modern statesmen and commentators usually made this distinction between absolute and despotic power. Bossuet, official theorist of Louis XIV's regime, insisted on it.[26] But the Sun King's enemies naturally thought more in terms of propaganda and dismissed him as a despot. More recently, the distinction has been ignored by historians who argue that early-modern absolute monarchy stood for untrammelled autocracy.[27] Whether argued by contemporaries then or historians now, this is a serious oversimplification. In the early-modern period neither in theory nor in practice was absolute monarchy defined by the absence of representative institutions. The reason was simple: nearly all European monarchies had them.[28] If an absolute monarch is defined in this way, then the number of early-modern absolute monarchs was few or none.[29] In what follows, 'absolute monarchy' will denote a strong royal prerogative with a consultative component, which contrasted it with despotism. Consistent with this usage, around the end of the period, Blackstone defined England's regime as an absolute monarchy.[30] The vital distinction was between absolute monarchy and despotic monarchy, which took opposite views of the rights of subjects – not between absolute monarchy and limited monarchy, which were two aspects of the same thing.

Even worse is the confusion generated by the word 'absolutism' and its sidekick 'absolutist'.[31] They were coined in the nineteenth century for nineteenth-century purposes and have subsequently been used with hopeless inconsistency. Sometimes they denote what has just been defined as 'absolute monarchy', consulting when appropriate. Usually they mean despotism or something very close to it.[32] Though they are sometimes unavoidable, where possible 'absolutism' and 'absolutist' are banished from the rest of the book.

Great Britain looms large, in spite of the influential myth of its 'exceptionalism' in the context of Europe, present and past. The claim that Britain was different was carefully crafted in the 1650–1750 period as part of its emerging national identity.[33] It has flourished ever since – an outcome facilitated by the fact that British and European histories have usually been written by different groups of historians. In spite of the fact that much of the culture which sustained Britain's nobility and monarchy was similar to elite culture on the Continent, both its king and aristocracy were contrasted with the European norm. Its elites were alleged to be far less privileged and more open to new recruits than their Continental opposite numbers. Its monarch was characterized as limited – not absolute like his European counterparts. Its common people were consequently free men – unlike those in Europe, who were slaves.

That was the majority view; and certainly the British nobility and monarchy possessed significant peculiarities. But so did every other European monarch and nobility.[34] Far from distancing Britain from the Continent, its significant peculiarities paradoxically brought Britain into line with it. More specifically, its monarchy was defined as absolute by the French philosopher Bodin in the sixteenth century and by Blackstone, Britain's most influential jurist, in the eighteenth.[35] In a European context Britain was far from exceptional in combining consultative assemblies with the strong royal prerogatives of absolute monarchy.[36] Whether its monarchy was or was not 'absolute' clearly depends on one's definition of the term. The one certain fact is that most British people avoided relating the word to their own system of government – and they still do.

Finally, what sort of states did these monarchs rule? They were not the unified nation-states of modern Europe. Instead we find 'composite states' consisting of several countries and peoples under one ruler. They were a patchwork of different legal, financial and administrative systems. This diversity was jealously defended by representative assemblies (Estates) in the provinces. It was a problem for monarchs who might prefer a neater arrangement.[37]

A composite state was quite different from a modern nation-state. The latter is, at least theoretically, ethnically and culturally homogeneous – literally, a state belonging to a race or nation. But a composite state was a far-flung multi-national, multi-ethnic, multi-lingual and multi-cultural entity, consisting of diverse communities or nations subordinated to a single ruler. In the early-modern period the term 'composite' was not used. A state of this kind was considered an empire, in fact, if not always in name. This terminology tends to be avoided by early-modern historians, presumably fearing confusion with 'empire' as later shorthand for state expansion outside Europe. But there is really no problem. Only in the nineteenth century did 'empire' acquire this meaning.[38]

## Composite States and Nationalist Historians

Clearly there was an urgent need after the mid-seventeenth-century crisis to restore order on a more permanent basis. But how? A long-established view, recently reasserted, is that many rulers now resolved to free themselves from dependence on unreliable provincial nobles, who were elites with power in their own right. The drawback of the latter was that they viewed government orders through the distorting prism of their own interest and could not be dismissed without political risk, even if they were defiant or incompetent.[39] An alleged solution was permanent use of bureaucratic officials from outside the elite. These had already been deployed before the mid-seventeenth-century crisis and, in combination with professional standing armies, arguably enabled rulers to coerce their subjects instead of consulting them.[40] Monarchs also claimed a sovereign power which transcended all other forms of authority and could override the rights and privileges of nobles and provinces when rulers considered it necessary (*raison d'état*). In short, the remedy favoured by monarchs for the havoc created in the 1640s and 1650s by their despotic policies was more of the same.[41] An autocratic crackdown was required.

Other authorities have suggested the precise opposite. They have argued that to restore their shaky inheritance absolute rulers needed to reinvent the co-operative relationship with their traditional support systems, territorial nobility and established church, and thus restore the productive symbiosis between them.[42] They have also asserted that in the context of composite states which valued their provincial and corporate privileges the notion of a royal sovereign power which trumped all other claims was dynamite – and almost certainly unworkable.[43] Fortunately elites were ready for compromise. Both during and after the mid-seventeenth-century crisis they remained shocked by two unwelcome realities. They had encountered a social challenge from below and, especially in Great Britain and France, they had divided against themselves.[44] They belatedly recognised monarchy as the keystone in the arch of power and privilege. Monarchs realised that keystones were little use without arches.

The first option was indeed a non-starter – but for a reason which has been widely overlooked. Indeed, many historians have added to the confusion by viewing early-modern states from the perspective of their modern boundaries. This creates an impression of integrated coherence which is totally misleading. Had monarchs ruled unified states with a single system of law, tax and administration, it would have been easier for them to impose their will throughout their realms. But most of them ruled composite states, each of which usually consisted of several countries under one ruler. The French monarch wore the crowns of France and Navarre, the Austrian monarch those of Hungary and the Holy Roman Empire, the Spanish monarch those of Castile, Aragon, Naples and Sicily and the British monarch those of England, Scotland and Ireland. They were usually obliged to have separate coronations in each of their realms.

Normal monarchy was not single but multiple. A composite state's components had different legal and financial systems, guarded by provincial representative assemblies or Estates. They were united only by their loyalty to the same ruling dynasty. To maintain this loyalty their unique rights and privileges were acknowledged by monarchs. If their rulers played the game of pass the parcel and swapped provinces, subjects could find themselves handed round foreign dynasties. When this happened, they retained their own laws and liberties. A state with uniform law and taxation throughout the realm was therefore an impossibility. France was a diverse collection of provinces and corporate bodies, all with their own legal traditions and dominated by independent-minded local elites. This made general policies launched by central government hard to frame and reformist change almost impossible to achieve. Most ministers settled for the status quo.[45] England is often proclaimed as the most unified state in Europe. Yet it was subdivided into the palatinates of Durham, Cheshire, the Isle of Man and the Channel Islands on the one hand and the remaining counties on the other. The former were run by their lords like semi-independent fiefdoms, royal power being much greater in the rest of the country. This administrative diversity was extended to parts of Britain's empire in North America. The semi-regal powers of Lord Baltimore, founder of the colony of Maryland, were modelled on those of the Bishop of Durham.[46]

Why has the composite character of early-modern states only recently been noticed? This can safely be blamed on the nationalist historians of the nineteenth century. In their eyes, the main development of the preceding four centuries was the rise of the all-powerful nation-states in which they lived.[47] Their mission was to create a pedigree for them. They have been described as 'among the most successful myth-makers of all time'.[48] The histories which they wrote imposed retrospectively their nineteenth-century nationalisms on seventeenth- and eighteenth-century Europe. They established the influential narrative of state formation and consolidation which survives among their modern successors.[49] In a recent and reputable history of modern France the pivotal chapter is entitled 'Louis XIV and the Creation of the Modern State'.[50] The emphasis is on administrative integration, and the dynastic imperatives of rulers tend to be minimized. Nationalist historians assumed that early-modern states had embarked on a project of consolidation which put them firmly on the road to becoming the unified nation-states of nineteenth-century Europe.[51] If their monarchs did not display awareness of this obligation, they were severely criticized. The pursuit of non-ethnic 'alien' territory was dismissed as a distraction from national destiny:

> Louis XI had contented himself with Anjou and Provence but his foolish and ambitious son [Charles VIII], fascinated with the dream of a southern kingdom which might serve as a starting-point for a new crusade against the Turk, was eager to enforce his claims in Italy. ... It does not seem altogether unfit that those Italian wars which caused such infinite misery in Italy, and were so disastrous to the best interests of France, should be associated with his name.[52]

The historiographical agenda of a century ago is clear. Early-modern monarchs who apparently pursued national consolidation received a tick. Those who ignored it got a smack.

The fact is that in the 1650–1750 period the urge for dynastic acquisition, regardless of strategic or territorial logic, constantly cut across the possibility of any internal cohesion.[53] Early-modern dynasts collected territories, peoples and provinces in the same way that rich individuals acquired antiquities, paintings and porcelain.[54] Reflecting these priorities, the historical education of princes hinged on dynastic rights and genealogies.[55] Much is heard in standard narratives of how the Great Elector of Brandenburg–Prussia devoted his energies to centralization and forged his scattered territories into some sort of unity. Less is heard of his will. It fails to fit the story, since it provided that on his death the territories should be divided between his sons. In 1688 his successor nullified these provisions, but the Great Elector's intention establishes that he failed to read the nineteenth-century script allocated to him.[56]

In fact the reach of nationalist historians extended further back than the seventeenth century. In AD 9, Arminius, better known as Herman 'the German', massacred the entire army of Quinctilius Varus in what is now north Germany. Six years later its whitened bones were discovered by the horrified army of Germanicus Caesar. But the Roman Empire rolled on and memories of Herman faded, to be rediscovered only in the Renaissance. Nineteenth-century nationalists selected him as Germany's greatest hero and supreme symbol of German nationhood. He was pronounced to have stopped the expansion of Rome in its tracks and drawn a permanent line between the Roman world of togas, towns and Latin and the barbarian world of warring tribes and blood feuds in defence of sacred Germanic soil. As described by Tacitus in his *Germania* of AD 98, Herman provides the birth certificate of the German nation.[57]

The real reason for this fault-line across Europe was probably Roman aversion to the poverty-stricken backwardness of territory north of the Rhine. But the Herman version made a better story – and one more relevant to nationalist concerns. In 1875, five years after German unification, a 28-metre statue of Herman was unveiled on top of a colossal column, itself on the summit of a 400-metre hill in the Teutoburger Wald. It turned out to be 70 kilometres south of the actual battlefield. In their anxiety to commemorate his achievements the Germans had built it in the wrong place.[58]

British historiography furnishes a further example. David Hume, writing in 1752, in five lines implicitly dismissed Boadicea (or Boudicca) as a savage.[59] For him the Roman Empire was benign, its paganism preferable to Christianity, and a Europe of nation-states not yet established as manifest destiny. A century later in 1851 a publication of the Society for Promoting Christian Knowledge hailed pagan Rome as a tyranny and Boadicea as the inspirational leader who roused her people against it. She thus displayed gratifying 'proof of the manliness and energy of the British character'.[60] Clearly the queen of the Iceni was already morphing into David Livingstone.

When nationalist historians turned their steely gaze on the early-modern period, they developed a simple criterion of significance. They assessed the importance of institutions in early-modern composite states according to how successfully they anticipated those of modern nation-states.[61] They thrilled to the embryonic bureaucracies and standing armies of the 1650–1750 period and greatly exaggerated their modernity.[62] In contrast they were unimpressed by royal courts, which they considered irrelevant to the creation of modern nation-states. These were written out of the story – just as, by some historians, they still are.[63] Unsurprisingly, early-modern composite states soon began to look very like modern nation-states. Nationalist historians forgot that early-modern rulers needed to make their territories work as composite states rather than nation-states. It slipped their collective mind that the required governmental techniques might have been different. Historians always need to beware of what a well-known evolutionary biologist has called 'the vanity of the present – of seeing the past as aimed at our own time, as though the characters in history's play had nothing better to do with their lives than foreshadow us'.[64]

There is one way in which the nationalist version of early-modern states did *not* look like modern states. There were no effective representative institutions. Nineteenth-century historians were blinkered by their nationalist agenda. They detested early-modern provincial and local representative bodies as obstacles to future national unification. Consequently they generally ignored them. But that was precisely the regional level at which consultative institutions representing the components of composite states could operate most effectively. The sidelining of consultation was not therefore the work of autocratic monarchs keen to flatten presumed rivals for power. It occurred mainly in the perception of nationalist historians who despised the lowly levels at which it operated.[65]

How has the multi-national character of early-modern states been so neglected? The answer is that for two centuries the history of Europe has been rewritten to conceal it. The government of composite states has never been properly studied. Attention has usually been focused only on those components which were ultimately to make it to nation-statehood. Nineteenth-century historians zeroed in on the peninsula to which Spain had been reduced by the time they were writing. They charted its growth from Roman *Hispania* to the Reconquest from Islam and through the union of Aragon and Castile under Ferdinand and Isabella. But its abandoned possessions in the southern Netherlands, eastern France, Naples and Sicily were largely ignored, since from the perspective of the Spanish nation-state of the nineteenth century they were a historical dead end. Admittedly it was hard to ignore the Americas; but as overseas colonies were written about by a different breed of imperial historian they were marginalized too. Similarly, England was targeted but not Ireland, Scotland or Wales – except by Irish, Scottish and Welsh historians with their own agenda. In recent decades there has been intensive examination of the part played by Scotland and Ireland in the rebellion against Charles I, but their role in the period from Charles II's Restoration to the Revolution of 1688 remains seriously understudied.[66]

So, apart from the Habsburg multiple monarchy, the only composite states which have been studied in depth are the minority which happened to become modern states (like Castile and Aragon), rather than the major- ity which failed to do so (like Saxony–Poland–Lithuania, Denmark–Norway, Sweden–Finland, Piedmont–Savoy and Britain–Hanover).[67] Nationalist his- torians have also tended to ignore European components which failed to become part of the equivalent modern nation-state. Early-modern Denmark has been closely investigated by its own historians, but its province of Norway has not – unless of course the historians happened to be Norwegians chart- ing the rise of their own nation-state, in which case they ignored Denmark. The multiple monarchy of Denmark–Norway has rarely been discussed. The two populations were roughly equal but the metropolitan centre was in Copenhagen in Denmark, and Norway has tended to disappear from the radar of Danish historians. One such author states in his introduction that Denmark was part of 'a larger multinational and multilingual united monar- chy' including Norway. Yet, in a book of 314 pages, Norway is subsequently mentioned on three. Two of its fleeting appearances are in the context of foreign countries.[68]

Nor is this oversight confined to historians writing about their own coun- try. Sweden–Finland was a united kingdom for six centuries before 1809. The standard history in English of the state in the early seventeenth century (pub- lished in the 1950s) doubles as a biography of Gustavus Adolphus, its greatest monarch. In the course of its 1,433 pages Finland, which contained a third of the total population, receives twenty mentions. Most of these consist of one or two lines of socio-economic comment.[69] In spite of raised awareness of composite states in subsequent decades, little has changed in general surveys of early-modern Europe. Their authors maintain a resolute focus on early- modern territories which happened to become modern nation-states. In a study of the usual regimes published in the 1990s Finland fails to make it into the index – or indeed into the book. The same work mentions the union of Denmark and Norway only twelve pages from the end of the text – in short, as an afterthought.[70] Only in 1997 did a book written in English tackle the complex relationship between Norway's elites and the Danish monarch.[71]

Few would guess from this long insistence on nationalist perspectives that ruling an early-modern composite monarchy posed challenges of unique managerial, constitutional and administrative complexity. Most of these have barely been investigated. What, for example, was supposed to happen when a monarch found himself presiding over different religions in different territories at a time when there was supposed to be only one version of religious truth? Even more perplexing, how could a ruler like Charles II of England justify tolerating a Christian sect in Scotland which he persecuted in England? The fact that he could use the resources of one country against dissidents in another would be cold comfort in the event of a general conflagration. Non-residence by the monarch was also a problem. We know that when George Elector of Hanover departed to rule Great Britain in 1714 he left behind his seven-year-old grandson, lest the Hanoverians should feel deprived if the whole family departed for London. He also arranged for his own portrait to sit on the throne in his place.[72]

The management of representative assemblies in composite states could be especially precarious. Estates frequently objected to the use of provincial armies for purposes which their monarch might favour but which the Estates deemed irrelevant to regional interests. They might also disagree about succession to the crown. In 1701 the English Parliament settled the English crown on the Hanoverian line: three years later the Scottish Estates selected a different descendant of the Stuarts. Estates might continue to meet together even after the component territory which they represented had been divided between different rulers. Finally, though it was accepted that Estates in one province had no authority over those in another, towards the end of the period some enlarged their ambitions. In 1720 the Westminster Parliament claimed authority over the Irish Parliament, with resultant ructions.[73]

The most problematic institutions were Estates Generals, combined meetings of representative assemblies for different territories of a composite monarchy. Though this was an obvious device for unifying a state, monarchs were as suspicious as provincial Estates. Both knew from experience that a centralized body representing the entire realm tended to exceed its powers, at the expense of ruler or provinces. In addition, Estates Generals tended to be ineffective in composite states with highly diversified laws, customs and economies, as well as regional and institutional rivalries.[74] Their members lacked the required degree of unity, co-operation and community consciousness. And European Estates Generals were constitutionally untidy. Unlike England's Parliament, they never had the authority to bind the whole realm. All decisions had to be referred back to provincial Estates. It did not take rulers long to reason that they might as well deal directly with representative bodies in the provinces: in the seventeenth century most Estates Generals disappeared. The most dramatic termination was that of the Danish *Rigsdag*, which was dismissed in 1660 and did not reassemble until 1835. A recent study of the Danish provinces of Schleswig and Holstein reveals that consultation was deliberately increased at a lower level, where representatives negotiated the amount of taxation directly with the king and accepted responsibility for collecting it.[75] That monarchs did not in all such cases intend to tax without consent is underlined by the Portuguese crown's refusal to summon the Cortes for over a century after 1698. The reason was not a new policy of despotic taxation. It was the discovery of Brazilian gold, which made the Cortes superfluous.[76]

The disappearance of Estates Generals has been much misunderstood. Philip IV of Spain's bitter announcement that 'states generals are pernicious at all times and in all monarchies without exception' has often been quoted.[77] A distinguished scholar has converted this into a denunciation of representative assemblies in general.[78] This meshes neatly with the traditional idea of despotic 'absolutism' and royal antipathy to political participation from below during the 1650–1750 period. The point missed in these examples is that consultation did not disappear. It was displaced to lower levels at which, in the context of composite states, it was less problematic. Far from setting out to subvert representation, monarchs shifted it to levels at which it was viable.

Early-modern composite states, with their privileged provinces and hypersensitive representative bodies, are now being rediscovered. It should be clear that the only solution to the complex problems they posed was for rulers to rely on regional elites. Without their co-operation monarchs had no chance. The only people qualified to rule a province of a composite state or empire were those whose power within it was ready-made and long-standing. A monarch aimed to hijack for his own purpose the local control conferred by their wealth, power and status. The kin, clients, landed influence and social standing of native elites provided a far firmer basis for political power than foreign officials sent in from the empire's metropolitan centre.[79] A ruler's objective was to persuade regional elites to collaborate with him. That was by far the most effective way of pulling together a composite state. It was also a question of numbers. The core bureaucracy of the Prussian Hohenzollerns consisted of only several hundred officials and was too small to rule at provincial and local level. Prussian absolute monarchy grew in step with the power and activity of the local landlords (Junkers) at those levels.[80]

But to secure the collaboration of local power groups a monarch had to permit a degree of local autonomy and respect their interests and privileges.

This was what the Habsburgs did when Philip IV of Spain recognized the liberties of the Catalans in 1652 after their mid-seventeenth-century revolt, and when Leopold I compromised with the Hungarian nobility three decades later. It was what James II of Great Britain signally failed to do in 1688, only to find elites united against him in a bloodless revolution. The Rakoczi revolt of 1703–11 against the Habsburgs demonstrated that aristocratic revolt was still not entirely a thing of the past, but in western and central Europe it rapidly died out. A ruler also had to channel favours for local communities through his chosen local bosses and thus reinforce their status. Finally he had to show respect for their privileged position by consulting them in Estates (representative assemblies) as and when appropriate. The programmed middle-class bureaucrats imagined by some historians to have ruled the provinces of composite states in the 1650–1750 period are therefore a sociological fantasy.[81]

So a brief period of despotism in the first half of the seventeenth century proved temporary and the old system of ruler–elite partnership returned. Recognition of the fractured nature of composite states meant that Estates Generals tended to disappear as too unwieldy, while the same recognition caused provincial Estates to remain as safety valves and points of contact with regional elites. There are many examples of monarchs backing off and pursuing a more 'softly, softly' approach. In France, Colbert's instructions to the intendants bristled with injunctions to respect local privileges and customs.[82] After decades of religious civil wars and political revolts, from the 1650s to the 1750s the reconciliation of crown and nobility was a main government priority.[83] But there was a new emphasis. Monarchs eagerly sought more strategies of compromise and co-operation. The less power rested on despotic force, the more they and elites needed to employ the arts of persuasion in their dealings with each other.

This may seem an odd assertion in a period when royal armies in most states grew exponentially and European warfare reached unprecedented levels of permanence and intensity. Was it not military factors which necessitated crown–elite partnership and supplied the means of imposing it? The explanation can be reversed. It has been cogently argued that larger armies and prolonged warfare were the *result* of the co-operation and consensus already negotiated between rulers and elites and not the cause of it. With the same demographic and tax base as his father, Louis XIV was able to assemble far larger armies and maintain them permanently after 1661. This was possible because he proved more sensitive to the family ambition of his nobles. Appointments to the high command within a hugely expanded army were made in ways which satisfied them. In other words, both he and they were dynasts and understood one another.[84] There is little evidence that elites were coerced into partnership by military force. The new standing armies were periodically deployed against revolting lower orders but rarely against elites, eastern Europe providing some exceptions to the rule.[85] Fiscal–military states (those whose resources were geared to maintaining large standing armies) needed to maintain the crown–elite alliance in other ways.

Monarchs of the 1650–1750 period therefore succeeded by recognizing that their composite states could not be ruled or held together by despotic force. The latter caused revolts which were too expensive to crush, too risky in possible outcome and too damaging to royal reputation. Instead the diverse provinces of their states had to be ruled in collaboration with their landed elites. The key to monarchs' success was skilful management of the nobility. To achieve it they relied on two mechanisms, one political and the other cultural.

To look briefly forwards, it is now accepted that, after 1789, French Revolutionaries expressed themselves in two ways – politically and culturally. They invented a cultural vocabulary based on the newly proclaimed nation and invested it with festivals, rituals and ceremonies. In doing so they adopted some of the techniques employed by the *ancien régime*, especially by the Catholic Church.[86] This was a compliment to the cultural strategies of the 1650–1750 period – though not to its ultimate objectives. It is beyond doubt that during the French Revolution political and cultural innovation buttressed each other, with cultural propaganda attempting to fill the gaps left by the political process.[87] I want to suggest that this is also an illuminating way of looking at the period that preceded the era of revolution – the age of the baroque state, as a few historians are now calling it.[88]

## Political Strategies: Monarchs and their Elites

The imperatives of order and stability imposed requirements. Monarchs and elites needed to join forces to negotiate deals and compromises, consolidate traditional socio-political power structures and open channels of communication between centre and provinces. The challenge to rulers was not to defeat local power groups but to secure a balanced relationship with them. In the 1650–1750 period strong government depended on a broad political consensus among those who mattered.

Consensus was a device for elite management: it was not a priority in treatment of the lower orders. Exactly the opposite was the case. The increased confidence and co-operation of crown and ruling orders facilitated forceful and decisive action against the threat of popular revolt. Attitudes to peasant unrest and revolt were uncompromising and coercive. Two dangerous French rebellions of the period reveal a significant contrast. When the peasants of Montpellier rioted against scarcity and war exactions in 1645, central and local authorities were too weak and divided to dare to deploy troops. In 1670, when the peasants round Aubenas in the Rhône valley launched a major insurrection against similar demands, the position was transformed. United in class solidarity, the local authorities played for time while a royal army approached Languedoc. The King's musketeers led by d'Artagnan, 1,500 cavalry and 2,300 infantry joined grateful provincial nobles, defeated the rebel army and butchered the fleeing peasantry. The leader, Roure, was broken on the wheel in front of the *hôtel de ville* in Montpellier. His body was exhibited on the Montpellier–Nîmes highway while his severed head looked down from the town gate where the trouble had begun.[89]

Contrary to the usual impression, the social basis of authority was essentially the same in Britain and France, namely a royal partnership with propertied elites.[90] It is true that the partnership was institutionalized by different mechanisms in different states – or even in different provinces within the same state. In Britain royal ministers formally consulted assemblies in London, Edinburgh and Dublin, while in France and the German states the procedure was carried out with less formality and with a greater variety of bodies. Consultation was institutionalized in France in 1789 and in the German states from the 1790s. This can be seen as a process by which more formal channels of consultation replace the informal bargaining arrangements of absolute monarchs.[91] Consultation was not lacking in the latter case: the mere assertion of authority was not enough. Power had to be negotiated. In short, the underlying relationship between monarchs and elites was similar everywhere, except in parts of northern and eastern Europe – and especially in Russia.

The search for new forms of taxation to fund the wars of the 1650–1750 period is usually thought to have pushed rulers into yet more authoritarian modes of statecraft. Estates were allegedly overridden or sidelined and taxation without consent established – hence the shift to 'absolutism'.[92] In a self-perpetuating cycle, rulers arguably established bureaucracies and standing armies, which enforced the extraction of yet more resources, to fund even greater armaments and wars. Victor Amadeus of Savoy–Piedmont, Charles XII of Sweden–Finland and Frederick William the Great Elector of Brandenburg–Prussia periodically fitted this pattern, but most rulers adopted the opposite tactic of calling Estates more regularly. This was true of many of the German rulers, who summoned annual parliaments like the English Hanoverians.

Much is heard of the Habsburgs' difficulties with the Estates in the eighteenth century; yet in the seventeenth they had conspicuously proved that consensus between monarch, nobility and church was a winning formula. The main tax, the Contribution, supported the standing army which rectified the shambles during the Thirty Years War, when Ferdinand II relied on Spain, the Catholic League and unreliable contractors like Wallenstein. By the 1680s inflation of state revenues had permitted the establishment of a 100,000-man standing army, funded from all Habsburg territories and large voluntary contributions from ecclesiastical bodies. The Bohemian and Austrian Estates had steadily increased levies of troops and taxes while Hungary and Tyrol, initially unwilling participants in the Habsburg enterprise, were making record contributions by the end of the century. The Habsburg Emperor Joseph I also saw the need to work with the Estates, especially during the Spanish Succession War. Royal deference paid dividends in the shape of aristocratic and civic loans, and the Estates increased the Contribution by another 60 per cent after his accession. With zero application of the force-and-centralization model, military taxation had been trebled in a single generation.[93]

Much has always been made of the contrast between the prestigious English Parliament, which enabled William III and his successors to borrow funds on the strength of its creditworthiness, and the ruinous deals that Louis XIV had to make with private fiscal contractors. In fact the provincial Estates in France raised loans for the monarch in essentially the same way as the English Parliament. The formers' regular meetings, reliable administration and guaranteed right to collect taxation created investor confidence, which led to lower interest rates.[94]

Rulers and elites therefore locked themselves into a collaboration based on what has recently been called 'negotiated power-sharing'. The alternative view is of the one-sided victory of allegedly despotic monarchical 'absolutism'[95] – and at precisely the same time that traditional elites were ascending to the summit of their power. That paradox should tell us something. It suggests that there was in fact no zero-sum game pitting rulers against elites. The zenith of absolute monarchy was also the zenith of its principal supporters. In relation to this period, despotic 'absolutism' is another nineteenth-century myth. Instead there was a mutually beneficial merging of different power structures which left monarchs and governing elites in most of Europe more united than ever before.[96] Monarchs intensified a previous trend of concentrating power into the hands of elite groups who were an ever smaller proportion of the population. This made negotiation of consensus more manageable. Self-perpetuating oligarchies sprang up in town and countryside, in the church and the law, and discovered a common interest in preserving the elite social, political and religious order.[97]

Rulers reconnected not only with the lords temporal, the landed elites who ruled the provinces, but also with the lords spiritual, the prelates who ruled the church. It is necessary to forget the enfeebled condition of the Christian churches in most twenty-first-century European states. In the 1650–1750 period the clergy at every level still constituted a formidable political, social, cultural and spiritual powerhouse, with which all, from peasants to kings, had to reckon. The church provided not only for the religious needs of the state's subjects but also for their education, health and welfare. The state certainly had too much of a vested interest in their education to leave it to chance, and the belief that it did so until the nineteenth century reflects neglect of the church's role as its social-services arm through many centuries. Only one monarch challenged this partnership. Victor Amadeus II of Savoy–Piedmont emitted a strong pre-echo of the Enlightened Despotism of the later eighteenth century when he attempted to free the content and personnel of higher and secondary education from clerical dominance. His achievement fell well short of his intention, but he made what has been called the first deliberate attempt to set up a system of secular education anywhere in Europe.[98]

Above all, however, churches in the 1650–1750 period were political institutions. They provided monarchs with divine approval (occasionally displeasure), inculcated respect for kings and the socio-political hierarchy which underpinned them, and placed their organization at royal disposal. Higher clergy moved easily between church and state. Most were part of the state's ruling elite twice over – by virtue both of their ecclesiastical offices and of their social origins. Ecclesiastical appointments were a key aspect of government policy, partly because they involved so many families from the governing elite. Prelates were usually great landowners as well. In the Holy Roman Empire they ruled the semi-independent ecclesiastical states known as prince-bishoprics. The majority of the Italian nobility inserted its members into bishoprics, cathedral chapters and abbeys. Its association with the ecclesiastical hierarchy gave it influence over the lower clergy.[99] The latter were deployed in every parish in the realm – an achievement totally beyond any government of the period. They supplied something which all monarchs and elites needed to exploit – supervision of the daily life of the entire population, and captive audiences for lengthy baroque sermons on the theme of obedience to kings and their nobles.

Until the middle of the eighteenth century rulers looked to religious rationale to justify political obligation. Monarchy was theocratic, underpinned by Christian theology. The King of France was 'the Very Christian Monarch', the Spanish 'the Catholic King' and the British 'Defender of the Faith'. Until c.1750 monarchs ruthlessly suppressed heretical challenges to this ideological marriage. This was partly because religious divisions were still believed to threaten political integrity, especially in composite states where religion was one of the few bonding agents available. More importantly, it was because church–state partnership could work only if religious unity (Catholic or Protestant) was maintained within each European state: the clergy were weakened as a monarch's allies unless they had contact with all his subjects. The church as the splintered body of Christ could not fulfil the role for which the state cast it – as the whole territorial membership conveniently organized in their capacity as Christians and handed to the state on a communion plate.

Kings and popes had locked horns in the past over ultimate supremacy and would do so again. The religious divisions which followed the Reformation precipitated between 1550 and 1650 a century of collapse in church–state relations. But in the 1650–1750 period, as if by magic, conflict was muted and co-operation flourished. The close relationship maintained between the institutions of church and state in most European monarchies mirrored the congruence between religious and political cultures in the realm of ideas. The result was a union of immense strength. With the predictable and temporary exception of Louis XIV's France, royal and ecclesiastical authorities in most states gave a convincing impression of being joined at the hip. Bishops controlled their dioceses partly on behalf of the state. They often headed the administration of a town or province and presided over provincial representative estates, with the aim of managing them in the interests of the monarchy.[100] In France, where future bishops might take the precaution of equipping themselves with degrees in law (sometimes canon law, sometimes not), the *parlements* and higher courts of justice reserved certain offices for clerics.[101] Every Catholic princely court teemed with a clerical high command of cardinals, abbots and confessors, while parish clergy were the indispensable infantry who transmitted ecclesiastical and political orders to the grass roots. The identification of monarch and church was often explicit. Habsburg military flags all carried embroidered pictures of the Virgin Mary, who held the military title of *Generalissima* in Charles VI's army.[102]

Monarchs were no longer threatened. The extremity of rebellion was increasingly avoided and overt opposition to royal policy accepted as treasonable – hence the eagerness of opposition politicians from Britain to Russia to secure the protection of the heir to the throne. Most monarchs also signed up to the rules: they had learned the hard way that absolute power stopped short of despotism. Government in this period worked through negotiated consensus between ruler and elites, apart from the free hand monarchs enjoyed with foreign policy and appointments. The 1650–1750 period, compared with previous and subsequent ones, is characterized by significantly fewer revolts. Nor did elites continue to support popular revolts, as they had often done. Deprived of their support, peasant rebellion swiftly fizzled out or failed to happen. Monarchs had learned lessons, forged links with local landowners and through them acquired greater regional control. Parish clergy were told by their superiors to stay out of local conflict. With elites safely on side, monarchs could be tough with increasingly rare plebeian revolt. Peasants who rose in Brittany in 1675 were hanged from trees and left there to rot.

Patrimonial mechanisms (patronage and clientage) were the lubricant of crown–elite relations and the key to successful government. From a modern perspective this was totally corrupt. But before the rise of democratic politics patrimonialism was universal as a means of achieving political and social ambition. In regimes based on the preservation of a privileged social order it was natural and appropriate.[103] Favour and influence were traded up and down the hierarchy from the monarch at the summit to town and village elites at the base. These networks of personal relationships are still believed by some authorities to have been eliminated by the rise of a bureaucratic and 'administrative' monarchy in the early-modern period.[104] But it is now clear that they extended their tentacles, unifying and consolidating the elite to an unprecedented degree. It has been argued that, in France at least, patrimonial mechanisms remained more vital than bureaucratic ones.[105]

Vertical ties of clientage and patronage linked mere provincial gentry with great aristocrats in government or court positions at the metropolitan centre. The former pledged local loyalty and support while the latter provided them with the opportunities and advancement they craved. Patronage brokers acted as middle-men to bridge the distance between them. Since powers of coercion and punishment were inadequate to command obedience, the bedrock of a superior's authority was his ability to give what his subordinates wanted to receive – promotion, opportunity and wealth for their families.[106] In many ways the dynastic ambitions of monarchs and their elites united this society and defined its political culture.[107] Elites indulged in cut-throat rivalries but, in most states, accepted the rules of the political game. A vital royal duty was to arbitrate over their disputes. Without that crucial function, in composite states where ancient areas of authority were untidily delineated, competing jurisdictions and overlapping authorities could bring orderly administration to a standstill. Government therefore depended on this mutual exchange between power elites at every level. Patronage and clientage served the needs of both state and elites.[108] The great majority of subjects, who had no power of consequence, were excluded.[109]

It is an old misconception that absolute monarchy rose upon the mangled remains of a troglodyte aristocracy.[110] France is a classic case, where the revolt of the Fronde is seen as the last gasp of the nobility – after which they meekly submitted to the power of an increasingly despotic and authoritarian crown and ceased to be a significant force in political life.[111] In fact they survived an adverse economic cycle surprisingly well and were not successfully challenged by a rising bourgeoisie for at least another century. Their elite status was defined by their role as warrior dynasties – one which was scarcely irrelevant in a monarchical state the main purpose of which was the waging of dynastic warfare.[112] The call for order in the form of rational administration modified the role of elites but certainly did not eliminate them. Rational methods boosted rapid growth in royal bureaucracy and standing armies, run by professionally trained staff and underpinned by the new mathematics (in the form of figures and statistics of some degree of accuracy). But increasingly in the 1650–1750 period they were led by old elites who had reinvented themselves as semi-professional service nobilities. Everywhere the nobility was re-educated in new values and skills.[113] Fresh from college, with diplomas in military training or political administration tucked in their belts, retrained elites were usually capable of what was required. In northern and eastern Europe this involved some restructuring of elites themselves, but only in Denmark–Norway was a new service nobility created from scratch and the old nobility sent packing.[114]

Elsewhere elites colonized the expanding state apparatus for its power and profit opportunities. Evidence so far studied confirms the tightening grip of old elites on army, church and bureaucracy. In France, significant numbers of officers were commoners in 1600 but by 1700 the army command was dominated by the nobility. In England, only 3 per cent of 188 officers serving with standing regiments between 1661 and 1685 were commoners.[115] By c.1800, 90 per cent of the Prussian officer corps were noble. This process meant that soldiering was transformed from an occasional occupation to a full-time job. Eastern European elites, in contrast, were conscripted into the army as ruthlessly as serfs. Russian nobles commonly wrote to the Tsar complaining that they had had no leave for twenty years. In 1716, names of Russian adolescents who had reported for duty were required to be posted in towns and villages, while those missing and in hiding were to be identified and denounced. Informers were encouraged by the offer of the draft-dodgers' estates.[116]

The area where co-operation between crown and elites was most crucial was military recruitment and command. The system of peasant conscripts and noble officers transferred to the army the serf–landlord nexus of the villages, the Junkers (landowners) and peasants of Prussia providing a classic instance. Historians are beginning to illuminate the mechanisms by which military structure mirrored the social relations of the countryside. This was also applicable to western Europe where voluntary enlistment was the rule. There a captain drew most of his company from the district where his family was influential. These devices neatly enacted the common interest between elites and the burgeoning state. They also demonstrate that the armies of absolute monarchs grew out of society rather than being imposed on it, thus reinforcing the argument in favour of consensual monarchy.[117]

Unprecedented opportunities were offered to elites by the state's failure to claim the monopoly of violence, which historians often attribute to it in this period. The state did not even own its armies. Even in the Prussian army the Junker perspective was one of private property and profit. This refutes the common notion that in this army, above all, the old royal procedure of contracting out to private enterprise had been discarded. Not until the mid-eighteenth century did European states monopolize all military functions. Like others in the 1650–1750 period, the Prussian army was a hybrid, combining the mercenary element of the Thirty Years War with centralized control by the state. Though European officers now led their monarch's armies in the monarch's name, companies continued to be held on a proprietary basis. But, whereas before the mid-seventeenth century a significant proportion of military entrepreneurs were non-noble, the 1650–1750 period saw their widespread replacement by the nobility. Rulers relied on landowners to raise, command, accommodate, clothe and equip military units. This was the case even in the Dutch Republic, the least aristocratic of European states.[118]

But, if elites had to invest considerable funds in their units, they also reckoned on a sizeable return. A Prussian subaltern could reach the rank of captain in four years in wartime and obtain proprietorship of his company, purchasing from his predecessor the right to farm his unit under the crown for profit. A captain who 'owned' his company received its finances and pay directly from the state and could take a hefty cut. He was paid three talers per month for each soldier, but during peacetime he could send half his 120 soldiers home to their agriculture and pocket their pay. To his annual salary of about 550 talers he could therefore add 2,000 talers a year from his *Kompagniewirtschaft* (company management). At the higher levels the Prussian army thus remained a means of making an elite family's fortune.[119]

The same dynastic considerations (rather than state-building) governed the army of France and the other European states.[120]

Another privatization from which elites benefited was royal finance. Dessert has shown that of the financiers with multiple contracts to bankroll Louis XIV, 85 per cent were noble, almost all held royal office and most were connected with clans of Colbert and his successors. Far from making the crown independent of the financiers, as can appear to historians who fail to look behind the scenes, like Richelieu and Mazarin he exploited his position to promote his own family and obstruct rivals. Any attack on the financiers who funded the monarchy would therefore threaten the social and political elite itself, just as any attack on privilege would threaten the basis of the credit needed to run the monarchy.[121]

A spectacular opportunity was presented to elites by the militarization of monarchs. What gave them an unmistakably military flavour in the 1650–1750 period was not their standing armies but their royal guards – a distinction few historians have made. Royal guards were the elite regiments, usually of noble composition, who protected the person of the monarch. They developed in the sixteenth and seventeenth centuries, before which monarchs had been guarded by the knights and gentlemen of their household. The intimate connection with the court remained, since the king was guarded day and night. The monarch was also more closely connected with his guards than with the rest of his army: instead of answering to a commander-in-chief or a minister of war they were usually under his direct control. By 1750 most rulers were colonels or captains of guard regiments and were frequently seen in uniform. Royal guards were increasingly distinguished from other troops by this personal connection with royalty, the magnificence of their uniform and the privileges they were accorded, as well as by being kept at full strength – a rare distinction in this ramshackle period of military history. The French Guards began to wear uniforms in the 1660s, when Louis XIV started to pay for them. From then on, as other royal guards followed the fashion, royalty acquired a spectacular military aspect from the number of guards surrounding it.[122]

In eastern and northern Europe, tables of rank were introduced. These were intended to encourage the nobility to perform more efficiently. This runs counter to the anachronism of interpreting them as an early modern version of the meritocratic society. They all stressed the crucial rule that only service rank (civil or military) bestowed eminence, regardless of social origins. But social elites still tended to finish at the top of the new system. As a contemporary spotted, the point was to encourage the nobility to 'distinguish themselves from common folk by merit as well as by birth'.[123]

Western European armies lacked such a system and experienced a conflict between the claims of social status and military rank. Though in France it was decided in 1676 that social status must defer to rank and seniority, many aristocrats were still resisting a generation later and socially superior persons continued to be of great military consequence. When Prince George of Hesse–Darmstadt was killed in the War of Spanish Succession in 1705, his heart was despatched in a casket to Germany. Unfortunately the English ship providing transport was captured by a French privateer and the heart taken prisoner. In view of the status of the body to which it had belonged, the French impounded it for six years and then succeeded in trading it for twenty captured French naval officers.[124]

In most European states during the 1650–1750 period, noble elites also established a virtual monopoly of the membership of the new permanent diplomatic corps.[125] At the same time they secured a more prominent role in the crucial leadership of the church in their respective states. As already recorded, four out of five bishops appointed by Louis XIV were of noble origin – far more than in previous or subsequent periods.[126] In short, by redefining themselves broadly as a service nobility, with the encouragement of monarchs, elites locked themselves into the royal dynastic state more totally than ever before, and helped it to survive.[127] The state did not expand at their expense but to their advantage, in the shape of patronage, positions and profit. Throughout Europe, from the shores of the Clyde to the Bay of Naples, elites began the 1650–1750 period by resisting the growth of state power and ended by embracing it.[128]

Elites brought with them un-bureaucratic methods. As explained, patronage and clientage were formerly assumed to have been terminated in the 1650–1750 period by the rise of impersonal bureaucracy, in which officials were obeyed by virtue of their office and not because they were part of a patron–client relationship. It is now clear that bureaucracy was not impersonal in this period. It was infiltrated from top to bottom by networks of elite personal relationships. They were deployed to reinforce royal administration in a world where social standing automatically conferred authority. Instinctive obedience to government administrators was not then a deeply rooted habit. Bureaucracies and standing armies had to go with the grain and operate as much through the social system as through the formal structures.[129] Administrative institutions could work only if they were reinforced by the patronage and clientage which acted as their instructional DNA.

If monarchs had to cut deals with elites in order to survive, in what sense was this period the zenith of absolute monarchy? It should not surprise us to learn that monarchs gained as much as elites. As partnership was restored and monarchs demonstrated that they could be trusted to respect the rights and privileges of composite states and their elites, they in their turn were increasingly entrusted with the traditional powers and prerogatives of monarchy. In recent decades this had not always been the case. In both Denmark–Norway and Sweden–Finland royal prerogatives had been subject to the veto of a council of nobles. In Brandenburg the ruler's right to declare war had been subject to the agreement of the elected Estates; soldiers had to take an oath to the Estates as well as to the ruler.[130] In Britain the monarch had lost all his prerogatives, followed by his head. Once elites no longer defined these royal powers as a threat, however, greater authority was invested in hereditary monarchs than at any time before or since.[131] Not only waging war but also diplomacy and treaty-making were royal prerogatives. Whole populations could be signed away by one ruler to another in the dynastic haggling which characterized *ancien régime* peace conferences. In the context of modern European democracy it seems incredible that the life and death of millions hung on the decision of one un-elected person. Such was absolute monarchy at its zenith.

## Cultural Strategies: Agendas, Media and Messages

Culture in the 1650–1750 period took many forms, whether ceremonial, propagandist, philosophical, visual, written, heard or built. These embrace culture in its more recent sense of all the arts – literature, music, painting and architecture. They also extend to culture in its older anthropological sense – beliefs, manners, morals and values, as well as the rituals, customs and institutions which embody them. Culture in all its forms was vital for political and social stability in what had proved inherently unstable regimes. Rulers had learned the hard way that despotic force could not be deployed in dynastic territorial patchworks dominated by independent-minded local elites.[132] Persuasive messages therefore needed to be transmitted and mental attitudes manipulated. In an age before the availability of mass media, high-level cultural strategies were essential for the consolidation of crown–elite co-operation and for the cohesion of elites themselves – both in their own perception and in that of the common people. The culture of this period has always been noted for its high political content. More than ever before, politics and culture became fused. Hence *The Politics of Culture* – the sub-title of this book, which explores the close relationship between them.

In the nineteenth century royal courts began to be discarded by scholars as unworthy of serious investigation – a trend which continued for much of the twentieth.[133] In recent decades historians have illuminated their culture in the early-modern period as a supreme instrument of persuasion and promotion.[134] Since 1996, a scholarly journal has successfully reinstated royal courts as vital rather than merely ornamental institutions.[135] Yet far less attention has been paid to elite culture in general, of which court culture was a vital and trend-setting part – but *only* a part. This neglect is unjustified. Between the 1650s and 1750s, partly boosted by the restoration of religious consensus, elite cultural cohesion performed a vital role in loosely-jointed composite states. It was a strong bonding agent in realms defined by diversity and difference. Increasingly adopting a common language in this period, a state's elites could link arms across all of a monarch's territorial possessions – an ability denied to the common people, most of whom spoke different languages within the same composite state. As they were increasingly cosmopolitan, elites could to some extent link arms across Europe. By the end of the period, European elites shared a cohesive cultural identity.[136]

Political elites had previously followed the cultural lead of others. Political and cultural elites now increasingly became the same people. To achieve this, political elites became better educated – a condition previously considered more suitable for clerks than for gentlemen. From Muscovy to Scotland there was a drive to raise elite educational standards. Nor was this merely about monarchs cracking down on elites: it was also about educated elites cracking down on boorish elites.[137] The arts and sciences were now released from the sixteenth-century stranglehold of professional university scholars and the way was opened to the gentleman amateur – and even to his wife. Many of them wrote poetry, novels and works of moral or political philosophy. Before the mid-seventeenth century most English dramatists had been professional writers like Shakespeare, but from the 1660s many leading London playwrights were gentlemen and the lives about which they wrote were their own.[138]

Elites made an even greater cultural impact as patrons and sponsors. The Grand Manner was invented as a style of painting and sculpture by Bernini and Poussin, both of whom were humbly born. But what mattered was that the Grand Manner supplied the style that elites overwhelmingly favoured, since it expressed their nobly heroic image of themselves. Unlike the romantic era which followed, this period was one of deference in which most artists submitted to the strongly articulated taste and requirements of their employers. Consequently, whether as active participants in cultural creativity or as patrons at one remove, elites communicated their values and concerns. In this sense they were the leading cultural voice, and aristocratic culture became something new in European history. In modern parlance, they invented their own cultural brand.

The importance and uniqueness of the 1650–1750 period in this respect have been insufficiently emphasized. This is partly because the social context of its culture has been studied far less than that of the Enlightened period which followed it.[139] It appears that an explicitly elitist culture was forged. This deliberately distanced itself from popular culture and thereby acquired a grandeur which overawed the common people, while in some crucial respects retaining an ability to communicate with them. There had always been a cultural gap between elites and common people, but until the seventeenth century elites had taken part in popular festivals, processions, theatricals and ceremonies. From the mid-seventeenth century this participation rapidly declined. At precisely the same time, French elites dropped their rich array of regional dialects and began to speak and write standard Parisian French. Local dialect was derided as 'patois' (from *patte*, an animal's paw). In a movement which was imitated all over Europe, French elite literature adopted a highly sophisticated vocabulary from which every hint of common usage was purged. The gap between elite and popular culture widened so dramatically, especially in France, that it seemed as if the country had split into two mutually incomprehensible cultural spheres. By the 1750s the *Encyclopédie* of Diderot and d'Alembert could comment with reference to the peasantry that 'many [educated] people see little difference between this class of men and the animals they use to farm our lands'.[140]

The phrase 'elite culture' as used here has nothing to do with the kind of highbrow culture which frightens *Sun* and *Mirror* readers – though they might well pigeon-hole Handel's operas under that category. It involves no value judgements. The phrase indicates the culture, of whatever quality, created or sponsored by monarchy, clergy and aristocracy. They had to achieve a difficult cultural balancing act. They wished to stress and define the superior values which separated them *from* the largely illiterate masses while simultaneously communicating *with* them. Luckily, the baroque style was available and they made it their own. Intellectually it was highly sophisticated and yet it made an instant appeal to the senses and emotions – even to the sentiments. Some historians have discerned an element of kitsch in baroque art, which enabled some of the world's greatest artists to communicate to an uneducated popular audience the values of ruling elites.[141]

Baroque was a perfect vehicle for cross-cultural communication.[142] Southern, central and eastern Europe responded with relish. Spain, Italy, the Spanish Netherlands, Germany, Bohemia, Hungary, Poland and Russia all succumbed between the 1650s and the 1750s to a mania for building baroque and rococo churches and palaces. They sweep up the beholder in a swirl of spiritual ecstasy. Educated taste is not obligatory. The abbey of Melk is built high on a cliff towering above the river Danube and shimmers with ornamented domes and gilded pinnacles. It celebrates the glory of God and the alliance of elites who built it. It was also intended to make a clear statement of the might of the world's spiritual rulers to the peasants who toiled in the fields below. Its structural and decorative scheme is pure Disneyland.

Elite culture attained its zenith in the 1650–1750 period. So did court culture. This suggests that both were a response to religious and political civil war and to the mid-seventeenth-century crisis – a tool in the same repair kit, in fact. The hypothesis is hard to prove conclusively. There was no documented high-level meeting at which a key player announced 'OK boys, here's the recovery plan.' One can only point to the culture's endlessly reiterated themes. The generations which remembered the 1640s were stricken by terror of anarchy for the rest of their lives and the renegotiated pact between rulers and their elites seems to have required expression in a strong corporate ideology.[143] The same courtly theme which fixated monarchs is a steady drumbeat throughout elite culture. This was a new conception of order, derived from the natural philosophers and their discovery of a demonstrable order in the universe. Shakespeare had much to say about order, but the revised version was pursued far more obsessively. Order in its many derivations became the mantra of monarchs and their elites – order in the state, order in administration, order in the church, order in society, order in the individual. It found its supreme expression in cultural style and content – whether it be reason's conquest of passion within the souls of Corneille's dramatic heroes, the noble proportions of an obelisk or the orotund flourishes of a baroque sermon. Its organizing principle was hierarchy. This ranked various social-status grades one above another, each performing its allotted role in the overall scheme of things. Monarchs showcased order and hierarchy in court spectaculars, aristocrats promoted them through their arts and 'sciences' (however disinterested the enquiries on which they were originally based) and prelates directed that they should be preached in their churches. It was a formidable team, which joined forces to promote the values on which it depended.

This elite collaboration was lucky to employ some of the greatest writers, painters, architects and musicians in European history, who raised a conservative cliché to a state of glory. Yet a degree of conformity was always expected: it is useless to trawl the period for rebel artists like Michelangelo and Beethoven. Members of the elite public seem to have had no objection to conventional themes and formulaic handling.[144] This clearly differentiates artists of the baroque era from their Renaissance predecessors. In the fifteenth and early sixteenth centuries architects and painters had competed to experiment and innovate, both in the forms they employed and in the themes they transmitted. Patrons made no attempt to impose conformity. Originality was perceived as an integral part of artistic genius. But not for long.

The launch of the Counter-Reformation, in the mid-sixteenth century, severely limited intellectual freedom for 200 years. After the mid-seventeenth century, elites were additionally determined to present a united cultural front. In the 1650–1750 period, conformity was increasingly shaken off in natural philosophy (ancestor of modern science) and to some extent in political culture; but it continued to prevail in much artistic and religious culture. The *ancien régime's* most oppressive weapon was the law, accompanied by the cosh of church or state censorship. A degree of conformity was imposed by the academies in which rulers as varied as Bourbons and Medicis corralled and rewarded their creative spirits. A further lever was elite social pressure, in the shape of the universal demand for decorum in style and subject matter – a constraint implicit in every act of elite financial patronage, along with a general obligation to glorify the sponsor. The willingness of artists to toe the line differentiates those of the baroque period not only from their Renaissance predecessors but also from their successors in the romantic era, which rapidly germinated from the 1750s. Only then were conventions and formulae again deemed an offence against authenticity, spontaneity and originality.[145]

The result was the development of a self-conscious ruling class with a distinctive culture which prescribed its rules, defined its values and distinguished it from commoners.[146] This culture may have conformed to strictly enunciated norms but it certainly stated its case. The churches of Wren and Bernini, Neumann's abbeys and palaces, Tiepolo's paintings, Racine's dramas and Handel's operas are available for our inspection three centuries later. Whatever the inner insecurities of elites, they projected through their chosen artists a dazzling display of self-confidence.

It is important not to weaken the argument by pushing it too far. Though the monarchs, aristocrats and prelates who controlled artistic patronage were a daunting partnership, it would be absurd to claim that no serious creative artists escaped their control. Watteau was recognized as one of the most gifted and original of French painters. Yet he never had a patron. Finding that friendly dealers offered him more freedom, he deliberately avoided commissions. His refusal to be embraced by the artistic establishment led to increasingly eccentric behaviour. At one point he went into hiding.[147]

The category of painting which he invented was the *fête galante*. It depicts fashionable people relaxing in an idyllic country landscape. They are making music, conversation and love. This is dreamy leisure with an erotic charge. Lulled in the soft afternoon air, Watteau's lovers seem to defy the passage of time – until one spots the stone figure reclining on a plinth, a lurking presence in all such paintings. It alone remains eternally, when the music has faded and the singers are gone. Watteau's innovation was imitated until he fell heavily from favour in the later eighteenth century; but now, again, he remains for many people one of the most familiar and attractive of eighteenth-century painters. Yet his work is outside the artistic mainstream of the period and corresponds to no aspect of elite iconography, whether historical, mythological, political or religious.[148]

On any definition, culture embraces religion. Yet the years between 1650 and 1750 have long been viewed as the period when the political grip of religion and the churches weakened. This is certainly true of foreign affairs, where confessional motives lessened and religion ceased to be a major cause of warfare between Christians. But revisionist historians have argued forcefully that political culture remained saturated in Christian values and beliefs.[149] Much the same is true of natural philosophy: as an alternative peephole into the mind of God, the natural world was studied as eagerly as the Christian scriptures. The widely perceived mental unison between religious, 'scientific', political and artistic cultures contrasts with the clashing ideologies of later eras. It mirrored the united front of monarchs, aristocrats and clergy. It also welded them into an even stronger power elite and helped them to weather the occasional squall in mutual relations.

The middle of the eighteenth century has recently been hailed as the climax of the Catholic Counter-Reformation, with Protestant missionary activity not far behind in central and eastern Europe.[150] In France, Louis XIV's reign saw the Catholic Reformation running at full tilt, with toleration of Protestants officially terminated and bishops displaying unprecedented determination to regulate religious and moral behaviour in encyclopaedic detail.[151] At the other end of Europe, most of Hungary and much of Poland were won back to Rome from Protestantism before the middle of the eighteenth century. The restoration of religious unity (Catholic or Protestant) within most states during the period strengthened the power of ruling dynasties, reunited them with their elites and gave composite states what little coherence they had.[152] Dynasties were the prime focus of loyalty, but their sovereignty rested on theological as much as on political foundations. Reinforced by divine sanction, they remained the focus of political obedience until the rise of nationalism in the late eighteenth century.[153]

## Royal Courts: Focus of Culture and Politics

The royal court was where power politics and culture met. Its functions were fourfold. It was the stage on which royalty and elites displayed and 'represented' themselves in the role which was theirs, spiritual Mecca and market place for cultural providers and consumers, political forum for decision-making and central switchboard for the operation of patronage networks. The first required magnificence, which Montesquieu pronounced to be an essential ingredient in royal power. It was an intrinsic part of the job and not a bolt-on accessory – hence a key task for the visual and auditory arts. As Louis XIV himself put it:

> Those people are gravely mistaken who imagine that all this is mere ceremony. The people over whom we rule, unable to see to the bottom of things, usually judge by what they see from outside, and most often it is by precedence and rank that they measure their respect and obedience.[154]

The second represented a powerful unifying role by forging the value system of *ancien régime* court society, largely based on the foundation of the ancient classics.[155] The third required elite factions to be manipulated and balanced in order to prevent any one of them dominating the monarch and to allow the latter to divide and rule. The last underlines an important shift in historical thinking. Since for much of the nineteenth and twentieth centuries historians believed that the rise of bureaucracy eliminated patronage and clientage, they also assumed that the patrimonial and administrative functions of the royal court disappeared with them. Obviously, if the former was not the case, neither was the latter.[156]

After the mid-seventeenth-century crisis, royal courts expanded their traditional role in order to project and enact the ruler's redefined mission as supporter of elites and supreme arbiter between them. A common interest in power obviously did not inoculate elites against rivalry. They competed fiercely for influence and royal favour, both outside the court and within it. An effective court was therefore never monolithic: it reflected elite divisions even as it sought to reconcile them.[157] Many of the elite aspired to influence or participate in the court's cultural and political roles. There was an insatiable demand for court offices – not because they carried large fees, which they did not, but because of the opportunity they presented for profitable networking. High-flying elites therefore needed to be present and the royal court was the most effective centralizing agency in the period. Its magnetic attraction pulled together the centrifugal components of a composite state as no other device could. The court reached its zenith in the 1650–1750 period, when the challenge of unifying composite states at some level was at its most urgent. For the Austrian Habsburgs their court in Vienna was an especially crucial linchpin: there was no other central institution with authority over the totality of the dynasty's territories. If provincial assemblies were sometimes a problem, the Bavarian Wittelsbachs had an answer to that. The highest court offices were held by the most august representatives of the Estates.[158]

The court was thus a mechanism for the management of elite provincial power structures. As the formal 'bureaucracy' could act effectively only when reinforced by these informal patronage systems, both needed to be focused on the same operational headquarters at court. Official ministers therefore needed to be courtiers as well, since they depended on the patronage networks to activate their administrative mechanisms.[159] In Vienna the contrast between noble courtiers and 'bourgeois' ministers makes no more sense than in France: they were often the same people.[160] The same is true in reverse. In France the main court factions of the 1730s, those led by the Noailles, the Belle-Isle, the d'Orléans and the Bourbon-Condé, had tap-roots in the provinces. Their in-fighting could not therefore be confined to the centre. Conflicts at court spilled over into Estates and *parlements*, as courtiers intrigued with their clients in corporate bodies to sabotage their rivals.[161]

The attendance of elites at court has been much misunderstood. Unfortunately, the historian who put the court back on the historical agenda after decades of neglect partly mistook its function. He launched the influential view that royal courts in this period were mechanisms for cutting off higher elites from their local power bases. Instead of devoting their energies to asserting semi-independence and plotting revolt, they were tamed and domesticated by involvement in prestigious but non-threatening activities under the royal eye.[162] This perspective tends to endorse the myth of monarchs and elites as antagonists rather than partners. It also misses the point that elites had their own courtly agendas. Attendance was just as likely to be an opportunity for them to influence or manipulate their ruler – or to use the court to establish their own status through the ceremony of presentation to the monarch.[163] Nor did elites neglect their local roots, since their usefulness to the monarch was based on their regional authority, which by this time could be reinforced and extended only with royal support. The greater nobility needed to acquire time-management skills. They had to spend time at court and in the capital as well as in the provinces. One of the habits which distinguished higher elites from commoners was their tendency to travel.

A royal court operated on subtler and more diverse levels than is evident from Elias. It performed two apparently opposite functions. It threw a protective cocoon around the monarch by erecting barriers between him and his subjects. These took the form of physical impediments like the guarded door of the royal chamber, and the magnificent ceremonial which created psychological distance when the monarch appeared in public. Obstacles were removed for those who belonged to his family or inner circle, and also for the chosen few who took turns to perform ritual duties for him. The honour of holding the voluminous royal nightshirt over the king's head while he discovered the sleeve openings is the classic and oft-quoted example. But from another perspective the court was the point of contact between the monarch and his elites. It connected the monarch to a larger political and social universe through forms of cultural representation that maintained his symbolic presence at a distance, and through patrimonial networks which radiated out to elites in the provinces.[164] The court thus achieved the difficult feat of elevating the monarch while simultaneously making him accessible.

At court most monarchs nevertheless spent much of their lives in the public eye. Like today's celebrities and politicians, they could claim no inner sphere as private – though their observers were omnipresent servants and courtiers rather than intrusive *paparazzi*. Most rulers ate in public and an audience was admitted to watch them do it. At Versailles, every time the king drank, a royal salvo was fired. Even royal couplings were regarded at Versailles as a matter of legitimate public interest – especially on wedding nights, when courtiers cupped their ears outside the door of the queen's bedchamber and monitored the stamina of her husband's performance.[165] Nine months later, if things went according to plan, they clambered onto ladders in the doorway of the same apartment to get a ringside view of the royal birth.

If political obedience was a religious duty, court ceremonial needed to fuse political and spiritual allegiance. Though the court as royal theatre has become a cliché, much of its ritual was in fact highly repetitive, potentially dull and quasi-liturgical. It presented the monarch as a sacred object to be venerated. Kings, whether sitting or standing in state or moving in procession, did so under the same type of canopy that was carried over the consecrated elements of the Mass. The triple bow or 'reverence', obligatory in most courts for persons who approached monarchs, echoed the obeisance performed to the consecrated bread. Perhaps surprisingly, the etiquette of Protestant courts reflected a religious emphasis similar to that of their Catholic opposite numbers. When the cultural climate began to change towards the end of the 1650–1750 period, it was in Protestant courts like Berlin and London that emphasis on sacral ceremonial was slimmed down or abolished. But this trend became general only from the 1750s.[166]

As royal courts widened their functions as focal points of composite states, we should expect them to expand physically as well. And indeed they did. Their growth seems to have climaxed in different places at different times during the decades around 1700.[167] So far the most detailed research has focused on the court of the Austrian Habsburgs. Their household personnel began to rise dramatically under Leopold I (1658–1705) and amounted to no fewer than 2,000–2,500 persons under Charles VI (1711–40). Expenditure on the court rose fivefold during Leopold's reign and had almost doubled again by the 1730s. The accession of Maria Theresa in 1740 stopped this trend in its tracks and reversed it. Habsburg court culture displayed a similar trajectory. From the mid-seventeenth century, there was a new emphasis on the precise codification of the court's ceremonial and on the expansion of its cultural activities – a development again arrested in the 1740s by the arrival of Maria Theresa.[168] The court of Bavaria shows a similar trajectory. It contracted during the Thirty Years War, grew steadily from the 1650s and reached its peak in the second half of the eighteenth century.[169]

This pattern of growth is related to two other factors. In the sixteenth century, and to a lesser extent in the early seventeenth, many great European aristocrats had maintained their own private courts on a scale which rivalled the monarch's court. By the later seventeenth and eighteenth centuries this was unknown outside Poland–Lithuania, where the crown was elective, penurious, and insignificant. Elsewhere the lives of European elites in the 1650–1750 period were dominated to an unprecedented extent by the courts of their monarchs – either directly by their own presence there or indirectly by their connection to someone from whose attendance they could benefit. At the same time the great royal courts of Europe became permanently located near the state capital rather then peripatetic as previously. The pioneers were the Spanish Habsburgs, who settled in Madrid in the sixteenth century and were followed by their elites in the seventeenth. In the later seventeenth century the Bourbon monarch settled at Versailles on the outskirts of Paris and leading nobles scrambled to catch up with their master by building luxury *hôtels* in the city. After the defeat of the Turkish siege in 1683 the Austrian Habsburgs and their elites finally settled in Vienna. In the first two decades of the eighteenth century the Romanovs moved to their newly built capital of St Petersburg. In a characteristically different procedure, they ordered their elites to follow.[170]

Not all royal courts were so successful. The early eighteenth century was not a golden period for the Stuart and Hanoverian court in London. It declined as a centre of cultural patronage and elites had to look elsewhere for entertainment.[171] By the early eighteenth century Britain had a strong monarchy for which existing royal palaces were perceived as inadequate. This was not primarily a reflection of the financial constraints on her monarchs. Continental rulers, including Louis XIV, spent far more than they could afford on palaces but believed magnificence justified debt. The ingredients missing in England were dynastic confidence and continuity. No family was on the throne for long enough to develop a style and momentum of palace building. The net result of dynastic convulsions in 1649, 1688 and 1714 was failure of nerve.[172]

The courts of George I and II consequently remained parasitic on the capital city. Versailles was a self-sufficient colony of 10,000 artists, cooks, stable boys, servants and courtiers, independent of Paris and providing employment for the town of Versailles. But when George II wanted to see a play or opera, he had to leave St James's and visit a London theatre, like the rest of the public. The Hanoverian court was never more than 1,500. It failed to generate its own large-scale entertainments and was one among other foci of social and cultural life. This weakened its hold on the loyalty of its courtiers, as a duchess demonstrated in a devastating snub to her monarch:

> The Duchess of Queensberry is surprised and well pleased that the King hath given her so agreeable a command as to stay from Court, where she never came for diversion, but to bestow a great civility on the King and Queen; she hopes that by such an unprecedented order as this is, the King will see as few as he wishes at Court, particularly such as dare to think or speak truth.[173]

## Summary

In most European composite states the crisis of the mid-seventeenth century had proved despotism to be unworkable. The wars of religion which preceded and overlapped with it had proved that religious diversity was fatal to state cohesiveness. To avoid a repetition of upheaval, elites closed ranks with their monarchs. Rather than ruler–elite deadlock there was now a desire for partnership, sustained by absolute royal authority redefined and deployed in a non-despotic manner. Religious cohesion was gradually restored as most states moved to impose either Catholic or Protestant religion, particularly amongst elites.[174] In the twenty-first century it seems unlikely that so simple a strategy could hold a massive socio-political structure in place. The brutal truth is that as long as royal, landed and ecclesiastical elites remained united there was little chance of successful revolution from below, since the great majority of the population were tradition-bound and semi-literate peasants.[175]

In contrast to their disarray in the preceding period, elites were now religiously unified, culturally reinforced, economically boosted and politically integrated into the state. The 1650–1750 period has been justly defined as a century of relative political and social stability – an *ancien régime* during which an unprecedented degree of unchallenged authority was concentrated in the hands of rulers, to be exercised in the interest of traditional elites who had cornered the market in power, status and wealth. From the mid-seventeenth century the lid was more or less closed on Pandora's box and the greatest age of monarchy, church and aristocracy was inaugurated.[176]

Historians are now becoming clearer about the basic priorities of monarchical states during the period. In the light of the new natural philosophy or 'science', updated state agendas were proposed by German Cameralists and others, though they had little practical impact until the later eighteenth century.[177] In the 1680s the Habsburg Emperor Leopold I's Cameralist minister Schröder anticipated Joseph II's arguments of a century later for the protection of the peasantry as the main source of production and tax revenue. His successor Joseph I endorsed a financial package proposed by his Cameralist minister Schierendorf. In many ways a pre-run of Joseph II's scheme of the 1780s, a 'universal excise' was to be levied uniformly throughout the hereditary lands, while peasants' labour services and taxes were to be reduced. It was vetoed by his successor, Charles VI (1705–40).[178]

The agenda that mattered between 1650 and 1750 was the traditional one. The partnership between monarch, nobles and church was more than a means of running an early modern state: it defined its essence. The dominant and privileged position of nobility and clergy was not merely a means of keeping the show on the road: it *was* the show. Maintenance of a social order based on the privileged position of the nobility, and of a spiritual order based on that of the church, remained the most fundamental purpose of government in this period. Its other basic purpose was waging dynastic war – a theatre in which the nobility again steps to the front. Though most wars in this period were initially fought to promote the dynastic ambitions of monarchs rather than nobles, military activity was a nobleman's *raison d'être* and army promotion a major strategy for boosting his own dynastic advancement.[179]

At the end of the period, however, monarchical despotism returned with a new ideological rationale in the shape of the European Enlightenment. It targeted the privileges of nobilities and churches. Elites now found themselves inhabiting a hostile environment. The churches ceased to expand and stalled. From the 1750s nobles began to be replaced in government at all levels by full-time professional bureaucrats – a development made possible by the spread of education beyond elites and by weakened belief in the idea of natural hierarchy.[180] Enlightened rulers who adopted the Habsburg Emperor Joseph II as a model were openly hostile to the aristocracy. The web of corporate, aristocratic and provincial privilege which festooned every state came to be viewed as a rationalists' nightmare inherited from the Middle Ages. Reason was hailed as a modern weapon to unify and equalize. This proved toxic. The traditional allies on which rulers had relied were alienated and undermined. The *ancien régime* was thus weakened from above by royal action and subsequently destroyed from below by revolution.

# Chapter 1: Key Themes of Elite Culture

## Truths Ancient and Modern

### The Christian religion: the foundation of everything

Samuel Hartlib is not a name that shouts from the page. Its owner was born in Polish Prussia and by the 1650s was highly influential in intellectual circles in London. His writings proclaimed the need for a nationwide news and information service, near-universal education and the harnessing of science to the improvement of human health. Historians who have heard of him tend to salute him as a pioneer of what was to become the modern welfare state.[1]

Yet his proposals were not as modern as they seem. Hartlib was not looking forward but back. He wanted to return to the golden age before the Fall of Man. He believed that implementation of his programme would re-establish the innocence and happiness that had vanished from the world when Eve tasted the forbidden fruit. This would herald nothing less than the Millennium in its original jaw-dropping sense: Christ would return to reign on earth with his saints for a thousand years.[2] Hartlib's inspiration is therefore the Bible – or, to be precise, chapter 20 of the Book of Revelation. And he was typical of his generation in setting firmly within the context of divine purpose what we regard as non-spiritual areas of policy and activity. There is no evidence that Hartlib's contemporaries classified him as a lunatic. On the contrary, he received a pension from Lord Protector Cromwell. Yet he was a direct descendant, though a more peaceful version, of the blood-spattered self-appointed prophets of the apocalypse who terrorized Europe between the eleventh and sixteenth centuries. They fizzed with religious frenzy and strove to establish heaven on earth. Instead they created hell.[3]

The moral of this tale is that we continuously rewrite the past to reflect, consciously or unconsciously, our own preoccupations. This creates a constant temptation to exaggerate its modernity. At a distance of three centuries the key role and visceral grip of early-modern religion are not always apparent to secular-minded modern people. We fail to realize that the rise of mathematics in the seventeenth century was partly driven by an urgent need to decode Biblical numerology and reveal the date of the Christ's Second Coming.[4] Few now know that Columbus (admittedly a little earlier) interpreted his discoveries in the Americas in exactly the same way that Hartlib viewed his welfare programme – as a divinely ordained precondition of the end of the world.[5]

Two generations ago the 1650–1750 period was widely regarded as an age of secularization, scepticism and toleration, in contrast to the religious wars which preceded it and the wars of political ideology which followed.[6] This was the impact of secular-minded historians of a later age who were keen to write religion out of history at the earliest possible stage. Yet Bach's *St Matthew Passion* and Handel's *Messiah* are towering musical monuments of the early eighteenth century – profoundly religious works in an age viewed until recently as increasingly dominated by reason, science and the calculations of the banking house. More fundamentally, either Protestantism or Catholicism was the official religion in most European states during the period. It was backed by the full force of the state and its morality was enforced in the church's courts. This was by no means a defining characteristic of absolute monarchies: the Venetian and Dutch republics were just as active in this respect. By the standards of modern liberal democracy, all states made outrageously totalitarian intrusions into the private life and conscience of their populations. This was still the era of medieval theocracies, where the state was in business to uphold a religion. The pioneers in the period who wished to separate church and state still had a long way to go.

The first key theme of the 1650–1750 period is therefore the centrality of the Christian religion, based on a medieval blend of the Bible and early Christian theologians. Later seventeenth- and earlier eighteenth-century thought was, in John Redwood's memorable phrase, 'God-ridden'. Whenever a man took up his quill and wrote about the weather or the seasons, the structure of the earth or the movement of the heavenly bodies, the power of rulers or the organization of society, he was by definition writing about God. The scholarly disciplines as we know them were, then, inseparable from theology and revolved round it. Whether experts argued about politics, philosophy, society or economics, it all boiled down to the same basic debate – the place of man in a Christian community in God's universe.[7] In this period religion often proved a far stronger bond than a common language or nation. French Protestants were merely following established custom when they signed up in the army of Protestant Brandenburg.[8]

Early-modern people of all classes therefore inhabited a lost mental world which disappeared somewhat suddenly in the second half of the eighteenth century. Historians working on Victorian England who visit the foreign country of the seventeenth and eighteenth centuries feel they might as well be studying the Middle Ages.[9] For much of the intervening period early-modern culture and ideas were ignored or misunderstood. Recovering them therefore involves an ongoing revolution in cultural historiography.

## The ancient classics: order and control

If the Christian religion was the intellectual cement of early-modern Europe, its clashing theological interpretations had ripped it apart. Confrontations between Catholic and Protestant, deadly offspring of sixteenth-century Reformations, partly fuelled the Thirty Years War and the General European Crisis which erupted at its climax. In contrast, in architecture and painting as much as literature and philosophy, classicism and its preoccupation with rules and conventions was perceived as a route to stability and order.[10] The second key theme of the period is therefore reverence for the culture of ancient Greece and Rome. The classics supplied the conceptual framework of all political debate, and command of Latin and/or Greek defined the crucial distinction between the educated elite and the plebeian 'lewd'. There was the tiny minority who were well enough educated to understood the classics and appreciate the values they embodied, and there were the 95 per cent or more of Europeans who were not.[11] The 1650–1750 period was unique in two respects. It was the age when Europe's landed elite was politically, socially, economically and culturally dominant.[12] It was also the period when the classical civilization of ancient Rome (and Greece to a far lesser extent) was revered as never before or since. This juxtaposition was no coincidence. Classical culture was suited to an aristocratic society, especially as it embraced a selective version of the classics which showcased harmony, balance and proportion – the qualities which an aristocratic society wanted to hear about. Maintaining an equipoise between extremes was an obvious way of avoiding further violent confrontations. The resulting stress on reason and emotional restraint appealed to an elite which prized order and control, in art as in life.[13] The darker and more irrational side of the ancient Greeks and Romans was ignored.

The claim that the appeal of classicism peaked in the 1650–1750 period requires justification. It is true that the Renaissance of the fifteenth and six-teenth centuries had anticipated this veneration of the classical culture of ancient Greece and Rome. But its early enthusiasts were grammarians, lin-guists and scholars and it began in one of the few Italian city states which had not fallen under the rule of a single prince. Bruni (the first translator of Plato and Aristotle into Latin) was a professional rhetorician, in the serv-ice of the Florentine republic and subsequently its Chancellor.[14] That repub-lic was governed by substantial merchants and craftsmen and had excluded the landed nobility from power.[15] The classics in their early-Renaissance phase therefore lacked the deliberate association with Europe's ruling elite which they acquired in the 1650–1750 period. It was then that they became the core of every gentleman's education – a tradition that lingered into the England of the 1950s.

It is also true that the neo-classical movement in architecture and painting was to prolong the worship of the classics into the later eighteenth and early nineteenth centuries. But by then classicism in literature was under increas-ingly heavy attack. In Germany the rigid classical rulebook, especially in the guise of French cultural dominance, was ripped up. Its supremacy was con-tested by growing enthusiasm for folk culture and its stress on reason, under-mined by Rousseau's cult of feeling and high-minded 'sensibility'.[16] But in the 1650–1750 period, in spite of a brief literary war between the 'Ancients and Moderns', classicism reigned almost unchallenged. Its touch conferred unique prestige. No gentleman's residence was complete without a classical portico above his door, classical texts in his library or a classical bust in his hall. A modern business mogul or celebrity cannot perform convincingly without a private jet, several Ferraris and a fleet of stretched limousines. Early-modern elites, in contrast, sensed a continuity of civilization extending over two thousand years. They preferred the prestige of classical Corinthian columns.

*Natural philosophy: the harmonious order of the cosmos*

These two previous themes represent the ancient source of supreme autho-rity in matters theological, moral, scientific and artistic. A new strand was derived from the natural philosophers, who had arrived on the scene in the seventeenth century. They aimed to discover the order that underlay God's apparently random universe and were inspired by a new sense of evidence based on what could be observed, counted and calculated by human reason.

They were what we should call scientists. These natural philosophers realized that the resulting knowledge offered huge potential. If they could understand the laws which governed the cosmos, there was a chance that they could harness its powers. Reason was seen as the ally rather than the enemy of religion, since it increased understanding of God's created universe. If we ignore a tiny minority of advanced thinkers who had the future on their side but were untypical of their own time, the tension between religion and science is revealed as an exaggeration, if not a myth, projected onto the 1650–1750 period by the century of Charles Darwin.

The swift and decisive advance of natural philosophy in the mid-seventeenth century is one of the mysteries of European history. Bacon had advocated much the same approach half a century before, with minimal impact. So had Galileo, pioneer physicist and astronomer. The Inquisition had placed him under house arrest for the rest of his life. Kepler, who revealed the laws of planetary motion in the 1620s, remained obscure – in spite of providing equations which were universal and verifiable. Why did natural philosophy triumph a mere forty years later? It would seem that, by then, natural philosophy told people what they wanted to hear. Both its champions and their audience had lived through bloody war and disruptive revolt. Natural philosophy responded to the same need as classicism – for order, harmony and certainty in a fractured world where all 'truths' were contested.[17] The quest for order and harmony in the universe was an old one, inherited from the Ancient Greeks via the Renaissance. Their location usually came vaguely packaged as 'the music of the spheres' and proved elusive. Only in the period 1650–1750 was the source of universal order discovered and universally accepted. This left its mark on the English language at precisely this time. From the mid-seventeenth century we find increasing use of the English word 'cosmos' as a synonym for 'universe'.[18] It was derived from the ancient Greek word meaning 'order'.

It did not take long for the various manifestations of order revealed by natural philosophers to be equated with order in state and church, as sustained by absolute monarchs, nobles and clergy. Order presupposed law. As God had given laws to the cosmos, so the sovereign ruler must give laws to the state. Therefore, for the first and last time in European history, most people now perceived political culture, science and religion as a seamless whole. It may seem odd that the climax of absolute monarchy, which allegedly told everyone what to do and think, coincided with the birth of science, which encouraged them to think for themselves. The truth is less simple. Subjects of absolute monarchs were not encouraged to think for themselves about religion, but other intellectual explorations were increasingly welcomed. Innovation, as opposed to tradition, was officially taboo before the seventeenth century. In this period it became a conceptual possibility. Cutting-edge thinkers proliferated and Europe pulsated from end to end with schemes for increasing the wisdom and happiness of mankind. Most of the new ideas, like those of Hartlib and the natural philosophers, were contained alongside the old ones within the prevailing religious culture. Religion was no mere brick in the cultural and ideological fabric: it was the mortar holding it together.

## Internationalism and its Alternatives

Rulers and elites in the 1650–1750 period were strengthened by their international connections. Since ruling dynasties intermarried, a handful of families ruled between them all European states. Foreign disputes were often merely family quarrels writ large. At bottom there was a bond between all elites, rulers included. They usually felt more in common with their opposite numbers in other states than with the common people in their own. Increasingly well-travelled, they were connected by common interests, a common culture and often a common language. They were more like members of an international club.

The Grand Tour was an elite practice which took off in the second half of the seventeenth century as a means of completing the education of young gentlemen, especially of English milords making their first visit to the Continent. Foreign travel had not previously attracted many Protestants since they risked being snatched by the Catholic Inquisition. But religious passions cooled after the Treaty of Westphalia in 1648 and the term 'Grand Tour' was first used in 1670.[19] Italy was always the ultimate destination and its aristocratic literary academies and colleges of education gave young nobles from all over Europe a veneer of common culture and deportment.[20] By the early eighteenth century, honour and politeness were Europe's international code of elite behaviour, French was its international language and the Grand Tour represented the international 'Gap Year' of its youth. In some ways Europe now became a fraternity of blue blood.[21] In contrast, while members of the lower orders could not afford to travel abroad, they were discouraged from travel of any sort. Whatever the practice, in theory they were supposed to remain in their villages. Plebeian travel was associated with social pests like rebels and vagrants.

Honour involves duelling. In its final genteel form this was another international feature which linked elites across national boundaries, both within multi-national states and between them. All members of the international elite already knew that an insult could be fatal and a challenge was hard to refuse, but not until this period were the rules definitively formulated. When the historical D'Artagnan (of *Three Musketeers* fame) arrived in Paris in the 1620s he immediately found himself participating in a three-a-side match, the seconds of himself and his opponent enthusiastically joining in. But by the second half of the century it was accepted that seconds were non-participating referees.[22] Not until after the Civil Wars was it grasped in England that peasants should not issue challenges – and that one refused to fight them if they did.[23]

Another cosmopolitan feature was the officer corps of most European armies. Throughout the period, nobles frequently served other rulers, especially when foreign monarchs provided military opportunities not available at home. Count Friedrich-Wilhelm von Schaumburg-Lippe-Bückeburg served with the Hanoverians at Dettingen (1743), with the Austrians in Italy (1745), with Ferdinand of Brunswick during the Seven Years War and finally in Portugal during the war against Spain (1762–3). Though untypical in his spectacular wanderlust, he and his type contributed to the cosmopolitanism of the upper ranks of both nobilities and armies.[24]

Of fundamental importance to the growing culture of internationalism was the adoption by European elites of the French language for certain government purposes. Diplomacy and foreign affairs were the key areas. In the 1650–1750 period diplomats from every state came to obey the same rules and conventions (French). They also came to speak the same language (French) as it gradually eclipsed Latin as the dominant medium of European elites. As states like Russia rose from obscurity, they embraced this culture. Between the 1670s and the 1720s all states apart from the Ottoman Empire established permanent embassies in most European capitals. Previous resident missions, where they existed, had been filled by persons of far lower social status, but the diplomatic corps who manned the new institutions were drawn overwhelmingly from the higher ranks of the nobility. Within the states in which they were resident they were now expected to spend much of their time attending the royal courts, thus reflecting and reinforcing the enhanced importance of the latter during the period. The new and larger agencies established at the same time to run foreign policy were also dominated by the nobility. Inevitably they identified with fellow-diplomats whose lifestyle and values they shared. During and after Louis XIV's reign, international diplomacy thus acquired the noble ethos which it was to retain until the First World War. And, as elite cultural values infiltrated and shaped the conduct of international diplomacy, the latter helped to consolidate and unify the grip of elites across Europe.[25]

Also important in maintaining a culture of internationalism was the weakness at elite level of national cultures. The rise of European nation-states in the nineteenth century was to prompt a proliferation of self-consciously national styles in literature, music and the visual arts. These contributed to the sense of national identity without which no nation-state can survive. But before the later eighteenth century, Europe was composed of composite states, each consisting of several nations in the sense of ethnic groups. A nation was a people, and a state a combination of nations. The 'state' was what mattered in the 1650–1750 period but it remained a dispiritingly abstract concept which excited only rulers and left the rest of the population unenthusiastic – if not hostile. The 'nation', in contrast, was a far more resonant and inspiring concept, which would rapidly come into its own – but mainly in the period which followed.[26] Between 1650 and 1750, in spite of some competition between French and Italian music, the nationality of a composite state's culture was therefore largely irrelevant to the state's survival – what mattered was what it proclaimed about the power and values of its ruling dynasty and elites. It was difficult to identify the nationality of many works of art.[27] Music in particular was an international language and probably the most cosmopolitan of the arts. Bach eagerly borrowed and modestly arranged the compositions of his more famous contemporary, the Venetian Vivaldi. He does not seem to have feared that the character of German music was thereby put under threat.

The weakness of national cultural styles in composite states had the result of boosting the international appeal of France and of its language, which was spoken by elites in most parts of Europe. The heroic classicism of French literature and painting and, to a lesser extent, of its architecture was widely admired and imitated. Music was its least successful export: the French could compete with the Italian product in France but not elsewhere. When French culture failed to colonize a location, Italian culture probably did. The result was that elites within composite states, as well as across Europe, were comfortable with a recognizably international cultural style – whether in language, literature, architecture, painting or music. This was one of the features of the 1650–1750 period which both drew elites together and set them apart.[28] Thankfully, it also removes the necessity for a cultural examination of every province of the European composite state system.

Since nations in the ethnic sense existed during the period, however, so did national identity. But it assumed an embryonic form which posed little threat to monarchs, who could even identify with it to the mutual benefit of both. It must be distinguished from a much more dangerous phenomenon, namely nationalism. This asserted the right of each nation to govern itself. There is currently much disagreement about whether this ideology existed before the later eighteenth century.[29] What seems certain is that it was not until then that nationalism became a problem for monarchs. Nationalism was usually a rival for their people's allegiance, since independent nation-states are incompatible with multi-national dynastic states. The former could only be constructed from the wreckage of the latter. The dynastic state system of the *ancien régime* was not convertible into one of nation-states.[30]

But nationalism barely ruffled the surface of the 1650–1750 period. When a national group like the Catalans revolted against the King of Spain in 1640, they do not appear to have done so because they wanted to express their nationhood in the form of political independence. They did so because their traditions and privileges were under attack. National identity might focus and energize their rebellion, but it did not cause it. In Marlborough's wars against Louis XIV (1702–13) it proved hard to rouse the English to the defence of their nation at all, whatever their sense of national identity. Recruiting officers began by tricking yokels into taking the queen's shilling and ended by offering condemned felons military service as an alternative to being hanged. This contrasts glaringly with the situation two centuries later in 1914, when Kitchener's call for men to fight the Kaiser's armies produced a million volunteers in a few weeks.[31]

The name 'Spain' is found on eighteenth-century maps. At first glance it bestows on the relevant area the aspect of a modern nation-state. Then it is realized that Italy and Germany are also labelled in this way, at a period when they were not states at all but parts of various empires. It becomes obvious that 'Spain' was used to describe the Iberian peninsula as a geographical unit but not a political one. Though all of what we call Spain was united under the same ruler, it remained fractured by different cultural, linguistic and historical traditions. The nation of Spain was yet to be born: Catalonia, Galicia and the Basque Country were the recognized terms. These were the 'nations' to which their inhabitants gave primary loyalty, though they acknowledged allegiance to their over-arching monarch. This usage long outlasted the early-modern period. The 1884 edition of the *Dictionary of the Royal Spanish Academy* was the first to define the word *nación* entirely in our sense. Before then, as well as carrying the modern meaning of 'country' or 'nation' it was defined as 'the inhabitants of a province'.[32] It has even been suggested that the real object of an early-modern Spaniard's loyalty, and therefore his *patria*, was a smaller unit than the province, namely the town or village.[33] Whatever the ultimate goal of this historiographical minimalism, in 1790 the Estates of Carniola, a none too significant outpost of the Habsburg central European territories, alluded to their province as *die Nation*, pure and simple.[34]

France can seem to defy the generalization that all states in this period were multi-national. Its core territories were compact and contiguous. Unlike almost every other ruling dynasty, including the families that ruled England during the 1650–1750 period, the Bourbons had not come to their throne from abroad. They identified themselves with the nation and the nation identified with them. The King's children and grandchildren were called 'enfants de France'.[35] At a deeper level, however, this perspective dissolves. France was not a unified nation-state at all. It was a composite state assembled like crazy paving out of bits and pieces of very different territories. Its varied origins were reflected in its chaotic system of government and administration. Seven archbishops claimed to be head of the Catholic Church in France.[36] The base of French national identity now also seems far less solid than it once appeared. Until the late nineteenth century 'France' meant nothing to most of its inhabitants, who had no conception of a world beyond their immediate locality. A sense of national identity was confined to the area round Paris and regional elites in contact with it. If France was a myriad of micro-cultures as late as that, what price national identity two centuries before?[37]

Crucial to national identity is national language. The fringes of France were dominated by foreign languages (Basque, Breton, Flemish and Alsatian), while two main languages were spoken in the rest of the country (French in the north and Occitan in the south). Each of the latter was a mishmash of mutually incomprehensible dialects. To glance briefly ahead, it is tempting to believe that the French Revolution of 1789–95 was enacted in French – and in Paris so it was. But revolutionary leaders were alarmed to discover that their vision of a republican nation, one and indivisible, was merely the fantasy of a small Parisian elite. According to their researches, more than six million out of thirty million French citizens were totally ignorant of the national language, while another six million could barely speak it. France had no more than three million 'pure' French-speakers and many of them could scarcely write it. Foreign visitors found Latin more useful than French. If the official idiom of the French Republic was a minority language, how could the people be taught that they were the proud possessors of liberty and equality – or even that they were French?[38] To look even further ahead, the places of birth and death of 527 architects, writers, composers and painters from the late seventeenth to the early twentieth centuries have been analysed. This demonstrates that the creators of 'French' culture tended to be born, work and spend most of their lives in Paris. Much of what came to be seen as French was peculiar to Paris or an imitation of it. Peasants living in the tens of thousands of semi-independent communities were scarcely aware of these matters. All they knew was that they detested Paris. Even today, the word *Parisien* is an insult in many parts of France.[39]

A nation has been defined as a body of people with a sense of belonging, based on shared historical, cultural, racial or linguistic identity.[40] A modern nation-state like Greece was a nation in this ethnic sense long before it was an independent state, since it spent millennia under foreign rule. Most modern nation-states reversed the process. France, Spain and Italy were states before they were ethno-cultural nations. Embarking on union merely as a hotchpotch of territories under the same ruler, they were forged into something like nation-states in the nineteenth century. After the political unification of Italy in 1870 a statesman remarked: 'We have made Italy: now we must make Italians.'[41] The national identity of these and similar states, in the shape of linguistic and cultural homogeneity, was not a natural phenomenon. It was largely manufactured and imposed, as nineteenth-century governments made successful efforts to homogenize the education and beliefs of the population. This was achieved by missionary zeal and methods which had hitherto been reserved for religious conversion.[42] In some states, especially in eastern Europe, where peoples were untidily intermingled, the process took the ugly form of ethnic cleansing (Spain having set the precedent in the fifteenth and sixteenth centuries).[43] Not until around 1900 could the Gallic mixed salad of Bretons, Auvergnacs and Gascons all be said to consider themselves Frenchmen. Few of them knew what France looked like before the 1880s, when wall maps were issued to schools.[44] The awakening arguably occurred even later for Spaniards, whose loyalties had remained stubbornly regional. In the 1650–1750 period a Spaniard might fight for his family or his home-town (which was his *patria*), his religion or his race, his lord or his king. He seldom fought for 'Spain'. The country seethed with internal rivalries. In 1689 Guipuzcoa threatened war against its neighbouring province of Vizcaya in an argument over iron ore.[45]

Yet many historians, both living and dead, believe that key early-modern European states were nation-states in the making.[46] This may well be true in retrospect. In terms of the objectives of early-modern rulers, however, these historians reverse the truth. They reduce the political history of Europe to the creation of its modern nation-states. This can be reflected in the nomenclature they use. Few historians, with honourable exceptions,[47] give Sweden–Finland and Denmark–Norway their correct names in this period. Instead they write 'Norway', 'Sweden', 'Denmark' and 'Finland', as though it made no difference that they were two composite monarchies rather than four nation-states. No wonder students become confused.

This argument embraces colonies as well as the continent of Europe. Overseas empire is rarely encountered in the standard narrative of absolute monarchy. Yet in this period, when absolute monarchy was at its height, the full intellectual significance of overseas contact and settlement was absorbed for the first time. It was between c.1600 and the 1720s that recognition of Europe as part of a wider world entered the moral, scientific and political consciousness of almost every educated person.[48] Overseas empire could therefore be incorporated into the rationale of the composite state more readily than ever before. Yet it is still assumed that European composite states and overseas empires represented competing historical processes, with the latter threatening the stability of the former.[49] This implies an unreal distinction – a misunderstanding perpetuated by the fact that state formation and colonialism are written about by different types of historian, with overseas empire the preserve of a separate group of 'imperial' historians. In fact, colonial empires were merely overseas extensions of European states by the addition of yet more pieces of territory, continuous with composite monarchy and not distinct from it.[50]

National identity, as it developed from roughly AD 1000, has been a fashionable line of study in recent decades.[51] But until recently no attention has been paid to a conceptual development far more appropriate to the composite states of the 1650–1750 period, namely the forging of over-arching identities for states containing several national identities. Periodically, rulers responded to the concept of rational order and uniformity espoused by natural philosophers. It was obviously helpful to promote some sense of a common culture among the ruling elites of a state's various territories. Sporadic efforts were made to replace the linguistic and political diversity inherited by the rulers of these states with something more unified. The problem of giving a cohesive identity to a supranational empire was addressed by Olivares at the start of the period, in the mid-seventeenth century. He condemned attachment to province as childish sentiment and awarded office without regard to province of origin. Most significantly, he declared that his Habsburg master Philip IV should no longer be 'King of Portugal, Aragon, Valencia and Count of Barcelona' but 'King of Spain'.[52] Unfortunately, the preferred method of Olivares for achieving closer union was despotically centralized uniformity. The resulting rebellion of Portugal and Barcelona were the exact opposite of what he intended, but the name 'Spain' finally stuck.

French Bourbons and Austrian Habsburgs both managed to consolidate their composite states in the 1650–1750 period on the basis of a common language and a re-imposed religious unity based on the Catholic faith. Louis XIV repealed the Edict of Nantes which had granted toleration to Protestants. He certainly appreciated the importance of noble elites sharing the language and culture of their monarch.[53] His minister Colbert pushed intermittently for greater linguistic, administrative and economic unity. Like the Bourbons, the Austrian Habsburgs trumpeted the link between their dynasty's destiny and the True Faith. By 1700, the triumph of their Counter-Reformation was evident. They also sought a symbol of closer integration between their territories but never came up with a snappier name than 'the lands of the House of Habsburg' or 'the lands of the [Holy Roman] Emperor'.[54] They did, however, succeed in making German the language of choice for most ruling elites throughout their empire. In an act of voluntary acculturation, nobles bought into an increasingly dominant Catholic German culture and into the imperial court in Vienna, with all the opportunities for advancement they offered.[55] In seeking to bind their provincial elites to the core territory, the Habsburgs relied for most of this period on cultural links as a substitute for institutional and administrative ones – a striking example of the key role of the arts. Their palaces in Vienna and Prague were extended in the early eighteenth century. The absence of any corresponding extension of governmental authority was concealed behind an intoxicating display of baroque grandeur.[56]

The greatest success in imposing a supranational identity onto older national identities was scored by the newly titled 'Great Britain' after the union of England and Scotland in 1707.[57] Unlike Spain's identity, which was largely focused on loyalty to its Catholic ruling dynasty, Britain's was grounded on a distinct ideology uniting peoples of the British Isles with their overseas dependencies. They were proclaimed to be Protestant, commercial, maritime and free. This owed less to empirical evidence than to Britons' determination to define themselves as the polar opposite of their arch-enemy the French.[58] By 1750 British identity was celebrated in iconic symbols such as Arne's 'Rule Britannia', the national anthem, the Union flag and the laws of cricket.[59]

Yet forging supranational identities was one thing and building nation-states was another. For one thing, rulers of empires and composite states were expected to embrace diversity. In practice they had to achieve an awkward compromise between irreconcilables – leaving their territories in their original state of infinite variation and imposing on them a despotic uniformity. The solution was usually a patience-tester, as rulers took every chance to nudge their territories closer together without causing too much offence. For another thing, nation-building was simply beyond the ken of anyone, however innovative, in the 1650–1750 period. Nations were seen as facts of nature, not human constructs.[60] Not until the later eighteenth century was nation-state building attempted in America and France. Integration had no simple upward and onward trajectory.

The reason for this is that the mindset of monarchs and their elites was dynastic. Their first priority was to expand the family firm. They were in business not to consolidate nation-states but to expand multi-national empires. Every time they did so, the addition of new territories threatened to dissolve any cohesion already achieved.[61] Yet in recent decades many historians have stressed 'state formation' and 'national security' as key objectives of monarchs.[62] Historians whose interests centre on the royal court have counterattacked with the claim that for most of the period they pursued goals which were incompatible with those priorities.[63] The composite states which continued to straddle Europe demonstrate that dynastic rights and claims were prioritized over strategic logic, territorial integrity and linguistic/cultural identity. Europe's sovereign families viewed their inherited personal claims as sacrosanct and their territories as resource bases for the advancement of dynastic honour. On them the entire currency of international relations, diplomacy and peace negotiations was based.[64]

So rulers in the 1650–1750 period were happy to make sporadic attempts to spread more widely the culture of the dominant core territory in order to tighten their grip over wider empires. Identities were not like hats: subjects could wear more than one at a time. Regional loyalties were compatible with the extension of allegiance to a wider community and even with absorption of its culture – but only as long as ruling elites considered the advantages to outweigh the disadvantages.[65] In elite minds at least, 'nations' in the old sense of major ethnic groupings (Catalans, Bretons or Scots) were fused into larger supranational communities (Spain, France or Great Britain). In the nineteenth century these in turn became modern nation-states. Britain and many others are now revealing their multi-national origins by looking fragile. Whatever their conceptual definition and in spite of having one dominant nationality, most modern nation-states are in fact ethnically diverse.[66]

The final result was not what some monarchs had intended or expected. They had presumably envisaged a composite identity which promoted cohesion and boosted dynastic prestige without creating a rival focus of loyalty. By the 1750s, in both Britain and France, a rival focus was what they got. The idea of the nation was acquiring a momentum of its own, at least among metropolitan elites. Before 1750 the term was a peripheral concept of debate but it was an increasingly central one thereafter. Reflecting on the debate about this issue in the 1750s the marquis d'Argenson asserted that the word 'nation' was never uttered under Louis XIV: even the idea of it was lacking.[67] The largest database of French writings reveals that between 1700 and 1800 use of the word *nation* in the enlarged sense increased more than fourfold.[68]

In the second half of the eighteenth century prestige and glory began to be seen in terms of the nation. This was now perceived as distinct from the monarch, who strove increasingly to be identified with it but did not always succeed.[69] In 1743, Pitt the Elder informed the British Parliament that George II was 'on the brink of losing the affections of his people' for his insistence on pursuing Hanoverian interests at the expense of British ones.[70] This antipathy proved temporary in Britain. In the second half of the century, George III managed to align monarchy and church with the national interest to form a tripod of rock-like stability. The nation was raised to a quasi-sacred level of devotion but had to share the honours with its more ancient partners.[71] But in France the monarch was increasingly perceived as the enemy of the national interest and the results were catastrophic.[72] French monarchs consistently failed to see the necessity of wrapping themselves in the flag – indeed, in France there was no national flag in which to wrap themselves.[73]

By the end of the period national identity had arrived on the European scene in its recognizably modern form. The thirty years after 1750 saw the creation of the British Museum, the *Encyclopaedia Britannica*, the *Biographia Britannica*, Hume's *History of England*, Johnson's *Dictionary of the English Language* and *The English Poets*, the canon of English literature, the rise of an English national historiography and the first histories of English painting and music.[74] All indicate a growing patriotic urge to glorify and define national identity and culture. The same impulse also energized France, Spain, the Dutch Republic and many parts of the Holy Roman Empire.[75] By the 1760s Mozart was writing *Bastien und Bastienne*. It was his first opera in German, his own language, previously deemed too uncouth to set to music. A decade later Vienna's first national opera theatre was founded by Joseph II.[76] In 1758 the *Académie Française* announced that the theme of its prestigious oratorical competition would be 'the great men of the nation'. Soon afterwards, the *Comédie Française* staged a series of plays to celebrate famous episodes of French national history. Voltaire quipped waspishly that audiences would prefer to be entertained rather than praised for their choice of nationality.[77]

## Conclusion

Modern political correctness decrees that it is unacceptable to stress congenital differences between members of the human species. Black and white, male and female, able and disabled, straight and gay are supposedly invisible attributes. Elite status was usually congenital in the 1650–1750 period but was stressed as never before or since. This was part of the conservative backlash and aristocratic revival after the terrors of the mid-seventeenth-century crisis. Few people in any class had qualms about the increasingly marked distinctions between people of 'quality' and 'the common sort'. The English were said to love a lord and much the same was true throughout Europe. Ruling elites were respectfully assumed to be superior not only politically and economically but also morally. Nobility of class was equated with nobility of character, while the masses were dismissed as insensitive and feral yobs – 'the swinish multitude', as an Irish politician termed them. As early as the fifteenth century this social/ moral connection had rubbed off onto the language of everyone's morality. A commendable deed had become 'noble' by association with the morals of the elite, regardless of who performed it.[78] A disreputable one was 'villainy', from the medieval word *villein* – a peasant. The same mental connection was responsible in the 1650–1750 period for the noble and heroic idiom of much of the art, music and literature of the period. This mode of expression was apparently adopted partly to benefit from the prestige of ruling elites and partly to reinforce it. Only deliberate subversives suggested that many gentlemen behaved like highwaymen and many highwaymen like gentlemen.

For most of the 1650–1750 period the nobility's power, wealth, status and moral worth were scarcely challenged. It was difficult to launch any cultural, economic or political project without the sponsorship of a nobleman. Rich bankers, brewers and merchants, having made their pile, could scarcely wait to buy country estates and turn themselves into gentlemen. Most novels told the tale of how a young man became a gentleman – either by learning to behave like one or by discovering he had been born into the gentry but been lost or disowned. Aristocratic fashion was imitated by all who could afford to do so. Even rulers could play copycat to the trend-setting aristocracy, the *Neues Palais* of Frederick the Great of Prussia almost certainly being modelled on the Earl of Carlisle's Castle Howard.[79]

But this aristocratic summer had all too short a lease. From the mid-eighteenth century, winter gradually set in and the idyll drew to its end (before yet another conservative backlash revived aristocratic fortunes in the early nineteenth century). In the 1750s Rousseau and his Enlightened contemporaries inaugurated an influential assault on the values and assumptions of the European nobilities. Elites attempted to adopt progressive causes as 'radical chic' but were soon to be perceived as the embodiment of social injustice, cultural decadence and moral vice. Meritocratic ideas prospered and deference declined.[80] Nor was the rest of the cultural and ideological fabric secure. The more radical elements of natural philosophy, which had buttressed Christianity, evolved into the Enlightenment, which undermined it – though not always intentionally. Classical and cosmopolitan ideals were challenged by emerging national cultures and identities. The European system of composite states failed to meet increasingly nationalist aspirations. On the contrary, it was seen as frustrating them.

# Chapter 2: The Formation of Elite Cultural Hegemony

The four previous cultural signposts obviously pre-dated the mid-seventeenth century. Elite identity incorporated them all, blended them into a distinctive new mix and became the dominant cultural force of the 1650–1750 period. When it began, a bonding agent of some sort was sorely needed. The Reformation of the sixteenth century had put Catholic monarchs and Protestant nobles on different sides, and vice versa. It had also driven a religious wedge between rulers of different confessions, as well as between members of their elites within most European states. Most seriously of all, it had presented subjects with an excuse (or in some cases prescribed for them a duty) to rebel against a ruler of a different religious persuasion from themselves – advice scarcely calculated to warm the cockles of a monarch's heart. In the General Crisis of the mid-seventeenth century the crown's natural allies were again in disarray and in conflict with their rulers, while rebels from the lower reaches of society spotted their chance to challenge ruling elites. Order and hierarchy had to be re-imposed on the state.

From the 1650s rattled elites therefore closed ranks, rejected former disruptive ambitions and re-imposed the order they had helped to undermine.[1] Traditional political and social power structures were reinforced. The renewed partnership of elites and monarchs coincided with increased emphasis on noble pedigree, as they now encased themselves in a hard shell of hierarchy, rank, title, precedence and deference. Requirements for entry into society's upper echelons were tightened up. Throughout Europe the identity of the landed elite was redefined and the bar raised for entry into the upper nobility. The latter became an elite within an elite, increasingly known during the 1650–1750 period as the 'aristocracy'. Aristocrats in this

56

sense (as opposed to 'aristocrats' standing for the whole elite) expected to be players at national level, while a member of the middling or lesser nobility (usually known as 'gentry') might dominate a region or a village.[2]

Given the European obsession in this period with status, it is hardly surprising that everyone wanted it. Elites obsessed with order and stability reacted by clamping down to an extent on social mobility, particularly at the top. In Denmark–Norway, Sweden–Finland and the Habsburg and Russian empires monarchs increasingly imposed rigid tables of rank which tended to lock their subjects into defined strata of society. In contrast, Britain propagated an official line about an elite open to men of business and finance, and a degree of social mobility which was unique in Europe. This has been exposed as myth. As on most of the Continent, social mobility flowed sluggishly; what little there was involved those enriched by the law and public office, not by business.[3] In France and Spain, however, owing to the sale of offices carrying noble privileges there was probably more mobility between the middle and upper ranks of society than in Britain. What can be said with certainty is that promotion into the elite was everywhere arduous and expensive, yet elite status was no longer determined solely by birth. Sale of offices and titles (venality) became the hot-air balloon of successful social climbers.

But the heavier the traffic on the social ladder, the clearer the labels on its rungs needed to be. Oddly, in some countries, new financial and legal safeguards for landed estates reduced the importance of medieval heraldic symbolism, as did the new emphasis on taste and manners as social separators.[4] But, generally, status indicators proliferated at elite level as never before or since – manor houses and gatehouses, artistic and architectural symbols, distinctive dress and headgear, fiscal privileges, seigneurial rights, family pedigrees, titles and coats-of-arms. They bolted into place 'a closely controlled and religiously observed hierarchy built both of real power and visible prestige'.[5] Yet there were limits to the tolerance of elites. They considered it inappropriate that those who made a successful ascent should have been launched at too low a depth. Walpole as Prime Minister of Great Britain made a snobbish comment which would have displeased the occupant of his office two and a half centuries later, had she heard it: 'A Gentleman of liberal Fortune and tolerable Education is fitter to serve his Country in Parliament than a Man bred to Trade and brought up in a Shop.'[6]

Much of elite self-definition amounted to physical and mental separation from tenants and social inferiors. Elites increasingly disengaged from those whom they ruled. From the later seventeenth century richer members of the landed class spent less time on their rural estates and more in local towns, in capital cities and at court. There they absorbed urban taste, manners and culture, which intensified the spiritual gulf between them and their inferiors. When they did reside in the countryside they were concealed in vaguely classical residences surrounded by large landscaped parks, whereas their sixteenth-century ancestors had often dwelt in a timber-framed manor house built on the village street. When they ventured out, they were curtained in coaches, hidden in private pews at church or mounted on horseback in hot pursuit of a fox.[7]

## The Novelty of Elite Cultural Identity and Leadership

As well as refining their exclusivity, elites introduced a crucially new cultural element. Some historians refer vaguely to early-modern culture as 'aristocratic', merely because the gentry and aristocracy were the political ruling class. This usage is too loose to be useful. Slightly tighter is 'elite culture' deployed as the opposite of 'popular culture'. But 'elite culture' in that sense does not have to be dominated by political elites. In fact, before the mid-seventeenth century, initiatives in 'high' culture were more likely to come from merchant dynasties or university-trained lawyers and theologians than from ill-educated aristocrats and gentry.[8] Most nobles had previously been cultural followers rather than leaders, and the language and idioms of respectable culture were by no means aimed at social elites. The most successful and influential writers, like Rabelais and Shakespeare, had used a language which was close to that of the common people.[9] Luther, the founder of Protestantism, was inspired by Renaissance humanists to develop a plain vernacular style which could bridge the gap between intellectuals and a far wider public – firstly half-educated readers and finally a large section of the illiterate masses. Rejecting the claims of such people to direct religious movements but desperate for his words to reach them, Luther invented and launched an idiom tailored to their needs.[10]

But around the middle of the seventeenth century a cultural revolution seems to have occurred and subsequently been little noticed by historians. Cultural leadership apparently passed to political elites. Several factors seem to have come into play. One was their improved education and their invasion of colleges and universities. Another was the reconciliation of religious and political culture as mutually supportive, rather than mutually destructive as they had proved for previous generations. This bound monarchy more closely to its time-honoured support systems, the mighty ranks of clergy and nobility. Finally, for the first time monarchs, nobles and prelates combined forces to assert their cultural dominance and to buttress their power after the events of the early and mid-seventeenth century had shaken it.

Key locations during the Renaissance and Reformation had been the commercial cities of the Holy Roman Empire – Netherlandish, Germanic and Italian. The Renaissance of the fifteenth and early-sixteenth centuries had largely been created by the merchant-controlled city states of Italy. But by the 1650–1750 period these had come under princely rule, lost most of their independence and fallen into economic and cultural decline. If republics survived it was under aristocratic control. In sixteenth-century Germany it had been Imperial Cities like Nuremberg and not princes which had set the cultural pace. They were small self-governing republics, subject only to the remote authority of the Holy Roman Emperor and ruled by rich merchants or even master craftsmen. This was reflected in the culture they produced. But the Thirty Years War had weakened these cities and they declined after 1650. Cultural leadership crucially switched location. For the first time it proceeded from the courts of the greater princes and the impact was far-reaching. German, the national vernacular language, dominant in the Middle Ages, was deliberately sidelined in favour of French. Nearly all the European towns and cities which still flourished in this period were courtly capitals like London, Paris, Mannheim, Vienna and St Petersburg. A few French cities, their merchants enriched by the Atlantic slave trade, were able to build magnificently. But throughout Europe in the 1650–1750 period there were few exceptions to the dominance of royal, aristocratic and ecclesiastical patrons.[11]

Between 1650 and 1750 political and social elites therefore had the opportunity to define the cultural agenda to an unprecedented and unrepeatable degree.[12] How did they do it? First, they actively participated at the cutting edge of contemporary culture as gentlemen amateurs, whether as poets, writers, critics, architects, musicians or natural philosophers.[13] Among elite families who spawned leading literary, artistic and 'scientific' figures in France and Britain alone were La Rochefoucauld, La Fayette, de Scudéry, Boileau, Milton, Dryden, Clarendon, Rochester, Dorset, Etheredge, Boyle, Burlington and Shaftesbury. Weston Park in Staffordshire appears to have been designed c.1670 by its owner, Lady Wilbraham, who possessed a heavily annotated 1663 edition of *The First Book of Architecture* by the Renaissance architect Palladio. She is possibly England's first woman architect.[14] Elites made a major personal contribution to literature, though painters and musical composers usually came from humbler backgrounds.[15] As natural philosophers, they also pioneered the rise of 'science' in the 1650–1750 period. The knowledge in which they specialized was essentially private and elitist, with Latin as its *lingua franca*, higher mathematics as its common currency and a small but international circle of gentlemen scholars as its target audience. Its restricted media contrast profoundly with the increasing commitment of 'scientists' in the second half of the eighteenth century to influence the new phenomenon of public opinion – hence the innovation of public lectures, laboratory demonstrations and introductory textbooks.[16]

Second, elites exercised indirect influence through patronage or its reverse – by funding, censoring or otherwise controlling most of the cultural productivity and media availability of the day. They enjoyed a near-monopoly of sponsorship and carefully chose what to promote and what to block. The miniature states of the Holy Roman Empire offered especially rich pickings to creative artists. A myriad of independent courts, many run by highly cultured princes, multiplied opportunities for cultural patronage. Artists depended on such courts but rarely functioned as mere executors of princely orders. The patron–employer relationship was more of a symbiosis, in which princes were open to suggestion from creative trend-setters but unlikely to commission anything which flouted their priorities or failed to implement their own agenda.[17] Similarly, courts and churches commanded a near-monopoly of the available media of communication, which in this period were few and controllable. The agenda was pursued in many ways, some blatant and others subtle. The aim was to define the threefold hierarchy, which had recently been challenged (monarch, clergy and nobility), and culturally underpin its value system. Order was not a new theme but the stress on it in this period was unprecedented. It was inspired partly by the natural philosophers' discovery of the order of the cosmos and partly by the catastrophic *lack* of order which had inaugurated the period. Throughout it the need for order in state, church and society was a steady bass drumbeat.

The outcome was spectacular and unprecedented. Uniquely, between the 1650s and 1750s the dominant cultural voices were those of monarchs, aristocrats, gentry and prelates. In this period European culture celebrated and promoted their taste, values and virtues. Their language and idioms, refined for the purpose, became uncontested norms of polite communication. An elite emerged with a sense of class solidarity and a distinct culture that divided it from the common people.[18] An aloof message was sent to those outside the magic circle of those who mattered. Elite culture made their power visible, tangible and convincing: their authority was simultaneously presented and legitimated. The aim was twofold – to deter elite troublemakers and to encourage those outside the elite to know their place and defer to their betters. In this sense elite culture reinforced socio-political stability. Though challenging innovations in literature and the arts were sometimes supported, direct attacks on elite values were discouraged. Those who failed to conform were marginalized or excluded. The hierarchical–noble conception of the socio-political order remained dominant into the later eighteenth century.[19]

In contrast, at the end of the 1650–1750 period elite cultural leadership was increasingly challenged. Its monopoly of the eighteenth-century media was broken by the rapid spread of new organs of communication like newspapers and various forms of discussion group. This expansion of a cultural 'public sphere' beyond its control offered a megaphone to anti-aristocratic writers like Rousseau, Beaumarchais and Paine. They grabbed it with both hands. From the 1750s a loss of aristocratic nerve was discernible, as leading members of the nobility began to parrot or embrace the meritocratic and libertarian values of the Enlightenment. Even in conservative England, where the aristocracy lasted longest, the hostile intellectual climate of the later eighteenth century can be gauged from a future Poet Laureate's open letter to the Bishop of Llandaff. At the age of 23 Wordsworth ridiculed the nobility's 'fictitious superiority' and called for its abolition, along with the institution of monarchy. Having more regard for his safety than his principles, he wisely left it unpublished.[20]

## The Creation of Elite Cultural Identity and Leadership

Elites had always had a certain *esprit de corps*. In the 1650–1750 period, however, they appear to have sought a deliberately crafted identity. Alarmed by the proven fragility of order in the preceding period, elites and those who ministered to their needs created a cultural style which asserted their leadership. Cultural superiority was deployed to fortify their political and social position against further challenge.[21] From the mid-seventeenth century elites began to look on their sixteenth- and early seventeenth-century ancestors as brutish, illiterate and uncultivated. They rejected the deplorable appetite of the latter for a literary drama presenting violent action and demanded something more refined and socially exclusive. The arts were increasingly required to function as both reflection and inculcator of a new system of elite values, centred on courtly manners and civility.[22]

In the course of the 1650–1750 period this development swept the Continent. The development is most obviously discernible in Britain, which had experienced the most catastrophic breakdown. But the other states of western and central Europe had to grapple with comparable problems, if less traumatic outcomes. More generally, and contrary to the myth of the British state's uniqueness, its similarities to its neighbours were striking. All shared a loose and composite structure in which the landed aristocracy was indispensable to government. In all, the main themes of elite nightmares were disorder and anarchy. Among the remedies adopted from Spain to Russia was a cultural compact which aimed to bond elites together as a powerfully united force for order and civility in a Europe of diversity and potential chaos. Thus Scottish, Welsh and Irish elites began in this period to shun the Celtic languages and to adopt English cultural norms and customs.[23] French elites probably pioneered the usage, throughout the realm, of the Parisian version of the language which by the end of the nineteenth century was to unify France.[24] Under the Habsburg monarchy German, Czech and Hungarian elites came increasingly to share a Catholic baroque culture which transcended their national differences. By the later seventeenth century this cultural bond between elites was a crucial element, along with political and economic developments, in reinforcing the cohesion of central Europe under the Habsburg dynasty.[25]

Even more important was the adoption of the French language in the area of foreign policy and diplomacy. In the 1650–1750 period diplomats from every state came to speak the same language as it gradually eclipsed Latin as the dominant medium of European elites. They came to behave in similar ways and obey the same French rules and conventions. As states like Russia rose from obscurity, they embraced this culture. Cosmopolitan contact was at its height. The scale of diplomatic interaction between the states of Europe was unprecedented: the period was an age of congresses and of intricate networks of alliances. Between the 1670s and 1720s all European states (apart from the Ottoman Empire) began to maintain permanent resident embassies in foreign capitals. Resident missions had previously been filled by persons of relatively low social status, but from the later seventeenth century, diplomats were drawn overwhelmingly from the higher ranks of the nobility. Elites also dominated the new state agencies established at the same time to handle foreign policy. Partly reflecting their enhanced importance in the period, royal courts assumed a greater role than before in diplomacy, and diplomats spent much of their time attending the courts of the states in which they were resident. They identified with fellow-diplomats, with whom they shared the same lifestyle and values: during and after Louis XIV's reign international diplomacy acquired the noble ethos which it was to retain until the First World War. Elite culture thus shaped foreign policy and diplomacy, which in turn helped to unify and consolidate elites across Europe.[26]

One of the great social escalators has always been education and a cultured elite must imply an educated elite. Literacy in Ur during the third millennium BC may have helped to define the aristocracy as a class.[27] From the mid-seventeenth century in Europe its education seems to have improved in scope and increased in urgency. In the mid-sixteenth century great French nobles were sometimes illiterate and few read books. Among 58 German nobles listing their losses after the Peasants' Revolt of 1525, only six had any books at all.[28] France was not considered the most backward of states; yet in the late sixteenth and early seventeenth centuries there was brisk debate about the education of its old military nobility, considered not as a fact but as a project worth attempting.[29] In the early seventeenth century most, from King Henry IV downwards, were characterized by coarse speech and aversion to intellectual and literary pursuits.[30] Yet by the second half of the same century the basic definition of the French nobility included an ingredient of cultural refinement.

Rabb has popularized the image of Condé leading a revolt against Louis XIV during the Fronde of 1649–53 and ending his days thirty years later rowing ladies round the lake at Versailles. This may be true of one member of the dynasty, who had become too elderly for treason. What Rabb does not mention is that Condé's descendants in Burgundy up to the 1740s gained and maintained influence from a large network of clients linked by marriage and office.[31] Their network was valued and exploited by the crown: otherwise it would have withered. In the 1640s Condé depended less on the royal court for his power and could therefore deploy it with more freedom. He certainly exemplified the cultural shift from the values of independent noble warrior to those of courtier gentleman.[32] The elite had already acquired the association it was to keep – with education, letters and literacy.[33] But it did not thereby become effete. It was still a ruling class.

Some European elites had been keen to acquire education before 1650. In the later sixteenth and early seventeenth centuries English elites had begun to take over the grammar schools and the universities of Oxford and Cambridge. Of 86 pupils at Bury St Edmunds Grammar School in 1656 over half were the sons of gentry. By 1584, 48 per cent of English MPs had experienced higher education, and in the seventeenth century Oxford and Cambridge became finishing schools for the ruling classes.[34] By 1640–42 the corresponding figure was 70 per cent, raising the suspicion among some contemporaries that elite education was not a response to the Great Rebellion and Civil Wars but a cause of them.[35] There were also earlier precedents for royal encouragement of higher education. Eleven new colleges were founded in Sweden between 1623 and 1643, with noble students predominating. There was a noticeable impact on the cultural spending of elites. By the mid-seventeenth century an educated noble in England or Germany might have a library of 100 volumes. Not all approved of the new bookish pursuits. 'In my time,' moaned an ancient French nobleman in 1656, 'one made gentlemen study only to join the church.'[36]

Between 1650 and 1750 the foundation of schools, colleges, academies and universities accelerated and elite take-up of places rocketed. As the seventeenth century advanced, the social exclusiveness of Oxford and Cambridge increased.[37] The ancient universities' acquaintance with new disciplines like natural philosophy, however, did not. It was the Continental universities which began to modernize their syllabuses and align them more precisely with the new demand for professional and technical skills. Where older institutions were unwilling to introduce new sciences and technology, rulers responded by founding specialized colleges, military academies and schools of administrative science (*Kameralwissenschaften*). These trained elites for state service, especially in northern, central and eastern Europe, though everywhere nobilities were encouraged to reinvent themselves as key personnel of the new state armies and bureaucracies.[38] In most states elites were encouraged to send their sons to military colleges. Russian recruitment policy went further. In 1714, Peter the Great made education compulsory for all Russian nobles between the ages of 10 and 15, after which age equally compulsory state service began.[39] In north Germany alone, local princes established the universities of Halle, Göttingen and Erlangen. Halle was even equipped with feeder-schools for orphaned sons of the nobility.[40]

Alternatively, old universities were newly colonized by elites. That of Aix-en-Provence was founded in 1409 but only in the seventeenth century did most nobles take advantage of its facilities. The prominence of its faculties of law, theology and medicine indicate professional as well as disinterestedly cultural motivation. Its seventeenth-century record shows that 30 of the 38 old noble families in the area had members who graduated from it. This shift in elite priorities closed the educational gap between the old military nobility and the new 'robe' nobility who owed their titles to legal and financial office – and who in older historical interpretations effectively superseded a redundant class in steep decline.[41]

More broadly, at university and college future elites were inducted into the standards and values of the socio-political system that they were to lead. Higher civil and ecclesiastical office throughout seventeenth- and eighteenth-century Europe was almost always reserved for a small elite connected by marriage or patronage; it was at university that the latest cohort would first encounter this network of relationships and interdependencies. Most significantly, university education created a greater degree of cultural cohesion among elites and crystallized their self-awareness as a ruling class.[42] Finally, the Grand Tour bestowed a networking opportunity that was international.[43] Cosmopolitan cultural affiliations helped to bond elites together, not only within European composite states but across their boundaries.[44] Sadly, travel did not always promote international sympathy. Sometimes it merely confirmed political and religious stereotypes and produced better-informed xenophobes.[45]

Elite educational imperatives were not new in the 1650–1750 period. Over a century before, Castiglione had updated medieval courtesy and chivalry in his best-selling *Book of the Courtier* by redefining the manners of a gentleman. His priorities were influenced by the Renaissance concept of the 'universal man' and the latter's potential for making of himself what he willed. Along with Erasmus's *De civilitate* of 1530, Castiglione's work was reprinted constantly throughout the seventeenth and eighteenth centuries. Both recommended the philosopher's morality and the artist's sensitivity as warmly as the warrior's toughness. Both insisted on the importance of social graces and basic taboos, especially at table. Spitting food into the faces of fellow diners was not encouraged.

This was an inclusive ideal, drawing self-made *nouveaux riches* into the same society as established elites and providing them with the necessary survival kit. But, like so much at the start of the 1650–1750 period, it was re-launched with a characteristic twist. Seventeenth-century France grafted onto the precepts of Castiglione and Erasmus the aristocratic ideal of the *honnête homme*, who owed his reputation less to his morals than to wit and social polish. Crucially, intellectual and aesthetic discernment was now seen as innate, though it required informing and refining. Good taste and good manners became the new criterion of social status and throughout Europe the cultivated gentleman was the supreme attainment target. In eighteenth-century Britain good manners were the most constantly mentioned characteristic of the military officer class, with courage and killing skills far behind.[46]

Like most things in the 1650–1750 period, social behaviour came under the sway of rules. Etiquette manuals legislated on good manners, while the houses of aristocracy and gentry were crowded with teachers of music, dancing and drawing. It must be admitted that a gentleman also needed a sense of his family's honour, and a fencing master to make him lithe-limbed in its defence. But honour, which could be dangerous, was now balanced by politeness, which was safe. 'Beau' Nash, master of ceremonies at the redeveloped spa of Bath, decreed that all admitted to polite society should stand on an equal footing and behave towards one another with exquisite *civilité*. Nobles and gentry were manoeuvred into mixing socially in his Assembly Rooms, conversing about fashionable novels and leaving their swords outside. But Nash exalted social differentiation by dictating who was admitted in the first place. Culture and manners were now the badge of acceptability – a means of social inclusion for those with them but of exclusion for those without. The drive to teach the European nobility good manners had intensified their exclusivity as a caste.[47]

This has implications for the relationship between elite culture and popular culture. The received wisdom is that there was, in the seventeenth century at least, no growing division between them.[48] The Christian religion was a broadly common bond, though it increasingly divided classes during the period.[49] It has also been argued that there was no clear divide where male activity was concerned. Upper-class men passed as polite in salon society, but outside it they shared with their lower-class contemporaries a culture of coarse speech and low behaviour. There was little to distinguish peer from plebeian in sexual and sporting contexts – least of all in their shared relish for public executions.[50]

This was much as it had been in previous periods. The educated classes had for centuries shared popular superstitions, read popular stories, attended popular sports, enjoyed street ballads and entertainments and normally spoken in regional accents. They had participated in the hedonistic Carnival which preceded the Lenten fast and in other rituals of the church's year.[51] From Madrid to London the aristocracy in their boxes and the populace in the pit all appreciated the plays of the great dramatists, if on different physical and intellectual levels.[52] In the early seventeenth century Shakespeare's plays were accessible to a broad social spectrum ranging from Westminster courtiers to City apprentices. Playgoers were drawn from all classes, except from vagrants and those who could barely earn or beg enough to eat.[53]

Recent research suggests that from the mid-seventeenth century much of this changed. As elites reshaped their own education and manners, it seems likely that the break with popular culture was much sharper than previously thought. Elites increasingly frowned on what the modern world calls 'cultural crossover'. The barriers between upper and lower levels of society were raised.[54] Lord Chesterfield, writing in the 1740s, advised his son to avoid common proverbs and trite sayings – otherwise people would assume he kept 'low company'.[55] Significantly, before the 1650–1750 period serious literature, theatre, music and painting had not been treated as a special category. They now acquired a collective identity which differentiated them from popular culture: the modern idea of 'high culture' is an eighteenth-century invention.[56] It helped to ensure that elite culture was better defined and more conscientiously adhered to by the mid-eighteenth century than ever before. By then there was an accepted ideal of what constituted a person of refinement, fashion and taste. Elite culture was no longer a miscellany drawn from other people's culture: it was firmly aristocratic.[57] The shadow of elite disapproval fell over popular sports. In 1711 the tutor of a young member of the Coke family (later Earls of Leicester) reported that though his pupil was dutiful he delighted in the wrong things, notably cockfighting. He had been rationed to one session a week, a total ban being impossible without risk of withdrawal symptoms.[58]

The same elite discrimination gentrified drama. Partly for religious reasons, London's open-air playhouses closed for ever in the 1640s – or at least until a replica of *The Globe* was built in the 1990s. Popular theatre disappeared with them. Nor was this phenomenon confined to England. By the second half of the seventeenth century, plays performed in the public theatres of Paris were written for an emphatically more restricted, sophisticated and aristocratic audience than previously. The same is true of the French book trade. This sidelining of the plebeian market made an indelible mark on the language and literature of France.[59] The gap was further widened by the classical literary standards launched in mid-seventeenth-century France and subsequently adopted throughout Europe. The poet and critic Boileau used the Pont Neuf, where popular ballad-singers performed in Paris, as a dire symbol of the vulgarity to be avoided. Danish gentry relished popular ballads until around 1700, when they succumbed to French behaviour models. By the mid-eighteenth century, Hungarian aristocrats were reading English novels and the Russian upper nobility was finally speaking French.

Much of elite self-definition involved an explicit rejection of popular culture: elites defined themselves against 'the common sort'.[60] The foundations of this attitude were laid in the sixteenth century with the overhaul of Christianity by the Reformation and Counter-Reformation. All over western and central Europe a growing cleavage had emerged between the pleasures and pastimes of social elites and those of the common people. Ecclesiastical elites condemned folk songs, folk tales, folk dances and folk festivals as violent or obscene perversions of religion. In the eyes of the godly, celebration of saints' days and of the Carnival period preceding Lent had degenerated into rowdy fairs, masquerades, plays, races, cockfights and football matches.[61] In Protestant lands many of these distressing phenomena had been confronted before 1650. In much of Catholic Europe, as well as outlying areas like Protestant Wales and Norway, the campaign was convincingly launched only after that date. From the mid-seventeenth century, elites increasingly attacked popular rituals as irrational and disorderly rather than ungodly.[62] But the result was the same: Lent triumphed over Carnival.

The rougher aspects of popular culture were especially targeted – particularly those like the Feast of Misrule, which inverted the social order and had social superiors serving their inferiors during the Christmas season. These were symptoms of disorder and therefore to be suppressed. From the mid-seventeenth century, participation in popular culture by members of the elite was usually an attempt to gain popularity or promote obedience. The result could be slightly paradoxical. Celebrations in England of St George's Day or the foiling of the Gunpowder Plot saw elites presiding from a great height and safe distance over what was nevertheless demonstrated to be one realm.[63] The ethic of respectability became prominent, and well-connected laymen joined the clergy in promoting virtue. In the 1690s local 'Societies for the Reformation of Manners' were founded in England, their membership extending from King William III to innumerable local Justices of the Peace. Their aim was to ensure that prosecutions were brought against lewdness, drunkenness, swearing, profanity, prostitution and gambling.[64] A similar organization in France, the Company of the Holy Sacrament, campaigned against Carnival and investigated the morals of rope-dancers.[65]

The consequences were partly unintended. Religious reform had a far greater impact on the manners and morals of the educated minority than on the behaviour of the masses. Elites were therefore cut off more sharply than before from popular tradition. But alongside this impulse were other culturally far-reaching developments. Natural philosophers ensured that among elites the new Latin names for plants devised by Linnaeus displaced the old English ones. Labels which polite society considered improper were now rejected. Plants quaintly categorized as priest's ballocks, horse pistle and prick madam were left for common folk to snigger over, while elites adopted a terminology of their own. This elevated Latinized nomenclature can be seen as part of an elite project to control scientific and public discourse.[66]

Even more fundamentally, mainly in the 1650–1750 period, elites throughout multi-national composite states began literally to speak another language – that of the royal court. They took up English instead of Welsh in Wales and of Gaelic in the Scottish Highlands, French instead of Occitan in Languedoc, German instead of Czech in Bohemia, Swedish instead of Finnish in Finland and Danish instead of Norwegian in Norway.[67] Sometimes there were particular historical reasons for this, as in the establishment of a German landed elite in Bohemia after the Czech revolt of 1620. It had happened stunningly and suddenly with the establishment of the Anglo-Norman composite state in 1066, when a Norman elite had replaced a Saxon one in England and monarchs and their officials had ceased to speak English for the next 350 years.[68] But the wholesale annihilation of one elite by another was untypical. The norm was more gradual acculturation, so that by 1750 culture in the widest sense was riddled with class distinctions unknown in 1650. This merely formalized an ancient mindset, since almost no one before the late nineteenth century believed the common people were fully rational human beings. That was why they had no vote. It was also why officers and gentlemen slain in warfare were the only ones commemorated. Private soldiers had no memorial and often no decent burial. Their bones were allegedly ground into fertiliser.[69]

The growing divide partly reflected the influential culture of the natural philosophers, which left the common people far behind. Their rational approach soon discredited longstanding popular superstitions. Browne's *Pseudodoxia Epidemica* (*Vulgar Errors*) of 1646 ridiculed the credulity of the masses, which exposed them to medical quacks and charlatans. After 1650, trials for witchcraft declined steeply because western European elites stopped believing in it, though in eastern Europe in the same period they peaked. Lord Chesterfield advised his son to avoid popular superstitions and common proverbs as they were proof of having kept low company, while the populist Rousseau denounced the snobbery that required persons of rank to 'speak, think, act, live differently from the people'. Even monarchs were lectured on inappropriate amusements. Charles I proved to be the last English king to employ anyone so vulgar as a court jester.[70]

Finally, if elites stressed their cultural distance from the lower orders, they also defined themselves by their antiquity. Aristocratic societies always looked back to the achievements of their ancestors – a key argument for maintaining the hierarchy of which they formed a vital part.[71] In the 1650–1750 period this reflex was accentuated. Noblemen had themselves painted in outdated armour, usually incongruously combined with lace ruffles and curled wigs. Artists in the late seventeenth and early eighteenth centuries kept helmets of vaguely medieval design in their studios, ready for aspirational clients. Even more significantly, it was from around the mid-seventeenth century that the houses of the nobility began to display portraits of ancestors as a demonstration of family pride, power and continuity.[72] As ruling dynasties began to take themselves more seriously, they also felt the lack of a fleshed-out pedigree. In 1688, Frederick I of Brandenburg–Prussia appointed Samuel von Pufendorf as Court Historiographer. His history of the Great Elector, Frederick's father, was the first to make systematic use of archived government papers.[73]

The only alternatives to this elite agenda were bourgeois and popular culture. A distinctively bourgeois culture is, however, hard to identify before the second half of the eighteenth century. The language of class did not develop in England until the mid-eighteenth century, with the phrase 'middle class' remaining unusual until the 1780s. The middle ranks of society were united mainly in their determination to identify with the upper classes and make themselves ladies and gentlemen.[74] They lacked the elite's means to communicate with one another and develop collective values and *esprit de corps*. Even in England, which probably anticipated more of modernity than most early-modern European states, there was no permanent, self-conscious urban class in opposition to the landed elite before the nineteenth century.[75]

What did exist in all European countries were many clearly defined status groups, each with a sharply delineated position in the hierarchy of respect. But, if social 'class' is defined in its modern sense of a group with the capacity for developing class consciousness and solidarity, in the old pre-industrial society there was only one class – the landed elite.[76] The notion of class conflict was not entertained. Partly inspired by distant memories of anarchy and instability, the accent was on the political necessity and divine demand for social subordination. Though a degree of social mobility was permitted, it did not extend to the great majority without property or education. Their status was viewed as permanent and unchanging. Social station was a given, whether as part of the divine plan, the natural world or well-organized society; class conflict was therefore unthinkable.[77]

For the most part the middle ranks therefore deferred to elite culture in the belief that they could benefit from mere association with its prestige (though not necessarily to court culture which, under the later Stuarts in England, was seen as disreputable). The anxiety of aspiring members of the bourgeoisie to emulate their betters was lethally skewered by Molière early in the period. His play *Le Bourgeois Gentilhomme* depicts a social climber who adopts the fashions, speech and cultural pursuits of his social superiors. He is desperate to behave like 'the quality' and engages masters of music, dancing and fencing to improve him. He also employs an elocutionist, who unveils the finer points of prose as a highly superior form of speech. The *bourgeois gentilhomme* is delighted to discover that he has been speaking prose all his life.[78]

Popular culture is easier to identify because contemporary elites were keen to distinguish it from their own. Before the 1650–1750 period, popular and high culture had overlapped. Gentlemen and artisans watched the same spectacles, whether tragic drama or religious festivities. But from the mid-seventeenth century high culture was remorselessly purged of its popular elements. A few educated eccentrics continued to find the latter quaintly interesting: it could inspire study occasionally but participation rarely. Only after the 1750s did German historians such as Herder look to the common people as the authentic voice of a new preoccupation – national culture. Only then were folk songs, folk poetry and folk dances eagerly observed and recorded for the first time. The native culture of the *Volk* and not the classical culture of the elite was hailed as the true source of the national spirit.[79] Significantly, therefore, the period 1650–1750 is the only one in which popular culture was neither shared by elites as previously, nor respected by them as afterwards.

# Chapter 3: Basic Agendas: 'Science', Political Culture and Religion

## Introduction

Most modern people consider it commendable to seek to understand their environment in order to improve it, whether by conserving the earth's resources or attempting to stabilize its climate. Three and a half centuries ago the general view was very different. The 1650–1750 period opens with a resonant reminder that human intellect was still in the grip of the Middle Ages.

In the 1650s Milton began to write *Paradise Lost*, his great epic of the Fall of Lucifer and the Fall of Man. It repeated in more grandiose form the world-view of St Augustine of Hippo, who died in the fifth century AD and was the most influential of the early Christian theologians. The morning star (now more accurately known as the planet Venus) rises in the east an hour or two before dawn – hence its ancient name of Lucifer, the light bearer. But when the sun appears in all its glory, Lucifer's presumption is rebuked and it vanishes, expelled from the heavens. This became a symbol for the fate of Satan, the fallen angel whose overweening ambition caused him to rebel against God. Pride brought low was also one of the great themes of ancient Greek mythology. The father of Icarus made a pair of wings for his son but he flew so close to the sun that it melted the wax that secured them and he crashed. Prometheus stole fire from the gods, gave it to mankind and was punished by being chained to a mountain while an eagle devoured his liver. Each night it regenerated and each day the torture was renewed. Such was the fate of those who sought to benefit mankind by technology.[1]

71

In the Christian version of the myth, Satan sought revenge for his expulsion from heaven. He tempted Adam and Eve, God's new creation, to seek forbidden knowledge. They in their turn were ejected from Paradise and their descendants doomed to the eternal consequences of their sin. From this Augustine concluded that human beings had a twofold nature. They were both body and spirit. While their body dwelt in the world, the City of Satan, their spirit aspired to Heaven, the City of God. No compromise between the two was possible, since the earthly city was founded on greed and appetite inherited from Adam and Eve by all their successors. The subjects of earthly monarchs were devilish sinners and needed to be governed with that fact in mind. Rulers had to make the best of a bad job.

Augustine viewed mankind as so corrupted that it would instantly misuse any knowledge it acquired. The reasoning faculties of the human mind were worthless: the only reliable source of knowledge about the human condition was the Bible. In around AD 600 Pope Gregory the Great accused a French bishop of devoting himself to 'the vanities of worldly learning', and a thousand years later there was no fundamental change in the church's position. Non-religious knowledge and enquiry were suspect and associated with diabolism. In Russia before Peter the Great's reign they were banned from educational institutions. They represented an attempt to push beyond the appointed limits of the human condition and attain knowledge and power that belonged to God alone. The end of man was to know God and enjoy Him for ever. Worldly wonders and phenomena represented an unhealthy distraction from that spiritual duty.

By the middle of the seventeenth century the world had for over a thousand years been regarded as a vale of tears in which human beings were at the mercy of a hostile environment and fit only to stay in that predicament. Those who attempted to understand or control the forces of nature in order to improve that environment were condemned by both Protestant and Catholic theologians as ungodly. Whether witch, sorcerer, conjuror, magus, alchemist or astrologer, only those in league with the devil had the key to nature's secrets. Their magic, whether black or white, was stamped with his mark. In the 1550–1650 period far more witches than heretics had been executed by the state.[2] Dark ancestral fears of forbidden knowledge prevailed at every level. Seventeenth-century 'science' was perceived as inseparable from magic: it is unclear whether even scientific giants like Newton drew a clear distinction. 'Science' and magic were coupled and damned together.

Throughout much of the seventeenth century most Europeans inhabited the same mental world as their medieval forebears. They believed in interwoven natural and supernatural worlds. Bodiless invisible spirits took up residence in material shells, while the walking dead might assume bodily form. Regardless of country, class or education, people were helpless spectators on a cosmic battlefield where angels and demons fought over individual human souls and rival spiritual influences intervened constantly in the natural order. In this crucial respect there was no cultural gap between masses and elites.[3] The mindset united all classes and cultures in a belief system inherited from the Middle Ages and similar to the animist beliefs of half the population of twenty-first-century Botswana. Anything else was considered tantamount to materialism and atheism.

Yet from the 1650s natural philosophers, ancestors of modern scientists, increasingly dared to know. They already had the word of God in the Bible but also wanted to 'read' and decode God's hand in nature. Under the protection of princes they slowly began to change attitudes. The churches gradually accepted their premises and permitted them to be taught in the universities which they controlled.[4] By the first half of the eighteenth century, unlike the second half of the seventeenth, natural philosophers could operate more freely. Their discoveries suggested that God had ordered the cosmos as a harmonious mechanism: a new player on the cosmic stage was launched – the Divine Watchmaker. This had obvious implications for the ordering of government and society. The result was a new intellectual fusion of religion, 'science' and political culture. The medieval argument for the divine sanction of all political authority (recently challenged in the Wars of Religion) was re-emphasized. It was coupled with the new 'scientific' perception that the ordering of earthly society and government must reflect the divine order and harmony of the cosmos. By the end of the 1650–1750 period Newton's exposition of the basic laws of physics had arguably reinforced Europe's socio-political fabric. And, on a more practical level, in most European states the formerly creaking partnership of monarch and clergy had been reinvigorated by the restoration of religious consensus between ruler and elites – though not always by methods of which modern liberal democracy would approve.[5] Only the dawning Enlightenment was to threaten this unprecedented and harmonious fusion of religion, natural philosophy and political culture.

## Natural Philosophy or 'Science'

By the middle of the seventeenth century, even as Milton was restating the Augustinian world-view, for the first time in a thousand years it was under serious threat. A growing minority of educated Europeans rejected the

Augustinian analysis of the human condition. They called themselves 'experimental philosophers' or 'natural philosophers' and were more widely known as the 'curious'.[6] They were the predecessors of modern scientists. This is why they are important now, but they mattered in the 1650–1750 period for a quite different reason. The natural philosophers perceived religion as a framework which gave meaning and context to their 'scientific' enquiries. They unveiled an exciting new revelation – that God had encoded his signature in the cosmos. This transmitted a message of order and harmony in what we should call the language of advanced mathematics. The new 'science' thereby reinforced the old dominance of religion.

So we need to be careful about the so-called Scientific Revolution. The concept is valid only in hindsight. It is tempting to assume that the early-modern period had a conception and valuation of the physical sciences roughly comparable to our own. In fact the word 'scientist' was not coined until the 1830s and it is reasonable to assume that no-one had previously experienced this linguistic gap.[7] The phrase 'Scientific Revolution' appeared another century later. The first priority of scientists as we know them is to discover the truth about the material world. If the main objective of a discipline is to discover the Mind of God, we should not normally call it science. Yet science and religion had been intertwined since ancient Egyptian and Babylonian astronomers scanned the night sky in the third millennium BC. The first astronomers had been priests of the god Ra.

The natural philosopher of the seventeenth century shared these dual priorities, if not their pagan embodiment. He studied one of God's books, the natural world, and the theologian the other, the Bible. Natural philosophy was an alternative route to religion and not (as increasingly after 1750) an alternative to it. There was no formal barrier between the subjects, and their objective now became the same.[8] Many natural philosophers were clergy. In the eighteenth century Robert Boyle, one of the greatest of them, was celebrated more for his sermons than for his experiments.[9] But the religion which appealed to many natural philosophers was a minimalist belief in a Creator God: it did not extend to the minutiae of theological dispute. With their philosophical friends they confined themselves to establishing scientific certainties on which they could agree and avoided theological speculations over which they might differ. Natural philosophy united people while theology divided them.[10]

The essential unity of 'science' and religion is neatly exemplified by an architect. There was no such thing in the seventeenth century as a professional designer of buildings. When Wren was appointed Surveyor General of the King's Works, he was a founder member of the Royal Society and

Professor of Astronomy at Oxford. His expertise also embraced anatomy, medicine, optics and mathematics. His many-sided genius enabled him to raise over the new St Paul's Cathedral the first monumental dome erected in England, intended from the start to dominate the London skyline. How to carry the load of a dome large and high enough to do so was an engineering challenge of the first magnitude, but at the same time Wren had to erect a building worthy of nearly two millennia of classical and Christian tradition. The result, mainly designed and built between 1700 and 1710, was an inspirational blend of his scientific, mathematical, historical and artistic skills. Even more significant was his plan for incorporating a vast astronomical telescope in the south-west tower of St Paul's. Eventually the instrument proved too long for its proposed location. Had it not, the cathedral would have symbolized the period's twin approach to the divine – hearing God's word in the nave and observing His works in the tower.[11]

The crucial distinction is between what was important then and what is important now. The latter is often mistaken for the former. The importance of natural philosophy in this period must not be exaggerated merely because the natural sciences, its successors, are significant to us. At the end of the seventeenth century natural philosophers were noted mainly as a buttress to religion. Those few who became famous, like Newton, were celebrated for their contribution to religious knowledge. Many read the European political crisis of the 1640s and 1650s as heralding the rule of Antichrist, the return of the Earthly Paradise and the Day of Judgement, as promised in the Book of Revelation. Newton saw scientific and mathematical advances as offering clues to decoding Biblical numerology and prophecy about the dating of these mystical events. For him and his pre-Enlightenment contemporaries the modern distinction between science and religion did not exist.[12]

If religion was a partner to early science, so was magic. Guided by ancient Hermetic writings and the Jewish Cabbala (both believed to be contemporary with the Bible), Newton and other natural philosophers believed that scientific study of the natural universe would reveal magic forces which could be harnessed by the magus (magician) for the benefit of mankind. In the last thirty years it has become generally accepted that the obsessive quest for these occult forces drove the rise of 'science'. Alchemy and astrology were based on magic and led to modern chemistry, astronomy and physics. The link of these early 'scientists' with magic was obscured until recently by the care with which they concealed it at the time.[13] Magic was forbidden knowledge and it remained dangerous to practise. Enthusiasts for the dark arts therefore covered their tracks and relied on the discreet patronage and protection of princes and elites.[14] Everyone knew what had happened to Bruno and Galileo, who fell victims to the Inquisition. Everyone also knew the legend of the sixteenth-century Doctor Faustus who intruded into nature's secrets and gained miraculous powers but lost his soul to the Devil. His story was still being enacted for popular audiences (by puppets) at the end of the period, in the 1740s.[15] In spite of the risk factor, therefore, science was not driving out magic – for much of this period they co-habited.[16]

This makes it easier to grasp how divine-right monarchy, appointed by God and enveloped in the aura of magic, could come to terms with the new ideas of the natural philosophers. In the twenty-first century some separation is expected between official government circles and New Age travellers who dance naked at the summer solstice. But after 1700 Newton was rewriting his work on mathematics and astronomy while Queen Anne, who had knighted him, was regularly laying her royal hands on sufferers from scrofula, who presented themselves in the firm belief that she could cure them. The point is that natural philosophers should not, strictly speaking, be called scientists. Their priorities were not primarily scientific but religious, and they dabbled, sometimes dangerously, with magic and the occult. There was a mystical element in their yearning to find a rational order in the universe. It would herald a Golden Age of certainty and harmony after the dispute and chaos of the previous period. It would also be a peephole into the Mind of God.

The natural philosophers were therefore multi-disciplinary, embracing what we call science, mathematics and metaphysics. And they proposed a new sort of evidence. When in the fourteenth century Chaucer wished to make a point about the natural world or anything else, he ransacked classical, Biblical and Early Christian authorities for quotations. Locke was one of the first political thinkers to avoid multiple references to what his predecessors had said and make his case by rational argument.[17] The natural philosophers also operated along different lines. They made personal observations, conducted experiments and gathered data. In the early seventeenth century they were hampered by inadequate equipment, but after 1650 the microscope, air pump and reflecting telescope were added to the tool kit, complemented by differential and integral calculus. Mathematics was honed as a language in which to express their observations and communicate conclusions to colleagues.

Armed with these techniques, natural philosophers proceeded to explore their terrestrial and astronomical environment. Aristotle, another supreme influence on medieval ideas, had pronounced terrestrial phenomena different in kind and quality from the heavenly bodies. The latter were eternal and unchanging, the former transient and in flux. Mathematics was therefore applicable to the heavens but not to the 'sublunar' world of humanity.

The experimental philosophers resolved to abolish this distinction and apply mathematics to both. Even apparently random events like the casting of dice were scrutinized by Pascal and Fermat, searching for the order which they were convinced must underlie them. The result was the mathematical law of probability.

Another contrast between natural philosophy and modern science is its social context. Until quite recently, far more has been known about the social nuances of Enlightened culture in the period which followed after 1750. The social profile of natural philosophy is not well known. To put it plainly, it was a pursuit for gentlemen and for those who behaved like gentlemen – and not merely because they were the only people with the necessary leisure. Credibility was vital for natural philosophers and the validity of an experiment depended on the authority for it. For this reason the social values of the period demanded that experiments be authenticated by those of gentlemanly stock or bearing. A crucial component of natural philosophy was therefore the conduct of gentlemen.[18]

Partly because of their social connections, monarchs and philosophers soon began to take an interest in each other. From the 1650s natural philosophers started to organize themselves into learned societies and seek the patronage and protection of royal courts. The first formally organized institution was the Academy of Experiments in Florence, founded in 1657 as a court academy by Prince Leopold de Medici of Tuscany. With their rich and influential backer, the academicians soon owned the finest collection of 'scientific' instruments in Europe.[19] Charles II founded the Royal Society in 1661 and Louis XIV the Académie des Sciences in 1666. The French King's motives were obvious. The engraving depicting his state visit to the Academy states that all excellence, achievement and distinction draws inspiration from the monarch and reflects glory upon him. In official eyes the French Academy of Sciences was an intellectual Versailles.[20]

From the start there was a strong international element. Italian precedents influenced the founding charter of the London Society and it in turn the French. The Dutch Huygens was a member of both the London and Paris academies. Members of different academies corresponded with one another. By the late seventeenth century most of the curious were members of these bodies, which began to publish journals of experimental reports. There were differences between them. The French Academy consisted of salaried professionals, while only a small fraction of the Fellows of the Royal Society earned their living from natural philosophy and aristocratic Fellows like Boyle did not need to earn a living at all. But throughout Europe they shared common features. They soon enjoyed more prestige than the universities, which had lost the intellectual lead they enjoyed during the Renaissance. Apart from those in Paris and Vienna, the old universities of northern, central and eastern Europe missed out on the rise of the great court cities – they were never in the right places to benefit from them.

The second generation of princely academies included Berlin in 1700, St Petersburg in 1724, Uppsala in 1728, Stockholm in 1739 and Munich in 1759. They underlined practical objectives more heavily than the disinterested pursuit of knowledge and the accent was less international. Peter the Great was obsessed with the practical advantages for the state of what we should call the promotion of science and technology. The creation in 1700 of the Berlin Academy, modelled on the French, was the work of one man, the natural philosopher Leibnitz. He was rapidly becoming the greatest living rival of Newton and claimed to have invented calculus before him. The experimental philosophers' most immediate impact on monarchs and their policies was their attempt to sell their 'projects' to royal courts. Experimental projectors wandered from country to country trying to catch monarchs' attention with cunning plans for improving the navigation of their ships or increasing their water supply.

Many had financial implications, promising riches straight from the realm of royal fantasy. Others were on apparently more solid ground. From 1716 to 1720 John Law, a self-proclaimed Scottish financial wizard, advised the French Regency government on monetary policy and promoted a raft of bold innovations. He was appointed to establish a national bank to manage (and eventually liquidate) the government's debt and create credit by issuing paper currency (in common only with England, Sweden and Europe's republics). He was also authorized to rationalize and centralize administration of the revenue by evicting the fiscal entrepreneurs who exploited the government's lack of a coherent tax-raising system. State creditors were encouraged to exchange their government IOUs for shares in the much-hyped Mississippi Company, which happened also to be run by the national bank. Much of the national debt was 'repaid' cheaply in shares whose value was inflated by public hysteria. The English government rushed prematurely to imitate Law's scheme with its own South Sea Company, but both projects collapsed within months of each other.

Yet the scale of Law's disaster has obscured the significance of his reforms. His *Mémoire* of 1719 represented the most radical proposals so far proposed by a leading government figure of the *ancien régime*.[21] Long before the advent of the post-1750s Enlightened despots, he proclaimed the necessity for rational uniformity in taxation at the expense of exempted classes and privileged provinces. Despotism was shrewdly assessed as a backup strategy where consent was unforthcoming: 'It is this despotic authority which is so much feared by individual enterprises opposed to the real or apparent good of the State.'[22] It is nevertheless true that he made future regimes wary of imposing rigid logic on political complexity. He also gave despotism an even worse reputation than it already had. At a time when people hoarded coin as a defence against the plummeting value of paper money, he had abused the absolute authority of the crown by deploying it against human instinct. Hoarding was banned by royal decree, and reinforced by arbitrary house searches. His failure probably helped to ensure that his methods were never subsequently deployed with consistency or tenacity in the 1650–1750 period. Furthermore, French monarchs were scared off establishing a national bank and centralized tax system until the Revolution. Revenue-raising was returned to private enterprise and monarchs submitted to renewed dependence on great financiers with semi-covert links to the rich nobility. Until the 1750s Bernard, Crozat and Pâris-Duverney retained their key role at the heart of state finance and the crown gave up attempts to remove its revenues from their sticky tentacles.[23]

Allegedly rational and scientific projects thus acquired an increasingly bad reputation during the 1650–1750 period. From the start the nerdy earnestness, dubious orthodoxy and often apparently useless investigations of humourless academics led to a spate of satire. The most notable example was Swift's *Gulliver's Travels* of 1726. He parodied the Royal Society as the Academy of Lagado, staffed by bumbling professors trying to make sunbeams out of cucumbers. Nevertheless, interest in the new methods caused most governments in the decades around 1700 to try to base policy on more rational administration and more accurate information. The fog of ignorance in which most had always worked began to lift. Data-gathering became fashionable and led to cycles of policy testing and amendment.[24] In 1681 the Danish crown began to measure and evaluate every piece of agricultural or forested land for a new land register and tax. The surveys and calculations took six years to complete and represented a huge administrative and scientific achievement. Christian V's *Matrikel* was not replaced until 1844.[25] English ministers like William Blathwayt and Samuel Pepys aimed to replicate the stability and efficiency of Louis XIV's regime. William Petty founded 'political arithmetic' (statistics) and in 1696 Gregory King first applied it to analysis of the population and wealth of the country. The latter also demonstrates how reason was deployed in the service of hierarchy. King arranged the population of England on twenty-six rungs – an apparently static structure with peers at the top and vagrants at the bottom. In terms of conditions making for political stability, a far stronger intellectual sense of the practical needs of government has been identified among those who wielded social and political power in the late seventeenth century than in their early seventeenth-century predecessors. Like their French models they were now seeking to build the foundations of good government on functional knowledge rather than constitutional arrangements and distribution of political power.[26]

These innovative achievements were possible only because the later seventeenth century saw the arrival of a new kind of official trained in rational methods, accurate record-keeping and strict administrative procedures. We can call it 'bureaucracy', but with three vital provisos. First, we put inverted commas around it. Second, we are aware that the concept was introduced only by Vincent de Gournay at the end of the 1650–1750 period and was therefore unknown during it.[27] Third, we realize that, according to Weber's definition of bureaucracy, suitability for appointment or promotion is determined by professional skill and not by considerations of patronage, clientage or status. Furthermore, authority must stem from the office rather than the status or patronage connection of the office-holder.[28] Defying this modern definition, early-modern 'bureaucracy' acquired clout only through reinforcement by patronage connection. Early-modern officials obeyed or were obeyed not because of their office but because of their status as clients or patrons. In short, modern bureaucratic routines and skills were combined with an early-modern patrimonial ethic.[29] The same can be said of the standing army, which was similarly subject to new disciplinary methods and equally integrated into the old patrimonial society.[30] The period 1650–1750 faced simultaneously backwards and forwards to a unique degree.

To turn to the supreme founder of modern science, Newton was not a scientist in our sense of the word.[31] He never called himself a scientist (the word had not been invented) and was never recognized as such in his lifetime. For many decades his main significance was considered to be religious. He was born in 1642, when Augustinian and Aristotelian attitudes were at their height. Only ten years before, the Pope had forced Galileo to recant his heretical views about the earth's rotation round the sun.

As for all natural philosophers, the modern distinction between science and religion did not exist for Newton.[32] The hand of God could be read in the mathematics of physics as clearly as in the Book of Genesis. Like many of his generation, Newton read both. A book of 1699 (not his) was significantly flagged up as *Mathematical Principles of Philosophy Or the Existence of God Geometrically Demonstrated.* Some of his secret and forgotten work touched on the dark arts, seriously so in the case of alchemy, the practice of which was a capital offence. Less controversial were his studies of biblical numerology and prophecy, his translation of Biblical words into their numerical coded equivalents, his search for the exact dimensions of Solomon's temple and his calculations derived from 666, the number of the Beast. As a millenarian, Newton believed that the return of Christ, heralded in the Book of Revelation, would begin with a period of a thousand years during which godly Christians would rule the earth. He ransacked the Bible for clues about this Second Coming and calculated that Christ's reign on earth would begin in 1937. Early scientists like Kepler had pictured nature's secrets partly in terms of magic numbers. In Newton's case the magic number was seven – hence the seven colours he detected in the spectrum, which could just as easily have been six.

His great book of 1687 was entitled *Mathematical Principles of Natural Philosophy (Philosophiae Naturalis Principia Mathematica)*. It has been judged by one who should know as 'the most important work in the history of science and the scientific foundation of the modern worldview'.[33] Its monumental achievement was to prove that motion on earth and in the heavens was determined by a single force of gravitational attraction which stretched throughout space. Newton's law mathematically united terrestrial and celestial realms and presented the universe as a unified structure, extending from planetary orbits to falling apples. This endorsed the Copernican view of the sun-centred universe, still rejected by the astronomy taught in seventeenth-century universities. It also removed at a stroke Aristotle's moral distinction between the inferior and irregular behaviour of the 'sublunar' earth and the perfect movements of the heavenly bodies.

This makes Newton sound like a convincingly modern man. Yet his Christian and occult priorities crucially affected what we now call his scientific work.[34] He was puzzled by the cause of attraction at a distance – as are modern scientists (including Einstein), who have still not found the subatomic particle which carries the gravitational force. According to Descartes' influential system of natural philosophy, action required some sort of physical contact: the universe was packed with tiny particles which pushed against each other and caused motion. This failed to satisfy Newton. It was probably his secret alchemical researches which triggered the crucial breakthrough. His familiarity with supposedly occult powers and his residual belief in animating spirits were revealed by the twentieth-century recovery of his papers, many of which had been hidden to preserve his reputation. This essentially religious starting point led him to guess at a mysterious force, which he could not explain, able to act without any apparent medium of transmission. His own story of watching the apple fall was probably invented to disguise the true origin of his intuition. In the last line of *Principia Mathematica* he cheerfully admitted that he had not the faintest idea of how 'this electric and elastic Spirit operates'.[35] He was thus able to write the equation for the force of gravitational pull, without having the least notion of what gravity actually was.

The *Principia Mathematica* ends with a resoundingly religious statement. 'This most beautiful system of the sun, planets and comets could only proceed from the counsel and dominion of an intelligent and powerful Being.'[36] But with the rise of the Enlightenment in the middle of the eighteenth century, Newton's dual approach (natural-cum-Biblical studies) passed out of fashion. Nature became an object of enquiry in its own right and the Bible was no longer seen as the best way to understand it.[37] After his death Newton's reputation was tailored to fit the emerging image of the 'scientist'. It was decided that his Biblical, millenarian and alchemical interests were sidelines to his real interests. His life and works were edited and inappropriate aspects simply deleted from the record. The imposition of modern academic categories on a pre-modern man has therefore obscured his aim – to unlock the secrets of nature by reading the message encoded by God in the universe.[38]

Whatever the grounds for Newton's subsequent reputation as a genius, it had to be manufactured by an energetic publicity machine working on his behalf. The champions of his fame were his fellow natural philosophers and himself. He was quick to deny his debt to those who arguably came before him in the field and most of his colleagues vigorously promoted his reputation. They did this partly because national rivalries were already kicking in. The British monarchy saw in Newton a handy status symbol to steal a march over other nations: it was important to champion him against the rival systems of France's Descartes and Germany's Leibnitz. Queen Anne knighted him in 1705. The pall-bearers at his funeral in 1727 were the Lord Chancellor, two dukes and three earls. Four years later his admirers erected a baroque monument in Westminster Abbey depicting Newton with his telescope and celestial globe, and cherubs in attendance. He leans regally on four books, representing Theology, Chronology, Optics and *Principia Mathematica*. Alchemy is conspicuous by its absence.[39]

Newton never ceased to believe in a universe of matter occupied by spirits. But in 1637 the French philosopher Descartes had published his *Discourse of Method*, which expelled spirits from the material universe. He established a rigid separation between mind and spirit on the one hand and matter on the other, the former having no direct impact on the latter. Whereas chemical bonding, for example, was previously attributed to the attractive power of spirit agents, Descartes reduced all natural phenomena to mere matter in motion. He was accused of reducing God, the designer, to a mere mechanic. But his ideas spread and for nearly a century after his death in 1650 he and Newton were rivals. National devotion to Descartes made French experimental philosophers (and Continental philosophers in general) reluctant to recognize Newton's achievements, just as the English scorned those of Descartes. But from the 1730s Voltaire championed Newton and gave him the edge. By 1750 Descartes' reputation had collapsed, partly owing to official opposition, and Newton had achieved celebrity status in France as well as England.

During this period 'science', religion and magic intermingled most obviously in medicine. The common cure for inflammation of the brain was to cut open a live bird and apply it to the head. It is now impossible to decide whether this was an empirical remedy utilizing the virtue of heat or a throwback to blood sacrifice. Healing also still overlapped with holiness. Much has been made of William III's refusal after 1688 to continue the practice of touching his subjects for scrofula, a skin disease which the hand of God's anointed monarch was believed to cure. To one insistent request he is reported to have replied: 'God give you better health and more sense.' Some historians have presented William's termination of the ritual as the end of divinely appointed monarchy in England and the start of something more contractual and down to earth – an interpretation weakened by the fact that Queen Anne revived it. In 1712 the mother of Samuel Johnson took a stage coach for the three-day journey from Lichfield to London, to return by a less costly stage wagon because she could not afford the coach fare twice. The purpose was to enable her infant son to be touched for scrofula by the Queen. The Hanoverians declined to have their sacred powers put so bluntly to the test, but the Bourbons continued the practice until 1825.[40]

Another aspect of the quest for order in the universe was the eighteenth-century drive to catalogue and classify. Things had barely progressed in this respect since the similar efforts of Aristotle and Theophrastus in the fourth century BC. Finding previous attempts to classify plants and animals too arbitrary to be useful, in 1735 the Swedish biologist Carl Linnaeus published his system for grouping similar plants in a genus, each different example of which was a species. He also established a precise system for naming plants and animals by using one Latin word to represent the genus and another to distinguish the species. This amounted to the creation of an international language – a sort of biological Esperanto. In all, he named and classified about 13,000 species. Others in the field were trying to do the same thing, but Linnaeus triumphed because only his system offered clarity and simplicity. Like Newton, he imposed rational order on chaos and diversity.

Underlying order is also the theme of Bernard de Mandeville, who in 1723 published the second edition of *The Fable of the Bees*. The resulting outcry was unprecedented.[41] The traditional Augustinian view was that since human nature was flawed, virtue required that natural human impulses be resisted. His fable tells of a hive that was successful but so full of vice that the chief bees decided to insist on virtue. The hive spiralled downhill. No more self-indulgence meant no more illness – hence no doctors. No more quarrels meant no more lawsuits – hence no more lawyers. Thrifty and sober bees stopped squandering their money – hence no luxuries, no arts and much unemployment among those who produced them. The bees ceased to covet wealth – hence no capitalists to supply society's needs. The hive swiftly collapsed.[42] The moral was that private vice and greed bring public benefits. It seemed scandalous at the time. But it was influenced by Leibnitz's optimistic conviction that even apparent evil was part of a greater and harmonious good.

To summarize, natural philosophy showcases the elite cultural project in several respects. It embodied the alliance with religion – if not always with religion of exemplary orthodoxy. And in its personnel, values and mode of address it was elite to its fingertips. At an early stage elites took control of the new philosophy (it originally sprang from Wadham College, Oxford, in the 1650s), and they retained it into the age of Darwin. Early seventeenth-century natural philosophers like Galileo and Kepler were humbly born: a century later most of them were gentlemen amateurs. They asserted triumphantly that the order required in the socio-political world was a reflection of the demonstrable order of the divinely created cosmos. Elite natural philosophers straddled the two spheres. This was a double boost to their prestige – in terms both of the cosmic knowledge they commanded and of the socio-political position they occupied.

## Political Culture

The claim that elite culture shared vital common values does not imply uniformity. The political culture of the Old Regime is the most spectacular illustration of variation. It was a contested area. It embraced a spectrum extending from those who placed total emphasis on the irresistibly absolute sovereignty of the monarch to those who swore by the inviolable privileges characterizing the composite state and its elites – and from those who believed that monarchs succeeded by divine hereditary right to those who asserted the right to remove them. The extreme wings of the British Whig and Tory parties exemplified these positions. Nevertheless, throughout the period the political culture of the educated held most of these perspectives in balance. This corresponded on an intellectual level with the very practical mixture of monarchical and republican elements in the institutional arrangements of most composite states, ensuring that elites were consulted about some of the decisions of the absolute monarchs they served.[43] Maintaining a balance between extremes was one of the key themes of elite culture.

The prevailing political culture of this period was a broad consensus – a bell curve with most elites towards the centre. This middle ground was capable of embracing rational innovation (represented in this case by the new theory of royal sovereignty) as well as respecting the traditional and customary (representing the ancient rights of provinces and corporate groups in composite states). Innovation had been acceptable since the Dark Ages, as long as it was rooted in tradition. As new ideas proliferated after 1650, those in the centre could subscribe to values that were both rational and sacred, mechanical and organic, bureaucratic and patrimonial. Exaggerated modern polarities like constitutional and 'absolutist', libertarian and authoritarian, are the fatal inheritance of the French Revolution and the nineteenth century. By imposing them on a period to which they were irrelevant we substitute our contemporary or relatively recent agendas for historical ones. Political thinkers at extreme ends of the spectrum, like Hobbes and Locke, have been adopted as representatives of opposite viewpoints. In fact they were totally untypical of the broad consensus. All historians are condemned to see though a glass darkly, but anachronistic categories turn the glass into a mirror onto which we merely project ourselves.[44]

Political culture naturally reflected the priorities on which the states of the 1650–1750 period were based. It has already been argued that monarchical states, unlike their nineteenth-century successors, were not in business to promote conceptions of national identity – and even less of nationalism. These ideas were in their infancy. Instead, their mission was to promote true religion and to wage dynastic war – an agenda which required the king to occupy two defining roles. The king as anointed leader defended the Christian faith and as supreme warlord upheld his dynastic interests by force of arms. Most wars were fought to settle disputed succession rights. Inherited dynastic claims were prioritized over territorial consolidation – hence the composite monarchies which straddled Europe.[45] The first role depended on his clergy and the second on his nobles. A third priority was therefore the maintenance of stable relations between monarch, church and nobility. This required a power base founded on crown–elite partnership, which needed to be wider and more durable than in the previous period. Otherwise disorder would return.[46]

Political culture in this period was therefore as much a part of religion as were the natural 'sciences'. In a bleak Augustinian universe evil would triumph unless firmly repressed. Corrupted human beings had to be clamped into a hierarchical and deferential political order or the moral and theological order would collapse. Religion therefore depended on earthly rulers and the elites on whom they relied. In turn it underpinned them. The states of Europe in this period were all officially Christian kingdoms. Their monarchs were believed to be divinely appointed, as were the elites who served them. Obedience to all of them was deemed a sacred duty. The socio-political order was envisaged as a 'Great Chain of Being', in which those in every rank of the hierarchy had a religious duty to defer to the ranks above. Before the rise of nationalism after the end of the period, a state was bonded together by loyalty to its ruling dynasty and elites – and by the divine sanction which empowered them. Politics and religion were therefore inseparable. Society was indoctrinated into a divinely ordained culture of deference. No alternative world-view was publicly presented.[47]

Nevertheless, the ideological divisions produced by the Reformation were catastrophic. The religious wars of the later sixteenth and earlier seventeenth centuries were followed by the revolts of the mid-seventeenth century. There was endless debate about whether resistance to a tyrannical or heretical ruler was legitimate. The Reformation generally strengthened Protestant monarchs by making them leaders of their churches and welding together state and religion in an unprecedented way. But that worked only with subjects who were also Protestants. In theory this meant all subjects, since minority religions were not tolerated. In practice it meant *most* subjects, since monarchs had no way of knowing what people were thinking. Those who remained Catholic were unsure whether they had to submit to a heretic king. Protestants living under Catholic rulers found themselves in a similar quandary.

The Bible failed to help. It ordered subjects to obey established governments but also to obey God rather than man. After the revolts of the 1640s these dilemmas were resolved by rulers with a resounding demand for submission. Such matters would be resolved in God's good time, not at the whim of the people. No monarch in the 1650–1750 period was prepared to recognize a right of resistance. Whatever their sins, rulers were answerable only to God and their subjects owed them obedience. This was scarcely an original theme. The court masques, festivals and ceremonials of the early seventeenth century had been crammed with allegories of anarchy averted and chaos replaced by order. But from the 1650s there was a difference: in Spain, France and Great Britain, not to mention other troubled locations, anarchy had actually occurred. What had previously been a polite refrain now became a deafening obsession.

The result was decisive for political culture. The priority was now to concentrate power to some degree in one pair of hands as a precaution against division and disorder. Monarchy was preferred to republics, where power was shared between members of a collective body or council. In contrast, few monarchs liked to share their sovereignty with councils or other institutions, as was the practice in some mid-seventeenth-century monarchical states where rulers were obliged to do so.[48] Power-sharing councils were considered appropriate only for states like the Dutch Republic. The resulting choice was what we can safely call 'absolute monarchy'.

This phrase was used during the 1650–1750 period to describe most European rulers. 'Absolute monarch' appropriately labelled a ruler who enjoyed absolute power in certain policy areas. Appointing ministers, promoting true religion and conducting war and peace were royal prerogatives – all areas where concentration of power in one person brought desirable speed and decision.[49] Prerogatives were absolute in the sense that they were shared with no one and there was no legitimate challenge to them.

But that is not quite the end of the story. In return the monarch was supposed to respect the property and privileges of his subjects. That was the deal between ruler and elites. Absolute power usually implied a monarch's right to obedience from his subjects in areas where he was entitled to demand it – not a right to dispose of their life, liberty and possessions.[50] A set of constitutional rules, usually unwritten, imposed observance of subjects' traditional liberties, with the expectation that the monarch would consult some sort of representative body over actions which affected those rights. Anything customary and hallowed by time compelled respect. This contrasted with the unlimited power of a ruler who recognized neither traditional privileges nor representative bodies and made whatever laws he saw fit. Such behaviour was condemned as despotism.[51]

It may be objected that this is not what most people understand by absolute monarchy. And it must be admitted that not all historians accept the picture of absolute monarchs operating in two zones, in one consulting a selection of their subjects and in the other acting alone or with their ministers. Some still endorse the traditional definition of absolute monarchy as rule *without* consultative and representative bodies.[52] But this clashes with the undoubted fact that most rulers in the 1650–1750 period expected to conduct foreign policy without consultation and to tax their subjects with the agreement of some sort of representative body.[53] It is hard to see any explanation for this other than the one that has been offered.

What seems to have happened is that in the late medieval period a compromise between monarchy and republicanism evolved. Monarchy appealed more naturally to the hierarchical spirit of the times. Kingship had many role models, from Christ as King of Heaven to the metaphor of the body politic with its head and members. Monarchy was also prized as an efficient and decisive concentration of power, especially in war. But subjects' life, liberty and property needed to be safeguarded and republics were traditionally their guardians. A republican component in the shape of consultative bodies was therefore inserted into the monarchical system, and representative assemblies and parliaments of various shapes and sizes appeared all over Europe. Hence the combination of absolute power with consultative organs – a puzzling mixture until it is realized that they operated in different spheres of activity.[54]

Representative parliamentary bodies like Diets and Estates therefore existed in most European monarchies and had prerogatives as well. One was the right to be consulted when a ruler changed the law, especially if it involved taxation. This would necessarily affect subjects' property rights, which were enshrined in custom and hallowed by the sanction of the past. The safeguarding of property rights was one of the most common justifications for the existence of kings. Representative bodies were also vital because all monarchs ruled what are now termed 'composite' states. As already explained, a composite state was a collection of separate provinces or countries, each with different laws, customs, ethnic groups and sense of identity but all ruled by one monarch. Most provinces had their own representative assembly, acting as a collective spokesman with which the ruler could negotiate. This defended the province's traditional rights against a ruler who might occasionally envisage more uniform arrangements for his patchwork of territories. Or it might agree to modify them, temporarily or permanently, in return for compensating benefits.

This runs contrary to a myth prevalent among English-speaking peoples since the late Middle Ages. It holds that the French and most other European peoples rejoiced in the autocratic power of their kings. In contrast, English monarchs were obliged to rule in consultation with the oldest of parliaments. This mythology dates back to Fortescue in the fifteenth century.[55] It exemplifies a more general insistence that England (or, after the Union of the Crowns in 1603, Great Britain) has always been unique, exceptional and different – a crucial part of the way her people have attempted to use their history to define their identity.[56] Until recently it was assumed that England had her own home-grown Reformation, owing little or nothing to other countries loosely known as 'the Continent'.[57] The parallel political narrative demonstrates the superiority to all others of the British constitution, founded as it was on parliamentary liberties.[58] The point in all cases is that Britain does these things better and gets them right.

This was and remains national propaganda. The British parliament was neither the first nor the only parliament. Early-modern Europe was awash with representative assemblies of every kind, some of them having a far more permanent presence than England's (which met for a few months each year if it was lucky). While it is undoubtedly true that taxation by consent was more obsessively upheld by the English parliament, the principle could be institutionalized in other ways, regional, local and 'virtual' (as the French termed the consent of the *parlements*, which acted in this respect for the absent Estates General). Nor did European people care to think of themselves as slaves to monarchs. 'The liberties of the French' and 'that liberty which is peculiarly French' were clarion calls that resounded many decades before the 1789 Revolution.[59] While civil liberties were probably more entrenched in England, there was arguably little to chose between the way Louis XIV treated the Protestants of the Cévennes, Leopold I those of Hungary and William III the Catholics of Ireland.

So most monarchs were absolute in prerogative matters (where they decided and others obeyed) but had limited power in other policy areas (where they were obliged to consult and negotiate). The snag was fuzzy definition of the boundary between rulers' unfettered prerogatives and subjects' traditional rights. There was a grey area that could be contested and cause conflict or in extreme cases revolt. Some monarchs found their rights of war- and peace-making subject to the veto of an aristocratic council or representative assembly. Montesquieu wrote in 1748 that monarchies were delicately poised. If intermediate institutions like *parlements* and representative assemblies wielded royal prerogatives, monarchy veered towards republicanism. If the ruler usurped the powers of intermediate institutions, it veered towards despotism.[60] Russians and Turks alone were perceived as sufficiently barbarous to tolerate a servitude fit for no one else.

One response to this ambiguity was to underline the urgent need for an undisputed sovereign authority, located at an identifiable point, to which everyone was subject. This reflected the imperative to take a firm stand against religious fanatics who thought it their duty to disobey or overthrow monarchs who failed to share their religion. The other response favoured a dispersal of authority among various power groups, with which monarchs needed to negotiate and co-operate in order to achieve a beneficial balance of forces within the socio-political system. The latter neatly mirrored, in medieval fashion, the contemporary theory of the human body's four chief fluids or 'humours' (blood, phlegm, yellow bile and black bile), a balance of which ensured health. The Hermetic secret knowledge which influenced Newton was an earlier intellectual current which postulated a parallel between the government of human society and the organization of the physical universe.[61] The mathematical cosmologies of Newton and Leibnitz blended with these previous trends to provide new models for human government. The order of the universe obviously equated with order in the state. Reason had revealed the law of gravity that governed the sun and planets. In the same way it would reveal the law which did or should govern states and the relations between them.[62]

Beyond that lay more differences of emphasis. Newton had postulated a universe of freely interacting independent particles, whose motion God continually intervened to correct. This supported notions of the balance of socio-political power groups maintained by the ruler. His rival Leibnitz had launched the idea of invisible particles called monads, pre-programmed by God to work together in harmony. This encouraged a contrary governmental ideal – that of bureaucratic power centralized in the hands of the ruler in the interests of uniform administration and operational efficiency.[63] The centralized bureaucratic model was soon advocated by the Cameralists, an important pressure group, heavily influenced by the new 'scientific' thinking. But, because it is now clear that they were heralds of the future, historians may have exaggerated their influence in this period. They offered a new view of the role of monarchy. It should be a machine for generating rational change and projecting effective power rather than a conservative repository of Christian piety and traditional rights. Cameralists outlined a conception of monarchy that was mechanical rather than sacred, uniform rather than diverse and bureaucratic rather than patrimonial (based on patronage and clientage).

Cameralists, who included Becher, Schröder and Hörnigk, criticized the confessional nature of the Habsburg monarchy under Leopold I. Its war effort from 1689 to 1712 was bankrolled by two dynamic Protestant states, England and the Dutch Republic. In 1740 it was forcibly deprived of Silesia by Brandenburg–Prussia, another dynamic Protestant state. Cameralists concluded that the intolerant Catholicism of the Habsburg monarchy was retarding beneficial social and economic development in its own state. They added social welfare to dynastic ambition as a legitimate and necessary aim of monarchy, whatever tradition it had inherited from the past. Inherited from the natural philosophers was the concept of a duty to take control of nature, while managing and exploiting its resources. Increased wealth would enable action by the state, on rational principles, to improve the condition of human society. This might mean overriding time-honoured provincial and corporate privileges, as well as defying obstruction by conservative nobles and representative bodies. By the 1740s there were two main factions among Habsburg ministers – those who clung to traditional values and those who wished to erode them.[64]

After around 1700 a few monarchs began to respond to the rationalizing natural philosophers and Cameralists. In some courts elaborate ceremonial began to decline and monarchs started to array themselves in more functional garb. Peter the Great in Russia and Charles XII in Sweden–Norway abandoned the flowing robes of their sacral predecessors and routinely wore military uniform. In 1740 the young Frederick II of Brandenburg–Prussia refused to have any coronation at all. A crown, he observed, was merely a hat that let the rain in. These were the first whispers of the demystification of monarchy, which were to become a roar after the 1750s. At the same time monarchs and their ministers began once again to consider the feasibility of imposing legal and administrative uniformity on the jumble of customs and institutions inherited from the past by their multi-national states. But until the 1750s these polarities were smudged. Only the Enlightenment was to make a virtue of stressing them.

Occasionally exponents of the new ideas pushed change too far and their relationship with rulers frayed. The philosopher Christian Wolff believed that God was the embodiment of reason and that everything in the world was as capable of rational explanation as the workings of a machine. He happily expounded the contract theory of government to Frederick II of Prussia, who appreciated a cutting-edge justification for royal power. His previous relations with Frederick's father were another story. Accused by the Pietists of atheism, in 1723 he was ordered by Frederick William I to leave Halle within 48 hours on pain of death by hanging.[65]

From around 1700 the favoured metaphor for government was clockwork. God was seen as a clockmaker: individuals were required to fulfil their allotted role and obey the authority of the system. Compulsion came not from the arbitrary will of a despot but from the order of the cosmos. It was a short step from God's laws ordering the universe to laws enacted by earthly monarchs, as explained in a memorandum usually attributed to Leibnitz and addressed to Peter the Great of Russia:

> God, as a God of order, rules everything wisely and in an orderly manner with his invisible hand. The gods of this world, or the likenesses of God's power ... have to establish their forms of government in accordance with this order if they wish to enjoy the sweet fruits of a flourishing state.[66]

Peter's edicts not only imposed rational reform. They also explained the rationale behind them, to which no obstruction was knowingly permitted.[67]

For him this necessitated a framework of government regulation which minimized the scope for laziness and incompetence by spelling out official duties in minute detail. Every manifestation of disorder was penalized and no detail was too small to catch his eye. Litter louts were to be flogged on sight. The printed regulations which he issued to his Admiralty college instructed the orderly to ensure that if anyone defecated in other than appointed places he was to be 'beaten with a cat-of-nine-tails and ordered to clean it up'.[68]

Far from undermining absolute monarchy, clockwork became a metaphor for its smooth effectiveness.[69] This was one of the principles behind the interlocking institutions of central and local government devised by Peter the Great in 1718–20. They were designed to work like a well-oiled machine without any need for the repeated intervention of its inventor.[70] Around 1750 von Justi announced:

A properly constituted state must be exactly analagous to a machine, in which all the wheels and gears are precisely adjusted to one another, and the ruler must be the foreman, the mainspring, or the soul – if one may use the expression – which sets everything in motion.

In his *Political Testament* of 1752, Frederick II went one stage further:

A well-run government must have a system as coherent as a system of philosophy. All the measures taken must be well reasoned; finances, foreign policy and military affairs must work to the same end, namely the consolidation of the State and the increase of its power. Now a system can only emanate from one mind, and this must be the monarch's. ... The monarch is the first servant of the State.[71]

Instead of identifying himself with the state, as Louis XIV had done, he saw it as a separate entity to which he was subservient. If God was reinvented as Supreme Engineer, some monarchs aped their master with their new image as humble mechanics.

By 1700 rulers in an increasingly rational world therefore confronted what has been called a 'crisis of representation'. The mechanical universe of Descartes, Leibnitz and Newton was rapidly undermining medieval notions of the cosmos (in which the motions of the stars and planets were attributable to their moral and spiritual qualities) and replacing them with a billiard-ball universe (in which nothing moved unless it was hit by something else or attracted by a force). In his early *Mémoires* Louis XIV had explained that the sun was an appropriate royal symbol as it was the 'most noble' of the heavenly bodies. Thirty years later this sounded a foolish description of an inanimate object. Also threatened were the mystical analogies between a monarch and various mythological heroes. He was not only compared to Jupiter or Hercules: some of their aura was believed to rub off on him. But circles round the king were aware of 'scientific' developments and bridged the gulf between old and new. The Perrault brothers were involved in the new science as well as management of the royal image. Furetière composed odes to the king's renown but also a famous dictionary which de-mythologized symbols. Fontenelle wrote operas which deployed classical mythology to glorify the king but also an essay which undermined the power of myth by reducing it to metaphor. It is therefore inaccurate to suggest, as some do, a neat polarization between retro royal court and progressive philosophers.[72]

Louis XIV's personal response to the new science was ambiguous. On the one hand he banned Descartes in French universities. On the other he was depicted in 1671 in the Academy of Sciences amid a vast assortment of mathematical instruments. Even more significant is that no such visit took place. This media pseudo-event demonstrates that the sciences were thought sufficiently prestigious to enhance the royal image. On the whole, absolute monarchs were responsive rather than hostile to the new climate.[73]

There were other harmless ways in which these ideas could be usefully applied. From the 1680s the royal image was partly revamped.[74] The original mythological design for the Grande Galerie at Versailles was focused on the feats of Hercules: it was dropped and replaced by paintings of the king's own achievements. Symbolic references elsewhere to planetary bodies and classical deities were replaced by recitals of newly fashionable statistical data – numbers of cities captured, prisoners taken, churches built and souls converted. At the same time Louis continued to touch the sick (1,800 on Easter Saturday 1701) and his *lever* still corresponded with sunrise. Most monarchs followed the same strategy and hedged their bets by adding the new mathematical vocabulary to the old sacred symbols. The Saxon court at Dresden updated less swiftly. The court ballet (*ballet de cour*) as performed in 1719 mirrored in dance the movements of the planets. But these were not state-of-the-art Newtonian bodies. In the medieval manner each symbolized a virtue, which was bestowed by the planetary performers, fairy godmother-like, on the Electoral Prince.[75]

After his coronation at Reims in 1654 Louis XIV never wore his crown again and his royal entry into Paris in 1660 was the last on the epic scale. For the last 42 years of his life the Sun King undertook no state ceremonial occasions whatsoever, as opposed to the elaborate court ceremonies which were daily routine.[76] His court was a mechanism designed to ensure that even the smallest domestic details contributed to his *maiestas* – the blend of power, dignity and magnificence which won the obedience of subjects and the respect of fellow monarchs. He lived mainly in public and statements of sovereignty were everywhere – in the procedure of a meal, the order of a procession, a royal bow of acknowledgement, the height of a dais. Specific occasions of state ceremonial faded during Louis XIV's reign, precisely because person and office had merged and his entire life was a state occasion.

When monarchs needed to talk up their authority (whether asserting their independence from the external control of Pope and Holy Roman Emperor or their authority over their own occasionally revolting subjects), they borrowed from political theorists. Bodin was one such source. He was a thinker of the sixteenth century who was more influential in the seventeenth. He tried to have it both ways. On the one hand he believed that the anarchy he witnessed during the French religious wars could be prevented only by an irresistible monarch – one who was not obliged to listen to the opinion of his subjects and whose power no man could legitimately limit or disobey. He was the source of the idea that sovereignty was an indivisible power, which subjects could not share with their monarchs. On the other hand he was keen to protect subjects' traditional rights, above all to their property. Taxation therefore required the assent of representative bodies. It is rarely noted that Bodin explicitly called the English monarchy absolute,[77] so, clearly, he considered this compatible with a ruler consulting parliaments (as English monarchs undoubtedly did). He regarded them as similar to absolute rulers in France and both of them as totally different from despotic Russian and Turkish monarchs, whose subjects' lives and properties were at the disposal of the ruler.

Though Bodin was obviously groping towards the idea of a monarch's twin powers (absolute and limited) operating in different spheres, he ended up by contradicting himself. Apparently his ideal monarch was to monopolize sovereignty and simultaneously share it with a representative body.[78] If some monarchs wanted to take their cue from Bodin's ideas, however, they should logically have used all of them and not cherry-picked. Predictably, they extracted what they wanted (the indivisible sovereignty) and ignored the rest (limitations concerning property rights). They thus made themselves advocates of despotism – a species of power that was generally supposed to be frowned on in the 1650–1750 period.[79] This conception of sovereignty had the attraction of trumping custom and tradition, especially when tax increases were on the agenda. But it was intrinsically contradictory in composite states dedicated to a socio-political order based on traditional privileges – namely those of ruling elites and of the component territories in which they acted as royal anchormen.

The exaggerated powers claimed by a few early-modern monarchs in turn misled a group of credulous nineteenth- and twentieth-century historians. They claimed to be writing early-modern history but were in fact seeking to chart the origins and development of the modern nation-state. A key feature of nation-states is sovereignty.[80] The concept was given its ultimate definition by John Austin in the 1820s. He was a disciple of Jeremy Bentham, who embodied the British Enlightenment's desire to clarify the elusive character of ultimate authority in the state. Austin asserted that every state required a sovereign power which was supreme and unlimited.[81] This was in the context of the modern nation-state, which he had now therefore declared to be omnipotent. But nineteenth-century historians were eager to reveal its origins and delved into the early-modern period. They discovered that Bodin had apparently said the same thing in the 1570s. He had written in a totally different context and with crucial qualifications. Both of these considerations were ignored and early-modern state sovereignty in approximately the modern sense became a historical 'fact'. The preoccupation with the formation of modern sovereign nation-states had been projected back onto the centuries allegedly being studied. Nationalist historians thus exaggerated notions of early-modern state sovereignty. They also understated the obstacles to it in the shape of composite states, consultative bodies and provincial privilege.[82] Bodin, Austin and the historians they inspired created historiographical havoc and befogged understanding of absolute monarchy for centuries.[83]

The concept of sovereignty was undoubtedly known in the 1650–1750 period. But, outside philosophical treatises, few used it in the modern sense of an irresistible and unlimited legislative authority. In all composite states the ruler's power was limited by corporate and provincial rights. In this context, whatever the natural philosophers' dynamic rationalism might urge, a sweeping authority which could impose significant change from above was inconceivable.[84] Early-modern sovereignty was much more about the king as fount of justice, which principally involved 'rendering to each what belonged to them'. This concept of sovereignty required that individuals, institutions and provinces be treated according to their different status and privileges – the exact opposite of the modern one, in which all are treated as equals by the sovereign power. If those privileges were to be altered, it must certainly be with their consent. To ignore these limitations was a negation of justice which exposed the monarch to the charge of despotism.[85] In the 1650–1750 period, except in the direst emergency, despotism was a step too far.

A fully sovereign state without democratic control presupposes some sort of autocracy or 'absolutism' – a term coined in the 1820s just as Austin was defining sovereignty. The obsession of many subsequent historians with 'absolutism' has proved another source of confusion. The term as they deployed it denoted a royal monopoly of power roughly equivalent to Bodin's indivisible sovereignty.[86] Most early-modern monarchies were labelled as 'absolutist' and their form of rule as 'absolutism'.

There are several objections to 'absolutism' as a concept. Its range of contradictory definitions has already been discussed (see Introduction). Under its usual dictionary definition of unlimited and despotic power, it cannot accurately describe an early-modern governmental norm. Until the mid-eighteenth century, monarchs had to operate in the context of a religious framework. A ruler failed to shine as a moral beacon if he trampled on his subjects' rights and liberties, since the political order was divinely ordained to uphold the Christian religious and moral order. Whatever he did in practice, no ruler could simultaneously claim divine sanction for his authority and also the right to deploy it in ways which flagrantly flouted divine law.[87] Machiavelli had argued to the contrary in the sixteenth century and his theory was still universally repudiated. For that reason despotism was a malfunction: absolute monarchy was the norm.

Finally, the concept of despotic 'absolutism' ignores the kind of state which monarchs in the 1650–1750 period actually ruled – and continued to rule until the coming of the French Revolution and Napoleon. Despotic 'absolutism' implies an all-embracing sovereignty. To repeat the point made earlier, this was inappropriate to the states of seventeenth- and early eighteenth-century Europe. These were multiple and composite rather than unitary and integrated. Monarchs had a problem listing all their titles succinctly. George II ruled Scotland, Ireland, the Channel Islands, the Isle of Man and Hanover as well as England and Wales. Printmakers preferred 'George the Second, King of Great Britain, &c, &c, &c'.[88]

Discussions about despotic 'absolutism' have usually been conducted in the context of what seems like a unified nation-state. This is normally France. Its relative unity makes it easier to import some aspects of the modern nation-state, until we recall that the French language was unknown to most of its inhabitants until the later nineteenth century. Like many early-modern rulers, the French king ruled a multiple monarchy. He was king of France and also king of Navarre (acquired only in the seventeenth century and ruled as a separate entity). Within the multiple monarchies of France and Navarre, France was a composite state consisting of many provinces and lacking a single uniform system of law – as, contrary to its cherished identity myth, was England.[89] Weights and measures varied crazily from region to region. So did taxation, and it also varied according to the social class of the payer. It was left for French Revolutionaries and statesmen of the Third Republic to impose a common law and culture on Frenchmen.[90]

The monarch could therefore have a double problem. He might find himself ruling several kingdoms with different constitutions in each; he would certainly encounter different laws and customs in provinces *within* those kingdoms. The system as it operated was deeply conservative and highly legalistic. It neurotically respected the traditional rights and liberties of existing social and corporate bodies. All early-modern states apart from Russia teemed with traditional judicial, financial, municipal, ecclesiastical, aristocratic or provincial privileges. All were fanatically defended if challenged, and all set firm limits to royal power. Though some rulers might seek to evade them or nudge them into a more acceptably rational shape, between 1650 and 1750 few or none directly attacked them.[91] Most provincial representative bodies, tasked with defending the liberties of composite states, survived throughout Europe. No French ruler in this period, or before, ever abolished an institution, since to do so would be interpreted as an attack on privilege.[92] After the end of the period, Choiseul, Louis XV's old minister, heard of the abolition of the *parlements* in 1771 – an early example of the new fashion for Enlightened Despotism. This would have solved many of the problems of his own ministry at one blow. He made a rueful and revealing comment: 'I never knew one *could* abolish the *parlements*.'[93]

The narrative of centralizing early-modern monarchs reaching out into the provinces at the expense of local privileges and powers is now increasingly challenged. The alleged ambition of rulers of composite states to integrate peripheral regions into a unified whole during the 1650–1750 period seems ever more problematic – especially as such attempts in the 1640s had proved to be highly destabilizing. Most rulers were cautious and they respected provincial rights, traditions and identities. Modest integration was achieved when it ran along the grain of provincial power politics and identities, and when there was active involvement by local elites and institutions. When rulers proceeded despotically and ignored regional sensibilities, the initiative was usually counter-productive. Now that the matter is under close investigation, historians are surprised by how limited centralization and standardization were in most early-modern states – in short, by how little the latter changed in the period.[94]

Yet this view of the 1650–1750 period is by no means accepted by all historians. The era continues to be depicted in many textbooks as the climax of despotic 'absolutism' – a view endorsed by a recent work of 'anti-revisionism' (i.e. criticizing historians who revise traditional interpretations).[95] Absolute monarchy is seen as independent of the elites on which it had previously leaned and that it was now intent on crushing. It is presented as a high-octane version of ordinary monarchy – an image that was partly its own creation. Though absolute monarchs had been dealt a poor hand and ruled loose empires sprawling half way across Europe, they nevertheless worked miracles. They levied and borrowed unprecedented funds, raised equally unprecedented armies and exerted their will to an extent on the battlefield and in the towns and villages of their realms.

But the achievements of absolute monarchy in this period do not justify repeating the mistakes of nineteenth-century historians. The exaggerated modernity of the infrastructure that supported these achievements is a scenario that few early-modern monarchs would have recognized in reality – though they might have recognized morsels of their own propaganda. The increased grip of absolute monarchy in this period seems to have been due to two factors. First, power at the summit was concentrated as never before by a new stress on royal prerogatives which centralized decision-making and speeded outcomes. Second, power at the base was anchored in co-operation rather than confrontation with elites – as was the epoch-making raising of funds and armies. Success was owed partly to cautious application of new rational ideas but mostly to smarter use of old mechanisms rather than innovation of new. At its zenith, absolute monarchy was a ramshackle affair, held together by a patchwork of partnerships, rivalries, power-sharing, compromises, muddle and corruption. It was less Thomas Hobbes than Heath Robinson.

Neither despotic 'absolutism' nor sovereignty in its modern sense will therefore work as a concept in early-modern composite states. It has already been shown that composite states, multi-national, multi-ethnic and lacking the integration and uniformity of nation-states, were, technically speaking, all empires. Empires have always lacked a clearly defined location of ultimate power. Instead they had multiple tiers of sovereignty, none of them fully sovereign, with the highest power replicating within this hierarchy scaled-down versions of itself.[96] Much the same is true of federations.[97] These multiple sovereignties within composite states partly reflected the need to accept limitations imposed by the size of empires. Distance had yet to be defeated. A letter from the Spanish government in Madrid took a minimum of three weeks to reach Vienna, two months to reach Mexico and nine months to reach the Philippines.[98] Decentralization in favour of regional power groups was required, as well as a degree of provincial autonomy to keep them on side.

The Holy Roman Empire illustrates how this could happen. In 1648 the Treaty of Westphalia granted sovereign status to the territorial princes of Germany and formally allowed them for the first time to pursue independent foreign policies – a traditional hallmark of sovereign kingship. But it did not allow them two other marks of sovereignty, the right to create nobles and the right to ultimate jurisdiction. Both of these were reserved for the Emperor and the *Reichshofrat,* increasingly the supreme imperial law court. The princes' sovereignty was therefore subject to a higher authority, which by nineteenth-century standards meant no sovereignty at all.[99] Furthermore, because of the way sovereignties could overlap and intersect with one another, monarchs did not have equal authority over all their territories. Early in the period the Duke of Nevers in France owed allegiance to the French king, his feudal overlord. But, as Nevers was also sovereign Duke of Mantua and therefore an independent prince in his own right, he could not be the French monarch's subject – a contradiction impossible in terms of modern sovereignty.[100] Early-modern sovereignty was a more untidy and ill-defined concept than its modern equivalent. In the 1650–1750 period it largely remained the exercise of authority in different spheres, seigneurial (feudal), ecclesiastical and judicial, which rarely coincided with one another. Much that we take for granted about it dates only from the rise of the nation-state in the late eighteenth century. Lines on a map matter; yet when sovereignties and jurisdictions overlapped and competed, particularly in borderlands, they mattered less.[101]

A key concept here is independence. A modern citizen is either a member of a particular state or he is not, subject to it or independent of it. Yet early-modern subjects like Nevers could enjoy a *semi*-independence. A modern nation-state is independent of other states; yet early-modern territories could be largely autonomous while under the authority of a larger empire. As with the authority wielded by the British Empire over the princes of eighteenth- and nineteenth-century India, more appropriate than the concept of sovereignty is that of suzerainty – a state's limited control of a territory which enjoys internal autonomy. Only with much sharpening of definitions could the concept of independence in the modern total sense exist. This is the legacy of the late eighteenth- and nineteenth-century nation-state. The model was fixed by the American Declaration of 1776. No document in world history before then had made an announcement of statehood in the language of independence.[102]

If we now look at detailed examples from the 1650–1750 period, it will be apparent that the precise implications of sovereignty and absolute power vary according to time and place. The political theorist Samuel Pufendorf, writing in the 1670s, refused to equate sovereignty with uniformly absolute power. Though a sovereign must have absolute power to enforce the law, he might be obliged to obtain the consent of the people's representatives to particular policy initiatives.[103] In his own *Mémoires*, of 1670, Louis XIV states that when he assumed full power in 1661 he aimed to make his will truly absolute, which sounds a little like Bodin. What is often missed is that he does not see this as anything new, but as a return to the situation prevalent before the rule of his chief minister Mazarin during the royal minority. His aim, as he states it, is merely to restore royal authority by recovering it from those who had usurped it (chief ministers, *parlements* and provincial assemblies) and redirect them to their legitimate role.[104]

In 1683, in contrast, the Danish crown promulgated a law code which has been identified as a classic statement of 'absolutism'. Its plagiarism of Bodin is blatant. It stated that the king

> alone has supreme authority to draw up laws and ordinances according to his will and pleasure, and to elaborate, change, extend, delimit and even entirely annul laws previously promulgated by himself or his ancestors. He can likewise exempt from the letter of the law whatsoever or whomsoever he wishes. He alone has supreme power and authority to appoint or dismiss at will all officials regardless of their rank, name or title; thus offices and functions of all kinds must derive their authority from the absolute power of the King. He has sole supreme authority over the entire clergy, from the highest to the lowest, in order to regulate church functions and divine service. He orders or prohibits as he sees fit all meetings and assemblies on religious affairs, in accordance with the word of God and the Augsburg Confession. He alone has the right to arm his subjects, to conduct war, and to conclude or abrogate alliances with whomever he wishes at any time. He can impose customs dues and taxes as he wishes.[105]

According to a recent authority, in theory Danish constitutional law hardly allowed a bird to fall to the ground without royal permission.[106] When it is realized that until 1660 the Danish crown had been one of the most limited in Europe, the 'absolutist' content dwindles to some extent. The monarchy had been elective and sovereignty was jointly vested in king and aristocratic council, from which the king had to obtain permission to declare war and make appointments. Much of the 1683 law can be seen as merely bringing the Danish king up to the level of the British monarch's prerogative, which was emphatically not 'absolutist'. The aristocratic council was abolished and the Danish crown declared hereditary, as were the crowns of Bohemia, Hungary and Russia in the course of the seventeenth century. This procedure was a normal part of the establishment of absolute monarchy.

But the first sentence is pure Bodin, minus the nuancing and interpretation he requires. The last sentence is also problematic, as it fails to say what sort of taxes the king could impose. If it refers to all taxation, then the Danish monarch was the only one in western or central Europe who announced a despotic claim to impose it 'as he wishes'. How could a monarch with such exorbitant powers ever be strapped for cash? Most rulers undoubtedly were – and for most of the time. Louis XIV's spokesman on such matters, Bossuet, pronounced invasion of subjects' property rights to be possible only for despotic Russian tsars. That is probably the appropriate Baltic company in which to put Denmark's absolute monarchy, especially as the Danish monarch did not merely recite this orgy of out-of-context quotation. He acted on it. In 1671 a new system of nobility was launched to replace the old, whom the crown regarded as usurpers of its power.[107] The position in Denmark–Norway is *sui generis* in that Danish 'absolutism' was partly a means of forcing the nobility out of a dominant position in government rather than binding them to it – a response to their proven incompetence.[108] Though this was also true of 'absolutism' in Sweden–Finland, on several counts we can conclude that Denmark–Norway was not the model of absolute monarchy for which it has often been taken. It merely bequeathed to future historians a definition of itself, henceforth misinterpreted as a norm. In fact it was a freak, along with Russia and Turkey – both considered by contemporaries to be the rogue despotisms of early-modern Europe.

Yet the centralization and unification of the composite state of Denmark–Norway never became serious priorities in the 1650–1750 period. The regime was, with the Russian, the most despotic in Europe and all royal decrees had the immediate force of law. But at the start of his reign the reluctant and paranoid Christian VII (1766–1808) was still 'King of Denmark, Norway, of the Goths and the Wends, Duke of Schleswig–Holstein, Stormarn and the Dittmarsches, Count of Oldenburg and Delmenhorst'.[109] An era of change arrived only with the ministry of his doctor and cuckolder, Struensee. Before the latter's grisly beheading and quartering in 1772, a succession of Enlightened ministers were able to deploy rational administrative methods against the patchwork conglomeration which prevailed.[110]

Denmark–Norway was the only state in the 1650–1750 period where despotic 'absolutism' became, in theory and in practice, a new system of government. Elsewhere, perhaps after an initial burst of despotic activity, the habit was to revert swiftly to more legal and consultative norms. At the heart of some rulers' tendency to despotic 'absolutism' lay a particular aim – to deal with the loose structure of composite states.[111] European warfare put periodic pressure on that structure and all rulers felt the strain. In order to extract more funds to meet the financial demands of the Thirty Years War of 1618 to 1648, monarchs wanted to tax their territories with less regard for the different privileges of every province. From the 1620s to the 1650s monarchs pushed rationalizing schemes to the brink and sought a tighter overall structure.[112] The dominance of the core territory was asserted and attempts were made to dismantle the barricade of fiscal privileges that the provinces had erected around themselves. Negotiation having hit the buffers, rulers seized on Bodin's theoretical justification of what they wanted to do anyway, and deployed the new claim to a transcendent sovereign power which overruled all others. During the Thirty Years War, Europe rang with denunciations of rulers' encroachment on the liberties of their provinces and subjects, as well as on the representative assemblies which defended them. In 1626, Sir Robert Phelips had bewailed the precarious position of the English Parliament: 'We are the last ... in Christendom that yet retain our ancient rights and privileges.'[113]

This was the background to the General Crisis of the 1640s and 1650s in its various forms. Attempts to encroach on provincial rights by force proved counter-productive and revolts were ignited. They taught most monarchs a salutary lesson right at the start of the 1650–1750 period. Most of them backed off. The revolts of the 1640s scared Spanish governments away from radical reform for half a century.[114] The new priority was to avoid provocation, stay within the traditional limits of royal power and respect the diversity of the composite state. Spanish political theorists like Palafox and Fajardo now argued that, if God had created provinces that were naturally different from one another, then the laws which governed them should conform to their distinctive character.[115] In Britain Charles II, who had spent 14 years in exile, expressed the mood of moderation and conciliation when he remarked that he had no wish to resume his travels. In the same way, memories of the French Fronde put the brake on Colbert's theoretically rational plan to re-order the laws and taxes of France – a blueprint which instantly collided with the proud attachment of the provinces to their ancient liberties and traditions. Contrary to 'absolutist' myth, he knew that despotic and autocratic methods had been tried by Cardinals Richelieu and Mazarin and found unacceptable. He therefore needed to sell the merits of his case to sceptical corporate groups such as trade guilds, town councils, local nobles and representative Estates. Hence the impatience and frustration expressed in Colbert's letters to his friends. His missives to his agents contain a skilful blend of stick and carrot, from flattery, cajolery and promises to pleas, threats and recriminations.[116] After scanning them, few would guess that Louis XIV was for three centuries the model of autocratic 'absolutism'.

This revisionist picture of management, compromise and co-operation has recently been challenged, in France at least. The older scenario of a harsh royal crackdown is now reasserted.[117] Examples have been detected in Louis XIV's France of a mailed fist in a velvet glove, especially in royal dealings with the law courts (*parlements*). The *parlement* of Paris had launched the Fronde of 1648 against Mazarin during Louis XIV's minority. In retaliation, his ordinance of 1673 obliged it to register royal legislation before protesting against it in the shape of remonstrances. At first glance this looks like an autocratic measure, but there is genuine debate about how much law-making was covered by its ambiguous text.[118] The claim that coercion was the only, or even the main, strategy employed seems dependent on selective choice of phases and episodes in Louis XIV's reign.[119] Louis XIV allegedly applied financial pressure to the *parlements* in order to swell his revenues and keep them submissive. It is claimed that by the time of his death in 1715 magistrates were worse off than previously, with their offices and the income derived from them both much reduced in value.[120] This is hard to square with the continued ability of the same people to fund lavish building projects and lifestyles in the capital and provinces.[121] The fact remains that coercion alone always proved counterproductive and was never maintained for long – which is why, during the Regency which followed, a determined if unsuccessful attempt was made to repair relations with the *parlements* and renew co-operation.

There is no doubt that the long period of warfare in Europe from the 1680s to the 1720s created another financial crisis for monarchs, along with further temptations to assert despotic powers. Again they clashed with the constraints imposed by composite states. This confrontation produced another of the few explicit statements of despotic 'absolutism' on record from the 1650–1750 period. This relates to Philip V's abolition of the liberties and privileges of Catalonia in 1707. Since the province was currently supporting a rival monarch against him during the War of Spanish Succession, Philip was well within his rights in responding as he did. Rebellion was an ancient way to forfeit ancient liberties. Furthermore, having confirmed Catalonia's rights on his accession in 1701, he had every excuse for being cross. But, while reminding his errant subjects of this fact, he proceeded to inform them of another justification for his action:

One of the principal offices and rights that attach to Kingship is that of Law Giver, wherein are comprehended both the prerogative of creating new laws and that of rescinding old ones. ... We are accordingly empowered to alter the Statutes of the Realm as circumstances themselves do alter.[122]

Like the Danish claim, this asserted a despotically unfettered power to rewrite the laws as the monarch saw fit – a sovereign power which transcended all other sovereignties. Macanaz, a political theorist working for Philip V, instructed his master that he could revoke traditional rights and privileges as he wished.[123] There is no hint of consensual process such as that associated with the French *parlements*, which traditionally had the right to accept or reject royal legislation.

But rulers in the 1650–1750 period rarely had full confidence in despotic power. Philip had hedged his bets in giving not one but two justifications for his action – always a sign of irresolution. And the aftermath proved that the Spanish bark was worse than its bite. Though Philip's unification (the *Nueva Planta*) suppressed for ever the distinctive provincial constitutions of the crown of Aragon, its impact was limited. When the small print was examined the Catalans retained their civil and most of their criminal law, while the compulsory use of the Castilian language was confined to government orders and correspondence.[124] By the mid-eighteenth century Philip V had again reverted to employing different titles for each of his territorial possessions. Instead of 'King of Spain' he was once more 'King of Castile, Leon, Aragon, Navarre, Valencia', and so on.[125]

Occasionally rulers of the period seriously pitted reason against custom and tradition in the manner that was to become common after 1750. In 1692, Frederick Karl of Württemberg dismissed the old constitution of his state as 'past history' irrelevant to new circumstances.[126] Yet most composite states survived the period 1650 to 1750, each with its multiplicity of legal, fiscal and institutional privileges largely intact.[127] Between those dates, composite states enjoyed a reasonably quiet life and basked in the broadly co-operative relationship prevalent between rulers and their provincial elites. Not until the rapid spread of Enlightened ideas after 1750 was their cultural and political diversity consistently attacked by an explicitly rational ideology. The result was another period of confrontation, a century after the General Crisis. 'Enlightened Despotism' was old mid-seventeenth-century despotism re-launched in the decades before the French Revolution with fashionable intellectual packaging. But not until Napoleon conquered the majority of Europe was the crazy diversity of most composite states finally doomed.

'Absolutism' in the despotic sense, with autocratic and irresistible powers extending to everything, can therefore be applied without serious inaccuracy to the periods immediately before 1650 and after 1750. But if it had been consistently operational *between* those dates, composite states could not have survived. Infinitely varied legal systems, constitutions, rights and privileges were as incompatible with Bodin's indivisible sovereignty as with the natural philosophers' commitment to rational order. An indivisible sovereignty presupposes a unitary state. Composite states were pluralist and not unitary. Their irrationalities and irregularities would have been easy meat for a powerful concentration of coercive authority, had Bodin's theory mirrored reality. But it did not.[128] Rather than impose, like Napoleon, a sweeping plan on France's disorderly historical inheritance, the tactic of his predecessors was to nudge, tweak and nibble at composite annoyances – anything but provocation. This is more consistent with absolute power in a limited sphere than with full-blown despotism. If Louis XIV and his contemporary rulers had an 'absolutist' script on their desks, most of them clearly never read it.[129]

Another issue addressed by political thinkers of the 1650–1750 period was the 'confessional' state, in which only one religion was permitted. The claims of Christianity were uncompromising and most monarchs refused to accept that there could legitimately be more than one mode of Christian belief and worship. Between 1550 and 1650 the result of this mindset had been bloody wars, motivated at least partly by religion, and made more deadly by adherents of minority creeds in one state who sought reinforcement from co-religionists in another. As a result, though most rulers continued to view toleration of religious minorities as abdication of their prime duty, after 1650 some highly innovative (and by definition untypical) thinkers concluded otherwise. They decided that the religious justification of the state was counter-productive and sought to give it a totally secular mission. The solution was to ground political legitimacy in rationality rather than theology.[130] A new basis was found in the hypothetical 'state of nature' (before the institution of government) in which its free and equal inhabitants were ruled only by their reason.

Two English philosophers, Thomas Hobbes and John Locke, developed this line of thought and arrived at opposite conclusions. Both denied that the salvation of souls was a legitimate objective of earthly government. A ruler's responsibility was his subjects' peace and security in the present world and not their condition in the next. Both believed that the state of nature was governed by the 'natural law' of human reason, which in turn endowed mankind with 'natural rights'. But without government this law and the rights it bestowed were not enforceable and human security was under threat. Hobbes and Locke therefore argued that people had agreed to an imaginary contract whereby they forfeited their independence and appointed a ruler in order to preserve their safety. At that point they parted company.

For Hobbes the contract was made between members of society, who surrendered their weapons and their rights to the ruler. His *Leviathan* was published immediately after the British Civil Wars, in 1652, and his priorities were peace, security and the ruler's capacity to deliver them. To maximize that capacity his subjects retained no rights against him, either to their property or to religious opinions – and certainly no right of resistance. Hobbes had no time for the old distinction between monarchs and despots. He pronounced tyranny to be merely 'monarchy misliked' – an exaggeration which distanced him from nearly all his contemporaries. Nor did he respect the reverence and sentiment on which monarchy had always rested: kings are to be obeyed only because they guarantee the security of their subjects. With him the power of tradition was for the first time challenged by a clear-headed and cold-hearted rationalism.[131] The result was something very like despotism. For Locke the contract was made between people and ruler. The latter's duty was to defend his subjects' natural rights to life, liberty and property inherited from the state of nature. If he failed to do so, he had broken the deal. The people could then revoke their allegiance and legitimately resist. This put Locke firmly into the 'anti-absolutist' camp.

The secular accent of Hobbes and especially Locke has probably been exaggerated. Their pessimistic descriptions of human life in the state of nature ('solitary, poor, nasty, brutish and short' according to Hobbes) retained much of the Christian basis of traditional political debate. But mid-eighteenth-century Enlightened writers co-opted the generation of the later seventeenth century as a dry run for the Enlightenment. Some historians have claimed that radical thinkers like Spinoza were indeed an early version of it.[132] Admittedly, Enlightened thinkers were slower to pick up on Locke than on Newton: Voltaire did not know his crucial *Treatises of Civil Government*.[133] But by the 1750s he had become an Enlightened icon.

Yet in promoting him to this position Enlightened thinkers distorted him. As with Newton, allowances have to be made for selective editing which presented him as far more irreligious than he was. Those in the later eighteenth century who viewed Locke from their own materialistic perspective ignored his sincere Christian convictions.[134] His original intention seems to have been to link intellectual and political development with a larger Christian purpose. He expelled monarchs from the religious lives of their subjects only because he believed no human being had privileged insight into divine realities, not because subjects' religious lives failed to matter. Yet the resulting transformation of the state into an exclusively terrestrial organization was and still is mistakenly taken to indicate similar priorities on the part of Locke himself.[135]

There were, however, two ways in which Locke undoubtedly intended to be a trailblazer. He broke with pessimistic Augustinian ideas and stressed that human beings were naturally lawful and co-operative. His *Essay Concerning Human Understanding* of 1690 argued that the contents of the human mind were derived entirely from sense impressions after birth. The Augustinian doctrine that 'original sin' was inherited from Adam and Eve was thus rejected. Governments should respect human natural rights because most people instinctively respected natural law, leaving only an anti-social minority who required government coercion. Locke trusted the people with defence of their own rights, if necessary by rebellion. This optimistic view of human nature was inherited by the Enlightenment.

Also destined to flower half a century later in the Enlightenment was Locke's conception of equal rights. Subjects' rights (and the liberty they embodied) were already supposed to be respected, but most rights belonged to corporate bodies or privileged provinces rather than to every individual. Locke injected a shot of equality into the concept – equal liberty for all rather than privileged liberty for the few. In proclaiming that rights were natural, his *Two Treatises of Civil Government* (published anonymously in 1688) were denying their origin as something artificial and unequal, created by governments. They pre-dated governments. Everyone possessed them equally in the state of nature before government began: 'All share in the same common nature, faculties and powers, are in nature equal and ought to partake in the same common rights and privileges.' Government was established by the people (not by God) to protect 'the equal right that every man hath to his natural freedom'. The starting point of previous political theories was the authority to which all were subject. Locke's theory began with the liberty to which all were entitled.

In the 1650–1750 period political thinkers like Hobbes and Bossuet are usually supposed to have produced a theory of 'absolutism' which became the blueprint for Louis XIV. Locke is commonly presented as their 'constitutional' opposite number. There are, however, a few considerations which bring the opposites closer together. Locke and Bossuet defined despotism in identical terms as encroachment by the ruler on the life, liberty and property of his subjects[136] – a view which commanded wide assent. Where they differed was in Locke's identification of despotic with absolute monarchy, whereas Bossuet contrasted them; but this slur was commonplace among the enemies of Louis XIV. Nor was Locke radically original in underlining consent of the governed as a condition of a ruler's political legitimacy. Contrary to modern perceptions, absolute (as opposed to despotic) monarchs usually needed the consent of some sort of legislative or constituted body before they could impose new taxes.[137] In spite of the authoritarianism of theorists like Hobbes, who was disowned by English royalists and largely ignored by Louis XIV's propagandists, there was among monarchs a strong sense of lawful rule, and of force as incompatible with it. Despotism should not be viewed as an early-modern norm. Despotic personalities might govern despotically and absolute monarchs might rule despotically in what they considered emergencies. But this was not the normal state of play. When the *parlements* attacked royal despotism they were not trying to destroy the French system of government but to implement it.[138]

## Religion

Most educated Europeans in 1700 inhabited the same spiritual world as their ancestors in 1600. In the early eighteenth century, ghosts, vampires and werewolves still scared elites as well as the masses. A mixture of the Christian religion and pagan magic equipped a superstitious population with charms and spells that could be deployed against a hostile environment. Church bells were often rung to drive away storms and in 1725 the bones of Sainte Geneviève were carried in procession to divert floods away from Paris.[139] Though the mental world of upper and lower classes was diverging in the 1650–1750 period, there was little fundamental difference between the superstitions of the ignorant and of the educated.[140] In a single year (1651), 200 witches were burned in the mountains of Bohemia – a holocaust presumably initiated by popular denunciation and supervised by local authorities.[141] In the 1740s the Jesuit confessor of Charles III of the Two Sicilies gave him a bag full of charms, which he was to wear continuously. If threatened by danger he was to swallow them.[142] Popular and elite tastes for less mechanical rituals were equally indistinguishable. Leopold I of Austria trod in the footsteps of countless thousands of his poorest subjects when he made repeated pilgrimages to Mariazell in Styria, the home of the Black Virgin. He was often accompanied by his entire court. To emphasize the simplicity and humility of his faith he signed the visitors' book as 'Leopold, the meanest and the least worthy of the Blessed Virgin Mary's serfs'.[143]

Educated and respectable people presumed that God intervened directly in human affairs, and they interpreted comets and natural disasters as signs of divine disapproval. Repeated earthquakes struck London in two successive months in 1750 and the streets were swiftly jammed with carriages making for the countryside. The Bishop of London did not loosen the gridlock by preaching a death-and-damnation sermon comparing the earthquakes to the divinely-inflicted Plagues of Egypt.[144] The tsunami which in 1755 destroyed Lisbon and killed 30,000 of its inhabitants was attributed by the Jesuit Malagrida and many other Christians to divine wrath. The Plague that ravaged England in 1665 evoked a modern response in the shape of accurate statistical records of the number of deaths per week but did not inspire either the king or his subjects to consult science and reason for a cure. Instead they appealed for divine intercession through penance, fasting and prayer. The tone had been set by the comet of 1664, the tail of which was instantly recognized as heralding the sign of the Beast. His diabolical number, as everyone knew, was 666. Sure enough, apparently erupting in September 1666 from the nether regions of hell, came the Great Fire of London.[145]

The impact of the natural philosophers on intolerant Augustinian Christianity should not be exaggerated. The Stuart monarch Charles II was happy to be patron of the Royal Society but giggled at the spectacle of grown men spending their time weighing air. Algarotti's *Newton for the Ladies* was placed on the Papal Index of banned books in the 1730s.[146] Locke's views on religious toleration remained largely unheeded for half a century after his death. A recent estimate is that as late as 1700, natural philosophers represented a tiny minority, albeit an influential one, among educated elites – perhaps a thousand activists and a wider circle of supporters.[147] Most of those found that their belief in a divine Creator of the cosmos was strengthened, albeit in an unorthodox manner – by 'science'. Contrary to recent claims, radical thinkers like Spinoza who veered towards materialism and atheism were an even more microscopic minority among a small minority of elites.[148] Innovators are by definition untypical of their age and the Augustinian consensus remained numerically dominant. Many resented the readiness of natural philosophers to undermine respect for established learning. This led to the 'Battle of the Ancients and Moderns', in which no quarter was given and minimal light shed. In 1700, therefore, most educated Europeans inhabited much the same spiritual world as their great-grandfathers.[149]

The eighteenth century, having been pigeon-holed as the Age of Reason, was formerly equated with a decline in the influence of religion and the churches. Modern research suggests that in the first half of the eighteenth century the grip of religion and the churches arguably achieved its tightest hold.[150] This was assisted by their continued and almost total monopoly of education at all levels in every European country. Education in Protestant Europe benefited additionally from the triumph of Pietism – a missionary and educational movement which radiated outwards from the powerhouse of Halle University, founded in 1694. Among its innovations were teacher training colleges, modern subjects like history and geography, new methods of instruction and the training of government officials. In Catholic states the Jesuits, supplying nearly all the book censors and university professors, maintained their educational stranglehold. The Jansenists, an unorthodox wing of the Catholic Church until they were expelled, stressed its social and educational responsibility rather than the sacraments.

The continuing grip of religion also influenced foreign policy. An older school of British and German historians maintained that 'wars of religion' ended after 1648. This contrast is overdrawn. Wars in the preceding period had never been exclusively about religion. Nor did foreign policy in the 1650–1750 period reflect exclusively secular concerns. Anxiety to present Britain in particular as different from absolute and Catholic states on the Continent has fostered the myth of its uniquely and obsessively colonial agenda throughout the period. It is now clear that religion remained an important influence on all monarchs' dynastic and foreign policies until the mid-eighteenth century. We now refer to the 'Hanoverian succession' of 1714. Contemporaries called it the 'Protestant succession'. The vital fact about the selection of George I was not where he came from but what religion he professed; 1714 was the third occasion in the period when British elites placed faith above birth in choosing their monarch.[151]

Nor did the impact of religious on dynastic concerns end there. In 1725, George I of Britain–Hanover vetoed a French offer of marriage between his granddaughter and the young Louis XV. His stated reason was that the alliance would be dynastically prestigious but spiritually unthinkable.[152] His son George II supported oppressed Protestants in Poland, Savoy–Piedmont and the Holy Roman Empire.[153] From the 1740s, however, the concept of an international Protestant interest was progressively shot to bits by the blatantly secular *Realpolitik* of Frederick II of Brandenburg–Prussia. His might-is-right approach was announced by a typically dry comment: 'Negotiations without arms produce as little impression as musical scores without instruments.' He inaugurated it within seven months of his accession with the morally indefensible seizure of Silesia. Allied in the Seven Years War (1756–63) to British and Hanoverians against Catholic Bourbons and Habsburgs, he was embarrassed to find himself cast in the role of Britain's Protestant hero. But this was merely a popular perception. By then most British ministers had ceased to view foreign policy in religious terms.[154.]

Most European monarchies were confessional states during the 1650–1750 period.[155] In other words, the early-modern state identified itself with one official religion, which was established and enforced by law while other faiths were banned. Though nothing else in these composite states was unified, in religion their rulers boasted theoretical uniformity. Their total identification with a chosen version of Christianity meant that a threat to their church was also a threat to their state – and vice versa. Those who rejected the claims of the religion would also defy the authority of the state, if only out of self-preservation. Heresy and treason were two sides of the same coin and fears of the one triggered paranoia about the other.

Rulers' operating principles were practical as well as spiritual. The Habsburg territories were bolted together mainly by Catholicism; England, Wales and Scotland only by Protestantism. In all cases, not only were deviant churches forbidden but attendance at the state church was, at least theoretically, prescribed. This presented monarchs with control of the early-modern period's only public-address system – the pulpit in every parish. Over and above practical necessity was spiritual mission. Modern states have been linked to several high-sounding objectives – to embody a nation in the nineteenth century and to achieve racial purity or proletarian supremacy in the twentieth. The supreme mission of almost every early-modern European state was religious and monarchs derived legitimacy from their commitment to maintain some version of Christianity. In an open letter, Charles I of Great Britain informed his son and heir that 'The true glory of princes consists in advancing God's glory, in the maintenance of true religion and the church's good.'[156] In contrast, modern liberal democracy, derived from the Enlightenment of the later eighteenth century, judges that there is no objective science of morals, society or religion. Governments therefore have no justification for imposing any religion, philosophy or ideology on the rest of society.[157] An early announcement of this approach was the First Amendment (1791) to the Constitution of the United States, which started a trend by stipulating that 'Congress shall make no law respecting an establishment of religion.'

But that still lay in the future. Early-modern monarchs believed themselves responsible to God for their subjects' spiritual well-being and in danger of damnation if they permitted non-believers to exist with impunity. The French King took a coronation oath to extirpate heresy. The English King was Head of the Church of England. The Prussian King was supreme bishop of the Lutheran church.[158] The period from 1650 to 1750 was the last in which monarchs took seriously the obligation to confront those who dissented from true religion – which in practice and in law meant the ruler's. Monarchs everywhere tried to restore religious consensus.[159] Persuasion was preferred, since it aroused less resentment. Established churches in most states were expected to undertake programmes of preaching and conversion.

Where they failed, force was applied. Persecution could take the form of civil disabilities, exile or capital punishment. To governing elites in church and state, toleration was a disreputably easy option leading to certain disaster. To religious minorities it could spell the difference between life and death.

The definition of punishable crimes was extended to embrace sins against God's law. Merrymaking of any kind on a Sunday was punished in most Catholic and Protestant countries by church courts which had the backing of monarchs. Between 1560 and 1690 Scotland's monarch supported its Parliament in making blasphemy, incest, adultery and fornication into statutory offences.[160] Not until 1771 did the Enlightened minister Struensee remove adultery, of which he was a vigorous practitioner, from the criminal code of Denmark–Norway.[161] Nation-states, based on race, had not yet been invented and there was a merciful absence of ethnic cleansing. But there was no shortage of spiritual cleansing. In this respect the states of early-modern Europe were very different from their modern counterparts and far nearer to the Islamic theocracy established in present-day Iran and admired by fundamentalist Muslims everywhere.

Exceptions were few and usually temporary. One was Brandenburg–Prussia, where a Calvinist monarch found himself ruling mainly Lutheran people. Another was France, where Catholics and Protestants had fought each other to a standstill in the Religious Wars of the sixteenth century and made some measure of toleration inevitable. But in 1685, Louis XIV reverted to the norm by revoking the tolerant Edict of Nantes, and Protestants were again persecuted. England was an exception after 1689, when the Toleration Act permitted select Protestant dissenters to worship outside the Anglican Church but denied them civil rights. English Nonconformists who had been driven into exile were, however, not an exception. Once they had the power to do so, they persecuted those who dissented from their own brand of religion. As Governor of Massachusetts at the time of Charles I's execution, John Winthrop tolerated colonial dissenters no more than his monarch had tolerated him. There was allegedly one Christian truth. Each of many different Christian states, churches and sects believed they monopolized it.

It remained dangerous to challenge Augustinian values without support from those in high places, though eastern Europe, with its harsh conditions and live-and-let-live mentality, was in many ways more tolerant than western Europe.[162] Newton wrote his occult works in code and escaped any physical threat during his lifetime. But within ten years of his death, Algarotti's beginner's guide to Newtonianism (*Newton for the Ladies*) was placed on the Papal Index of forbidden books.[163] Locke considered it prudent to publish his two most controversial works anonymously. There was no repetition of the free-for-all in published opinion which accompanied the mid-seventeenth-century crisis in several countries. In 1671, Louis XIV forbade the teaching of Descartes' ideas in French colleges and universities, though his books were not banned.[164]

It is often supposed that the heat went out of religious rivalries in the mid-seventeenth century. Neither literally nor metaphorically was this the case. In 1724, thousands poured into Palermo from the countryside to watch Father Romualdo and Sister Gertrude burn alive at the stake.[165] Portuguese heretics were incinerated for unorthodox Christian belief as late as 1761.[166] Intolerant Catholicism was still advancing. Though the Treaty of Westphalia of 1648 had vaguely encouraged toleration of religious minorities, by the early eighteenth century this was far from universal in the Empire and little known elsewhere. French Protestants were savagely persecuted. Protestants in Hungary and Poland succumbed to a combination of force and conversion. In 1731, Leopold Firmian, Prince-archbishop of Salzburg, expelled 30,000 Protestants. This represented one seventh of the population of his state. It can be argued that the Counter-Reformation peaked not in the mid-seventeenth but in the mid-eighteenth century.[167]

All available indicators point to the same conclusion. The proportion of non-monastic priests in relation to the general population reached its highest known level in France, Spain and Italy. Monastic numbers also increased until around 1750. The Capuchins increased from 22,000 in 1650 to nearly 33,000 in 1754. The number of Polish monasteries rocketed by two-thirds between 1700 and 1773, and in Hungary almost doubled. The wealth of the Catholic Church was still growing. In France it held over 10 per cent of the land, in Austria 40 per cent and in Bavaria 50 per cent. The great abbey of Melk on the Danube commanded an income drawn from rents, tithes, feudal services and dues. It amounted to 1 per cent of the revenue of the entire province of Lower Austria.[168] The Church was still strengthening its hold on elites as well as on the lower orders. Historians have measured the proportion of books of theology, sermons, prayers and lives of saints in libraries of nobles in western France. It increased until the mid-eighteenth century. The cult of the Virgin grew apace. Her main shrine in Austria was visited by 120,000–150,000 annually in the seventeenth century, 188,000 in 1725 and 373,000 in jubilee year 1753. The seventeenth-century devotion to the Sacred Heart of Jesus inspired the foundation of 1,088 confraternities in France and Italy between 1694 and 1769. There was little sign of a church in retreat.[169]

The trajectory of witchcraft trials partially mirrors the same chronology, though less so in western Europe, where they ended earlier than in central and eastern parts of the Continent. Moravia witnessed a full-blown witch craze in the 1680s, complete with black sabbaths and obscene activities. While a trickle of isolated trials continued there until 1740, in the early eighteenth century the craze in Hungary took off. Discoveries of nocturnal meetings and pacts with the devil were followed by a spectacular series of *autos-da-fé* (burnings at the stake). Intensive trials and executions continued until the 1750s, when they suddenly stopped.[170] Official termination of witch trials came everywhere after they had ended in practice – in France in 1682, in Prussia in 1721, in England and Scotland in 1736, in Austria and Hungary between 1755 and 1768, and in Poland in 1776.[171]

Even in western Europe there were some sensational cases. From 1679 to 1682 the specially appointed *Chambre Ardente* presided in Paris over a flurry of assorted witchcraft and murder trials. Accusations extended to the royal mistress, Mme de Montespan, who was accused of administering poison to the king and lending her body to the devil. Others with court connections were accused of sacrificing children to Satan, poisoning their rivals and sticking pins in wax effigies. The tribunal issued 319 arrest warrants, took 194 persons into custody, held 210 sittings, tried 104 people and executed 34 of them, variously hanging, burning, beheading or strangling them. A few were broken on the wheel. The episode has never been given a high profile, possibly because 27 years later Louis XIV himself burned the records of the proceedings. What it proves beyond doubt is that the educated and hard-bitten courtly elite at Versailles could respond to the same irrationality, hysteria and superstition which dominated popular culture.[172]

From a liberal perspective, an advance by 1750 was that in both Protestant and Catholic states, censorship was run by the state rather than the churches, and in France it was run by the royal administration rather than the *parlements*. But, especially in France, this reduced the need for compromises between competing jurisdictions, and censorship merely became more efficient.[173] There was also a discernible softening of hostility between Catholic and Protestant elites. At the end of the Thirty Years War in 1648 they could not bring themselves to negotiate together. The Emperor's representatives had to meet them in two different German cities thirty miles apart, Catholics at Münster and Protestants at Osnabrück. But, having fought one another to a standstill, rulers were henceforth less inclined to embark on crusades against other Christian monarchs and more willing to do business in government and diplomacy. By the end of the 1670s Catholic and Protestant representatives felt able to sit down with each other face to face and hammer out a peace treaty ending Louis XIV's Dutch War.[174]

Attempting to control opinion is often presented as a defining habit of absolute monarchs. There is a time-honoured contrast between repression of unorthodox opinions by Catholic absolute monarchies and toleration by Protestant republics (or alleged quasi-republics like Britain). There is some truth in this generalization but it should not be pushed too far. Two radical writers, at the beginning and end of the period, were oppressed by very different authorities, but with the same result. In 1750 it was the Enlightened thinker Diderot, newly released from imprisonment in Vincennes by the French Catholic absolute monarchy; in 1650 it was natural philosopher Descartes, on the run from the Calvinist Dutch Republic. This suggests on the face of it that Protestant and Catholic authorities were equally opposed to freedom of thought and publication and that in this respect little changed in a hundred years. So, apparently, were monarchies and republics. This impression is confirmed by one of the responses to Rousseau's publication of *The Social Contract* in 1762. It was examined with interest by the republican government of Geneva, the Protestant city-state where he had been born half a century before. Its oligarchs were the only government in Europe to burn and ban the book on publication.[175] The Catholic republic of Venice was no less active in repression. In 1755 its three Inquisitors of State arrested and imprisoned the renowned sexual athlete Casanova for dabbling in alchemy and the occult. Their general feeling seems to have been that he was both spiritually and sexually out of control.

The relative freedom of the late seventeenth-century British state and of the Dutch Republic is usually exaggerated by English-speaking historians. In fact France moved nearer to their position after Louis XIV's death in 1715, when the government began to recognize a category of book which had been neither officially licensed nor expressly forbidden (though this left writers and publishers trying to second-guess the government's response).[176] In the Dutch Republic, war was declared on Anti-Trinitarian views and the atheism allegedly advocated by the Dutch philosopher Spinoza.[177] In Britain, much is heard of the English Parliament's Toleration Act of 1689 and the termination of its Licensing Act in 1695. Less celebrated is its Blasphemy Act of 1698, which outlawed denial of the divinity of Christ or of the Holy Trinity. Toland's *Christianity not Mysterious* was burned by the common hangman on the orders of the English and Irish Parliaments.[178] It was worse in Scotland. Whereas the last heretics had been burned in England in 1612, in 1697 the Scots hanged Thomas Aikenhead for denying the Trinity.[179] In 1694 the Dutch Calvinist cleric Balthazar Bekker, who doubted the existence of the devil, was suspended – but unlike poor Aikenhead, not in thin air.

The Swedish monarchy in its less absolute phase of the mid-eighteenth century was unabashed in its opposition to the circulation of dangerous opinions. In 1743, Samuel Klingenstierna, a Swedish follower of the mechanistic German philosopher Christian Wolff, asserted that three classes of book must be eradicated – those that damaged the state, good morals or religion. The most absolute monarch in the period, Frederick II of Prussia, was also the most liberal. He loathed the priorities of the confessional state and relaxed the censorship laws. But even he cracked down on inappropriate material printed in the language of the common people. The luxury of access to radical and irreligious publications was confined to the safe obscurity of Latin and French.

## Conclusion

Compared with what preceded and what followed it, the socio-political stability of the 1650–1750 period was remarkable. A key explanation is arguably the cultural base on which it was partly grounded. The new amalgam of 'scientific', religious and political cultures was launched as an elite project in the second half of the seventeenth century and became increasingly dominant among elites in the first half of the eighteenth. Rather miraculously, these three cultural activities supported rather than undermined one another. In a classic synergy, they interlocked to form a whole greater than its parts. In contrast to the harassing of early seventeenth-century natural scientists, no serious collision was allowed between 'science' and the churches: the discovery of God's mathematical signature in the cosmos was welcome news to both. This was partly because of the prestige of icons like Newton, who applied rational methods to the heavenly bodies while remaining reassuringly within the framework of the Christian religion. Similarly, elite social values were embraced by the new 'scientific' community and its cosmological discoveries in turn endorsed the existing socio-political order. Finally, church and state sealed a deal which endured for a century until, after the 1750s, the Enlightened despots broke it.

The new 'scientific' methods were employed selectively by governments – enough to be useful in the shape of rational administrative methods but not enough to threaten the socio-political order. Until the 1750s monarchs, ministers and elites could work selectively and pragmatically with these ideas, while managing to avoid potential collisions between innovative and traditional values. Rulers in the 1650–1750 period never seriously addressed the issue raised by a looming confrontation – that between the rational order of Cameralists and natural philosophers on one side and the composite state's privileged diversity on the other. Respect for ancient custom was so ingrained that the incompatibility was ignored rather than shoved into the spotlight. If Cameralist ideas had been pushed to their logical conclusion, European states would probably have reverted to the chaos prevailing in the 1640s when the period began. That was precisely the situation which had scared generations of rulers away from the risk of doing any such thing.

The only major ruler of the period to produce a comprehensive and coherent plan for change was Peter the Great of Russia. It represented the most determined and explicit application of the new rational philosophy – and consequently the most radical break with the past. This was due partly to personal temperament and partly to the circumstances in which he found himself. Any decree (*ukaz*) issued by the Tsar automatically had the force of law without further procedures. Russia possessed neither privileged persons, groups or provinces, though where non-Russian areas had special rights even Peter respected them.[180] As a composite state without the usual barriers to royal authority, Russia could have become a laboratory specimen of rational reconstruction. But even here there was a spectacular gap between reform on paper and in practice. Away from the centre the Tsar's autocratic command was diluted. Nobles took the law into their own hands – literally.[181]

In general the new rationalism was deployed to improve the old system rather than invent a new one. Useful practical applications followed. Bureaucracies and standing armies, dating from the sixteenth and early seventeenth centuries, were underpinned by the new statistical mathematics and increasingly run by professionally trained staff (usually educated or re-educated elites). Despotic moves to unify composite states were unsuccessful and short-lived. This cautious approach and cultural mix of old and new elements enabled positive potential to be at least partly exploited and negative outcomes largely avoided. Above all, the idea of a rational and harmonious order in the universe, mirrored in religion, government and society, assisted the acceptance of monarchs, nobles and prelates as an effectively regenerated elite.

But from the 1750s some rulers would push these ideas to their logical conclusion and embrace reason in the more doctrinaire form associated with the Enlightenment. Their insistent demands for more uniform taxation would offend privileged nobilities with tax immunities and threaten the royal alliance with landed and office-holding elites. In 1773, under pressure from the rulers of Spain, Portugal, France and Naples, Pope Clement XIV would abolish the Jesuits – a body-blow to the Catholic Church and its Counter-Reformation missionary institutions. At the same time monarchs and ministers would begin to look at a new relationship between church and state. Tighter control of clerical activities and toleration of religious dissent would be imposed in Austria, Prussia, Russia, Scotland and finally France (two years before the Revolution). The confessional state would be widely dismantled, with destabilizing results for the alliance between clergy and absolute monarchs.[182] Above all, monarchs would be largely demystified. That would enable French Revolutionaries to return to the ruthlessly unsentimental mindset of Cromwell's faction in late-1640s England. Hume's account of the beheading of Charles I was the last book that the condemned Louis XVI would read before his own decapitation in 1793.[183] The wheel would thus come full circle.

# Chapter 4:  Media and Messages: the Arts

## Introduction

Three centuries ago art followed power. If modern European people want to view a town's art treasures, they head for its art gallery. But in 1700 those with similar intent visited its richly decorated churches, monasteries and nunneries. If they were in the countryside they headed for the nearest residence of a nobleman. In a capital city they paid their respects to the royal court.

Between the mid-seventeenth and mid-eighteenth centuries the alliance between art and power was as crucial as that of crown and altar. It will be argued here that the arts of that era had two agendas. The first was to buttress elites by projecting the power, merits, magnificence and god-like status of monarchy, church and aristocracy. The second was to inculcate the belief which underpinned them – that the hierarchical order in church, state and society reflected the divinely ordained order of the universe. Neither of these messages was entirely novel. But the clarity and force of their combination, as well as the scale and sophistication of their delivery, were unprecedented.

Around the middle of the seventeenth century the Spanish writer Cellorigo described the three orders of society as

> the one of priests and the other two of nobles and plebs, which the prince has to work with so that they do not become changed, disturbed, mixed up or equivalent, but that each one preserves its place, order and harmony, so that the diverse voices will make a perfect consonance.[1]

According to Carballo, a writer of the same period, poets and painters had to depict their subjects in a manner and with a 'decorum' which indicated their position in the social and political pecking order. Anything inappropriate to their status must be avoided by

> attributing the wise with wise sayings and deeds, the rustic with rustic words and deeds; the scholar deals with his school, the pastor with his flocks, the Prince with his government, the vassal with his family, the seignior orders and the slave obeys.[2]

These concepts of order, harmony, balance and decorum resonated during a period of unexpected stability sandwiched between two eras of political turmoil. To establish this point, the arts of the time must be examined, as well as contrasted with what came before and after.

For much of the nineteenth century it was impossible to make a valid assessment of royal, aristocratic and clerical culture in the 1650–1750 period – what we now know as baroque culture. This was because soon after the 1750s most of its greatest painters, architects and musicians disappeared from the radar. Not only did most of them swiftly die: changes in artistic fashion and political culture caused their achievement to be denigrated, despised or forgotten. This revolution in taste is an impressive indicator of the elitist flavour of that vanished cultural world and of how swiftly its ceremonial grandeur and religiosity came to be seen as musty and archaic.[3] It is now necessary to evaluate the political significance of baroque culture on its own terms and not on those of a later era which despised it.

Forty years ago, histories of European countries contained chapters on cultural developments, written more dutifully than enthusiastically to inform readers what was happening in the arts during the period. Unfortunately, historians tended to know less about the arts than they did about war and politics. Cultural historians had similar limitations. Their knowledge of political history (and especially of concepts like 'absolutism') was always hopelessly outdated. The disciplines are now coming together. With a little help from their friends in fine arts and literature faculties, historians are now using culture as historical evidence.[4]

Their method has, however, become more sophisticated than half a century ago, when the works of Defoe were deployed as a social report.[5] Interpreting any of the arts as a snapshot of reality can be perilous if they embodied other agendas or were specifically intended to create illusion. Historians are now more aware that writers and painters did not merely record history. Their role as persuasive propagandists made them players in it. Creative artists and those who sponsored them were activists as well as onlookers. The meaning a society identified for itself is encoded in its paintings, buildings, processions, rituals, music and written texts. These art forms can be made to reveal how elites used them and how they wished to be seen by their equals and inferiors. Culture is therefore inseparable from socio-political power and historians now view images and texts as socio-political sources. Furthermore, power, was inseparable from all aspects of culture. Monarchs and their elites employed every form of communication from painting, music, architecture, horticulture and the printed book to live drama, dance, mime and pageantry. We therefore have to put together what has been separated by different academic disciplines. Any analysis of early-modern monarchy must be multi-disciplinary.

In early-modern Europe, power rarely came out of a gun barrel. Police forces were little more than neighbourhood watch schemes. Though the standing armies of the 1650–1750 period were unprecedented in their scale and effectiveness, by modern standards they were small, ill-disciplined and of doubtful loyalty. They disliked being deployed against native nobles and were not reliable if used against a monarch's own people. Yet at the same time absolute monarchs were making unheard-of claims for their own role and authority. To fill the gap between what their theory of monarchy proclaimed and what their physical power could deliver they had to employ the black arts of media manipulation. Because early-modern power structures lacked a convincing apparatus of force, they were dependent on the projection and perception of monarchy. Enlarged Habsburg palaces, extended in a swaggeringly baroque manner, concealed the absence of an equally impressive extension of administrative or military capacity.[6] Similar media strategies massaged the creaking joints of Louis XIV's regime with such spectacular invention that it persuaded contemporary rulers that France was a far greater threat than it was. It also fooled historians for the next three centuries into erecting the myth of Louis's so-called 'absolutism'.[7]

Much of the apparent increase in state power in seventeenth-century Europe is therefore a confidence trick consciously perpetrated by rulers on their subjects: it creates the visual impression that they wielded greater political power than they possessed.[8] The myth of 'absolutism' was itself a cultural construct.[9] Many insignificant princes were extravagant patrons of the arts. The stability of 1650–1750 often seems hard to explain with total conviction. One of the reasons is that, if not all done with mirrors, it was less complete than it looked – more of a precarious balance than a stable equilibrium.[10] The claims made by the arts were often in inverse proportion to reality. There is no doubt that where monarchy was least firmly established, its projection was most self-conscious. Highlighting the splendour of the crown could conceal the weakness, whether personal or institutional, of the wearer. Monarchs had long realized that the arts were a useful means of trumpeting what was not automatically taken for granted. But where real power was obvious, décor could be downplayed. The special relationship between God and the Catholic kings of Spain was certainly taken for granted: the unique empire with which they had been endowed was matched by their obligation to promote God's cause. Predictably, the Spanish kings had no coronation ceremony and, for much of the seventeenth century, no throne, no sceptre and no crown. No powers of divine healing were attributed to them: Spaniards with a health problem went to Paris rather than Madrid. Court access was confined to a tiny elite of grandees, and public sightings of royalty were minimal. Their sacred persons were surrounded by the same few officials, in a cavernous court which was more like a monastery than a palace. Indeed, the Escorial *was* a monastery.[11]

The opposite tendency is illustrated by the Prince-bishop of Würzburg, Carl Philipp von Greiffenklau. In 1750 a great Venetian painter arrived there to decorate the newly-built *Residenz*. As the visitor ascends Neumann's sumptuous staircase, Tiepolo's vast ceiling fresco floats above like an aerial ballet. Nothing less than the four continents of the world do homage to the reigning prince, whose ermine-draped portrait is upheld by cherubs while the figure of Fame trumpets his name to the ends of the earth. Von Greiffenklau was optimistic to imagine that posterity would be impressed by his obscure mediocrity. Amid the critical chill factor which enveloped princes in the later eighteenth century, such personages seemed merely ridiculous.[12]

Exploitation by monarchs and their elites of the media of baroque Europe was unprecedented. They formed close relationships with baroque artists and architects, Victor Amadeus with Juvarra, the Austrian Habsburgs with Hildebrandt and von Erlach, Louis XIV with Le Vau, Le Brun and Le Nôtre. Baroque and its rococo spin-off scored dazzling success as propaganda for rulers struggling to restore their authority after decades of crippling warfare and civil revolt. But as the royal image was polished and promoted in a new and self-conscious way, there is a temptation to project onto the early-modern period our current obsession with image-makers, media management and spin doctors. Has Colbert, Louis's minister of culture, been updated into something suspiciously like a modern Prime Minister's press officer? In fact Louis *did* have an organization whose sole responsibility was the projection of a favourable royal image. It was called the *petite académie* and met every Tuesday and Friday, vetted designs, wrote inscriptions and planned what we should call media events.[13]

The danger is that our modern obsession with spin doctors enables the early-modern propaganda machine to impress us more than those at whom it was directed. Then and now, the exercise of power amounts to more than the manipulation of images. When the distance between image and reality became too great and a credibility gap appeared, image-making became counter-productive.[14] Because of the least-mighty/loudest-noise rule, this was a constant risk. The House of Savoy got away with it when it employed court culture to press its campaign for a royal crown.[15] But in the 1640s Olivares suffered from the discrepancy between the proclaimed unity and strength of Spain and the self-evident reality of its disintegration and defeat. Every shred of his credibility evaporated.

The arts in the 1650–1750 period lacked one important role later allocated to them – that of bonding together state and society by expressing a common allegiance to the nation in the form of a national culture. Early-modern culture at this level was far more cosmopolitan and bonded together international elites, not national units. Creative artists had less sense of duty to a single national culture than nineteenth-century successors like Chopin or Smetana, who considered themselves the voices respectively of Poland and Bohemia. This makes it possible to generalize far more accurately about European culture as a whole in this period than in later ones. Only in Britain, which staged an austere revival of Palladian architecture while the rest of the Continent was festooning itself in baroque and rococo, was there a major departure from European styles. Since artists worked within multi-cultural and multi-national states and empires, they could enrich their work by acquaintance with several national cultures. Vivaldi began as a servant of the Catholic Church in Venice and ended seeking employment from the Holy Roman Emperor in Vienna. There was brisk relocation within the components of multiple monarchies. The Scandinavian dramatist Holberg was born in Norway but made his career in the metropolitan centre of the composite monarchy in Copenhagen, Denmark. Handel started his career in Hanover and then preceded his master the Elector to London, four years before the latter became King of Great Britain.

A useful example of the way patronage networks operated within multinational monarchies is provided by Gluck, the composer who in his final years was to sweep away baroque opera. He was born in the Habsburg empire in the Upper Palatinate on the borders of Bohemia. Since his father was a forester his origins can be safely described as humble. Fortunately his parent's employer was Prince Lobkowitz, whose tentacles extended throughout the Habsburg empire. Sniffing musical potential, the prince moved the young man around his palaces, first in Prague and then in Vienna. From there Gluck was sent to complete his musical studies in Habsburg Milan, where he began to write successful operas. Once his reputation was made, he could break into the international scene, and invitations to London and Paris duly followed. He succeeded by successfully blending influences absorbed from his cosmopolitan background, at a time when the cry was for a fusion of Italian, German and French music rather than separate national styles.[16]

There were 'nationalist' exceptions to this thinking. Literature obviously did not travel as well as painting or music, though by the mid-eighteenth century French was the *lingua franca* of Europe. There was also brisk competition between French and Italian culture under Louis XIV and Louis XV. The librettist Perrin informed the king that his own glory and that of France 'make it unseemly that a nation otherwise invincible should be ruled by foreigners in matters pertaining to the fine arts, poetry and music'.[17] Yet such opinions were less usual before the 1750s than after. Elites generally regarded xenophobia as a vulgar outcome of popular ignorance. And though national identities were being defined they were still too weak, and regional identities too strong, to enable them to act as a strong focus of political or cultural loyalty – especially in multi-national monarchies where national feeling was obviously a centrifugal and counter-productive force. Much of that focus was provided by the state church, whether Catholic or Protestant. For this reason monarchs buttressed religious unity with continued determination. Churches were the main public assembly point, where ordinary people experienced most of their cultural life. Protestant churches were in this respect scaled down but not dissimilar versions of Catholic ones. The partnership between the arts and religion was so close that the join was seamless – an alliance assisted by the absence of a clear division between religious and secular art during the period.[18] Equally vital to state cohesion were quasi-feudal loyalties to dynastic monarchs, though they were not treason-proof – any more than loyalty to the church was heresy-proof. And finally the role of elites as regional anchormen in composite states was indispensable. For these reasons monarchs and their elites could commandeer an unprecedented degree of cultural support.

Most serious painting, architecture, music and literature were created for the benefit of these three ruling powers and only indirectly for those to whom they wished to project their message. The arts had not been democratized. The performing and visual arts now occupy impressive public buildings. This reflects the status attained by the arts in the nineteenth century, when they became in part a substitute for religion in the minds of a growing intelligentsia. The building of art galleries and museums was that century's substitute for cathedral and palace construction: the former were consequently designed to look like the latter. But culture in the baroque period was not presented in public buildings intended to be palace and church lookalikes. It was displayed in buildings which *were* palaces and churches, since it existed mainly for the purposes of those who occupied them.[19] Only from the middle of the eighteenth century did monarchs gradually recognize that the arts had a validity in their own right. At this point they began to separate the arts from their palaces and allow them an independent status of their own. The first freestanding opera house in Europe was built by Frederick the Great of Prussia in the 1740s and the first free-standing museum by Frederick of Kassel in the 1770s. At an early stage on their journey to nineteenth-century sacralization, the arts were carving out their own dedicated space.[20]

But between 1650 and 1750 the main purpose of the arts was to represent the power and values of monarchy, church and aristocracy.[21] 'Represent' in this context implies projecting an image. The means could be visual, literary, musical or ceremonial – statue, portrait, coin, building, ritual or anything else which enhanced the prestige of the person referred to.[22] A royal or aristocratic palace, for example, worked on two levels. It transmitted a spectacular (and usually exaggerated) impression of the power, wealth and status of its owner. It also functioned as a theatre where its semi-divine occupant acted out his 'representative' role with elaborate ceremony. By the same token, a church was a theatre where God and his Church were seen to be glorified.[23]

Royal entries, coronations, processions, festivals and fireworks were all 'representations of power', loaded with political messages and symbolism designed to impress royal authority even on uneducated subjects. Every known visual, literary and musical medium was exploited by royal publicity machines – portraits, coins, medals, statues, tapestries, dramas, operas and assorted spectacles and entertainments. In the case of Louis XIV they added up to a conscious attempt to invent a royal image of the king, which was constantly revised as circumstances changed. Though we know less about the 'PR teams' of other rulers, they undoubtedly imitated the Sun King's methods.[24] A classic instance was the royal entry into capital or other cities. Rulers sometimes went to extraordinary lengths to make a public statement of a political point. During the Fronde the loyalties of the city of Marseilles had occasionally wobbled. When Louis XIV visited it long afterwards, he offered it the ostentatious insult of refusing to enter by the city gate. Instead he arrived like a conqueror, through a breach in the wall specially made for the occasion.[25]

The increasing elaboration of the ceremonial surrounding executions has recently attracted attention, especially since it was orchestrated like a performance art. Details of everyday life which previous historians considered insignificant have recently been shown to be clues to greater things. They offer tangible contact with a remote mental world. As the ultimate demonstration of sovereign power, executions always had special significance and there was a logical link between king and executioner. Without the latter, according to the early nineteenth-century political writer de Maistre, 'order yields to chaos, thrones fall and society is extinguished'. Increased initiative from above probably reflected the eagerness of central government's spin machine to seize a chance rather than its determination to interfere in local affairs. Absolute monarchs wished to stage executions as ritual displays of the power and majesty of the state, rather than acts of the community. Medieval illustrations reveal that executions were casual affairs, with few spectators, little solemnity and less spectacle. In the late seventeenth and eighteenth century, monarchs ensured that executions were rarer but more intensively orchestrated, as execution rituals, elaborate processions and scaffold ceremonial ensured that the ultimate power of the state over its subjects was demonstrated with due pomp and circumstance. Punishment also had to be seen to proceed directly from the state through its servant, the executioner, whether by beheading as in most of the Continental states or by hanging as in Britain. This eliminated punishments which could be seen as invoking the power of the natural elements, such as fire (burning at the stake), earth (burial alive) and water (drowning).[26] The same propaganda motive is seen in the eagerness of the state to execute effigies and corpses when the actual criminal had escaped or died. In an age attuned to symbolism all these points were noticed – though presumably less so by victims whose attention was otherwise engaged.

This is a reminder that for monarchs and elites to address an exclusively elite audience would have been self-defeating. They had to achieve a delicate balance. They wished to articulate the superior values which distanced them from the masses, but at the same time they needed to communicate with them. In the case of the church there was obviously a popular element, since the clergy (Catholic more enthusiastically than Protestant) used religious art to inform and inspire the faith of simple folk, just as monarchs and nobility used grandiose architecture to inspire their loyalty. Visual and musical imagery was especially important for a European population of which over half were illiterate. The perfect medium for this cross-cultural communication was the new artistic style of the seventeenth century known loosely as 'baroque'. It began as a weapon of the Counter-Reformation of the sixteenth century, but adapted as easily to the Protestantism of Dresden as to the Russian Orthodoxy of St Petersburg. Intellectually it was highly sophisticated, but it could also make an immediate impact via the senses on the raw emotions of uneducated observers. This made it particularly effective as an active and dramatic transmitter of new values. Before the mid-seventeenth century it was confined mainly to Italy but afterwards rapidly became a must-have commodity for European monarchs, aristocrats and prelates. In the rebuilding of Vienna after the siege of 1683, baroque pictorial and architectural imagery celebrated the elite alliance which had saved the city, and it communicated the power of that alliance to the masses.[27] Its splendour and exuberance represented a triumphant proclamation by princes and prelates reaching their zenith.[28]

More generally, the arts existed for the entertainment of elites, who before the mid-eighteenth century had a near monopoly of the media. Only they could afford to provide a reliable market for the work of architects, composers, painters, sculptors and writers. Patronage and connection were essential features of the system. Vanbrugh was chosen by Lord Carlisle to design Castle Howard only because they were both members of the Kit-Cat Club.[29] Freelance artists could avoid elite patronage only if they were prepared to tolerate the hazards of employment elsewhere. Street musicians had no aristocratic dominance to endure but no regular salary cheque either. Town 'waits' (bands of musicians employed for civic ceremonies) were marginally more secure, but had to supplement their official wage by teaching or playing at private functions. One of the main attractions of elite patronage was the opportunity offered for travel, work abroad and absorption of foreign influences.[30] Only the growth of an educated public in the later eighteenth and nineteenth centuries could free creative artists from dependence on royal, ecclesiastical or aristocratic patronage. This launched a public sphere in which that public could sponsor the arts collectively rather than as individuals. Only then came the invention of the romantic image of the artist as rebel and outsider, serving nothing but his own genius. But the artists of the baroque period were (for the last time) worldly, courtly, establishment figures, respectful to those who provided their livelihood. And he who paid the piper called the tune.

None of this means that all elite culture was an explicit propaganda exercise on behalf of nobles, princes and churchmen. Educated people did not require an obvious sales pitch. They were quick to pick up coded messages, like the parallel between order in the state and order in the metrical structure of a poem or in the musical form of a concerto. Nor were palaces designed only to shout 'Look at me!' Elites required quality housing for their own comfort, as well as to accommodate those who served them. And though they wanted to impress contemporaries, their concept of fame was not ours. Royal PR agendas were not dominated by quick fixes which brought fleeting recognition from the fickle multitude. Popularity (literally, the admiration of the common people) was disdained. Instead, one of the key images of elite culture in this period was the winged goddess of Fame who trumpets great deeds down the centuries.[31] In 1663 Colbert wrote to Louis XIV:

> Your Majesty knows that in lieu of magnificent acts of warfare, nothing betokens more the grandeur and the spirit of princes than buildings; and all of posterity measures them by the standard of these superb buildings that they have erected during their lives.[32]

What mattered to elites was reputation with their peers and with the future. Hence the obsession with status, a new feature. By contrast, Leonardo's *Mona Lisa* of *c.*1502 gives no indication of the subject's rank.

Some historians have suggested that governments, especially in France, exerted an almost totalitarian Goebbels-type grip on cultural activity.[33] Yet the royal court had little influence over what sort of art municipal dignitaries or nobility chose to patronize. The fact that monarchs and their elites shared common cultural values did not prevent them from being cultural rivals. Occasionally, especially in France, this appeared in the guise of the classical versus the baroque style. More generally, it was easier to contest the supremacy of a regional lord or a distant monarch by issuing a cultural challenge than by staging an overtly hostile political act. In the same way, princes and monarchs found it cheaper and less risky to assert their superiority by building more grandiose palaces than by putting bigger armies on the battlefield. Building was part of the profession of ruler, on a par with statecraft, warfare and hunting.[34] The arts were an extension of politics by other means. Rival courts whose authority overlapped, rival cities who clashed over provincial supremacy or joined forces to defend provincial privilege against the king, rival families competing for status or rival bishops disputing primacy – all regarded iconography as part of their armament. Visual weaponry was used to protect cultural identity, rights and privileges and to further corporate and family ambition. The arts thus move from being a backdrop to political events and become a political player. It was invariably simpler to make a visual statement about power than to exercise it.[35]

Clearly monarchs and elites had the power to censor culture and to forbid any serious alternative. Royal intervention was expected in all direct promotion of the royal image. On the other hand a genius like Poussin, for whose services competing patrons would metaphorically kill, refused to allow them to determine the subjects that he would paint.[36] He was an extreme case and in the last analysis most patrons would insist on their own wishes. Less celebrated names would be deferential to their patrons. But many of the latter probably felt they were more likely to enhance elite prestige by recruiting the best performers rather than by force-feeding them their lines. The amount of explicit propaganda was probably reduced by the willingness of patrons to step back from the actual creative process. The reputation of elites was boosted as much by the superlative quality of what was sponsored as by its precise message. Political debates of great importance were conducted in much of the art and literature of the period. In his later years, Louis XIV was subject to constructive criticism from within elite circles and accepted it in that spirit.[37]

Monarchs, nobles and churchmen had been surrounded by art and ceremony since the early Middle Ages. Several changes now raised their game. One was the tendency of the royal court to settle in the capital city rather than itinerantly sponging off the nobility. The establishment of a permanent residence like Versailles enabled monarchs to develop the arts of presentation on an unprecedented scale. It also permitted etiquette to be elaborated to levels previously prevented by the unmanageable state of temporary royal and aristocratic residences – always assuming they had escaped being wrecked by warfare.

An even more significant change was the adoption by elites of a new cultural style. Between 1650 and 1750 the arts were shaped by a uniquely elevated idiom known as the Grand Manner or the Grand Style. The elite patrons who invested and participated in high culture saw in it a reflection of their taste, interests and supposedly high moral tone. Its aim was to idealize the subject and present it as heroic and noble. It exaggerated what was fine, minimized what was ugly and added a splash of grandeur. The Grand Manner in painting was mirrored by the Grand Style in literature, and both clearly demarcated elite from commoners. The style had two variants. One was the baroque strand, derived from Bernini and characterized by movement – rearing horses, theatrical gestures and billowing draperies. The other was the classical strand launched by the painter Poussin and the dramatist Corneille in the 1630s. It was characterized by calm dignity, restrained gestures and greater concern for what was true, natural or plausible.[38] It repudiated the low, undisciplined and mean, and condemned displays of uninhibited emotion as unseemly and plebeian.[39] Both strands were derived from the fifteenth-century Renaissance concept of 'decorum' (literally, finding a style appropriate to the content – high style for noble heroes and low for vulgar peasants). But Renaissance artists had deployed a flexible visual and literary vocabulary and never subscribed to a single, 'grand' style. Instead there were three – a low style increasingly frowned on, a graceful style derived from Raphael and a heroic style invented by Michelangelo. It was debated whether the heroic style was in good taste, since it could be alarmingly unrestrained. It was said at the time that while Raphael painted elegant gentlemen, Michelangelo painted muscle-bound dockers.[40]

The Renaissance had also re-launched the classical virtues associated with the patricians of ancient Rome: *gravitas, dignitas* and *severitas*. Swayed by these prestigious abstractions, artists now tweaked the concept of decorum to widen the gap between elite and popular culture: everyone in a painting was made to behave like heroes and gentlemen.[41] Though there were precedents for this in the sixteenth century, in the seventeenth it became a compulsory formula. In this respect the Grand Manner and Grand Style were typical of the culture of the 1650–1750 period. Both were based on artistic trends present before the Thirty Years War and the Crisis of the 1640s, during the course of which those trends were redirected to a new purpose. Both offered parallels to the grandeur of baroque architecture, a late-Renaissance device which gave the classical style a new twist and developed a life of its own. All were ultimately products of the Italian Renaissance and were hijacked throughout Europe. The Grand Manner and Grand Style were linked with a conception of harmonious order embodied in heroic elites, and reappeared as a cultural buttress of royal, noble and ecclesiastical power. By the mid-seventeenth century the aristocratic style had developed originality, independence and force: it was attracting the best minds and artists to its cause.[42] By the late seventeenth century it had solidified everywhere into a set of moral and cultural imperatives and become an international orthodoxy. It was imposed, like modern political correctness, with the ferocity of a criminal code.

The possible Marxist connotation of a concept like aristocratic culture raises the hackles of some eminent cultural historians.[43] Yet this slur should not be deployed too loosely, since there is little about the concept which is Marxist. Marx asserted that 'the ruling ideas *of each age have ever been* [my italics] the ideas of its ruling class'.[44] It has just been explained how, on the contrary, cultural leadership by elites in the 1650–1750 period was a new phenomenon. Marx also argued that 'the mode of production of material life conditions the social, political and intellectual life process in general'.[45] That goes a lot farther than the claim that the class which creates, sponsors and censors intellectual production conditions its nature. Marx further alleged that 'the history of all hitherto existing society is the history of class struggles'.[46] This book makes no suggestion of a class struggle in the 1650–1750 period. Though there was keen rivalry between vertically bonded groupings of elites and their clients, this was a one-class society in which there could be no conflict between interest groups organized as horizontal classes. In the old pre-industrial society only the landed elite was capable of class solidarity, of banding together in the exercise of its political, social and economic power.[47] Thus, in the context of this book, an 'aristocratic culture' is merely one that embodies the values and ideals of elites. It is a descriptive phrase – not a call to arms.

In summary, there was nothing new about an alliance between artists and elites. The novelty of the 1650–1750 period was the deployment and monopolization of the arts by monarchs and elites to define themselves in terms of distinctive values and priorities. This was a project without parallel before or since. That is not to say that it was conceived and launched in an artistic vacuum. Every aspect of it had precedents which inspired its patrons and practitioners and which they turned to their own purposes. The Habsburgs had deployed Titian, and Charles I of Great Britain had seized on Rubens and Van Dyck for urgent image repair work. But these examples were geographically isolated, if only because artists of their stature were thin on the ground before the mid-seventeenth century. Between 1650 and 1750 baroque art went global. From the heights of Rio de Janeiro to the marshes of St Petersburg, a glittering retinue of highly gifted painters, architects, writers and composers collaborated to enable monarchs and elites to immortalize themselves.

## Literature

Between 1650 and 1750 European literature was under new management. Proceeding mainly from the courts of the greater princes and the patronage of the nobility, it celebrated the virtues, taste and values of ruling elites. An immediate symptom of the new regime was that literature became classical and cosmopolitan. In some parts of Europe vernacular languages were sidelined. The influence of French literature pervaded the territories of Britain, the German states and the Spanish and Austrian Habsburgs. Count Kaunitz, Maria Theresa's Chancellor, was reported to speak perfect French, Italian and Spanish – but to maul his German to demonstrate his distance from the common herd.[48] This Francophone culture also informed the mindset of Frederick the Great of Brandenburg–Prussia, though he always disliked French music. In 1743 he revived the Prussian Academy (abolished by his father) and entitled it the *Académie Royale des Sciences et Belles-Lettres*. He gave it French statutes, a French president, a mainly French membership and an order to communicate in the French language. Three centuries later, French culture continues to dominate the language of crafts and skills that it made uniquely its own – diplomacy, fortification, fashion (*haute couture*) and cookery (*haute cuisine*).

In literature, as in architecture, Italy was losing its cultural leadership to France. Italian men of letters retreated into cultural isolation and continued to recycle various strands of the classical tradition inherited from their late-medieval Renaissance.[49] Most states were more cosmopolitan. German and Spanish literature was heavily influenced by French models and therefore reflected elite classical values. Ruling elites, especially in central and eastern Europe, usually spoke and wrote a different language from the common people. Most generally this was French, though Latin was preferred for government purposes in Hungary and Poland, as was German in northern Europe and Russia. Literature had only just begun to be written in native languages like Magyar.[50] Language and literature in this period therefore reflected class far more than nationhood, though this changed towards the end of the eighteenth century.[51] In 1784, Joseph II decreed that German was to be the official language in most of the Habsburg territories and would act as a bonding agent for his unwieldy composite state. When the Hungarians objected, they were informed that their use of a dead language like Latin proved the inadequacy of Hungarian and put them in the same category as the Poles, whom they despised. Rational, unifying, Enlightened approaches invariably proved risky and tactless when they were implemented after the 1750s. The hypersensitive Hungarians, already angry enough, were now aware that in their ruler's perception they shared a cultural dustbin with their Polish neighbours.[52]

Many of the attitudes of the new literary regime can be identified in the Republic of Letters. In the 1650–1750 period this was a community of writers, scholars and 'scientists' with no institutional existence. Unlike an academy or literary society, it existed only in the minds of its members and in the values which shaped them. It was vigorously cosmopolitan and yet inward-looking. Its boundaries were international, yet its members did not address the public or a 'public sphere', which did not yet exist – they addressed one another. Though often radical in religious and philosophical belief, politically and socially they favoured a conservative stress on stability. Many of the Republic's members were bourgeois by origin but their values were emphatically not. Most of them at some stage taught in aristocratic universities, worked in aristocratic libraries or tutored aristocratic children. To give authority to their utterances, members were expected to communicate with gentlemanly decorum (an ideal admittedly more honoured in the breach than the observance). They therefore embraced the new refinement of manners with its elaborate codes of courtesy. The Republic of Letters thus esteemed civility as a mode of discourse as well as a means of social cohesion.[53] Formed in much the same spirit was the Kit-Cat Club, dominated by Addison and Steele, the great English essayists. Though both commoners, they were steeped in aristocratic connections and aimed to disseminate the values of 'polite' culture and steer a middle course between political extremes. They adopted the rhetoric of balance, learned from the ancient Romans. This always set one element against its antithesis: 'To appear free and open without Danger of Intrusion, and to be cautious without seeming reserved'.[54]

A clear sign of elite priorities was the appearance of the first dictionaries. Their aim was to regulate the languages of the European states by imposing structure, organization and standards. The Florentine Academy had published an Italian *Vocabolario* as early as 1623. In 1694, after 55 years of work by an academic team of 40, the French Academy produced its *Dictionnaire*. The original members took five years to complete the letter A and some wondered whether they would live long enough to reach G, let alone Z. Its declared intention was to promote 'nobility and elegance of speech', partly by omitting words avoided by well-bred persons.[55] The result was a verbal hierarchy which mirrored the social hierarchy – noble, bourgeois and plebeian. Henceforth serious literature had a duty to employ the first and shun the rest. A similar objective activated the Italian Academy of Arcadia, founded at Rome in 1690 with the express purpose of exterminating 'bad taste'. In 1697 the writer Defoe proposed a similar body to monitor the English language. This took the shape of a Society 'whereof Twelve to be of the Nobility, if possible, and Twelve Private Gentlemen, and a Class of Twelve to be left open for meer merit'. In England as elsewhere, the pre-eminent model was the speech of the royal court – 'the King's English'.[56]

In 1755 the English essayist and critic Samuel Johnson published his *Dictionary of the English Language*. A tortured and disorderly soul who alternated between sociability and melancholia, he experienced an obsessive compulsion to touch every lamp post as he walked down Fleet Street. He was an improbable performer of a supremely methodical labour. But after seven years of almost single-handed toil he had mapped the contours of the English language and fixed it.[57] His avowed aim was to stabilize and purify it by rounding up and defining 43,000 key words. By the end of his labours he realized that no book could embalm a living language but his stated intention, however hopeless, was to armour-plate it against foreign borrowings, fashionable fads and the fast-changing diction of 'the laborious and mercantile part of the people'.[58]

In France, the royal court had no monopoly of literature in this period, as cultural and intellectual life in Paris began to rival it. The most significant venues were the salons of society ladies. The Marquise de Rambouillet encouraged a social mix of men of letters and aristocratic leaders of society, allowed women to meet men on equal terms and imposed feminine values. Writers and scholars were forced to wear their learning lightly and conversation had to be witty, charming and pleasurable, never dull or pedantic. Though free of the restrictions imposed by court hierarchy and etiquette, the ideal remained aristocratic. The most famous salon of Louis XIV's reign, the Duchesse du Maine's at Sceaux, was a private court which rapidly became the intellectual and social substitute for the gloomy conformity of the ageing monarch's Versailles.[59] But she was a tyrant who regarded her literary discoveries as extensions of her aristocratic ego. As in other salons, bourgeois writers were acceptable only on the elite's terms and invited merely as exhibits. English ladies acquired the salon habit rather later. The famous Blue Stocking circle became established only at the end of the period, in the 1750s.

Equally aristocratic was the language in which salon conversation was conducted and admired works were written. Standards were deliberately set for society at large and there was a growing conviction that polite language needed cleaning up. A verbal apartheid increasingly segregated elites from their inferiors, as seventeenth-century salons and academies launched the linguistic hierarchy which soon dominated literature. It aimed at elegance and refinement of language, distanced from the chatter of common people. As one expert announced, 'good usage is that of an elite, bad usage that of the masses'.[60] Popular speech was accordingly banned from serious drama and poetry. Mere words now exhibited social status – or lack of it. Sixteenth- and early seventeenth-century writers had cheerfully incorporated into their work provincial and plebeian expressions. By the 1660s Shakespeare's vocabulary of only fifty years before was seen as insufficiently class-conscious: the change in taste had occurred swiftly. Davenant claimed to be his illegiti-mate son and revised several of his plays, including *The Tempest* of 1611, with Stratford usages deleted.[61] The language of the populace continued in the broader kinds of comedy, which was regarded as an inferior literary form, but realistic words from everyday life dropped totally out of tragedy. By the late seventeenth century there was a sense of mission accomplished. In 1686, Racine delivered the funeral oration on Corneille, who had from around 1640 established the appropriately heroic themes of tragedy – aristocratic duty and honour subverted by unbridled passion.

> You know in what a condition the stage was when he began to write. ... All the rules of art, and even those of decency and decorum, broken every-where. ... Corneille, after having for some time sought the right path and struggled against the bad taste of his day, inspired by extraordinary gen-ius and helped by the study of the ancients, at last brought reason on the stage.[62]

Acceptable language had contracted. Shakespeare had deployed an unparal-leled vocabulary of over 21,000 words. Racine used fewer than 2,000.[63]

A further innovation of the ladies' salons was to redefine the new ideal of the gentleman – the *honnête homme*, whose virtues were not military but social.[64] Its pioneering manifesto was published in 1632 by Faret. Manuals of gentlemanly behaviour had been written since the Middle Ages, but their aim was to produce an amalgam of soldier and scholar. Despite all attempts to the contrary, most members of the male elite remained more of the former than the latter. Faret's text was partly a translation of Castiglione's *Courtier*, its sixteenth-century equivalent, but Faret was more emphatic in valuing wit, taste and *politesse* higher than warlike bellicosity. He knocked the rough edges off the old military role-model and demanded a male who could hold his own in manners and conversation rather than in battle – a more exclusively aristocratic ideal than martial arts. This was a code of polite social behaviour that entrenched social divisions and clearly distinguished elites from the rest.[65] It would dominate first French and then European attitudes until the 1750s, when it began to be undermined by Rousseau's glorification of peasants' simplicity, warm hearts and guileless sincerity.

Another device to mark off educated elites from unlettered multitudes was knowledge of the culture of ancient Greece and Rome. Their language and literature, especially tragic drama and epic poetry, contributed to the Grand Style – the literary equivalent of the Grand Manner in painting. Its first appearance in English was in the heroic or epic poems re-created from classical models in the 1650s and 1660s by Milton. One of his aims in *Paradise Lost* and *Paradise Regained* was apparently to raise the tone of English literature, to enable it to stand alongside that of that ancient world. He looked back far beyond Shakespeare and Chaucer to Homer and Virgil. His template was Virgil's *Aeneid*. Its key classical features were nobility of language and majestic themes, designed to associate human beings with divinities and heroes. Though his family originated on both paternal and maternal sides as landed gentry, Milton himself became a revolutionary republican. His political attitudes were democratic rather than aristocratic and he worked for England's regicide regime in the 1650s. After the restoration of the monarchy in 1660 his name was on the official list of those being considered for the death penalty.[66] Though he denounced political elitism, his style was based on the classical and Renaissance concept of cultural 'decorum'. This implied the need to elevate his medium until it was worthy of the classical epic tradition and of his own mighty theme of Christian sin and redemption.

For Milton this meant forcing Latinate vocabulary and syntax onto the English language. Though capable of writing with great simplicity, even in *Paradise Lost*, he tended to shun the diction of everyday life and preferred resonant polysyllables derived from Latin to simple monosyllables from Anglo-Saxon – 'contention' rather than 'fight' and 'exalted' rather than 'high'. Words derived from Latin appeared in their original Latin sense (in Miltonic English 'admire' meant 'wonder at' rather than 'approve of'). He crafted long, rolling Virgilian periods which crammed as much as possible into each sentence, and imposed a Latinate word order, often with the verb clinching the meaning only at the end.[67] The opening of *Paradise Lost* illustrates the point:

> Of Man's first disobedience and the fruit
> Of that forbidden tree, whose mortal taste
> Brought death into the world and all our woe,
> With loss of Eden, till one greater Man
> Restore us and regain the blissful seat,
> Sing heav'nly Muse. ...

This immediately sets the poem in the heroic classical mode. Not only is the word order strongly reminiscent of Virgil, but the Muse of poetry is invoked as at the start of the first literary work of European civilization – Homer's *Iliad* of over two thousand years before. Milton managed to be both radical and traditionalist. His astonishing intellectual scope enabled him to embrace millennia of classical and Judaeo-Christian thought, as well as to anticipate political and cultural ideas which would dominate future centuries.[68]

What is certain is that Milton's re-telling of the Christian story in the style of the ancient classics thus represented a major departure from popular culture.[69] In this respect he was the opposite of Bunyan, his approximate contemporary and author of *The Pilgrim's Progress*. Uniquely, this son of a tinker invented an eloquent version of the language of the people and wrote one of the few literary masterpieces to be found in the cottages of the barely literate – a destination which Milton would have coveted. Though politically no supporter of aristocracy, Milton had a stubborn streak of cultural and spiritual elitism. His introduction to *Paradise Lost* made no secret of his target audience. His rejection of 'the jingling sound' of rhyming couplets was no defect, he asserts, 'though it may seem so perhaps to vulgar readers'. Distancing himself from what had gone before, he dismissed rhyme as 'the invention of a barbarous age'.[70]

Whatever his original intention, Milton's insistence on unprecedented dignity and loftiness of language elevated literature to a realm apart and profoundly influenced writers for at least the next hundred years.[71] Even if, like Dr Johnson, they disliked his distortion of English by confining it in a Latinate straitjacket, they admitted that the result was sublime. The iambic pentameter (five beats to the line), previously used mainly in drama, was extended by Milton's example to any poetic subject of sufficient grandeur and solemnity. Nor were English writers his only disciples. *Paradise Lost* was translated into French prose by Louis Racine, son of the dramatist who performed the same refining surgery on French tragedy.[72]

Milton invented the Grand Style because it suited his theme. The poets and patrons who followed him employed it partly to voice their elite aspirations. Classical epics were, by definition, about royal princes and nobles like Hector and Achilles, whose heroic example fuelled the cult of elite leadership and excellence. There can be no doubt about the propaganda value of these prestigious classical icons. When Dryden translated Virgil's *Aeneid* into English rhyming couplets, its illustrations made the point. Aeneas, heroic founder of Rome, was endowed with the unmistakable facial features of the current monarch, William III.[73]

Pope, the greatest English poet of the early eighteenth century, was the son of a linen merchant but succeeded as a writer and soon moved in aristocratic circles. He translated Homer's *Iliad* and *Odyssey* (which represent the birth of European literature) from ancient Greek into English. Sales amongst his aristocratic friends were so spectacular that the proceeds amounted to £10,000 (the equivalent of £1,000,000 now). He became the first English writer to achieve financial independence. So accurately had Pope assessed what elites wanted that he no longer needed them.

Another influential classical text was Aristotle's *Poetics*, dating from the fourth century BC. This provided rules for tragedy and poetry. Chief of these were the so-called unities of time, place and action, which meant that there must be only one plot and that it must take place in one location and on one day 'within a single circuit of the sun'.[74] Aristotle also decreed that tragic heroes should be leaders and aristocrats, while persons of less importance were fit only to feature as figures of fun in raucous comedies. Finally, actors in tragedy had to speak not in prose but in verse. The *Poetics* had been discovered at the time of the Renaissance in the sixteenth century, but the 'cultural police' did not enforce Aristotle's literary laws until around the middle of the seventeenth century. Significantly, that was when elites were looking for ways to define their brand. After Corneille's tragedy *Le Cid* had sparked a row by ignoring some of Aristotle's rules, a consensus for strict obedience to them emerged in France. Boileau, arbiter of French taste, extended them from tragedy to other literary forms. What had been an option in the first half of the century solidified into an obligation in the second.[75]

It was France which set the pace in this elite cultural surge. Molière included low-life characters in his plays but aimed for elite appeal and frequently performed at court. Racine moved effortlessly between the Paris theatres and Versailles. His tragic dramas achieve a suitably aristocratic bearing by deploying the alexandrine metre (six beats to the line rather than Shakespeare's five), which slows the tempo to inject greater solemnity. Propriety (*bienséance*) is invariably observed and there are no facile effects.

Screams and wild gesticulations are banned. Violent action is described but never seen. Outward restraint is maintained at all times and nothing permitted to ruffle the surface of formal politeness. In all this, Racine showed awareness that his most important audience was at court, where self-control and concealment were required for survival.[76]

Before the publication of Rousseau's *Confessions* in 1781, the personal emotions of a unique individual were considered inappropriate vehicles for art. Its proper subject was the study of Man in general, and suitable exemplars of the species were the noblest available – kings, princes, aristocrats and classical heroes. Racine's stage is therefore dominated by the heroes and heroines of history and mythology. All were tragic and never comic. Comedy remained in prose because it was, by definition, not about kings and nobles, even though it was performed at court. Lesage's *Turcaret* of 1709 recounts the life and loves of a tax farmer, and the title Molière gave to *Le Bourgeois Gentilhomme* speaks for itself. Within the 1650–1750 period the class distinctions implicit in French literature grew even sharper: the social status of characters in comedies of the early eighteenth century was higher than in those of Molière. Seventeenth-century literary conventions dominated the first half of the eighteenth century. Corneille and Racine reigned from the grave as the tragic dramatists of the 1700–1750 period, and French tragedy's rigid conventions continued to prevail.[77]

English literature followed a similar trajectory. Charles II returned from exile in 1660 and brought French classical taste with him. Half a century before, English Renaissance writers had cheerfully ignored classical literary rules. Only two of Shakespeare's 37 plays had observed the classical unities of time, place and action.[78] Furthermore, though much influenced by the Roman dramatist Seneca, whose tragedies were sensationally bloody, Shakespeare missed the point about patrician classical reticence. While Seneca arranged for grisly deaths to be reported by messengers, Shakespeare enacted them on stage for an unsophisticated audience which paid a penny for standing room and liked to witness murders for their money. His plots also relied heavily on disguises, changes of identity, confusion of twins, and improbable coincidences – all of which offended against French insistence on *vraisemblance* (plausibility). With the arrival of classical taste in the mid-seventeenth century, most English writers obeyed the rules more conscientiously, though still less rigidly than on the Continent. The audience for drama became smaller and more select. England's Parliament had closed all theatres in 1642 at the start of the Civil Wars. When they re-opened in London in 1660, the Crown issued patents to only two theatres, both indoors. The smaller Tudor city had supported six. The open-air playhouses beloved by Shakespeare's plebeian 'groundlings' disappeared and the popular theatrical tradition which appealed to all comers died with them.[79]

This broadly classical culture proved censorious and intolerant. In an unprecedented development the new literary standards triggered criticism and rejection of previously admired writers who lacked them. English so-called 'metaphysical' poets like Donne were noted for their tortuous logic, far-fetched imagery and colloquial or even coarse diction. They fell out of favour for the next two and a half centuries.[80] The reputation of Rabelais, a highly educated French writer and leading lawyer, collapsed for similar reasons. Over a century before, like many of his contemporaries, he had plundered popular culture for inspiration. A peasant's relish for the graphic language and frank physicality of sex was cheerfully incorporated into his work. In 1690 he was accused by La Bruyère of typifying 'the wild and barbaric sixteenth century' and of having sown filth in his writings – *d'avoir semé l'ordure*.[81]

As an alternative strategy the works of dead writers were retrospectively improved to make them acceptable to refined taste, just as the twenty-first century now sanitizes the writings of the past to render them politically correct. The Restoration generation was targeting a more educated, discriminating and upper-class audience than previously.[82] Shakespeare, for all his genius, was seen as 'irregular', flawed by the barbarous age in which he had unfortunately lived.[83] As we have seen, French taste demanded *bienséance* (propriety) in word and deed. Davenant had produced the first cleaned-up version of Shakespeare in the 1660s and Tate produced a new version of *King Lear* in 1681. He revealingly claimed to find the play 'a heap of jewels, unstrung and unpolished, yet dazzling in their disorder'. He deleted the folksy Fool (along with his obscenities) as unsuitable company for a monarch, had Gloucester's eyes gouged out by a servant rather than a nobleman and created a happy ending in which the bad were punished and the good rewarded – a conclusion alien to Shakespeare's dark vision.[84] New tragedies were now entirely in verse, as befitted the nobility of their characters. Half a century before, Shakespeare's heroes had spoken poetry but mingled it with less elevated speech. The choice was determined by the importance of the speaker's subject rather than by his social status. King Lear employs iambic pentameters to curse his daughters but prose to order his dinner.

Writers sensed that they were breaking with the cultural past. Dryden argued that a new age of refinement was inaugurated in England when Charles II regained his throne in 1660. He identified it with the cultural glories of Rome under the Emperor Augustus and launched the concept of a new 'Augustan Age' possessing the aristocratic qualities associated with admired classical writers like Virgil and Horace.[85] These were taste, decorum, elegance and sophistication – all the virtues conspicuously lacking in popular culture as well as much previous literature. This literary period is judged to extend to the mid-eighteenth century and include classically-based writers like Pope and Swift, just as in France the influence of Corneille and Racine in the seventeenth century dominated the first half of the eighteenth.

It is no coincidence that the 1650–1750 period was the greatest age of satire since the decline of ancient classical culture. Satire requires accepted social norms against which to measure the vice or folly it seeks to ridicule. Such norms were now in place and Boileau in France and Dryden in England were supreme masters of this art. Much of their satirical energy was devoted to literary criticism, based on their standards of refinement and good taste. This criterion banned direct representation of the vulgarity of ordinary people – violent behaviour, low buffoonery and foul language. Also prohibited were typically Shakespearian plots involving confusion of twins, changes of identity and incredible coincidences. In enforcing these standards Boileau wielded an elegantly destructive wit which, it has been claimed, earned for satire its own metaphorical title of nobility.[86] In England a favourite satirical weapon was the mock-heroic (or mock-epic) style, which described low characters, trivial subjects or inferior talent in the epic manner. This was a clever device. It dodged the ban on base subjects by portraying them in polite terms and heightened the contrast between noble ideal and brutal reality. A few lines from Dryden's attack on a rival dramatist give the flavour:

> The rest to some faint meaning make pretence,
> But Shadwell never deviates into sense.
> Some beams of wit on other souls may fall,
> Strike through and make a lucid interval;
> But Shadwell's genuine night admits no ray,
> His rising fogs prevail upon the day.
>
> (*Macflecknoe*, 1682)

Like his contemporaries, Dryden drew an analogy between order in literature and in the state.[87] He was descended from the conservative knights and squires of Northamptonshire. Even though some of them had fought for Parliament in the British Civil Wars, all were appalled by their outcome – the beheading of Charles I. They were also determined to maintain their elevated status above the common people. Like many of the gentry in this period, members of Dryden's family constructed an exclusive pew for themselves in their parish church at Titchmarsh. It was built over the south porch, reached by a private staircase, heated by its own fireplace and well apart from their tenants in the nave.[88] By the mid-eighteenth century most parish churches were equipped with similar squirarchical installations. Reflecting his background, Dryden identified order and hierarchy as essential to a harmonious society, state and culture. For him a jarring rhyme or rhythm in a poem was the literary equivalent of rebellion in the state.[89]

Dryden found a worthy successor in Pope, a supreme master of the mock-heroic style. In his hands it presents aristocratic manners with lightness and wit. *The Rape of the Lock*, which he published in 1712, acknowledges lords and ladies as social arbiters and glamorizes their lifestyle. Their rituals of tea-taking, card-playing and love-making are painted in seductive tones, the heroine being first revealed in the alluring intimacy of her elegantly aristocratic 'toilette'. The *Dunciad* of 1728, a more serious mock-epic, attacks the subversion of literature by plebeian influences and equates cultural and moral excellence with aristocratic values. Both poems ransack Virgil and Homer for prestigiously classical parallels, epic similes and heroic themes of battle and contest.

One apparent exception to the dominance of elite culture was the rise of the novel in England. It has been argued that it appealed to a rising middle class with the means and leisure to form a new reading public.[90] There are three issues here – the social and moral values promoted, the social class of the writers, and the profile of their readership. Firstly, though bourgeois novelists were often critical of the Court aristocracy, they usually accepted gentry values and *esprit de corps*.[91] Tom Jones and Joseph Andrews, the engaging heroes of Fielding's greatest novels, both turn out in the denouement to have been born gentlemen. The heroine of Richardson's novel *Clarissa* is a gentlewoman who has her creator's sympathy when under pressure to marry a man socially beneath her. Richardson's Pamela, a well-educated and highly principled servant girl who marries her master, is a more ambivalent creation. Richardson seems to suggest that on the one hand moral worth levels social rank but that in other ways Pamela was an unsuitable wife for a squire.[92]

Secondly, it can be doubted whether an early eighteenth-century bourgeois readership alone was enough to initiate a literary revolution.[93] The middle classes relied heavily for their reading on the spread of public and circulating libraries, which were a feature of the later eighteenth century. A public library opened in Bristol in 1740 and the first circulating library in 1757.[94] Nor were the bourgeoisie the only class addicted to the latest novel. Many of the genre were written for the landed gentry.[95] Their libraries contained rows of the commodity. It was probably for them that the Greek and Latin quotations which adorned many early eighteenth-century title pages were intended. The market might extend to the bourgeoisie but the tone remained aristocratic. As for the novelists, though Fielding attended Eton (already an elite school), it is true that most of the accepted canon of great writers can be classified as bourgeois. But many of the minor and forgotten writers who created the bulk of the available novels cannot. Some were far humbler and others (like Horace Walpole, son of Sir Robert) were gentry.[96] And, if the famous English novelists were bourgeois, their French equivalents were certainly not. The most celebrated early novelists in France were Madame de Lafayette, whose *La Princesse de Clèves* of 1677 portrayed the aristocratic society to which she belonged, and her contemporary Mademoiselle de Scudéry. The latter's 'oriental' novels were spiced with slyly disguised but revealing portraits of personages from the elite salon society to which she herself belonged. Unsurprisingly, she was a bestseller.

The aristocratic elite were not only the practitioners of good taste. They were its arbiter. A theatre crowd assessed the quality of a performance by watching the nobility in their boxes. It was impertinent to express approval before a 'person of quality' had done so. It was an outrage to do so before a monarch or prince (if present) had started the applause. Yet by the later eighteenth century the aristocracy's role as cultural dictator began to falter and the monopoly position of the classical style was challenged.[97] The ground was shifting from the 1750s, but this was merely the start of a long period of erosion. Elite priorities were more deeply ingrained in literary culture than in the other arts. A century passed before such unassailable assumptions were totally shattered.

A pioneer work in the assault on elite values was Gay's *The Beggar's Opera* of 1728. It mischievously suggested that politicians often behaved like criminals and highwaymen like heroes. But not until 1751 did Rousseau turn the system of gentlemanly values upside down with the publication of his *Discourse on the Arts and Sciences*. This claimed that peasants were more natural, spontaneous and unsophisticated than nobles – and therefore more virtuous.

> It is under the homespun of the labourer, and not beneath the gilt and tinsel of the courtier, that we should look for strength and vigour of body. ... Before art had moulded our behaviour, and taught our passions to speak an artificial language, our morals were rustic but natural.

In 1761 he commented in *La Nouvelle Héloïse* on the socially exclusive personnel of current literature: 'You would think that France is populated only with counts and *chevaliers*.' But it was not until 1784 that Beaumarchais put an unworthy nobleman on the stage in his comedy *Le Mariage de Figaro*. In pursuing the object of his lust the count stoops to low cunning, is outwitted even by his own servants and ends up looking ridiculous. Up to that point an ignoble nobleman was a contradiction in terms. Louis XVI was initially unwilling to have the play performed, since it publicly lampooned the pillars of state and society. Hence the scramble for seats at the first performance, in which several theatre-goers were crushed to death.

A century before, German baroque literature was dominated by French classical models. It was largely confined to courtly romances and the pastoral romps of shepherds and shepherdesses in unreal arcadian settings. The one novel of the period which has survived as readable today is Grimmelshausen's *Simplicissimus* of 1669.[98] It issued a challenge by being entirely different. Instead of cultivating elite gentility the hero rubs shoulders with soldiers and peasants, slips in and out of the Thirty Years War and charts the horrors of the times. German writers did not address their own reality again until the 1750s. By then a rising group of dramatists led by Lessing was regenerating German national literature. In order to inspire a return to their own roots, they deployed the unruly genius of Shakespeare as a card with which to trump classical rules and French cultural hegemony. For the first time, the Bard of Avon was launched as literature's supreme god.[99] Lessing and his compatriots also fatally discredited the elite speech and taste which had downgraded him and they turned to the exploration of what they considered middle-class values.[100] Even German poets who continued to honour French classical models became more selective in their borrowings and less merely imitative. Whatever the source of their literary forms, what emerged were specific German themes.[101] The crumbling of French classical literary influence in Germany horrified Frederick the Great. 'You will see the abominable plays of Shakespeare being performed in German translations and the audiences deriving great pleasure from these ridiculous farces, which merit only to be performed in front of savages in Canada.' He reserved the German language for corresponding with his officials and shouting at his soldiers.[102]

German was previously dismissed as too uncouth to be set to music. In 1768 Mozart set an opera text in German (his native language) for the first time, after he had already composed two operas in Italian. His third engaged with the life and love of peasants. Its lyrics included dialect and popular expressions which sent up the elegant language previously spoken by supposedly bucolic shepherds and shepherdesses.[103] Shortly after, Goethe rejected the literary rules favoured by Francophile elites and gave Germans a literary voice of their own. In his play of 1773, *Götz von Berlichingen*, the action defiantly sprawled over several months, changes of scene were endless and there were at least two different plots. He thus offended against the three classical unities of time, place and action. The dialogue was even more provocative. Much of it was either lifted from the sixteenth-century sources of the story (when there was less linguistic class distinction) or written in the regional dialect of Goethe's home town of Frankfurt am Main – in both cases equally uncouth to an aristocratic ear.[104] For Goethe, poetry was 'the common property of all mankind, not the private possession of a few refined, cultured individuals'.[105] It seemed that he had written *Götz* in order to flout as many elite literary conventions as possible.

In England the grip of elite diction weakened from the mid-eighteenth century. In 1798, Wordsworth's *Lyrical Ballads* explicitly endorsed the emotions and language of the common people as poetic matter and medium. Even then there were protests from Whig grandees like Charles Fox – self-proclaimed Man of the People who admired the politics of the French Revolution but deplored the democratization of language.[106] As late as 1817–18, *Blackwood's Magazine* attacked the poet Keats and his mentor Hunt for their cockney origins and ignorance of literary decorum.[107]

> All the great poets of our country have been men of some rank in society, and there is no vulgarity in any of their writings; but Mr Hunt cannot utter a dedication, or even a note, without betraying the Shibboleth of low birth and low habits.[108]

Yet in 1838 Shakespeare's King Lear recovered his Fool, who had been banned from the English stage in the early eighteenth century on the grounds that tragic heroes and vulgar entertainers did not mix.[109] Finally in France itself, also in the 1830s, Hugo's *Hernani* successfully defied the ban on the vocabulary of everyday life. It caused a riot in the theatre and was considered revolutionary, but it ended the long reign of elite speech in French culture. Yet even Hugo accepted the convention that tragic heroes were always noblemen reciting verse. Another half-century was to roll by before Ibsen's *Ghosts* proved for the first time that tragic heights could be scaled by ordinary people speaking prose.[110]

## Architecture

As with much of its painting and music, the buildings of the 1650–1750 period fell heavily from favour for a century and a half. Its architects were not taken seriously until the twentieth century. Borromini, now considered one of the greatest of them, was dismissed as the 'anarchist of architecture', who overthrew all the laws of the ancient classical masters and replaced them with disorder and chaos.[111] Only recently has it become possible to assess the art of the period from the perspective of its own values and in the context of the mental world it inhabited.

The great age of public or civic buildings had not yet arrived, apart from a few German town halls in imperial free cities. After 1750, public libraries, theatres and museums hit the drawing board with increasing frequency, as did palaces for *arriviste* bourgeois like the Schätzler Haus of the 1760s in Augsburg. But before that date the most notable buildings in the period were erected for monarchs, bishops, abbots and nobles. Triumphant assertions of grandeur, they proclaimed their owners' supremacy over a locality, region or country. Between the 1650s and the 1750s the pace of building was breathtaking. The period saw a glut of new royal and ducal residential cities, as well as one new capital, St Petersburg, founded by Peter the Great. Versailles was built by Louis XIV near Paris, Schönbrunn by the Holy Roman Emperor near Vienna, Nymphenburg by the Elector of Bavaria near Munich, Potsdam by Frederick the Great near Berlin, Caserta by Charles III of the Two Sicilies near Naples, and Ludwigsburg by the Duke of Württemberg near Stuttgart. Some of these were summer residences built away from the capital, where the full rigours of court etiquette were somewhat relaxed. Not to be outdone, nobles and churchmen hastened to join the collective rush to build.

Palace-building is part of the dynastic history of Europe. Great houses had been built in Europe since the eleventh century, but they were austere, functional and defensive. They were, in short, fortified castles. In contrast, the monumental residences built between 1650 and 1750 for monarchs and their lay and clerical elites radiate magnificence, strength and confidence. The aim was clearly not defensive as there are no fortifications. Instead, architects filled walls with windows and concentrated on the grandeur of the interiors and of the approaches. Design thus reflected increasing social and political stability. Rather than barricading themselves against rival robber barons, the landed classes now distanced themselves from the lower orders and physically marked and reinforced the barrier between them.[112] Monumental architecture and exquisitely landscaped parks and gardens proclaimed the power and immutability of ruling elites.[113] Great estates were now clearly etched on the landscape by endless walls, punctuated by impressively escutcheoned gatehouses and lodges. These power bases strike a new note – an arrogant and defiant trumpet blast.

This consideration also altered the way elites updated their homes. Their ancestors would have cheerfully tacked on random extensions to a medieval castle or timber-framed hall, which were consequently left looking like the handiwork of visually-challenged architects. But rulers in the 1650–1750 period respected a rational order in architecture as in all else. More great European houses were rebuilt between these dates than in any other period. A coherently planned and symmetrical rebuilding projected the core message – a new dawn of harmony and tranquillity after the Thirty Years War and mid-century crisis.[114] The architecture of the period was the stage for sculpture, painting, music, drama and ceremonial. All these projected with incomparable impact the power and prestige of the creators of the new social and political order – monarchs and their elites, who were thereby distanced from the rest of creation. The divinely ordained social hierarchy positioned the masses closest to the beasts, incapable of rational thought and swayed by appearances. Baroque architecture thus performed two tricks in the same flourish. It physically separated the few from the many and projected, in terms that none could misinterpret, the myth of power behind the hierarchical social and political order.[115]

Instead of single-mindedly establishing the monarch as military and political supremo, the design of royal dwellings could now reflect and enhance his cultural and religious leadership. The pace was set in the sixteenth century by the Habsburg rulers of Spain. Near Madrid, Philip II had built the Escorial, a monster of thirteen courtyards and eighty miles of corridor crammed with thousands of sacred relics and works of art. In the 1630s his successor Philip IV erected the Buen Retiro, a country retreat to which the court could retire for a few weeks each summer. It was comparably stuffed with about 800 Spanish and Italian paintings.[116] Like these predecessors, the palace of Versailles was an art gallery for living in. Yet, when its final stage was begun around 1670, the Fronde was only twenty years in the past and France was still studded with moated and castellated *châteaux*. Though domestic peace seemed established, the palace was still a magnificent gamble, built by an insecure ruler eager to create a bold impression. That is part of its artistic purpose. Projecting an impression of confidence, whatever its basis in fact, can never be a miscalculation for a ruler or a ruling class. Hence the achievement of art historians in distinguishing between art as a report on reality and as a representation of themselves which contemporaries wished for various reasons to create.

As with all the other arts, the underlying theme was order. But order in architecture came in two variants, corresponding to those of the Grand Manner in Painting. One was the baroque version, characterized by intoxicating ornament, mystical complexity and swaying movement. It made a powerful appeal to the emotions and senses – order at its most gripping and cryptic, needing to be decoded. Like most aspects of elite culture in the 1650–1750 period, baroque architecture pre-dated the mid-seventeenth-century crisis. But before that crisis it had barely advanced beyond Rome. From the 1640s it rapidly penetrated the rest of Italy, France, Spain, Germany, Bohemia and eastern Europe. It was this flamboyantly assertive variant which most perfectly matched the troubled times to which it was seen as an answer.[117] The other was the classical version, simple, plain and static – order rational in its clarity and satisfying to the intellect, with all the building's components politely deferring to the balanced and harmonious proportions of the whole. Both variants deployed the same basic vocabulary of classical columns, domes, porticoes and pediments. In practice they overlapped and interlocked, especially in France, so that what mattered was whether the emotional or intellectual components were uppermost. Only from the 1750s was there a demand for a totally pure classicism in architecture – hence the neo-classical movement. It is unnecessary to unpick the separate strands in each building considered in this section, though lurches to the baroque and classical extremities will be noted when they occur.

After conquering Italy, baroque architecture spread to France, where in the second half of the century its exuberance was soon tamed by the austerely classical tradition it encountered there. By the late seventeenth century the flow was being reversed. Bernini, the greatest Italian sculptor and architect of the 1650–1750 period, was representative of his artistic generation in signing up to the *status quo*. He accepted all the philosophies and theologies of the absolute state and translated them into baroque visual images of unforgettable power and grandeur.[118] But his design for the Louvre was rejected in favour of a French rival's more classical design. At the same time Louis XIV's designer Le Brun was elected president of a prestigious Roman Academy, and French buildings were being imitated in Rome. Bellori, the Italian who re-launched and consolidated the Grand Manner in his *Lives of the Artists* of 1672, dedicated the volume to Colbert, Louis XIV's culture minister. Paris and its monarch began to replace Rome as the artistic role-model for Europe and great artistic patronage passed from Italy to France.[119]

As in France, baroque order collided in Britain with the classical variant and produced a century of architectural ping-pong. Classicism had already been established in the early seventeenth century by Inigo Jones. His version was Palladianism, derived directly from the Renaissance architect Palladio. It was based on accurate replicas of classical columns, porticos and pediments, deployed with minimal ornament. Components related to each other in a clearly symmetrical way and produced instant harmony between all the parts. But the building of Wilton House around 1650 announced that English architecture was joining the European baroque mainstream.[120] Its 'double-cube' room was constructed to display Van Dyck's portraits of the Earl of Pembroke's family, and its baroque style was imported from France. Festooned with garlands, fruit and cherubs created in fresco and white-and-gilded stucco, the result was the most richly decorated room yet built in the country. Yet this early example of baroque was only one room and was not followed up for fifty years. Wren managed to blend baroque and classical variants but his successors leaned more wholeheartedly to the Continental model. Finally, in 1700, Vanbrugh began Castle Howard, the first great house in England that could be accurately described as baroque. To arrive at the European party over half a century late was insular indeed.[121]

Then in the first half of the eighteenth century the classical option hit back and a revived Palladianism gradually squeezed out baroque. This may have reflected the preference of the new Hanoverian dynasty for the Palladian style.[122] It was highly appropriate for a period dedicated to refining the cultural level of elites. Palladio himself had argued that stately buildings displayed the 'greatness of soul' of the princes who built them and held that harmonious and balanced architecture had a benign effect on the spiritual values of its occupants.[123] After 1714 the ruling Whig elite equated baroque with allegedly despotic Catholic monarchy and reinvented the British monarchy as robustly Protestant and limited.[124] But classical architecture was not the only input. Britain is a fine example of the many influences that played on architects of this period, from distant memories of native traditions to the all-pervading need to detect religious origins. John Wood the Elder, who built most of Bath, managed to convince himself that the Palladian classical style he employed was derived ultimately from more significant sources than pagan Rome. With the help of a friend of Newton, the Freemasons and some pseudo-history, he argued that both Greek and Roman classical architecture and Celtic buildings like Stonehenge derived from a Biblical source – nothing less than Solomon's temple. Having experienced this revelation, he proceeded to substitute houses for monoliths and built a stone circle of 648 classical columns, superimposed in three tiers, in the middle of eighteenth-century Bath. The result was Bath's Circus – the Colosseum turned inside out (or, to be more precise, outside in) to create the first circular classical terrace in Britain.[125]

In the late seventeenth and early eighteenth centuries the baroque style charged into Spain, the Germanic lands, Bohemia and eastern Europe. Its victory was far more emphatic than in France and Britain. In central and eastern Europe architecture and sculpture developed a distinctive regional character, partly inherited from the curling, flame-like Gothic style dominant in the area two to three centuries before.[126] It achieved its final luxuriant flowering in the triumphalism which followed the raising of the Turkish siege of Vienna in 1683. The threat from Islam had delayed the surge of building confidence experienced earlier in the west. It was therefore the baroque rather than the Renaissance style which transformed many of the towns and cities of central and eastern Europe into something like their present glory. The medieval mishmash of crooked streets and timber-framed houses was replaced by symmetrical squares and axial vistas, crowned with classical buildings and matching pediments and pilasters. The architectural shift was so dramatic that by the mid-eighteenth century Mozart's father could dismiss the ancient medieval city of Ulm as lacking *Regularität* (proportion, balance and harmony of elements). It was, he groaned, 'dreadful, old-fashioned and tastelessly built'.[127] The same was true of upper-class domestic housing. In the first half of the seventeenth century symmetry was optional. By the second half, elites were expected to endorse the universal merits of harmony and balance. Cultural correctness was well-nigh compulsory.

Since baroque was the Continent's dominant architectural style during the 1650–1750 period, we had better take a closer look. The most obvious features of baroque architecture are richness of ornamentation and fusion of masonry, marble, moulding, sculpture and paint. Baroque exploits its own version of multi-media technology. The aim of both churches and palaces is to create theatrical spaces and vistas which overpower spectators with a vision of material and spiritual splendour, so that they appear to be looking through solid ceilings into the heavens. Much of baroque architecture is illusion. *Trompe l'oeil* effects leave the spectator uncertain whether domes, cornices and balustrades are paint or masonry. Much illusion is literally done by mirrors, extensively installed to double the size of rooms and reflect tinkling chandeliers. Opulence and display are *de rigueur*. Architects and craftsmen went to extraordinary lengths to ensure perfection. To achieve a high gloss uncontaminated by dust, the oriental lacquered panels for Maria Theresa's palace of Schönbrunn were painted at sea.[128]

But baroque architects have further and greater objectives.[129] They use the essential elements of the classical style – columns, arches, domes, porticoes and pediments. Their aim is to hijack for propaganda purposes the dignity and grandeur of the ancient Roman Empire. But having deployed the key classical components they have another trick up their sleeve: they play fast and loose with them. At Emmanuel College in Cambridge Wren pierced a classical pediment to insert a modern clock. Architectural lines are deliberately disrupted to suggest forces in conflict and reveal opposites in confrontation. The classical and Renaissance emphasis on static repose is abandoned: the classical elements are apparently set in motion. Baroque columns twist and bulge. Façades recede and advance, moving rhythmically in convex and concave undulation, like a membrane that is pushed out or sucked in. Baroque buildings have been aptly described as classical ones viewed through a sheet of rippling water. Yet, contrary to surface appearances, all is finally seen as an ordered whole. Disorder is tamed and made beautiful. For a building mastering its components read absolute monarchy healing a fissured society.[130] Baroque architecture does not merely symbolize the triumph of order. It enacts it.

At first sight this makes a baroque building baffling and disorienting – a factor in its later fall from favour. The clean straight lines and plain surfaces of the later neo-classical style are almost entirely missing. But art historians have now penetrated a little deeper. The baroque architect Borromini is revealed as a master of hidden meanings and mathematical puzzles – of rational order underlying apparent disorder. At first glance, his college church of St Ivo della Sapienza in Rome looks like a roughly assembled wedding cake. Rational restraint is the last quality with which English-speaking people would associate it. But at a profounder level, restraint results from the application of logical control, of which baroque has an abundance. On closer inspection its ground plan is based on two equilateral triangles which overlap to form a six-pointed star on the outer periphery and a regular hexagon as the central space. Every detail of the design is derived from this first geometrical concept. Another layer of meaning is added when it is realized that the six-pointed star is the star of David, who was a symbol of wisdom and therefore appropriate to a university church.[131] St Ivo is the perfect marriage of mystery and reason, dominant in the period.

The rococo style between the 1720s and 1750s was merely a final variation of baroque. It was intended to inspire pleasure rather than solemnity. Baroque buildings always appear solid and cavernous, however richly ornamented. In rococo buildings solidity seems to dissolve in an exuberant riot of surface decoration. Lightness and whiteness replace weight and shadow. Classical ornament was previously confined to the capitals at the top of the columns and the entablature above them. In a rococo ensemble it overflows from its original perch, cascading downwards or spiralling upwards.[132] Expression of structure is minimized. In monumental interiors the real building materials are always encased in a skin of stucco, creating the impression that it has been added to the structure rather than integrated with it. This carries the frothy decoration, reminiscent of rampant vegetable growth creeping over everything. Ceilings swarm with rosy-faced cherubs, and walls are encrusted with gilded C-curves and S-curves. Rococo is terrified of a straight line.

In many ways rococo architecture is a sham. Nothing in an interior is quite what it seems. Mirrors dissolve the solidity of walls, walls turn imperceptibly into ceilings and ceilings with aerial paintings soar into infinity. Wood is disguised with white paint, and glue-and-plaster scagliola masquerades as marble.

The magnificent dome at Die Wies in Bavaria is at first reminiscent of St Paul's in London. On closer inspection it turns out to be made of plastered wood.[133] On one level a rococo church is pure fantasy. The altar of the Bavarian pilgrimage church of Vierzehnheiligen looks like a combination of coral reef and mermaid throne.[134] The observer has an intoxicating sense of undulating movement, of volumes and spaces flowing into one another without any clearly defined divisions between aisles and transept, nave or choir. Yet, like St Ivo, the building's construction is based on hidden mathematics: unpack its geometry and order is revealed. A deliberately complex visual pattern is underpinned by clear structural logic, since the ground plan reveals seven neatly intersecting circles and ovals. Again, simple reason lies beneath apparent chaos.[135]

The purpose of royal baroque and rococo palaces is presentation of the monarch. They are theatres in which the drama of absolute monarchy can be staged and the monarch's public role acted out with elaborate ceremony and ritual. In this context monarchy is a performance. Similar considerations applied to other occupiers of palatial premises – aristocrats, abbots and bishops. They all claimed to be raised above ordinary mortals to semi-divine status and the palace represented them as such. Staircases in monumental houses had previously been insignificant and utilitarian. Towards the end of the seventeenth century, designers spotted their potential as a thrilling preliminary drum roll to the even greater spectacle in store, as the vision of Majesty was approached. In baroque palaces they rise in exhilarating curves from the depths of vaulted halls so as to provide the perfect stage for aristocrats needing to make theatrical entrances.

Baroque houses did something else of great significance. Unlike previous elite dwellings, and in line with the increased emphasis on hierarchy and deference, they were designed to separate servants more totally from their masters. Servants had formerly dined in the great hall with their betters and used the same stairs. Many servants in great houses had been gentlemen themselves, eager to secure the protection of a great lord. In the 1650–1750 period, as rulers came to possess enough physical force to maintain law and order, it was considered increasingly demeaning for a gentleman to be in service. Servants were now kept out of sight unless they were actually about their business. They lived and ate in the basement. Servants' backstairs were installed to ensure that their employers did not have to meet or converse with them unless they were performing their duties. Off the backstairs were servants' rooms, where they now slept rather than at the foot of their master's bed. Above all, gentry ascending the main staircase did not have to meet their last night's faeces coming down.[136]

Baroque houses were designed to underline hierarchy and status in other ways. It was important to express the etiquette that was vital to gentlemen's honour and therefore also to rulers as a disciplinary device. As each room in a sequence of apartments was more exclusive than the last, the host's compliments to a visitor were gauged by how far he allowed the visitor to penetrate along it and how far he came out in the other direction to welcome him. If the visitor's status was lower than the host's, he hoped to penetrate as far as possible but might not succeed. If it was higher he would be invited to the inner sanctuary but might not accept. We get something of the flavour in a contemporary account of the visit of Philip V of Spain to the Duke of Somerset at Petworth in 1703. The official host was, however, Prince George of Denmark, husband of Queen Anne. The Duke's main role seems to have been paying the bill.

The Prince welcomed the King at the door and escorted him to the entrance of his apartment. A series of 'state' visits were then paid. First the Prince sent a message to the King to ask if he could call on him. Permission being given, the Prince proceeded through the ante-room to the door of the King's bedchamber. The King, who was sitting in an armchair, rose and came to the door – but no further – to welcome him. He then invited the Prince to sit in another armchair, this being one rank above a chair without arms and two ranks above a stool (which was all the Duke would have got). Shortly after returning to his apartment the Prince received a message from the King asking permission to return the visit. Being an inferior grade of royalty, the Prince came out of his apartment to the top of the stairs to greet him and then conducted him to his own bedchamber. Later the King asked the Duke's permission to call on the Duchess and proceeded down to her apartment on the ground floor. The Duchess 'came forward several rooms, even to the bottom of the stairs, to meet the King, and making a very low obeisance she received a kiss from him'. The King, however, advanced no further into her apartment than a small antechamber. Everyone now having called on everyone else, King, Prince, Duke and Duchess emerged from their various apartments to have supper together in the saloon.[137]

The fashion for baroque palaces was set by France. It was first seen at the château of Vaux-le-Vicomte, built from 1657 to 1661 by Louis XIV's Overseer of Finance, Fouquet.[138] At the time the most magnificent château in France, it was intended for royal visits and became the prototype for Louis XIV's palace of Versailles. Its interior decoration was based on a combination of gilding, paint and stucco (painted plaster moulding) and copied from a Florentine palace of the 1640s.[139] Vaux-le-Vicomte inaugurated the distinction between gates and gravel on the one side and lawns, flowers and fountains on the other. It also invented the pattern of grand apartments to house royalty on state visits, with its sequence of ante-room, bedroom and closet. The King's bedroom was decorated with gilded and painted stucco in the current Italian style. Crystallizing a custom developing from the 1640s, the royal bed was placed behind a proscenium arch in an alcove separated from the room by a low balustrade, like altar rails in a church. Courtiers who had right of access within the balustrade were known as *seigneurs à balustrade*. Members of the social elite were accustomed to receive honoured visitors in their bedchambers, and it was vital to keep all but the most favoured from contact with the royal person. A great house was by definition open house, and grubby specimens might gain access.[140]

Palace design, whether royal or aristocratic, was intended to emphasize the ordered hierarchy inseparable from royal and aristocratic stateliness. Vaux-le-Vicomte was the first palace constructed in France after the Fronde of 1648–51. It became the blueprint for all that followed. Its first priority was clear signposts of who was who and what was what. At the state centre, where the King would preside if in residence, was the saloon – a domed hall of dazzling magnificence designed for great balls and dinners, and the centre of social life for the court aristocracy. It proclaims its importance at the relevant point on the façade by a huge portico of Corinthian classical columns surmounted by a triangular pediment, while in the rooms behind the façade a hierarchy of space is created. The prestige of the Roman classical orders is thus evoked to define the monarchical centre of state.

On either side stretch two sets of state apartments strung out in a straight line on an axis of honour. Doorways are cunningly lined up to offer an awesome vista down the whole length of the building, further demonstrating that impressive display was the first priority rather than comfort (informal private rooms bypassed by corridors had to await the nineteenth century). First comes the antechamber, then the chamber and finally the closet (*cabinet*). On the prestige scale those who penetrated to the great man's closet had arrived, while those who reached only the antechamber needed to reassess their political significance. On the façade, therefore, the antechambers are treated plainly, while the chambers and closets at the privileged end of each set of apartments are punctuated by pilasters and separate roofs, forming majestic terminal pavilions. Aesthetic appearance and political function are perfectly fused.

Louis XIV decided that he would never again be upstaged by a subject. He first destroyed Fouquet and then hired the team which had created his palace – Le Vau the architect, Le Brun the interior decorator and Le Nôtre the garden designer. All its features were replicated at Versailles, a modest hunting-lodge enlarged between 1670 and 1710 into the grandest palace complex in Europe. Its fundamental purpose was to create physical and psychological distance between the monarch and the over-mighty subjects who had caused mayhem during the previous century, most recently during the civil wars of 1648–53.[141] The project was masterminded by Colbert, the minister responsible for this glorification of an absolute monarch.[142] With Apollo the mighty sun god perched on the ceilings of the King's apartments, it is clear that baroque art did not represent the reality of royal power, in spite of widespread presumptions to the contrary. It created the illusion of it.[143]

The château of Versailles was positioned on the principal axial vista of a vast formal landscape, continued by the town of Versailles to a total length of eight miles. In 1701, Louis moved his bedroom to the centre of this axis, thus symbolizing the monarch as the source of order and proclaiming that all power and influence converged on and radiated from him. Louis's contemporaries were more alert to symbolic nuance than ourselves. They realized that he had compelled nature to do what did not come naturally, whether in the shape of water flowing upwards or hedges and plants regimented into straight lines. After Versailles, palaces throughout Europe were required to be strung out on long axial vistas which were extended into the surrounding gardens and countryside. A quarter of a mile distant from his window, still on the same axis, the Sun King was mirrored by the sun god, source of light, harmony and order. There, in a magnificent sculptural group, Apollo rose in his chariot from the water amid the spray of fountains while tritons sounded their horns to announce the return of day.[144]

At one level this is clearly an absolute monarch controlling nature by imposing a rational order upon it. But that is probably not the only debt landscape planning owed to the natural philosophers. For them nature was one of the books in which the mind of God could be read. As secular theories of political authority began to challenge the divine right of Kings, it has been argued that nature was seen as a new way of legitimating royal authority. It was therefore important for the ruler to establish a physical bond with nature by imprinting himself on his territory. This also partly explains the obsession of rulers of the period with maps, plans, models and globes, as well as their interest in measurement of land, calculation of longitude, surveying, canals and other civil engineering projects. It may also account for their alliance with 'scientists' like Huygens. The works done at Louis XIV's Observatory linked astronomy to cartography and destroyed any lingering beliefs about the laws of the heavens being different in kind from those of the earth. Measuring and charting the King's territory became one continuous activity, as natural philosophers linked God's works in heaven to the King's works on earth.[145] The maps of the period reveal an increasing emphasis on the state and its infrastructure as a territorial unit, and they were usually commissioned by or dedicated to the monarch. In 1675 Ogilvy's map of England and Wales represented the first national road-atlas of any country in western Europe.[146]

Yet, whatever its precise intention, by the 1730s this approach to gardening looked like a monstrous imposition on the spontaneity of human life and nature. First in England and later elsewhere, the ordered symmetry of baroque yielded to something less artificial. Strict geometry was replaced by irregular lakes, meandering paths and apparently random groupings of trees. The aim was to create a landscaped arcadia, with winding walks, groves, grottoes, seats and temples offering places for contemplation. The source was Virgil's *Georgics* and *Eclogues*, which provided a literary agenda capable of working on two levels. It advertised the classical culture of elites and distanced them from the uneducated who lacked it. It also supplied the ancient credentials on which all educated elites could agree. However deep their rivalries or party differences, they could present a united and homogeneous appearance to outsiders in the shape of garden design.[147] It remained just as rational as the one it replaced, but it freed nature to follow its inner logic rather than imposing it from without. The poet Pope explained in his *Essay on Criticism* of 1711:

Nature, like Liberty, is but restrained
By the same Laws which first herself ordained.

Just as surely as Newton found hidden order in the movement of the planets, English garden designers found it in vegetable growth.[148]

At the turn of the century the baroque baton passed to other contemporary rulers who had shadowed Louis XIV's every architectural move, including his new development at the Paris Louvre in the 1670s. The baroque palaces built around 1700 in turn launched a mania for palace-building which lasted for fifty years, evaporating only in the 1750s and 1760s. Emperor Leopold I started building the palace of Schönbrunn in 1695 specifically to stake out his own claim to equality with the Sun King. In an unmistakable political statement the plan of Versailles is echoed to the letter. Leopold even adopted the sun as his own logo. Another monarch who wished to draw an analogy between the Sun King and himself was Charles XI of Sweden. Recently acknowledged to wield absolute power, he required visual underpinning for his new status. The first palace burned down in 1697 but under Charles XII its replacement soon rose. Being a town palace in Stockholm it was modelled not on Louis XIV's Versailles but on the Louvre. It replicated Versailles only with its line of King's Presence,

Guard and Bed Chambers, mirrored by the identical parade of the Queen's chambers opposite.

This correlation between palace construction and periods of intense political competition is again seen in the methods employed by four new royal dynasties to win their crowns – itself a symptom of the revived cult of monarchy and huge appetite for Kingly titles. Their building spree started well before their crowning success and was obviously intended to support their bid.[149] Here architecture was deployed not to enhance political power but as a substitute for it. It was cheaper and less deadly to outperform a rival Prince on a building site than a battlefield.

In 1701, Frederick III of Brandenburg became Frederick I, King of Prussia. He immediately felt architecturally challenged and required a capital fit for a King. His palace was begun in 1698 and finished in the years after his success. The result was another enormous imitation of the Louvre. It may or may not be coincidence that it was slightly longer, and exactly the width of, the Stockholm palace.[150] The Hohenzollern palace was one of the glories of the new, grandiose Berlin. Victor Amadeus II of Savoy became King of Sicily in 1713. In 1714 he brought Juvarra, a rising architect, to Turin and gave him the task of transforming it from a ducal to a royal capital. One of his greatest creations was the Queen Mother's Palazzo Madama. It incorporated what was then the grandest staircase in Italy, swiftly imitated elsewhere. It was an issue of prestigious importance to determine how far down such a staircase the host should descend to meet his guests. Status would be lost if he overstepped the mark.[151] More fundamentally, Juvarra transformed the street plan and built or remodelled sixteen palaces and eight churches. The result was a showcase of royal baroque town planning. To this day, Turin's rational geometric grid plan communicates the cultural and political order that its ruler was striving to impose on his territory.[152] A lesser project was the rebuilding of the summer palace of Herrenhausen in Brunswick by another new recruit to royalty, the Elector of Hanover, who became King of Great Britain and Ireland in 1714.

Augustus the Strong of Saxony was elected King of Poland–Lithuania in 1697 and alternately lost and regained his crown for thirty years before his death in 1733. On his accession in 1694, with the site conveniently cleared by a serious fire in the previous decade, he immediately started to rebuild Dresden, his Saxon capital. The project continued until 1750 and created in the *Neustadt* one of the gems of baroque Europe.[153] Augustus's confident gesture paid off when he snatched the Polish crown in the face of stiff competition. One of his architect's most spectacular inventions was the Zwinger – an open-air extension, separate from the main royal palace, for tournaments, festivals, pageants and court celebrations. Walls dissolve into sculpture so that it is impossible to see where the architect stops and the sculptor begins. Its sole purpose is extravagant display. Building was part of the power game, just as geometrical royal gardens with axes, eye lines and vistas were nothing less than power planting. If it was impossible to play the game satisfactorily on the battlefields of Europe, the arts enabled it to be played out in virtual reality.[154] Augustus had not proved a successful European soldier or statesman. But as the most spectacular of Europe's royal philanderers, with a fabled brood of 354 illegitimate children, his spermatozoa hit their targets more frequently than his political projects.[155]

The German Schönborn family were well-known building fanatics. A glance at them reveals that baroque splendour, though never intended to reflect political realities accurately, was sometimes total myth. The head of the dynasty was Lothar Franz von Schönborn (1655–1729), Prince-archbishop-elector of Mainz and Prince-bishop of Bamberg – and quite capable of designing rooms for his own palaces. One of his nephews, Johann Philipp Franz von Schönborn, was Prince-bishop of Würzburg, and another, Damian Hugo, was Prince-bishop of Speyer. Lothar Franz built Pommersfelden (1711–18), Johann Philipp the Würzburg Residenz (1719–37) and Damian Hugo the palace of Bruchsal (1720–32). They passed round the family circle three of the most influential architects of the day, Neumann, von Hildebrandt and Dientzenhofer, the latter brought from distant Prague and introducing the inventive spirit of Bohemian baroque to Franconia. While no remaining staircase at Versailles makes the ceremonial statement associated with baroque palaces, those at Würzburg, Pommersfelden and Bruchsal are the central event of the building. They introduce the state rooms with a deafening visual fanfare. Yet, though Lothar Franz was influential in the election of Charles VI in 1711, none of the Schönborn princes was of first consequence in Germany. They presented the image rather than the reality of greatness.[156]

If the architectural statements of individual churchmen seem to exceed the facts, the Catholic Church in general was merely celebrating its continued wealth and onward spiritual march by launching its greatest building boom since the Middle Ages. In this it was joined by the territorial aristocracy. These two emerged as joint-victors from the chaos and artistic sterility of the Thirty Years War (1618–48), but celebration was delayed by the Ottoman onslaught (1667–83). Once the Turks had been defeated, central Europe fizzed with ecclesiastical and aristocratic building projects. They were a breathtaking announcement of the new partnership between ruler, church and elites – and of the new ideology which expressed and buttressed it:

The Church entered an age of frenzied ostentation, building and rebuilding with unexampled haste ... its pilgrimage churches, votive altars and statuary creating a dense ecclesiastical landscape in country as well as town. It used the plastic arts, like the literary dramas enacted in its schools and colleges, to emphasize the sacred harmony of the world and its absolute order behind the shifting façade of human frailties.[157]

In 1713, the Habsburg Emperor Charles VI made a vow to build a church dedicated to St Charles Borromeo if God spared Vienna from the plague then threatening to engulf the city. On its obedient retreat the Emperor dutifully began to build the Karlskirche, which was completed over 20 years later. The centrepiece is a temple-front portico copied from the Roman Pantheon of AD 120. This is surmounted by a baroque drum and dome, flanked on either side by twin towers, all derived from the mid-seventeenth-century work of Borromini. On either side, between portico and towers, are inserted two copies of Trajan's column of AD 113, both bearing a spiralling bas-relief which depicts the achievements of the saint.[158] As well as evoking the grandeur of ancient Rome, they were intended by their scholarly architect to suggest minarets shooting upwards beside a mosque.[159] What can be the meaning of this miscellany of cultural and historical reference? Or should that be dog's breakfast?

In fact the diverse elements all work together. Architect Fischer von Erlach intended the church to embody the architecture of the ages by successfully harmonizing elements from different styles and eras, as well as synthesizing pagan, Islamic, Jewish and Christian resonances. The goals towards which all this pointed were the universal harmony and order sought by natural philosophers and now happily embodied in the alliance between Habsburg Empire and Catholic Church. Lest this seems to push too far the message capable of architectural transmission, there is evidence that the philosopher Leibnitz advised on the iconography.[160] There is yet more. The architect was also affirming the symbiosis of Holy Roman Emperor (donor), Roman Catholic Church (recipient) and their jointly prestigious Roman inheritance (imperial power).[161] Finally, the interior reverts once more to the dedicatee of the whole project, who is painted in the dome fresco and sculpted over the high altar beneath stucco clouds pierced with gilded rays. Though few people then or now would read every layer of meaning, the Karlskirche gives baroque a modern flavour – multi-faith, multi-cultural and multi-disciplinary.

In the half-century after 1683 approximately 300 palaces were built in and around Vienna and hundreds of new churches and abbeys mushroomed in Bavaria and the Habsburg territories. This embodied, in the most ostentatious form possible, the renewed alliance between Habsburg Emperors and their elites. It also enunciated their mutual interdependence. Only the higher nobility had the political clout and the material resources to lead the recovery. The latter thereby advanced their social, economic and political position at the expense of other social groups and became even more necessary to the Emperor than they were before. But they were equally dependent on him. He had the international connections which enabled them to defeat their enemies, whether Turks, Protestants, lesser nobility or revolting peasants. He was also the source of the imperial patronage available at the Habsburg court in Vienna to those ready to travel. Most of the higher nobility were more than ready. Loyalty to the Habsburg dynasty and the Catholic Church was the price they paid: that was the deal. In just a century this arrangement elevated the Esterhazys of Hungary from minor gentry to princes owning an estate the size of Wales.[162]

Though in terms of their own building programme the Habsburgs lost the battle of the palaces to Louis XIV, in visual terms the rock-solid bond between monarch, church and nobility was announced more eye-catchingly in central than in western Europe. In Tudor and Stuart England the monarch's portrait or coat of arms might be displayed as an emblem of loyalty in churches and the houses of landed elites. But in the 1650–1750 period, when British or French elites installed smart new baroque ceiling paintings, royal portraiture was scarcely their iconography of choice. They normally preferred classical mythology – or, even better, representations of themselves. But in *Mitteleuropa* nobles and prelates created the sumptuous Emperor's Halls (*Kaisersäle*) erected to host personal visitations by the Holy Roman Emperor – in effect, imperial spaces within their own palaces. A ceiling fresco in the monastery of St Florian near Linz presented the Habsburgs as heirs of the four great empires of the past – Babylon, Persia, Greece and Rome. The proclamation of the mutual dependence of monarchs, prelates and nobles has been called royal 'representation at one remove', namely of monarchs by their subordinates.[163] But this golden Habsburg moment did not last. By the 1780s the monks of Prague's Strahov monastery were decorating their library ceiling with key figures of the French Enlightenment.

Equally attuned to a different sort of reality, political and military in this case, were the palaces built around 1700 for the victors of war and revolution. The baroque palace reflected absolute monarchy and the society that went with it. Louis XIV had set the fashion. His enemies followed it regardless – William III at Hampton Court, the Duke of Marlborough at Blenheim and Prince Eugene at the Viennese Belvedere. Their core values were the same.[164] Marlborough's Blenheim Palace and Eugene's Upper

Belvedere in Vienna were high-profile projects intended to exalt the successful generals of the Spanish Succession War. Marlborough was an upstart from a family of mere gentry. The baroque was a heaven-sent medium for projecting his new-found power and erasing the modest origins of England's latest ducal creation. Eugene underlined his international significance and military impact in two ways. He employed part of the same team which had constructed the gardens of Versailles and ensured that the roof line was designed to suggest a tented military encampment.[165] Additionally, Chatsworth House in Derbyshire was built for the same Earl (later Duke) of Devonshire who had helped to engineer the 1688 Revolution which installed William III. All represented genuine power bases, though Blenheim and the Upper Belvedere also gave a hint of glorified retirement homes.

A final aspect of palace-building was the influential stylistic pace it set. Because of the enhanced prestige of the ultra-elite with which it was associated, everyone wanted to participate in the status contest. The result was the palace-fronted terrace. This was a terraced row of town houses designed to look like one classical, baroque or Palladian palace.[166] It bestowed on its occupiers a collective sense of superiority, if not an individual one. In the modest version architects simply plonked a pediment on the centre of a standard London terrace – the merest reminder of classical style and sophistication, but enough to impart prestige. On the monumentally Palladian scale it produced the north side of Bath's Queen Square (*c*.1730). This was elite housing for the many – and especially for upwardly mobile merchants to whom appearances were important. It brought the style and grandeur of an aristocratic country house to the urban middle classes.[167]

A leading baroque invention was the visual dependence of a town street plan on a building in which sovereign authority was vested. To the west, Versailles commanded a geometrically ordered park, and to the east, a town of corresponding regularity. The symbolic point is obvious: if nature can follow superior orders, so can buildings and so can people. Princely publicity was taken a stage further in 1709 when Duke Eberhard Ludwig of Württemberg launched the construction of a *Residenzstadt* at Ludwigsburg near Stuttgart – a new town laid out alongside his palace, a monster with 452 rooms. In 1715 the Margrave of Baden–Durlach began to lay out his own Versailles at Karlsruhe. Symmetrically radiating from the central octagonal tower of the palace are no fewer than thirty-two avenues.[168] It had few imitators. Most monarchs had presumably pondered the implications of a palace located at the centre of a spider's web.

This is part of a larger development – the invention of town planning based on what has been called 'baroque order'.[169] Like most cultural aspects of the

1650–1750 period, it depended heavily on earlier Renaissance initiatives. In the late sixteenth century, Pope Pius V and his immediate predecessors had sliced through the city of Rome with a series of axial avenues, whose sight lines all converged on focal points punctuated by great churches or obelisks. This project blended artistic, practical and political objectives, not least of which was the visual assertion of power and control. But it was never carried through with theoretical consistency and its geographical reach was limited.[170] By the mid-seventeenth century such experiments remained rare in southern Europe and non-existent in the north. Evelyn, diarist and antiquarian, escaped in 1643 from the English Civil War and headed for Rome. He waxed so lyrical over the half-mile vista along the Via Pia to the ceremonial gateway crowning its terminus that it is clear he had seen nothing like it before.[171] Rectifying this oversight became the mission of most European monarchies in the period which followed. Imposing visual order on their cities was the counterpart of restoring political order in their states. Straight avenues multiplied, uniform architectural elements were repeated along their length and roof lines became a continuous horizontal. In short, the order with which absolute rulers liked to associate themselves was imposed on the architectural jumble inherited from medieval cities.[172]

Yet the obsession with order was not confined to monarchs who conspicuously promoted themselves as absolute. It also gripped their elites. It can be placed in the same context as their orchestration of house and landscape into one harmonious whole and their need to rebuild country houses to a coherent plan. Rigorously ordered planning could therefore characterize regimes of different hues. Wren was obliged to negotiate with four competing authorities in rebuilding London and St Paul's Cathedral after the Great Fire of 1666 – Crown, church, Parliament and City. Yet the outcome was almost Stalinist in the thoroughness of its regulation. Inflexible rules governed the height of not only each house but each storey. Even 'mansion houses of the greatest bigness', no matter how secluded, were forbidden to exceed the uniform height regulations, while street lines were staked out and builders who tried to ignore them were disciplined by official surveyors. Gutters and downspouts were obligatory for health reasons, and brick or stone rather than wood for obvious ones. Not so much as a window sill might protrude beyond the foundation line.[173] It has been suggested that the explanation for these obsessive rules and regulations is to be found in the early life of the generation responsible. Wren and Hooke, fellow members of the planning team, were children of the Civil War. The former found his childhood experience of it too distressing to talk about. But they discovered in the new natural philosophy the foundation of certainty on which to base their quest for order after chaos – whether in state, society or the streets of London. The present St Paul's Cathedral, classical, rational and ordered, is arguably a monument to a traumatized generation.[174]

The attempt to present Britain as an exception to the rest of the European continent has continued from the late seventeenth century to the present day. This apparently has implications even for townscapes. It is usually alleged that there was a negligible royal building programme under the restored monarchy after 1660 and that the baroque model was rejected. This is difficult to square with Charles II's Royal Hospital at Chelsea and even more grandiose palace at Winchester, or with William III's Greenwich Hospital and huge extension to Hampton Court Palace.[175] As to the style, Winchester, Hampton Court and Chelsea were directly derived from Louis XIV's projects at Versailles and Les Invalides. Greenwich is notable for Wren's colossal baroque ensemble and for Thornhill's painted ceiling over the Hall of Greenwich Hospital, which rivals the most extravagant baroque to be found in Catholic Europe.

Furthermore, London may have been the source of the building regulations imposed by a highly despotic regime. Peter the Great had plenty of opportunity to note its methods during his visit of 1698. Monarchical urban planning subsequently reached its apogee in St Petersburg. In 1711, Peter had a model cottage built and ordered the inhabitants to copy it when erecting their own homes. In 1714 he went one better. All were to conform to standard patterns drawn up by official architects, one for each social class. In 1715, the interventionist climactic, all building was forbidden unless the plans were approved by the government.[176] Inevitably this drive for uniformity broke down, but the city's roof line remains more harmonious than that of any other European capital.

In Turin a grid-iron street layout was imposed by the architects of an absolute (as opposed to despotic) monarch, Victor Amadeus II of Piedmont–Savoy. Each new grid was aligned with the previous ones. His palace square, laid out in the decades before and after 1700, was innovatory in accommodating government administration. Between about 1670 and 1720 the Savoyard army quadrupled and the increasing weight of administration was making it difficult for ministers to run departments from their private residences in the traditional way. The new square therefore incorporated a group of purpose-built government offices, housing the rapidly expanding state apparatus of staff and records. The central position of the complex next to the palace was symbolic, as was the relegation of the city hall to a peripheral position.[177] Yet other absolute rulers displayed more respect for developers' individualism. In Paris, smaller unaligned grid developments were the result of independent property speculators laying out separate areas, as in developments on the Ile St Louis. Monarchs tend to jump out of the pigeon-holes fashioned for them by 'absolutist' clichés.[178]

It has been suggested that palaces were not built in countries where dynastic issues were settled.[179] By contrast, the more precarious the socio-political equilibrium, the more extravagant its visual representation. This would explain the building spree on which Britain embarked before 1700, when the succession was less secure than after the passing of the Act of Succession in 1701. The only major royal work after that date was a suite of state rooms at Kensington Palace in the 1720s. But it can also be argued that, though to us the 1688 Revolution is Britain's last revolution, to the men of 1701 it was merely the most recent. The dearth of royal building after the 1720s may owe something to the miserly philistinism of George I, who announced that he hated 'Boets and Bainters' (a sentiment echoed by his son George II). The latter had much in common with his equally uncultured cousin, Frederick William I of Brandenburg–Prussia, and exhibited no discernible interest or taste in architecture.[180] Finance is unlikely to have been the key factor. The British population was about half that of France (under 10 million as opposed to 20 million) and the government's tax base therefore lower. But there was little unique about the financial constraints that applied in Britain, since lavish building projects threw most European rulers into debt.

Though rulers were potentially a key cultural driving force, they had to work within the context of a socio-political elite. No absolute monarch could impose a cultural dictatorship and few attempted to. As usual, Peter the Great comes nearest, with his orders to his nobles to wear western dress and remove their beards. The alleged cultural straitjacket into which rulers clamped their subjects was a spin-off of the concept of despotic 'absolutism'. The standard authority on architecture under Louis XIV delivers the following judgement:

Owing to the dictatorship of Colbert and Lebrun this style was imposed all over France. In this period everyone accepted the official doctrine about the arts; all were orthodox and there were no heretics. All the great commissions emanated from the crown, and any artist who aspired to success had to obtain such a commission, which generally speaking only came through the official channels of the Academy or the Gobelins. The standards of Paris and Versailles were accepted all over France, and we find little independent initiative in the provinces.[181]

This is the cultural dimension of the centralized autocracy and bureaucracy that Louis XIV was once imagined to have imposed on France. Not only the arts but 'all activities throughout France' were controlled by 'an almost uniform system, dependent on the central authority'.[182] Clearly, in some academic circles of the 1950s and 1960s the Sun King was being re-launched as a prototype for the totalitarianism of Joseph Stalin.

Art historians are now catching up with the implications of the unravelling of the 'absolutist' concept. The gap between art history and socio-political history is being bridged. But the focus has been on a limited area which has long been recognized as multi-disciplinary, the royal court. It is now extending to the much wider area of provincial power struggles and their relation to central government. Power elites and their rivalries are the focus. In spite of the alleged rise of 'absolutism', extensive power remained with traditional aristocratic, judicial, municipal and ecclesiastical elites. A monarch could therefore implement his cultural projects only with their co-operation and hence through negotiation and avoidance of force. The monarch was one of the players, and not a solo performer.

The truth is that provincial and urban elites did not have to be yes-men of the royal court. If they could object vociferously to royal fiscal policy, they could do the same to royal cultural projects – especially since culture was in this period a political weapon. As with rivalry between rulers in search of crowns, cultural competition was the extension of politics by other means. Rival courts whose authority overlapped, rival families competing for status or rival bishops disputing primacy, rival cities who clashed over provincial supremacy or joined forces to defend provincial privilege against the king – all regarded iconography as part of their armament. Visual weaponry was used to protect cultural identity, rights and privileges and also to further corporate and family ambition. For the historian, architecture again moves from being a backdrop to political events and becomes a political player. Competition for political power could be fought with buildings and become a battle for sight lines. Whether a disputed authority emanated from the monarch or another institution, it was easier to challenge it in architectural imagery than in the courts. It was also simpler to make a visual statement about power than to exercise it – and sometimes, in the case of the monarch, more judicious. The arts have long been regarded as a valuable addition to the limited repertoire of physical power. To repeat the point, they were often a substitute for it.

The battle for visual pre-eminence involved competition for prime building sites and vantage points near city gates with instant impact on visitors. An extended archiepiscopal palace would instantly incite a visual counter-attack from the town council (with an enlarged *hôtel de ville*) and from the courts (with a beautified *palais de justice*). The study of cultural politics evokes a world of long-vanished nuance. Visual deference to Kings and bishops was, for example, inappropriate in a building dedicated to civic dignity. Much hung on whether a civic or royal building should dominate a public space, and a city council which erected a grandiose building opposite a royal palace was issuing a cultural challenge. This was a battle Louis XIV and Victor Amadeus II could win in their own capitals, but at a distance of 400 miles the outcome was unpredictable. In Montpellier a crisis was precipitated when civic buildings faced the threat of being upstaged by a statue of the King. When it was relegated to a site outside the city walls, royal officials announced that to force royalty to overlook fields was architectural *lèse-majesté*.

The paintings which adorn civic buildings also tell a story. Those which record the city fathers of Toulouse participating in royal visits have been interpreted as humble tributes to monarchy. But royal personages were often exploited to enhance the city fathers' own civic prestige. Their brilliantly coloured robes of office dominate the foreground, while royal visitors are invariably relegated to the back. The civic dignitaries are frequently gazing out at the spectator, while their distinguished guests are ignored. If monarchs themselves were depicted, they were usually safe historical figures rather than potentially threatening contemporary ones. City councils considered the merits of living Kings greatly inferior to those of dead ones.

Municipalities developed strategies for reconciling opposites – desire to please a King whose help might some day be needed, and abhorrence of a grovelling stance incompatible with corporate dignity. Public statues of Kings were a Bourbon innovation.[183] Innumerable city councils therefore announced plans for equestrian statues of Louis XIV, only to stall their erection indefinitely. In one case there was a delay of 27 years, while the intended artwork reposed forgotten in a village barn between Paris and Dijon.[184]

## Painting

There can be no better evidence of elite cultural dominance than the Grand Manner. Though historians have had little to say about it, it played a central role in painting during the 1650–1750 period – and its weighty influence lingered for many decades afterwards. With a few notable exceptions, painters embraced it or conformed to it. The term was first applied to painting in the later seventeenth century and ancient Greek and Roman art was hailed as its model of excellence.[185] The style's two variants have already been mentioned. The baroque version, a very free interpretation of classical standards, was derived from the sculptor and architect Bernini. He favoured dramatic movement, heroic gestures, exaggerated expression and emotional impact. A more austerely classical version was launched at the same time by the painter Poussin, who chose instead to appeal to the intellect. He preferred a calmer heroism with restrained gestures, noble profiles and blank faces.[186]

Both repudiated the low and vulgar and preferred the aristocratic and noble.[187] The latter alone was defined as heroic. The Grand Manner was the logical climax of the traditional identification before the 1750s of moral qualities with social classes – noble deeds with knights and aristocrats and base deeds with peasants ('villeins'). It clearly demarcated elites from commoners and was the perfect visual imagery for an elite society. The hero was portrayed in a dignified and impressive pose, as if he had already become a public statue. The difficulty was that nature rarely came up to scratch and actual specimens of the human body were always blighted by imperfections. Painters (and sculptors) therefore felt bound to raise the heroic content by depicting ideal body types as seen in modern health and fashion magazines. Though the surface of the baroque version tends to swirl with visual energy, this does not detract from the dignity of the subject since an orderly design underlies apparent chaos. Rational and mathematical, this order is always based on circles, rectangles and pyramids – or even corkscrews.

The highest categories of painting were religious, mythological and historical.[188] Religious pictures celebrated the Christian religion and, in Catholic countries, the Catholic Church (with heavy emphasis on saints, early Christian theologians and Madonna and Child). Mythological pictures depicted Greek and Roman gods and goddesses in their various escapades and pastimes. Historical pictures celebrated monarchs, victorious generals, great battles and spectacular sieges. As Samuel Johnson argued, 'whatever makes the past, the distant or the future predominate over the present advances us in the dignity of thinking beings'.[189] The reality displayed less moral uplift. It was often a thinly veiled excuse for praising royal or aristocratic elites or removing clothing. In the most familiar scenario, naked classical deities mingle with male royalty, who display minimal clothing and improbable muscles.

Portraits came lower in the hierarchy and were of two kinds. Public portraits were commissioned by a corporation or institution, and private, by rich art collectors, the latter being more informal in style. The Grand Manner was applied less to private portraits than public. This sometimes caused problems. The need to flatter monarchs and bishops by presenting them as glorious and god-like clashed with the lowly Augustinian assessment of human dignity and potential. Artists ensured that visually the former priority prevailed, but only because these worldly powers were divinely appointed agents for the repression of sinful humanity.[190] European academies ruled that large full-length portraits were merited only by morally uplifting royal and religious subjects. Gradually this privilege became less exclusive. It was extended first to the high aristocracy and from the 1750s to the English country gentry by Reynolds and Gainsborough.[191] Other forms of painting were considered minor. Paintings of fruit and flowers, non-gentlemen and servants always had to be small. There was little demand for landscapes and genre paintings (scenes from ordinary life), unless they depicted shepherds and shepherd-esses in a highly idealized state of pastoral bliss. In the lowest category of all came sculpture. The challenge lay in mastering a difficult medium (marble, stone or bronze), and the creator of the finished product was considered a craftsman rather than an artist.[192]

Monarchical and aristocratic values emerge more clearly in contrast to those of the Dutch Republic, which reversed them.[193] Whereas the bedrock of monarchical states was royal and aristocratic dynasties and great corporations of clergy and lawyers, in the Dutch Republic it was family households. Between artisans and trading merchants was a broad class of the population (in England known as 'the middling sort') which, while not rich, prided itself on being decently housed. Domestic cleanliness was therefore a national obsession and homes were scrubbed, scoured and swept with military precision. Dutch streets were the only ones in Europe in which people could walk without plunging their feet into filth and ordure thrown from the houses. Consequently, Dutch genre painting contrasted serenely conscientious house-wives cleansing their homes with merrily carefree ones who neglected them. Cleanliness was a patriotic and moral duty – next to godliness, in fact.[194]

The main painted representation of monarchs, nobles and prelates was the baroque state portrait. It had two sources. One was the Renaissance state portrait, with billowing velvet curtain and classical column as stage props. Classical columns conferred status on the sitter. (They are still added to the porches of suburban dwellings which aspire to be something more.) The other source was the early baroque painter Van Dyck, who worked for Charles I before the British Civil Wars. In the Middle Ages monarchs were usually depicted crowned and enthroned. It was the achievement of Van Dyck to invent a royal iconography which simultaneously exalted the subject and relaxed the pose. He invested his subjects with unprecedented glamour and swagger but caught them in casual mode. In the 1630s he painted Charles I on the hunting field, dismounted, restful, yet magnificent.[195] A repertoire of *trompe l'oeil* techniques was perfected. In a full-length portrait the subject was always painted life-size, but as it appeared set back from the front of the picture a larger-than-life impression was created – a trick still employed by Reynolds over a century later. Were his sitters to walk out of their frames, they would be seven feet tall.[196] The state portrait was invariably painted in the Grand Manner. This involved a dignified but leisured pose, feet poised in a heel-to-toe right-angled position and one hand on hip. Today it can look comically camp. The fingers of the hand had to be elegantly splayed out and the facial expression to be solemn: smiling at the camera was considered naff.

The Renaissance state portrait from which that of the 1650–1750 period descended was fully developed by the sixteenth century.[197] Italy (especially the Venetians) and the Netherlands had evolved a style of three-dimensional modelling in which oil paint and *chiaroscuro* (manipulation of light and shade) gave lifelike depth and space to the subject. The convention was established that the reality of an unimpressive royal subject must be modified by the need to depict majesty and nobility: the deficiencies of nature had to be improved if necessary. But this Renaissance formula was by no means universally accepted. In the England of Elizabeth I, partly owing to the taste of the queen herself, state portraits remained as flat, wooden and unreal as paintings of medieval monarchs. The same was true of much of northern Europe from Scandinavia to Russia. Only in the late sixteenth and early seventeenth centuries did the Renaissance style begin to spread all over Europe, regardless of political and religious frontiers. This was partly owing to the extensive influence of Rubens. He helped to transmit the achievement of the great Venetian painters throughout the Continent and to their ravishing colour he added swirling rhythm and dynamic movement.[198] Rubens worked for many rulers and was the pivot between High Renaissance and baroque. From the mid-seventeenth century the baroque portrait became the norm in monarchies everywhere and rulers moved to exercise unprecedented control over their royal image. Artistic backwaters like Brandenburg–Prussia hastened to raise their game. Previous portraits of mousy-looking Hohenzollern rulers were over-painted with the baroque swagger and grandeur now considered essential.[199]

Rigaud's state portrait of Louis XIV of around 1700 accordingly blends the solemn Renaissance symbols with the laid-back dignity of Van Dyck. There is constant image repair work. The symbols of kingship are updated as Rigaud refreshes the traditional image by an injection of modernity. He depicts the king in his coronation robes, surrounded by his regalia, the symbols of power. The curtains and obligatory chunk of classical column are prominent. But the pose is identical to that of Van Dyck's Charles I and hence informal. Louis does not wear his crown, which reposes on a cushion. The medieval sword of justice is three-quarters invisible, as though an ordinary weapon and not a mystical one. He holds his sceptre upside down and leans on it like a walking cane or golf club.[200] Louis and his ministers certainly demonstrated their awareness of living in a new age.[201]

This is the pattern for an endless series of baroque state portraits in western and central Europe. The formula remains the same – crown on cushion or table, hints of throne and other coronation regalia, swirling draperies probably representing the royal canopy over the monarch's head, and Majesty itself in relaxed but imposing posture. Van Loo's Louis XV in 1761 and Duplessis's Louis XVI in 1774 are mere reworkings of Rigaud. Monarchs competed as keenly for great painters as they did for victory in battle and an acknowledged genius like Velazquez was not obliged to flatter his royal sitter. His portrait of Philip IV of Spain at the age of fifty unflinchingly depicts sagging flesh and puffy eyelids.[202] Yet state portraits were often treated as totemic substitutes for the monarch. The Rigaud painting took Louis XIV's place in the throne room at Versailles when the King was absent. To turn one's back on it was a calculated insult. Other portraits presided over festivals in the King's honour in the provinces.[203]

This formula was reserved for royal, noble or ecclesiastical dignitaries. But in 1729, nearly thirty years after his ground-breaking portrait of Louis XIV, Rigaud extended the same treatment to Bernard, a banker. Globe and fleet were substituted for crown and sceptre as accessories. This was the same erosion of formal indicators of social differentiation that Boswell noted in eighteenth-century England, where the gentrified title 'esquire' was being slapped on everybody.[204] When the assumptions which shaped the baroque state portrait could embrace a financier, however rich, the rules were clearly starting to slacken.

The Grand Manner was further undermined a decade later in England. In the icy winter of 1740 in his studio in Leicester Fields, London, Hogarth was painting a sitter who was, by aristocratic standards, a nobody. According to the rules, only his head and shoulders should have been depicted, with one hand thrown in if he was lucky. But the painter was planning to cover an area eight feet high and five wide with a state portrait of a commoner. The result was *Captain Thomas Coram*, Hogarth's monumental image of a great benefactor. Coram had made a fortune building ships in Massachusetts. On his return to London he walked into the City each day from Rotherhithe and was dismayed to see the corpses of abandoned bastard babies in the gutter. He turned himself into a fund-raiser and lobbyist, caught the attention of the great and the good, and launched an appeal for a Foundling Hospital in Bloomsbury. George II incorporated the resulting institution by royal charter in 1739. Artists were persuaded to donate works of art to raise its profile and attract people of quality. Hogarth's contribution still hangs at the top of the stairs and is the first English state portrait of a commoner.

An engraving of Rigaud's Bernard was Hogarth's main source.[205] Yet his portrait looks nothing like Rigaud's. He pinches Rigaud's baroque draperies, hanging from nowhere, his over-sized classical column and his epic background vista, while the captain's billowing coat recalls the fluttering robes of a bronze baroque bishop. But after the fanfare of his grandiose set and props, Coram himself is a deliberate anti-climax. Whereas Bernard is festooned in full-bottomed wig, sash of the order of the Saint-Esprit and all the accoutrements of an aristocratic status which he did not have, Coram is unmistakably a jolly little man with a coarse, weatherbeaten face and short legs, whose feet barely touch the dais on which he sits. No ruffles impede his heavily veined, practical hands and his hair is an untidy mop of his own, rather than the powdered wig of a grandee. While books of manners required a gentleman to turn his feet elegantly outwards at a balletic angle like Bernard's, Coram's are plonked down in parallel. While Bernard is kitted out with dress and body language proclaiming aristocratic status, Coram is allowed to remain a sea captain.[206]

Yet his benevolently good humour and honesty of demeanour make clear that the artist regarded him as unequivocally admirable. Like Rousseau, Hogarth proclaimed that heroic moral stature deserves high social status. In the 1750s the novelist Richardson made the same point in a different way. At the start of *Sir Charles Grandison* he broke with convention by listing his characters in order of moral worth rather than social rank.[207] Hogarth, however, accepted that only an elite artistic convention can confer the deserved moral status – hence he gives Coram the full baroque treatment of a state portrait in the Grand Manner. Yet the latter begins to lose its original justification as the medium of the nobility when the claims of mere merit are advanced. Bernard could join the company of the elite only by pretending to be aristocratic. Coram enters the exclusive club as himself.

Portraiture underlined elite class values in other ways. This was the greatest age of power dressing, when costume as a social and political indicator almost became an art form in itself. Modern male dress may have owed its origin to Charles II's wish to make a political point. It may also have a religious motivation. The Plague and Fire of 1665–6 were widely perceived as God's judgement on the luxury of a dissolute court. In late 1666 Charles launched a reform of traditional upper-class male dress. The court abandoned the elaborate costume of short doublet down to the waist, combined with ballooning petticoat breeches (something like women's culottes) and lavishly adorned with yards of ribbon. The substitution of a simpler combination of narrow knee-breeches, frock-coat and long vest (waistcoat) reaching below the waist heralded the essentials of the modern three-piece suit. It seems to have arrived from Persia and was regarded as a deliberate attempt to break away from French fashion. Pepys claimed that Louis XIV swiftly adopted it. French historians naturally assert that the Sun King wore it first.[208]

If the lines of this new elite dress were simpler, the fabrics were certainly not. Portraits showcased the gorgeousness of its embroidered silks, shot satins and lace ruffles. Elites distinguished themselves from the labouring poor by arraying themselves in the most ornate and impractical finery in the history of costume. It defined their status and made it impossible for them to perform one minute's physical work. It also made it difficult for them to walk. Gentlemen ventured through ordure-infested streets in coaches and sedan chairs, or on horseback. Only lesser mortals went on foot. It was the time, in the immortal words of Beatrix Potter's *The Tailor of Gloucester*, 'of swords and periwigs and full-skirted coats with flowered lappets – when gentlemen wore ruffles and gold-laced waistcoats of paduasoy and taffeta'. Royalty and aristocracy spent astounding amounts on clothes. The Duke of Bedford shelled out an estimated £500 (about £35,000 in modern values) for a suit to wear at the court of George III, when nearly 90 per cent of British families had an income of under £50 a year. The Empress Elizabeth of Russia rarely wore the same dress twice. When she died in 1761, 15,000 dresses were discovered in her wardrobe.[209] This was power dressing on an unprecedented scale.

The celebrity status of elites in this period is indicated by the desperation with which their dress and lifestyle were imitated. Sumptuary law had previously forbidden the 'lower orders' to ape the dress of 'people of quality'. This had been abandoned in western Europe before the period began – prematurely, as it turned out.[210] In England the poor saved their pennies in order to dress above their station and by the early eighteenth century were able to imitate the costume of their betters in simplified versions and cheaper fabrics. But around the middle of the century the process was reversed. Elites began to dress down.[211] Gentlemen adopted as country wear the round hats worn by working men, and aped their habit of going wigless. A simultaneous shift in the public's attitude to elite ostentation was underlined in 1789, when the procession of elected representatives at the opening of the French Estates General triggered a sartorial disaster. The traditionally lavish costumes of the nobility were jeered and every European elite took note. By the late 1770s peacock fashion-statements were rapidly giving way to a vogue for something stylish but simple – and, compared with the glory of what preceded it, rather boring. The magic of sumptuous display had ceased to impress spectators who had learned to add up the cost.[212]

Wigs merit closer attention. Portraiture paid special attention to headgear. From the mid-seventeenth to the mid-eighteenth centuries most members of the elite shaved off their hair and wore wigs. These were the full-bottomed variety, with rows of curls descending well below the wearer's chin and looking vaguely like a spaniel's ears. They were a symbol of authority, which is why they are still worn by British judges. Wigs were also visible signals of social order. To lose his wig made a member of the elite look ridiculous. Social chaos was invariably depicted by gentlemen's wigs falling off. James Boswell describes in his journal how the loss of his headgear obliged him to make a twenty-five-mile journey to buy another before he could appear in polite society.

After the 1750s wigs began to decline – a development flagged up in 1765 when the peruke makers petitioned the British king because of their business recession.[213] First, wigs became smaller, with a single sausage-roll curl above each ear. Towards the end of the century gentlemen began to wear their own hair lightly powdered and tied back in a ribbon to give a mere hint of a wig. In order to display solidarity with the more egalitarian spirit of the age, their sons omitted the powder and let their hair fall naturally on their shoulders. Rear-Admiral Nelson was still insisting on the wearing of pigtails in 1799, but it was by then a hairstyle which his younger officers viewed as archaic.[214]

It seems that quite ordinary people could 'read' a baroque painting in a way their twenty-first-century descendants have never learned. They could identify standard personifications and allegories which are now forgotten and appreciate subtle devices by which a person's status could be underlined. On the west wall of Thornhill's Painted Hall at Greenwich, created around 1720, the motto on the architrave proclaims 'Now a new race from Heaven … '. Beneath it, somewhat anticlimactically, appears the rather ordinary figure of George I. To make him look majestic and heroic Thornhill equips him with the full kit of crown, sceptre, ermine and armour. The future George II stands at his side attended by a portly female triumphantly waving a trident, identifying her as Naval Victory. Reposing on cushions of cloud are the figures of Justice, complete with sword and scales, and Time with his scythe, watching over a cornucopia from which flows a stream of gold, thus stressing the benefits of the new Hanoverian regime. On the highest cloud of all floats a voluptuous woman in a topless dress. She is leaning against an obelisk to signify the stability of the new order.[215] In the foreground stands Thornhill, who has deferentially painted himself smaller than royal personages sitting further back. This makes them seem monumental. His left hand is behind his back, palm up. As a result he looks like a dwarf requesting a tip. Grossly underpaid (he requested £5 a yard for the ceiling but had to settle for £3), he probably felt like one.

Having ascended with his brushes from the west wall to the ceiling, Thornhill proceeds to make extravagantly symbolic claims for the superiority of Great Britain's system of government. Attended by all the Virtues in heaven, William III and Mary II restore the cap of liberty to a grateful Europe. William's feet trample on despotism in the shape of a cowering Louis XIV.[216] The disintegration of tyranny is underlined by the broken sword of the now-eclipsed Sun King, whom Thornhill has thoughtfully rendered in a hue reminiscent of rotting human flesh.

This visual language was universal throughout Europe in the period. In 1711, at the other end of the Continent in the monarchy of Saxony–Poland–Lithuania, a large print was published to broadcast the glories of the newly completed Zwinger, itself part of the grandiose plan for transforming Dresden into a royal capital. The centre of the composition is crammed with an awestruck crowd inspecting the new Orangery. In the foreground an ornate cartouche attributes the initiative for the enterprise to the King of Poland and Elector of Saxony, Augustus II, and the designs to his talented architect, Matthias Pöppelmann. Above the clouds an airborne team of cherubs, angels and goddesses thrills to the architects' original drawings, which they have somehow acquired, and brandish potted plants.[217]

Turning from the content of painting to the people who looked at it, we see that the elite stranglehold was loosened in other ways towards the middle of the eighteenth century. Nobles and monarchs had their own art galleries but other people needed galleries which admitted the public. The annual Parisian exhibitions of painting and sculpture known as the 'Salons' fitted this description and began in 1663. But they were often postponed. After 1704 there were no Salons until 1737, when they became biennial. By the 1750s attendances were 15,000, with 30,000 by the 1780s. This spectacular lift-off deposited royal, ecclesiastical and aristocratic collectors firmly on the back seat and transferred to the public the aesthetic judgement that mattered.[218]

In England, Hogarth had a key role in extending to the middle classes what had previously been aristocratic and courtly. Engraved prints had been around since the fifteenth century as a means of producing works of graphic art in quantity. But Hogarth was the first to spot their commercial potential and exploit it with flair. For every painting he sold the gentry, he could sell hundreds of printed copies to a mass market. *The Harlot's Progress* started in 1731 as six paintings. He then engraved a limited number for upper-class enthusiasts who had subscribed to his project, and finally authorized cheap prints for the masses. Like modern reproductions, prints projected his paintings far beyond the aristocratic clients for whom they were created, and communicated his moral and political message to a wider public. In 1735 they were sufficiently plentiful to justify an Act of Parliament banning cheap copies of prints unauthorized by the artist, though in practice pirated versions easily dodged it by incorporating minor differences from the original.

This culture of print belonged to the bourgeois 'public sphere', challenging the dominance of a court culture defined in terms flattering to the interests of crown, church and nobility. By the mid-eighteenth century the middle orders were finding an independent voice. Historians of modern state formation present Britain's expanding print culture as more evidence of her progressive socio-political system. But this development was not unique to England, since Hogarth himself found a lucrative market in Germany. Its bourgeoisie subscribed to literate activities in sufficient numbers to prompt Georg Lichtenberg to hail the mid-eighteenth century as the 'Paper Age of the World'.[219] And British innovations pale into insignificance in comparison with cultural developments in the Netherlands. The 1698 inventory of a Flemish merchant records that he owned 'An Old Woman Cooking Eggs', one of the most celebrated paintings by Velazquez.[220]

If that was unusual, the art market of the Dutch Republic was unique. Surviving household inventories of c.1650 suggest that 2,500,000 paintings existed there, two-thirds of them the work of around 500 living artists who produced about 50,000 canvases a year.[221] Ownership extended to most of the middle classes. Inventories from Delft prove that pictures of some kind hung in two-thirds of all houses, while in 1717 a tailor on the Prinsengracht in Amsterdam who traded in his house had five paintings worth five guilders in total. Landscape and genre paintings of everyday middle-class life, the categories downgraded by elites of the monarchical states, were precisely those most valued by the more equal society of the Dutch Republic. A foreign visitor commented that 'pictures are very common here, there being scarce an ordinary tradesman whose house is not decorated with them'. The Republic's population had no need of cheap prints: most of them had original paintings. This was the first mass consumers' art market in European history. Dutch literary culture too was remarkably unified, with fuzzy boundaries between the elite and the popular. In 1655 Jacob Cats's marriage manual was published in two parallel editions – with fine engravings in large folio for the grand and with crude woodcuts in a format a quarter of that size for the humble. A text common to both strongly suggests that the reading public was not bound by class distinctions.[222]

The contrast with non-republics is obvious. Britain was similar to other western European monarchies in having a culture dominated by aristocratic and clerical elites, who until the 1750s alone possessed the means for major cultural patronage.[223] But the Dutch concentration of economic power made their republic different from all other states in baroque Europe. In two generations it had become a world empire stretching from the West Indies to the East Indies. The wealth drawn from it was finally sucked into a cramped space roughly the size of Wales.[224] Most of its people were rich in comparison with other European populations and could afford commodities beyond popular reach elsewhere. If we seek signs of modernity, we should look at the Dutch Republic. In this period that is where the true 'public sphere' has to be.

Yet even there, symptoms of the Grand Manner are discernible. Rembrandt's most controversial painting is now known as *The Night Watch*, a group portrait of the 1640s depicting the members of Amsterdam's Guard. It reveals which elite conventions, now being established, the artist respected and which he flouted. He upheld the rule that social elites should occupy the most prominent positions in a composition. It is often forgotten that, though the Dutch Republic by definition lacked a monarchy, it did have an aristocratic elite.[225] This ensured that the cultural tone of Europe's other aristocracies was not lacking in Amsterdam. The niceties of the social pecking order are observed by Rembrandt, and the two aristocratic commanders of the military company emerge with stunning visual force. They are resplendently arrayed in sparkling colours and have just marched into the light source of the picture. They dominate its centre and are the focus of several parallelograms (created by the lines of pikes, muskets and flagpoles) which structure its composition. One of them was so pleased with the original that he ordered two copies.[226]

But Rembrandt broke with the venerable tradition of group portraits. Instead of an impressive if static line-up of members, it was the *action* of the group to which Rembrandt subordinated all the individuals. He was determined to dramatize the march of Amsterdam's guard with fairly gritty realism: a tiny powder monkey is seen running out of the picture. He had never subscribed to the classical imperative of idealizing his subject by editing nature.[227] The commanders are at least shown at the front, but instead of striking statuesque poses they are marching out of the picture towards the spectator. The rest of the company probably expected to be immortalized in the conventional manner – as a row of heroic individual portraits. Instead they are emerging from the shadows and are depicted as mere animated shade. Rembrandt was also becoming bored with grand baroque gestures at a time when they were taking a firmer hold on elite culture. Contrary to legend, objections that *The Night Watch* lacked taste and decorum emerged only after Rembrandt's death. But fourteen years after painting the picture he became bankrupt. The reasons were not exclusively artistic, but by the 1660s his style clashed with the new cultural climate and commissions dwindled. Neither development was likely to have enhanced his financial status.[228]

The Protestant Dutch Republic, where ownership of paintings was endemic, lacked the stimulus given to artists by the Catholic Church. Clerical demand for pictures, frescoes and sculptures for cathedrals, churches, convents, abbeys and chapels made the latter far and away the greatest patron of painting. More broadly, nine-tenths of all Spanish art seems to have been religious; in Italy and the Spanish Netherlands the proportion was almost as high and in Poland and the Habsburg lands even higher.[229] The baroque style was a perfect medium for whipping up the emotions in order to maximize spectator response to the demands of religion. The passions of saints and martyrs were rendered in paint or marble with graphic realism. Baroque art frequently exploited the power of the forces of nature. One of Bernini's sculptural groups, commissioned by a rich patron for a Roman church, was the ecstasy of St Teresa. It depicts the moment when an angel allegedly pierced the saint's heart with a golden flaming arrow. Her dress, though solid marble, seems to quiver. It is as though it has been energized by an electric charge, or even a naked flame. Another favourite of baroque artists was wind. One of the focal points of St Peter's in Rome is Bernini's sculptural group known as the Apostle's Throne. At first glance the ensemble apparently depicts a force-10 gale. Clouds scud across the scene, the robes and beards of attendant bishops billow magnificently and St Peter's throne seems to take off into pell-mell flight. But all these items turn out to be reassuringly solid. It is the spectator who is 'blown away'. Here Bernini has merely used the wind machine to ramp up the excitement level, rather as Hollywood films feature powerful cars chasing each other at extreme speeds and periodically exploding.[230]

In contrast, Protestants tended to separate art from religion. Their horror at the worship of inanimate images led to a very different conception of art – not as a route to God but as a spiritual road block. Painting and sculpture were violently rejected whenever they attempted to mediate between God and man. The result had been most devastating in Britain. Much medieval painting and sculpture was destroyed between 1536, when Henry VIII dissolved the monasteries, and 1658, when Cromwell died.[231] These savage attitudes had subsequently softened, but nothing created in the 1650–1750 period came near to replacing what had been obliterated.

By the middle of the eighteenth century even greater change was under way throughout Europe. There was an unmistakable sense of overdosing on grandeur and sensation. The theatrical solemnity of the Grand Manner in painting was challenged. Though that style had itself loosened the stiff ceremonial of Renaissance art, there was now a shift to a more informal portraiture which punctured baroque pomposity. The insistence of the Grand Manner on status and authority was downplayed as elites were increasingly depicted in more relaxed mode. From the mid-eighteenth century intimate 'conversation pieces' presented prestigious sitters in cosy family groups rather than as awesome icons of power.[232] At precisely the same time the boundary wall between portrait painting (elites) and genre painting (ordinary life and people) began to come down.[233] Even royal portraits began to lay less emphasis on allegories of sacral rule, divine origins and dynastic heroism.[234] Instead they presented intimate paparazzi-like glimpses of off-duty monarchs enjoying the affection of their children in a setting of cosy domesticity. By the 1760s the Wittelsbach ruling family of Bavaria could be depicted drinking coffee and playing instruments like members of their musical staff.[235] In short, Rousseau's endorsement of the natural and spontaneous above the artificial and sophisticated was taking hold.

The arts were now demystifying heads of state and turning them into employees working for their people. Simultaneously, in real life, monarchs like Frederick II of Brandenburg–Prussia and Joseph II of Austria were repackaging themselves as busy rulers with neither time nor inclination for stuffy ceremony. It is never clear whether life follows art or vice versa, but the message was that kings and queens were simply people.[236] This represented the harnessing of art to political needs in a new intellectual climate. Yet it was an uneasy presentational compromise for monarchy, wanting to appear part of society yet be necessarily removed from it.[237] A generation before the Age of Revolution, power was descending to earth.

After 1750 the letters of British painters start to quiver with resentment against the repetitive drudgery of endlessly painting the aristocracy, its wife and its dog. Leading artists began to form a resistance movement against what they increasingly saw as the cultural tyranny of elites.[238] Gainsborough famously expostulated: 'Damn gentlemen! There is not such a set of enemies to a real artist in the world as they are, if not kept at a proper distance.' Reynolds continued as late as 1790 to employ and defend the Grand Manner with its heroically noble poses, inherited via the Renaissance from classical antiquity and embodying the latter's *gravitas*.[239] He urged the painter to conform to this convention, even if it meant falsifying the known appearance of historical figures: 'He cannot make his hero talk like a great man; he must make him look like one'.[240] Nevertheless, with contemporary elites and celebrities persuaded to pose for him as classical deities, sprites and wood nymphs, many of his state portraits verge on tongue-in-cheek satire. The pomposity of the Grand Manner in its glory days is punctured by irony and humour. Reynolds's image of Lord Cawdor shows him throwing out his arm in a grandiose gesture, seeming to indicate the breadth of his ample acres. On closer inspection, he has thrown a stick for his dog to retrieve and the animal has dismissively turned its back on the missile.[241]

In the early nineteenth century the Grand Manner was revived throughout Europe as part of the attempt to reinstate old ruling elites after their catastrophic mauling by the French Revolution and (to a lesser extent) by Napoleon. But the life had gone out of it and it was soon applied to very different artistic purposes. It was appropriated by rich commoners who merely featured as themselves, whether successful writers or Lancashire cotton magnates. It was also deployed subversively. The socialist painter Courbet used it to bestow moral dignity and grandeur on provincial nobodies, previously thought incapable of either.[242]

To return to the later eighteenth century, a cult of *Bürgerlichkeit* took hold in Germany. This represented a reaction against French culture, manners and morals.[243] One of its greatest illustrators was the German artist Chodowiecki, who in 1779 published a set of engravings entitled 'Natural and Affected Acts of Life'. Two couples are depicted, one representing plain German honesty of feeling and the other French artificiality and sophistication. The first couple are natural to a point just short of indecency. The youth conceals his genitals with a mere wisp of fabric, while the girl wears a loose and flimsily transparent dress from which both breasts have joyfully escaped. In contrast, the second couple are stiffly correct in deportment, grotesquely overdressed and festooned with bows and baubles like a pair of courting Christmas trees.[244]

The change in taste had profound implications. Tiepolo was the greatest decorator of the palaces and churches of the baroque and rococo period. By the middle decades of the eighteenth century he was internationally famous and employed throughout Europe, yet shortly after his death in 1770 he went out of fashion. Purely from his imagination he had crafted a world of illusion, an alternative universe where angels and gods, both classical and Christian, gambolled in the clouds with rosy-cheeked nymphs and cherubs. Heavily perfumed and artificial, Tiepolo's work was detested by the neo-classical champions of truth to nature who followed him. The courtly and aristocratic culture which he helped to create was viewed by the Revolutionary Era as frivolous, hedonistic, decadent and doomed. He was perceived as subservient to the pomp and pretensions of tyrannical princes, who in turn were denounced as periwigged anachronisms resisting the spirit of the age destined shortly to sweep them away. His paintings survived but their creator was forgotten. No book on Tiepolo was published in any language between his death and the 1880s.[245] Totalitarian dictatorships are not the only regimes to airbrush their victims from history.

## Music

Here, as decisively as in the other arts, elite patrons called the tune. Music in this period, apart from popular dance and ballads, was dominated by their taste. Most baroque music was written for royal, aristocratic and ecclesiastical courts, churches and chapels. Its main small-scale instrumental forms were labelled *sonata da camera* and *sonata da chiesa* – court and church sonatas. By 1700 these were less clearly distinguished and known simply as sonatas, but their origin in the two main early-modern performance venues is apparent.[246] Choral music was even more exclusively the servant of the church. Until Haydn performed *The Creation* in Vienna in 1799, few choral concerts were public.[247]

A composer like Albinoni was lucky. Born into a rich family, he never needed court or church employment. He went on to write the first set of oboe concertos by an Italian composer to be printed and published. But only rare musicians with independent means could escape the clutches of royal, aristocratic or clerical elites. Most respectable performers and composers served them in the style of which their employers approved, with some concession to popular styles for church congregations. They had no alternative audience. The newly literate 'middling sort' were still not collectively rich or numerous enough to support them. Peasants, craftsmen and tradesmen had their own popular entertainers who sprang from their midst and provided the musical accompaniment to popular ballad (often printed), folk legend, myth and ritual. Their social status was low. Though the blind ballad-singers of eighteenth-century Palermo had their own craft guild, along with the usual bunch of privileges, most travelling performers were regarded as beggars.[248]

There is little sign at any time in the early-modern period of a reverential attitude to the music of the past.[249] Its literature, architecture, painting and sculpture were venerated because their tangible remains were available, broadcast by the printing press and displayed in churches and other public places. In the 1620s Charles I of England bought nearly 400 paintings and classical statues from the bankrupt Gonzagas of Mantua for over £18,000 – a huge sum in seventeenth-century terms.[250] All this art was at least a century old. In contrast, there were few ways of hearing yesterday's music because little was perpetuated by publication. Furthermore, apart from the Christian religion, the main inspiration for all the arts in this period was the classical civilization of ancient Greece and Rome. Continual variations on the same theme presupposed a basic vocabulary, written or visual, which remained familiar. But there was no common musical thread linking the generations, since no one knew what ancient Greek and Roman music sounded like.[251]

Within the context of music as a transient art, it was nevertheless true that some composers were consigned to more total oblivion than others – none more so than those active in the 1650–1750 period. As with the other arts, baroque music was a near-terminal casualty of the revolution in taste that followed in the later eighteenth century. Only in the last half-century has it returned to favour in music libraries and recording studios. We now recognize Vivaldi as a great baroque composer and Johann Sebastian Bach as possibly the greatest of any period. Yet within fifty years of their deaths their names vanished from musical bibliographies and dictionaries. Bach's reputation survived only in aristocratic musical circles and his great choral works appeared in print only in the 1830s. By the early nineteenth century Vivaldi, like Tiepolo, was forgotten. His *Four Seasons* was not rediscovered until 1929.[252] Handel managed to retain popularity on the strength of his choral oratorios but his operas were consigned to the musical bin. *Julius Caesar*, one of his greatest, was first performed in 1724 and revived several times while he lived. His death sent it into total eclipse until 1922. At Baron van Swieten's Sunday-morning parties in the 1780s Mozart discussed and performed the works of Handel, Bach and their baroque contemporaries like so many antique museum pieces.[253]

It can be suggested that one reason for this was the incomprehension of listeners in the period which followed the baroque, when religion was severed from other spheres of thought and activity. In the 1650–1750 period there was no distinction between sacred and secular musical styles. Bach incorporated dance idioms into his church cantatas and no one was shocked to hear soloists performing operatic vocal acrobatics in church music. Yet, when in 1874 Verdi wrote his *Requiem Mass* in an operatic style, there was an outcry from religious quarters.[254]

Baroque music was functional. It was not absolute music in the manner of a Beethoven piano concerto but designed for a practical purpose. Composers supplied a commodity for the present rather than immortal masterpieces for posterity. The status of early-modern music as a contemporary art form meant that patrons tended to employ musicians who could write the music which they played, rather than borrowing it from the past. The reason baroque composers gave little indication of tempo and dynamics in their scores was that they usually performed their own music. Most princely courts had their own orchestra. The first permanent one in Western music was assembled for Louis XIV in the early 1650s when his musical director, Lully, established an ensemble of 21 string players. By the 1670s he was virtual dictator of French music with ultimate authority over all theatrical productions which included it. No company could employ more than six violins without his consent.[255]

Royal and aristocratic patrons wanted birthday odes, wedding songs, funeral dirges, ceremonial welcomes, military marches, fanfares and fireworks music. Many eighteenth-century composers were *Kapellmeister*, musicians employed to organize what was sung and played in a court chapel. Assisted by court composers with similar duties, they supplied the ceremonial soundtrack. In France, as in most courts, the *lever*, the *coucher* and the Mass took place to the accompaniment of appropriate mood music. Musicians were also required to perform at assorted low-grade events. Serenades or *Tafelmusik* were designed to accompany eating or conversation. Only a few eccentric monarchs preferred to concentrate all their spending on military might; most regarded cultural spending as a prestigious substitute for hiring yet more regiments. None the less, in 1713 Frederick William I of Brandenburg–Prussia effectively closed down his father's court and disbanded his orchestra. In a supreme snub to the Berlin Academy which his father had founded, he appointed his court dwarf as its President.[256]

Music also had a key role in the royal hunt. This was at the heart of court life and a central part of the *métier du roi*.[257] It facilitated access to the monarch, provided space for intimate requests and 'networking', signalled shifts in favour by inclusion or exclusion from the hunting party and displayed courtly magnificence to a wider public. Throughout Europe the Stables were one of the great departments of the royal court. The Master of the Horse, one of its leading officials, was usually responsible for the sovereign's service as soon as he set foot outside the palace.[258] Most monarchs hunted each day in season and the highlight was *la vénerie*, the staghunt. The stag was a noble animal and therefore worthy prey of kings and nobles. Oudry's tapestries of 1743, *Les chasses de Louis XV*, present the royal hunt in the Grand Manner as a state occasion, on a par with visiting a port or besieging a town. Clearly it was regarded as mimic war. As well as underlining the king's nobility, the hunt was also a symbol of privilege. By the sixteenth century, royal law excluded commoners from hunting, even beyond the royal forests – hence the eternal feud between noble huntsmen and starving poachers.

A royal hunt had a highly characteristic musical score, though its prestigious associations caused it to spread far more widely among elites during the 1650–1750 period. It was accompanied by the music of huntsmen blowing their horns, answering one another across the forest. They proclaimed the different stages of the hunt. The instruments encircled the bodies of huntsmen in blue and scarlet livery and four of these announced in a unison fanfare the scented quarry. When it took to the water they played the melody *La Reine* and when it was killed they sounded *Le Mort*. Their last duty was to serenade its end, as the corpse was flayed and disembowelled, like a rival for the royal mantle. Finally the antlers were cut off – a resonant and primeval symbol of the removal of the dead contender's crown, while the carcass was desecrated by the hounds.[259]

A musician's work was heartbreakingly repetitive and music a disposable commodity. Mozart's father alleged in 1757 that he (not his more famous son) had written over thirty grand serenades for the Prince-archbishop of Salzburg. Only one has ever been found, and recently at that.[260] Telemann's composition of 600 overtures in the Italian style puzzles self-important modern composers until they realize, to their horror, that each was intended to be played once and forgotten. It was lucky that composition had a significant mechanical component. Vivaldi composed over 500 concertos, but all his works were variations on a handful of simple forms. Rather than a composer in the modern sense he was clearly a one-man production line. The huge numbers of compositions were the result of the drudge-like status of musicians and the grovelling contracts they had to agree to. At one stage in his career Handel had to write a new oratorio every month, and J. S. Bach had an equally major deadline to meet every Sunday. Not only did he have to write each week a cantata lasting around 20 to 30 minutes. Among many other duties, he also supervised the copying of the parts, organized choir and orchestra, rehearsed them on Saturday afternoons and directed the performance on Sunday mornings.[261]

Work overload was eased by baroque recycling techniques. These could take the form of shameless repetition of whole sections of music, or arrangement for new instrumental combinations of the composer's previous works – or even (amazingly, in the light of modern copyright law) of works by other composers. Baroque composers had a down-to-earth attitude to their compositions, which were initiated by financial contract rather than spiritual inspiration. Bach once complained that the mild weather had cost him 100 thaler – he preferred unhealthy temperatures and brisker demand for funeral music.[262]

The social status of musicians was low because most were merely attendants of kings, lords or higher clergy. Unlike celebrated nineteenth-century composers, who expected to dine at the tables of the mighty, they ate in the servants' hall with the staff. It is necessary to forget the exalted status attained by nineteenth- and twentieth-century musicians like Beethoven and the Beatles.[263] In the 1650–1750 period many of their predecessors had to double as valets or bureaucrats. Most were treated by their employers as indentured servants. In 1717, J. S. Bach was disappointed at not being appointed *Kapellmeister* after nine years at the court of Saxe-Weimar and he accepted a post at the nearby court of Cöthen. The Duke of Saxe-Weimar imprisoned him for a month. Princes expected supplicants for their patronage to perform grovels of epic proportions. Bach forced himself in 1721 to write a humble dedication to the Margrave of Brandenburg, who had shown an interest in the concertos named in his honour. He begged the Margrave 'not to judge their imperfection by the strict measure of the refined and delicate taste in musical pieces that everyone knows you possess, but rather to consider kindly the deep respect and the most humble obedience which I am thereby attempting to show to you'.[264] And Bach was a proud and difficult man, to whom nauseating self-abasement did not come naturally. Unfortunately he had nine children to feed.

Forty years later a musician's lot had scarcely improved. A manual issued by the Austrian Empress to define the social hierarchy placed musicians at the bottom, along with actors and beggars.[265] A celebrated musician like Haydn was irked by the subservient status he had to accept. He had to sign a contract specifying the dress code he was obliged to observe when performing for Prince Esterhazy. This included the livery of his master, a dark crimson-and-gold uniform. In addition he was to appear 'neatly in white stockings, white linen, powdered, and either with pigtail or hair-bag, but otherwise of identical appearance'. He could not travel without the prince's permission, his compositions were exclusively the property of his patron and he had to perform where, when and what he commanded.[266] The tone of their relationship is indicated by the obsequious message that Haydn appended to the pieces composed for Esterhazy's birthday:

The most welcome arrival of my patron's name day (which may Divine Grace let Your Serene Highness spend in perfect well-being and happiness) causes me not only to offer to Your Serenity in dutiful submission six new divertimenti, but also to kiss the hem of your robe.[267]

This highly unequal relationship resulted in 126 pieces for baryton, which Haydn composed for his master. The baryton was an ugly-sounding instrument which would long ago have been consigned to the museum, had Haydn's compositions not preserved it. Sadly for him, Esterhazy was one of the few people who played it.[268]

Yet after the 1750s there were signs of change. In the baroque world people were far more interested in the dignitary for whom the music was written than in the composer who wrote it. This contrasted with the treatment accorded to the seven-year-old musical prodigy Mozart when in the 1760s he triumphantly toured the royal courts of Europe and was fêted as a celebrity. But aristocratic arrogance reasserted itself and his luck did not last. In 1781 he took a decision which liberated him from the whims of elite employers but ensured that the rest of his short existence would be precarious. He demanded more dignified terms of employment from the Archbishop of Salzburg. Even for Mozart, this proved premature. The Archbishop's steward kicked him out of the palace. Literally.

Music was the medium which audibly trumpeted the period's fervent religious faith. The supreme musical patron was the Catholic Church, whose liturgy was set to music by many of the musicians it employed. Professional musicians were often ordained priests. Vivaldi received the tonsure in 1693 at the age of fifteen and a half; he spent most of his life teaching the violin at a Catholic girls' orphanage in Venice.[269] The Catholic Church was musically enterprising. It banned opera during Lent but was thoughtful enough to sanction a substitute in the form of oratorio. This was like opera but composed on sacred themes and performed without action, scenery or dance. It originated in Italy, spread to other countries and was taken up by the Catholic courts of central Europe. Even Protestant states, where music had a less prominent religious role, caught the habit. By the 1740s Handel's oratorios were so successful that they replaced opera on the London stage. The Protestant churches, in spite of fears that music could distract from the true purpose of worship, also gave extensive financial support to players, singers and composers. J. S. Bach worked at St Thomas's church in Leipzig for the last 27 years of his life. Like several other baroque composers, he wrote all his music (not just the intentionally sacred pieces) to celebrate God's greatness. At the end of many of his scores was inscribed *Soli Deo Gloria* – 'To the glory of God alone'.[270]

It is hard for modern ears to hear how baroque composers achieved their effects. The tricks are too subtle for ears attuned to the insistent beat of rock music. At the end of their operas Lully and Rameau often placed a dance called a chaconne. This was constructed on a continually repeated theme in the bass, above which the upper parts wove varying patterns of sound. Though the chaconne had been around since the sixteenth century, it attained its greatest popularity in the 1650–1750 period. A suggested explanation is that sensitive seventeenth-century ears were attuned to symbolic nuance. The firm and unchanging bass line represented the constancy of kingly power, the rule of eternal law and the foundation of the state. On that secure footing the dancing bodies of the people could move freely and gratefully in infinite variation.

Baroque music's ability to represent order emerging from chaos is illustrated by the canon. In this a short melody was played. It could then be accompanied only by exact repetition of itself, or by itself played upside down. Making this accompaniment sound right harmonically involved solving a mathematical puzzle: how many beats after the original melody should it start and how many notes distant from its pitch? The result was scientific, mystical and cosmic – or, as Bach's colleague Walther expressed it, 'a heavenly-philosophical and specifically mathematical science'. Earthly music became celestial harmony. The canonic voices wove in and around one another like orbiting planets, eternally in motion, sometimes varying and yet eternally the same.[271] Bach himself made a supreme contribution to musical order when he composed his 48 Keyboard Preludes and Fugues specifically to fix the European key system and reveal the tonal and harmonic logic behind it. Rising through the 24 major and minor keys, they defined the language of music for two hundred years.

Harmony, along with melody and rhythm, is one of music's basic elements. It was inevitable that musical harmony would become a metaphor for cosmic harmony. Dryden immortalized this identification in his *Song for St Cecilia's Day* of 1687. In it, as the Creator imposes order on inert and shapeless matter, music becomes the mouthpiece of the divine voice:

> From Harmony to heavenly Harmony
> This universal Frame began;
> When Nature underneath a heap
> Of jarring Atomes lay,
> And could not heave her Head,
> The tuneful Voice was heard from high,
> Arise, ye more than dead.
> Then cold and hot and moist and dry
> In order to their Stations leap,
> And MUSICK'S pow'r obey....
> From Harmony to Harmony
> Thro' all the Compass of the Notes it ran,
> The Diapason closing full in Man.

The text depicts to perfection the unity of religion, 'science' and political culture: as harmony sustains the divinely ordained cosmos, so it will irradiate the realm of humankind. Half a century later, Handel was inspired to provide the music which is the poem's main theme. He set the 'jarring Atomes' section to grinding discords, only to resolve them in the final 'Harmony' section with a sunburst of radiant major chords. What Dryden's verses did *not* say was that music can make a point more directly than words.

The most important form of music for combined instruments was the baroque suite. Derived from the court sonata, it was introduced by dancing masters of the early seventeenth-century French court.[272] It consisted of several movements, each in the style of an aristocratic dance. Sarabande and gavotte followed one another in stately sequence. Also included in the suite was the minuet. Performed by one couple at a time, it was the favourite aristocratic dance of the late seventeenth and early eighteenth centuries. One exception was the gigue – a fast country dance often employed to bring proceedings to a rousing conclusion. It was usually in 6/8 time, which was considered a rustic metre suitable for peasants or hunters.[273] It enabled a composer to court applause by letting his hair down – almost literally, in the era of curled and powdered wigs. Most of this musical language was that of elites, and its influence is heard more widely than in the suite. At the opposite end of the musical spectrum was J. S. Bach's austerely Protestant *St Matthew Passion*. Yet in most of its arias we hear the solemn motion of slow, courtly dances such as the allemande and the sarabande. One of the founding moments of Christianity, the inauguration by Christ of the Eucharist (the eating of the bread and the drinking of the wine), is set to the stately rhythm of the minuet.[274]

Yet by the mid-eighteenth century the growth of music publishing and the opening of public concert halls were widening the performing and listening public. The suite was consequently replaced by less aristocratic musical forms – the classical sonata, symphony and string quartet. After the 1750s composing suites rapidly became an archaic exercise and only the minuet survived.[275] Haydn and Mozart retained it in their symphonies but took such liberties with its rhythm that its character as a courtly dance was destroyed. Anyone attempting to dance to it would have needed to be an acrobat rather than an aristocrat.

The clearest indication of the domination of music by royal courts and aristocracies in the 1650–1750 period was the rise of opera. It was ideally suited to absolute monarchs and their elites. It enjoyed the prestige of descent from classical Greek tragedy, the chorus of which had expressed itself in some form of singing or chanting.[276] As a lavishly spectacular multimedia entertainment it was an effective demonstration of the wealth, power and magnificence of its patrons. Its stylized staging mirrored the hierarchical social order. Its plot usually transmitted a direct political message, with titles and themes reflecting contemporary political events – as we should say, it responded to the news agenda.[277]

In seventeenth-century Italy, where opera began, it was (and still is) part of popular culture. It was thoroughly Shakespearian in its mixture of tragedy and comedy. In Venice, opera had enough popular support to sustain seven opera houses. In Italy and Germany, commoners were also likely to be admitted to the opera houses attached to royal and ducal courts. Their rulers were often minor princes whose armies were too small to sustain an independent voice in European politics. Instead they competed culturally.[278] Building an opera house gave them a space primarily dedicated to projecting their majesty, as the gilded glory of the centrally placed royal or ducal box proclaimed. An opera house also reinforced the social hierarchy by replicating the protocols of rank and etiquette prevalent at court. The priority was not to see the stage but to be seen by the rest of the audience. These considerations meant that the scale of building had to be colossal. Where the available courtiers and aristocrats were insufficient to fill the seats, the public had to be admitted and the cost shared with a wider slice of the population.[279] Few German or Italian opera houses were aristocratic preserves. Elsewhere it was different. A great city's opera house was usually attached to the royal court and was mainly reserved for elites.[280]

In France, from the 1660s, Lully established for Louis XIV a distinctively French operatic form which included dance and ballet and was specifically designed as a representational display of royal and aristocratic grandeur. This was *tragédie lyrique*. It was much like *opera seria*, its Italian opposite number, which denoted serious opera addressing a tragic or heroic theme. Both were grand, formal, classical, elitist and hierarchical – and ideally suited to projecting the virtues of the existing social and political order and celebrating the triumph of absolute power and harmony over rebellion and discord.[281] By the early eighteenth century most royal courts had their own opera houses, usually with professional musicians permanently attached to them. Librettists (text writers) like Zeno and Metastasio imposed on operatic themes and procedures the aristocratic restraint, formality and solemnity that had already shifted painting and literature on to a higher social plane. Opera was refined and cleansed of plebeian impurities. Their texts for composers to set to music delivered high moral content – usually the admirable deeds of classical gods and heroes, supposedly reflected in the lives of early-modern princes. There was no hint of humour. Omitted from the new operatic agenda were also the farce, rape, incest, torture and murder which were all the rage in Italy – the sort of thing lower-class audiences did not get enough of at home.[282]

A good example of the direction of modern scholarship is our new appreciation of Metastasio. Until interdisciplinary studies had dissolved the boundaries between areas of specialization, he was ignored.[283] His 200 operatic texts were too literary to interest musicologists and too inseparable from their musical setting to attract historians. For two centuries he has been regarded as responsible for the formal conventions and boring pomposity from which Mozart rescued the operatic public. By the time of his death he represented an artificial aristocratic court culture which had passed out of fashion. But in the context of the aristocracy's post-1650 recovery he looks more interesting.

According to the *opera seria* convention which Metastasio established, the plot was invariably some variation on the clash between private passion and the aristocratic code of public duty and honour (as in Corneille's tragedies). The hero was usually played by a castrated male singer, whose voice combined the sweetness and agility of a woman's larynx with the power and clarity of a man's. No-one in the early eighteenth century thought it odd that a great historical figure like Julius Caesar should be played on stage by a eunuch.[284] He would stand centre-stage in a Roman toga, explain his dilemma in an aria displaying glittering vocal gymnastics and then march off majestically. *Castrati* were cult figures, prized for the unearthly timbre of the male soprano sound and paid telephone-number fees. One of them, Farinelli, was the first international musical celebrity. He sang in Madrid in 1737 and Philip V offered him the equivalent of 50,000 francs a year to stay. He did so for 25 years and trilled the same four songs each night to the king.

Yet Metastasio bestrode the culture of the *ancien régime* like a colossus, and any attempt to recapture that lost world must take account of him. As Imperial Court Poet to Habsburg rulers Charles VI, Maria Theresa and Joseph II, he wrote hundreds of pieces for their court. He was so famous as an opera librettist that his texts attracted over 400 composers (one was set 70 times) and were heard from Lisbon to St Petersburg. His Viennese works were written to celebrate dynastic birthdays, name days, weddings and coronations, or as part of the court observance of Holy Week. The texts projected the Habsburg image in the context of the court and church ceremonial with which they surrounded themselves. Key themes were power, order and divine favour bestowed on the dynasty for its piety. Far from being empty display, this reflected its political, social and economic agenda. Only grants of favour and privilege could secure the support of noble and clerical elites in the multi-ethnic scatter of Habsburg territories. Privilege required an ordered hierarchy headed by the monarch, and music underlined the point with pageantry and ceremonial.[285] Metastasio's plots ransacked classical history and mythology for high-profile opportunities to display the aristocratic ethos of the period. Characters were required to be moral and heroic in the face of danger and temptation. Happy endings were the natural consequence of the triumph of right and reason over adversity.[286] Metastasio's texts were always in Italian, thus distancing his aristocratic, classically educated audience from its more ignorant social inferiors.[287]

The tradition in most courts was that royalty should take leading parts. Louis XIV starred in the 1650s in masques and *ballets de cour* (court ballets). In these he took, among other glittering roles, that of Apollo and the rising sun, resplendent in a golden wig. But historians have failed to stress his really significant interest, which was to end the confusing lack of rules governing a key aristocratic activity. Ballet had originated in the sixteenth century as a courtly entertainment. By the seventeenth, dancing was a necessary accomplishment of every gentleman and a crucial part of the *esprit de corps* of the court nobility. In 1661 Louis took an important step in the cultural consolidation of the aristocracy when he founded the Academy of Dancing, subsequently attached to the Academy of Music and charged with codifying the approved steps and movements. His founding charter explained the motivation, which smacks more of the modern gym than of a classical art form:

> The art of dance has ever been acknowledged to be one of the most suitable and necessary arts for physical development and for affording the primary and most natural preparation for all bodily exercises, and among others, those concerning the use of weapons; and consequently it is one of the most valuable and most useful arts for nobles and others who have the honour to enter our presence not only in time of war in our armies, but even in time of peace in our ballets.[288]

This was all part of the process by which royal courts defined and cultivated what the French called the *honnête homme*, the ideal gentleman and courtier. He was gallant, strong, brave and honourable, but also well-read, graceful, polite, witty and entertaining – as deadly with the killer one-liner at a dinner table as with the rapier in a duel.[289]

A century later, royalty and aristocracy were still participating. When in 1751 Metastasio wrote *Il Rè Pastore* for the theatre in the palace of Schönbrunn, five of Maria Theresa's children were prominently cast. The future Emperor Joseph II, aged fourteen, played Alexander the Great. The content of these dramas had to glorify monarchy, inspire the performers with admirable ethical and diplomatic principles, announce dynastic superiority and remain scrupulously decorous. No villain could be portrayed, since this would discredit the royal impersonator. As it was shameful for child-actors to display their legs, characters had to be taken from countries and periods offering the possibility of ankle-length robes.[290]

The virtues and achievements of ruling dynasties were still centre-stage and rarely did these entertainments stray off-message. But the propagandist agenda of court masques and operas must not be exaggerated. Though any self-styled gentleman could enter Versailles as long as he was wearing a sword, concerts and the sort of ceremonial that was accompanied by music were the preserve of a real elite. The message was largely preached to the converted.[291] But, away from court, music throughout this period underpinned the same elite ideology. In the opera houses of mid-eighteenth-century Paris it remained much the same as under Louis XIV and Lully. It asserted the same Bourbon myths of *gloire* and splendour, as well as the now rather faded triumph of order over chaos. Princes were still represented on stage in the image of gods. Music also underscored the gulf between nobles and lower orders. Aristocratic characters sang stately and florid airs and, in triumphant mode, were accompanied by drums and trumpets. In contrast, when common persons came on stage they were depicted by simple plebeian dance or street tunes.[292] The orchestral texture was thinned down, fewer instruments were deployed and half the players escaped temporarily to the bar.

By 1750 challenge was imminent in France. In 1752 Italian *opera buffa* (comic opera) arrived in Paris, with subversive undertones. Originating in an area where royal and princely courts were thinner on the ground, its themes were familiar, proletarian and contemporary instead of remote, lordly and historical. Its answer to the stately measures of Rameau was hummable tunes and catchy rhythms. Pergolesi's *La serva padrona* (*The Maid as Mistress*) took Paris by storm. The plot concerns a bachelor who democratically accepts his maidservant as his wife, thus overturning social hierarchies. Rousseau was currently composing his *Discourse on the Origins of Inequality* and spotted the opera's relevance. He rushed into print to champion the Italian invasion. Rameau defended his own brand of traditional French opera – the pompously aristocratic *tragédie lyrique*, the French counterpart of Italian *opera seria*. Rousseau thereupon attacked Rameau as well. To show how effective a simple folksy style of music could be, he wrote his own comic opera, *Le Devin du Village* (*The Village Soothsayer*). It was performed before the king at Fontainebleau in 1752. To all appearances an exposé of aristocratic decadence, it proclaimed the victory of spontaneous peasant hearts over aristocratic guile and sophistication. In spite of sending up everything the court stood for, it was a huge success. Louis XV was alleged to have gone around for days singing its arias 'with the worst voice in his kingdom'.[293] More significantly, it celebrated innocent rural simplicity and the beginning of the end of aristocratic values.

Rousseau describes in his *Confessions* the ferocity of this battle of the muses. Allowing for the writer's aversion to understatement, at stake was not a musical style but a clash of value systems – one ceremonial and royal and the other informal and egalitarian.[294] Apparently it divided Paris into two camps and aroused more passion than the concurrent dispute between the Paris *parlement* and the Crown. It started with two parties in the Paris Opéra – the Italian party which sat near the Queen's box, and the French near the King's. It ended with Rousseau needing an armed guard when he attended the theatre. At that point Rousseau greatly complicated things by writing a pamphlet attacking the French language as inappropriate for opera. This was an unexpected development, since he had written his own opera in French. Rousseau had raised two contentious issues. The first was the liberty of outsiders to challenge the musical monopoly of an elitist royal court and those it licensed. The second was his insult to the national pride of the French in their culture. Those who had supported him when he attacked French opera for being elitist opposed him when he attacked it for being French.[295] The whole explosive row is proof of how heavily music, like all the arts, was politicized in this period. It is also incontestable evidence of the passionate response which the arts could inspire. Monarchs and elites who prioritized them so highly knew what they were about.

Thus, like the Grand Manner in painting, in the 1750s courtly theatre and the aristocratic ethic enacted in it started to lose their dominance.[296] After holding the stage since the seventeenth century, the operas that Lully had composed for Louis XIV were now performed to a diminishing audience. Grimm, a literary correspondent resident in Paris, caught the note of stultifying boredom:

> For two and a half hours I was wearied by a collection of minuets, gavottes, rigaudons, tambourins and contredanses, interspersed with some scenes of plainsong that seemed to come straight from the evening service. I noted that in France this was called Opera.[297]

As a consequence of the plummeting popularity of these works, the bourgeoisie were permitted for the first time to buy tickets for court theatres. In Munich its members felt confident enough to hiss the performers, ignore their prince's appeal for silence and inform a remonstrating official that they would take orders from no one as they had paid for their seats.[298] In the growing number of public theatres it became even harder to exercise control. Of 135 annual subscribers to the best (first-level) boxes at the Paris Opéra in the 1750s, all except seven were aristocrats. The second and third levels were dominated by lesser nobility and rich commoners. Though not riotous, even 'the quality' was not especially attentive. Their boxes were equipped with curtains to enable the occupants to eat or play cards without being distracted by proceedings on the stage. But the real threat came from the lower orders at stage level. Standing without seats was a crowd around a thousand strong – a cross-section of the rest of French society, from dandies aspiring to be members of the elite to drunken servants. They signalled a return of the 'groundlings' of Shakespeare's period but their behaviour was far worse. Their shouting and singing frequently drowned the performance on stage and their pets ran amok, defecating copiously while armed guards strove to restore order.[299]

As opera began to move from the court to private enterprise, the subject matter changed accordingly. In Vienna from the 1750s Gluck's operas abandoned the narrowly aristocratic ethical code of *opera seria* for psychological music drama that was universal in theme. Gluck also replaced vocal fireworks with simple, unadorned melodies. Metastasio regarded him as a mad barbarian. In 1764, Saxony's Frederick Augustus III deleted the court's *opera seria* company from the royal expenditure list, installed an Italian comic opera troupe in its place and invited the public to the Zwinger palace to hear it. His baroque grandfather, Augustus II, must have been spinning in his grave.

So musical culture extended its reach. With the rise of the classical style from the 1740s, music moved closer to the masses. Punctuating soft passages with an unexpectedly loud *forte* maintained even unsophisticated interest. Simple melodies, easily identified, became the key to musical structure. Composers began to incorporate folk elements, which their early eighteenth-century predecessors would have dismissed as pandering to plebeians. Before the end of the century, Mozart, a court composer, wrote *Die Zauberflöte* ( *The Magic Flute*) for the public Theater an der Wien. The opera's sublime medley of operatic aria, folk song, slap-stick and pantomime accurately identifies the wide cross-section of society at which it was aimed.[300] The wheel had come full circle and audiences again began to look like the social miscellany at Shakespeare's Globe two centuries before.

The *Allgemeine Musikalische Zeitung*, greatest of all musical periodicals, reviewed the eighteenth century at its close in 1800. It claimed that until around the 1750s serious music in Germany had been confined to the topmost ranks of society, but that by the century's end, public concerts and private music-making ensured that aristocrats and connoisseurs were losing their monopoly and music had become an integral part of the expanding culture of the middle classes.[301] The growth of a bourgeois audience for music thus seems to have been a development of the later eighteenth and early nineteenth centuries – not of the later seventeenth and early eighteenth.

# Chapter 5: The End of an Age: the Mid-eighteenth Century

## The Public Sphere

During the 1650–1750 period Europe remained a society dominated by courtly and aristocratic cultures. Admittedly, there were bourgeois exceptions.[1] The urban centres of the Dutch Republic and the 51 Free Imperial Cities of the Holy Roman Empire, independent of princely rule, represented rare alternatives to elite patronage.[2] Civic officials enveloped themselves in music and pageantry, beadles and insignia, pomposity and ceremonial. Handel began his musical career as a player in the orchestra of Hamburg's public opera house. Leipzig is an interesting case. Its city council employed J. S. Bach for the last 27 years of his life and, though part of the Electorate of Saxony, it controlled its own cultural affairs. Yet there, as almost everywhere, the musical lead was given not by burghers but by nobles.[3] And most of these cities had to recognize that their best days were behind them. Cultural leadership and innovation had moved to the princely and aristocratic courts.[4]

Yet it has been argued that during the 1650–1750 period the few bourgeois exceptions were becoming the rule as the rise of a 'public sphere' broke the cultural stranglehold of the court and aristocracy.[5] It began in a humble way. Though seventeenth-century popular culture (like late medieval culture) was still intensely visual, the uneducated 95 per cent or more were not entirely strangers to books. Cheaply produced 'chapbooks' catered for a mass market of the half-literate and even the totally illiterate by combining image with print. They peddled astrology, fairy tales and old legends, as well as advice on household and health matters. But their value in broadcasting useful information was limited. In a world of simple people, where novelty aroused hostility and incomprehension, the content never changed. A book on health care, *L'Escole de Salerne*, was first published in 1474. It went, without update, through nearly 300 editions by 1846.[6]

Only during the eighteenth century did the printed word, as opposed to printed image, cease to be the preserve of a small elite. As the means of access to knowledge and advancement, it became accepted as a desirable focal point for all. But at what point in the eighteenth century did this development occur? Some European governments, especially the French, began seriously to promote education. In 1698 the Christian Brothers persuaded Louis XIV to decree that all children from the age of 7 to 14 should enrol in a Catholic school – an initiative made even more effective by their innovatory instruction of 30–40 pupils simultaneously, rather than of each individually.[7] Early-modern literacy levels were rising. Though we have only random snapshots rather than systematic figures, it seems clear that by the end of the eighteenth century literacy exceeded 50 per cent in many parts of western and northern Europe.

But a century before, things were rather different. In France around 1690 only 27 per cent of men and 14 per cent of women could sign their names to a marriage contract (that being no proof that they had fully mastered either reading or writing).[8] Between the 1680s and the 1780s French literacy rates rose from 29 to 47 per cent for men and from 14 to 27 per cent for women. A less progressive picture emerges if regional differences are considered. Between 1786 and 1790 in northern France (the cultural heart of the country), 71 per cent of men and 44 per cent of women could write their names. This was a higher percentage than in contemporary England, Scotland and the Austrian Netherlands (60–65 per cent for men and 37–42 for women). But in southern France during the same period only 27 per cent of men and 12 per cent of women could sign – similar to the national male average a century before.[9] Figures for German-speaking Europe suggest a slow increase from 10 per cent of the adult population in 1700 to 15 per cent in 1770, with a rapid acceleration to 25 per cent by 1800. In East Prussia the figures are even more telling. Only 10 per cent of male adult peasants could sign their names in 1750, a figure which had shot up to 40 per cent by 1800.[10] Excepting men in northern France, therefore, literacy before the mid-eighteenth century should not be exaggerated.

Matching these developments came an unprecedented expansion of print culture, as a torrent of books, periodicals, pamphlets and newspapers gushed from the presses to meet the needs of the newly literate. In France, the number of titles doubled between 1750 and 1789.[11] This correlates with the expansion of literacy elsewhere after the middle of the century.

The middle of the eighteenth century was also the tipping point for music printing. Not until then did some approximation of a mass market begin to develop, whereas previously music had circulated in manuscript copies. The printing press gave Haydn's career a major boost and he was probably the first great musician so to benefit; yet as late as 1768 his works were advertised for sale in manuscript only. By then Europe was changing fast, with the growth of literacy, expansion of towns and bourgeois values, commercialization of leisure and rise of consumerism, as well as faster communications and a proliferation of choral societies – all of these now created a new cultural space, which musical entrepreneurs instantly moved to occupy.[12]

Equally significant was the medium in which print culture was communicated – for most of the period predominantly Latin. In much of Europe this was the language of the law, the church and intellectual life and it confined print largely to the highly educated.[13] In the France of 1650 even pornography was published in Latin (though by 1700 an incredible 90 per cent of titles were in French). In the German-speaking world Latin titles fell from 67 per cent in 1650 to 38 per cent by 1700, 28 per cent by 1740, and 4 per cent by 1800. This correlates well with the accelerating literacy trajectory.[14] To balance the picture, only in 1784 did German replace Latin as the language of administration for Hungary and the eastern parts of the Habsburg empire.[15]

The result of all these developments was another new feature in the political and cultural landscape. This was public opinion, a force which monarchs had increasingly to recognize, as target of their own propaganda and also as potential challenger to it.[16] The exception is Russia, as usual, where little approximating to an opinion anywhere outside government circles can be detected before the nineteenth century. In a highly influential pioneering work, Habermas has suggested that a 'public sphere' was growing in this period. It was free of the control which monarchs, clergy and nobility exercised through their patronage and was colonized by the bourgeoisie (defined not as the Marxist capitalist class but as all those between landed elite and rural peasantry – merchants, professionals and intellectuals).[17] This larger public could not afford to patronize culture as individuals but they could do so collectively. In other words, culture became commercialized and available to the public like everything else on the market. For musicians, writers and artists this offered release from subservience to culturally dominant elites.[18]

It has been argued that during the eighteenth century the public sphere escaped and finally eclipsed the court and its aristocratic and ecclesiastical allies. It was a forum between the private world of the family and the official world of the state, where individuals could meet to exchange ideas and information. It was a meeting of minds, either spiritually in print or physically in clubs and coffee houses. It embraced the growing print culture of newspapers and novels, masonic lodges, subscription concerts, publicly funded museums and art galleries. This was the world of the salons and art market of Paris, the clubs and reading societies of Germany, the provincial academies and literary societies of France and England, the public concerts and theatres of London, Berlin, Paris and Frankfurt, and the coffee houses of Venice, London and Vienna.[19]

Coffee houses were an innovation of this period. The first opened in Venice in 1647, the first in England in Oxford in the 1650s, and the Café Procope in Paris in 1660. By 1739, London had 551. Their success seems based on two attractions: they provided newspapers and pamphlets and were centres of conversation and commerce, where goods, ideas and information were exchanged. Because they effectively usurped the prerogative of the monarch by debating politics and religion, they were initially disliked by royal governments. In 1675, Charles II issued a proclamation closing down all London's coffee houses. They were already so popular that he was forced to withdraw it a few days later.[20] Coffee houses were typical of the public sphere in recognizing 'no distinction of persons'. They replaced hierarchy with meritocracy. As they were open to all who could pay, dukes and gentlemen mingled with their social inferiors on equal terms. It is surely significant that these egalitarian institutions emerged precisely when hierarchical space was being mapped out and regulated as never before. As courtly and aristocratic etiquette solidified it became important to demarcate areas of escape.

To Habermas and his followers the growth of a public sphere implied a critical bourgeois culture. Consumerism was making the 'middling orders' the cultural driving force of the eighteenth century, initially in England and then more gradually throughout Europe.[21] But several aspects of this are questionable. First, the concept of consumerism is a very broad brush, which conveniently blurs and underplays political, religious and social divisions.[22] Second, the public sphere was not an agenda. It was a space in which many shades of opinion could be expressed.[23] Third, the middle classes might now have their own media outlets, but they were not necessarily hostile to the elites who had previously monopolized them or to the government itself. Much of the culture of the 'middling orders' was subject to a trickle-down effect from elite culture.[24] The years after 1730 saw a new culture of moralizing sentiment, improving as well as entertaining, which has been identified as bourgeois. This is misleading if it implies a bourgeois reaction against courtly, aristocratic culture, since the nobility sponsored it as well. It can be more accurately identified as a shift in sensibility common to both. Some of the most artistically progressive work, with apparently bourgeois subject matter, was patronized by the Crown and court aristocracy. Among purchasers of the paintings of Chardin, with their genre and still-life scenes of humble kitchen tasks, serving maids, fruit and vegetables, were ambassadors like the Prince of Liechtenstein and Louis XV himself.[25]

By the same token, it now seems naive of historians to have supposed that a newly literate bourgeoisie wanted to read about itself, rather than the rich and famous. As we have seen, novels like Fielding's *Tom Jones* (1749) have been hailed as a key stage in the rise of bourgeois mentality. But even when his heroes were ostensibly plebeian they invariably turned out to be gentlemen, muddled or mislaid at birth. And there is little indication that, once the middle classes had the purchasing power, they sponsored anything very different from elites (who bought novels too). The values and content of their favoured painters, writers and musicians replicated aristocratic taste – unsurprisingly, since the nobility were everywhere the social elite and therefore automatic role models. There was evidently an element of social escapism. The emphasis on upper-class leisure and fashion was an irresistible contrast to humdrum middle-class routine.[26] Bourgeois reading matter evidently approximated, in its obsession with social elites, to *Hello!* magazine.

Fourth, there is no reason why the new public sphere should have been accessed exclusively by bourgeois intruders. Its space was extensively colonized by existing politicians and provided a new platform for old debates.[27] With the public sphere's emergence in the seventeenth century, the anxiety of monarchical governments to promote their views had been a great impetus to the rise of newspapers. The National Library at Paris has copies of over half a million printed papers issued by the state between 1598 and 1643. In 1631, Cardinal Richelieu had supported the foundation of the *Gazette de France*, a weekly newspaper which gave the government a platform as well as supplying factual information. The coverage of what we should call political news was, however, next to nil.

The crisis of the mid-seventeenth century changed all that. The English Civil War spawned nearly 2,000 pamphlets in 1642 alone, an average of almost six publications a day. Similarly in France, the Fronde from 1649 to 1652 detonated one of the first explosions of printed revolutionary propaganda, with over 4,000 attacks against Cardinal Mazarin. It was clear that a line had been crossed. Contemporaries were alarmed that rebel leaders had invited the masses to participate in the mysteries of high politics. 'The people entered into the holy of holies,' Cardinal de Retz commented smugly on the Fronde.[28] But it was a false dawn. As the dust of the mid-seventeenth-century crisis settled and the agents of order re-established control, consumption of newsprint plummeted. In France the total output of pamphlets from 1661 to 1715 was about 1,500 titles – fewer than the number of *mazarinades* that appeared in 1649 alone.[29] The public sphere was again dominated, if not monopolized, by elites. Eighteenth-century nobles and monarchs colonized it as eagerly as their competitors. To Louis XIV, books were prestigious works of art and their contents were secondary. By contrast, his successor Louis XV was trained to compose a text for printing. Many of his nobles owned presses and became expert in preferred typographies. They also commissioned books and illustrations and promoted their success competitively. In many ways the public sphere was merely another arena for elite activity.[30]

Much of the case for the growth of the eighteenth-century public sphere hinges on Britain, allegedly its trailblazer and first embodiment.[31] Claims for Britain's precocious public sphere are an update of a long-established historical orthodoxy – that maritime Protestant states like the Dutch Republic and Britain, where monarchy had been ousted or allegedly neutered, were progressive, bourgeois and on the side of the future, while 'absolutist' Catholic states like Spain and Austria remained aristocratic, conservative and stagnant.[32]

There is lively debate about how far the British press was ahead of the French in the reach and volume of its newsprint. Some authorities continue to insist that in its freedom from government intervention and high circulation and readership the British press had far more impact than the French.[33] Britain was certainly foremost in the field with the first national daily newspaper, *The Daily Courant*, which appeared in London in 1702. By 1724 there were three in London and by 1750 twelve, either daily, bi-weekly or tri-weekly. By 1753 there were 32 provincial newspapers, though a further 30 had folded – an indication of their precarious commercial basis.[34] It can, however, be argued that too much has been made of adverse conditions in France, from the severity of its political restrictions to its lack of coffee houses (in fact, Paris had 380 by 1723[35]). Britain had comparable disadvantages, while the vigour of the French press before 1789 has arguably been underrated.[36] Before the turnpike revolution of the mid-eighteenth century, Britain's poor communication system meant that news was out of date before it was published. And in the first half of the eighteenth century its government, in common with others, drastically curtailed domestic news coverage. Only after 1750 did governments, especially the British and French, begin to abandon their previous insistence that the mysteries of high policy and affairs of state should be decorously screened from public view. It was precisely in that period that the public sphere took off.[37]

Furthermore, before the 1750s British newspapers, in places other than large towns and cities, tended to be distributed through elite channels. Far from increasing the political independence of social inferiors, the early eighteenth-century press probably increased their reliance on local notables for news of national events. Some of the leading papers sponsored by political parties mainly targeted gentry and clergymen, in the expectation that they would relay news at local level. The exclusiveness of politics was to an extent retained. Newsprint may have expanded, but before 1750 the British public sphere as a forum for independent opinion was not necessarily enhanced.[38]

Periodical and newspaper figures for France show a similar profile. It had fewer than a dozen titles in 1715 and still only 20 in 1750. But by 1785 there were 82. From the 1750s publications oriented to current affairs proliferated. There were five political newspapers in 1750, 12 in 1770 and 19 in 1785. In addition there were the *affiches* – provincial advertiser-cum-newssheets. Originating in 1751, there were 16 in 1770 and 44 in 1789. They were one of the big newspaper successes of the period after 1750 but continued to devote many column inches to false teeth and horse manure.[39]

One of the features of the period was the rise of public concerts, theatres and opera houses. They represented the widening of access to the arts in the eighteenth century as culture became a commodity – an item or event to be bought by the wider public as opposed to patronized by elites. This is usually hailed as evidence of an expanding public sphere and the bursting of elite monopolies.[40] The first public opera house opened in Hamburg in 1678 and Copenhagen had a public theatre by 1747, while by the early eighteenth century London had many. It was this that attracted Handel to leave Hanover and settle in the city. With the benefit of hindsight, his commercial success clearly pointed to a future in which control of culture would slip from crown, aristocracy and church and become subject to the free market of public supply and demand.[41] The public sphere in Britain is usually linked to the predominance of commercial wealth in the City of London, to the rise of bourgeois culture and to the uniqueness of Britain generally.

The linking of these broad cultural developments with the familiar narrative of the rise of the bourgeoisie has long been accepted.[42] It is alleged that from early in the eighteenth century the middle classes collectively patronized the performing arts and thus broke the cultural monopoly of royal courts, prelates and nobilities. This neatly corresponds with, for example, Handel's abandonment of Italian opera composed for aristocratic patrons and his subsequent dedication to oratorios in English for a presumably more bourgeois crowd. The scenario has long gone unchallenged, since most historians know little about the history of music.

Fortunately a few of them do. Tim Blanning lethally skewers the myth of an eighteenth-century bourgeoisie calling the cultural shots, especially in relation to the rise of public concerts. The first public concerts took place in seventeenth-century England and were dominated by nobility and gentry, as were those which followed in France from 1725 and the Habsburg empire after 1745. The words and music performed were submissively dedicated to the glory of the ruling dynasty and the elite patrons who sponsored these entertainments: eighteenth-century concert life was neither created nor sustained by mainly bourgeois audiences. Whether the venue was a public concert hall or a private palace, the audience was equally aristocratic and musicians remained vulnerable to the whims of elites.[43] Handel's British public, both before and after his conversion to oratorio, turns out to have been overwhelmingly 'people of quality'. His oratorios had the sponsorship of neither church nor civic authorities. Provincial concerts were underwritten by gentry patrons and were timed to coincide with quarter sessions, race meetings and assorted events that brought the landed classes to town.[44] Furthermore, this elite audience profile continued longer than in the other arts and well beyond the end of the 1650–1750 period – at least into the 1780s. The success of Haydn, Mozart and the young Beethoven owed far more to Viennese aristocrats like Thun, Galitzin and Lichnowsky than to a middle-class public. Whether Mozart was performing in palaces or public rooms, nobles made up the bulk of his audience. Though it has become fashionable to stress his contempt for the *status quo*, for a rebel he displayed indecent eagerness to send his father a complete list of 176 prestigious sponsors for his benefit concerts in Vienna. It reads like a roll call of the higher nobility.[45]

It is true that by the mid-eighteenth century an artisan earning around £50 a year could get into most London theatres after the second act for the price of two quarts of ale.[46] But entry into the pit offered no control over what was on the stage. In some ways London's theatres can be viewed as more royal sphere than public sphere. Courtly, ecclesiastical and public performance did not operate separately. Instrumentalists in London theatres were also employed as Royal Musicians under the Master of the King's Music.[47] More importantly, whereas in Paris the stage was regulated by the *parlement*, in London it was controlled not by Parliament but by the king's prerogative powers. The right to perform was restricted to those to whom the crown granted patents or licences, while the content of performance was subject to the approval of the Master of the Revels. In 1737 he was replaced by the Lord Chamberlain after Prime Minister Walpole read to a shocked House of Commons insulting stage references to George II's piles and farting.[48]

The Master of the Revels and the Lord Chamberlain were both officials of the royal court. Monarchs and their elites in most states were intolerant of attempts to challenge their own cultural norms. Spiritual, moral, religious and aesthetic values were upheld to some extent by selective sponsorship, the weight of influential opinion and the 'laws' of good taste. Where those failed, the criminal code was deployed without hesitation. All early-modern European states, Protestant as well as Catholic, republics as well as monarchies, were anxious and willing to purge unacceptable views.[49] The rise of natural philosophy made no difference in this respect. In politics as well as religion, in England as well as on the Continent, there was a feeling that reason would lead all right-thinking people to the same truth. Ideological dissent, parties and factions were therefore disreputable. Obsessive maintenance of homogeneous opinion seems to have been broadly successful till after the 1750s, when the walls were gradually breached. The system of licensing books before publication broke down and governments had to rely on prosecuting them afterwards, as the British government had done since 1695. By the 1770s forbidden material appeared in France faster than Louis XVI's agents could raid the Paris bookshops.[50]

Apart from the disciplinary function, royal and aristocratic support for theatres was crucial throughout Europe. In the German states, musical patronage came mainly from the princely courts. Venice's profusion of public opera houses were all owned by the nobility, who appointed a director to run them or leased them to an independent impresario or group of businessmen.[51] In 1719 the Royal Academy of Music was founded in London to stage Italian opera at the King's Theatre, Haymarket. Essential to its initial success was the financial backing of a prestigious group of nobility and gentry led by the Prince of Wales. They subscribed what was then the enormous sum of £100 each, while George I gave £1,000 per annum.[52] The nascent public sphere was therefore far from independent. It is more accurate to view it as an adjunct of the elite from which it sprang. Public concerts were not a bourgeois creation but part of an aristocratic culture, which the middle classes merely emulated and expanded.[53]

British cultural novelties are sometimes mistaken for British norms. London's theatres always lived on the edge of financial crisis. At the height of the craze for aristocratic *opera seria* several went bankrupt and in the 1740s it fell from favour. It is true that Handel was the first great composer to escape from dependence on royal, aristocratic and ecclesiastical patronage. He pulled off this feat by making substantial profits in the free marketplace of public music-making. But it is less stressed that in this period he remained the only one who did so and that he lost almost as much money as he made.[54] Nor has it been sufficiently emphasized that, if some of his projects were independent of aristocratic support, many others were not.[55]

Handel's publisher was a crafty entrepreneur called Walsh. He is credited with publishing music on a scale previously unknown in England, assisted by slick sales promotions and free copies. But another of his innovations was the subscription lists printed in most of the major scores he published. These listed the nobility and gentry who had sponsored the publication. A similar point can be made about the provision of public concert halls. There were few before the later eighteenth century. Composers who wished to introduce their own music had to find a church, royal palace or aristocratic salon willing to host their audience.[56] J. S. Bach relied on a wide range of patrons.[57] Like most baroque composers, he started his career in the *Kapelle* (chapel) of a prince, the Duke of Saxe-Weimar. He then became *Kapellmeister* to the Prince of Anhalt-Cöthen but never obtained a major court appointment. For the last 27 years of his life he was Kantor (musical director) at St Thomas's church, Leipzig, with additional responsibility for other churches in the city. He was lucky. Few city authorities were rich or powerful enough to employ a major artist like Bach for over a quarter of a century.[58] In this post he was able to buck the trend towards elite exclusivity by producing sublimely spiritual music with its tap root in Lutheran popular culture.[59]

Finally, it is claimed by historians of the public sphere that London's public opera houses were exceptional in northern Europe. But France had them as well – London simply had more. The greatest French composer of the period was Rameau, who in his early years benefited from the support of several patrons, namely the financier La Poupelinière and assorted bishops who employed him as organist in their cathedrals. But he had no court appointment. He managed to have his first opera (*Hippolyte et Aricie*) performed in 1733 at the Paris Opéra, a public theatre which acclaimed the quality of this and later works. Only at the age of 62 did he secure a court appointment and become chamber music composer to Louis XV, whose favour ensured that his later works were premièred at court theatres. So, though royal, aristocratic and ecclesiastical patronage was predominant, there were already alternatives on the Continent as well as England, especially in the great metropolitan areas. The similarities of the musical scene in England, France and Germany are arguably more prominent than the contrasts. As we have seen, Handel and even Mozart were more dependent on royal and aristocratic support than historians usually acknowledge and until the 1750s elite sponsorship was essential for most musicians. The truth is that outside London and Paris the musical public sphere in the mid-eighteenth century was still in its infancy.[60]

Much the same is true of literature. Throughout most of the period its public was too small to enable writers to make a living with their pens. They therefore needed nobles, courtiers or monarchs as patrons to subsidize them or they had to have private means – which meant they had to be nobles or courtiers themselves. None of the most successful French novelists and playwrights of the early eighteenth century, Prévost, Lesage and Marivaux, was able to make a living from his works. In England, Alexander Pope did so, but he was the only one. 'I take myself to be the only scribbler of my time, of any degree of distinction, who never received any places from the establishment, any pension from a court, or any presents from a ministry.'[61] But he scarcely rose to financial independence on the back of his bourgeois readers. Pope's translation of Homer's *Iliad* sold for six guineas in the 1720s – a price then far beyond an average member of the bourgeoisie (multiply by about 100 for modern values). A breakdown of any subscription list establishes how far this end of the publishing trade remained dominated by social and economic elites. Pope was only one step down from a writer patronized by an individual aristocrat.[62]

Even if it is conceded that eighteenth-century Britain was to some extent a pioneer of the expanding 'public sphere' with its allegedly bourgeois accent, most of the relevant developments lay outside the 1650–1750 period. Within it, even British culture remained stubbornly upper-class. A coherent and powerful elite of noblemen, MPs, upper clergy and well-born academics dominated the period's culture as philosophical, scientific, literary and architectural practitioners. The high-profile Kit-Cat Club united literary and political top people and was dominated by titled and landed names. The subscription list of the *Tatler*, a periodical published between 1709 and 1711, boasted 166 aristocrats out of a total of 752 and many of the rest were genteel.[63] The first commercial targeting of a mass readership occurred in the 1740s, when Wesley and his followers promoted Methodism by printing unprecedented numbers of booklets and pamphlets on their own press. Such enormous print-runs did not recur for half a century.[64] In the 1750s circulating libraries began to charge a fee of a few pennies to loan a book and achieved spectacular success in expanding the reading public. Before these two breakthroughs, London alone could sustain a market for literary works aimed at the bourgeoisie.[65]

Even more persuasively, a recent work of superlative scholarship and interpretation has rewritten the history of reading in Britain.[66] Though there are no comparable authorities for the rest of Europe, it may be that there also our knowledge has suffered from the mindless repetition of stale clichés. What we now know for certain is that the traditional narrative of a steady rise in readership in eighteenth-century Britain does not fit well with what the archives say. In fact there was a sudden 'explosion of reading' towards the end of the eighteenth century.[67] In the first three-quarters of the century, book production in England showed only modest growth. If anything, it declined. This was because everything else (income per head, population, markets and transport) grew steadily: a modest increase in book production in absolute terms therefore represents a fall in real terms. In reality there was a long, slow, downward trend as the book market focused even more on upper-income groups.[68]

The main cause of this was the concept of perpetual copyright in intellectual property. It meant that certain publishers owned certain texts (of Shakespeare, Milton or whomever) and other publishers could not reprint or abridge them. From the 1630s enforcement was tightened up. There was a deliberate attempt to prevent selections or extracts from reaching a poorer and less educated readership. Between the early seventeenth century and 1774 not a single mainstream English literary work (with negligible exceptions) was published in a popular format, whether ballad or chapbook. This divided the reading nation by socio-economic class into those who could access such literature and those who could not.[69] There was a wide consensus that cheap availability of reading matter would make the poor discontented with their appointed station in life. In 1757 a certain Jenyns argued that to 'encourage the poor man to read and think, and thus to become more conscious of his misery, would be to fly in the face of divine intention'.[70]

In a landmark ruling of 1773–4 the English and Scottish judiciaries rejected as unlawful the concept of perpetual copyright in intellectual property. In effect they threw open to all publishers the right to print the literature of the past, and to all people the right to read it. The legal battle and its repercussions have been described in justifiably momentous terms:

> The scene was now set for the most decisive event in the history of reading in England since the arrival of printing 300 years before. It was a struggle between the ancient guild approach to economic management and the emerging world of free trade and economic competition, between entrenched interests and challenging innovatory forces ... between a static *ancien régime* view of society based on hierarchy, heredity, property and allocation of roles, and the new Enlightenment science of political economy that aimed to use the power of reason to bring about social and economic improvement.[71]

As a result, in the last quarter of the eighteenth century the number of British men, women and children reading printed texts suddenly began to grow swiftly. The better educated read more books, journals and newspapers than ever before, on a wider range of subjects. And book-length literary texts became accessible to lower-income groups whose reading had previously been confined to the English Bible, short chapbooks and popular ballads.[72] The book industry at the time estimated a fourfold increase in output during the last quarter of the century. This represents an increase in individual acts of book-reading of around fifty times. If we seek a watershed, here surely it is. By the late 1770s Thomson's *The Seasons* was reported to have been found among shepherds who had never seen any other book but the Bible. In the 1780s a German tourist was thunderstruck to find his landlady, a tailor's widow, reading Milton.[73]

To summarize, the crucial question is how far the growth of the European public sphere had dented the elite's near-monopoly of culture and the arts by 1750. If traditional socio-political structures were still holding, can the same be said of traditional socio-cultural relationships? The evidence offered here suggests that the public sphere took off dramatically from the 1750s onwards, a trend which accelerated towards the end of the century.[74] This furnished opportunities to air newly broached national and Enlightened concerns, not all of them congenial to elites. But in the 1650–1750 period the impact of the public sphere was far less marked, leaving elites substantially in control of the cultural agenda. Britain was exceptional, but less so than has traditionally been maintained. Though the origins of a middle-class culture were certainly discernible there by the mid-eighteenth century, British cultural taste was still established and cultural fashion set in circles which remained defiantly aristocratic.[75] This situation is reflected in politics. Only in the 1760s did John Wilkes build up a following among England's 'middling sort' which seriously challenged the aristocratic political establishment.[76]

## The Enlightenment

After the mid-eighteenth century the churches, and especially the Catholic Church, were in retreat on every front. The Jesuits, who dominated education and missionary activity throughout Catholic Europe, were expelled from Portugal in 1759, from France in 1765 and from Spain and Naples in 1767. The whole Order was dissolved by the Pope in 1773. In France and the Habsburg lands, hundreds of monasteries were dissolved from the 1760s to the 1780s. Catholic rulers severely curtailed papal power over the church in their states and granted toleration to Protestants. Bequests and recruitment to the church fell. Clerical numbers, religious intolerance, the confessional state and monarchs' respect for ecclesiastical authority all declined spectacularly.[77] If the altar was in trouble, so was that other component of the age-old alliance – the throne. Respect for monarchs, especially in France and Britain, plummeted from the 1750s.[78] It is worth remembering that until the late 1780s revolution was widely expected in the latter.[79] Some historians have reached for words like 'dechristianization' or 'desacralization'. Others consider this language too sensational. But whatever terminology is used to describe the process, it was happening.[80]

A major reason for this was the rapidly increasing impact in the middle of the eighteenth century of so-called 'Enlightened' ideas which had been fermenting before that date. Historians have generally been keen to push back the origins of elite secularism. The date when most educated people ceased to believe in fairies, ghosts and witches, along with the all-embracing reach of religion and personal interventions by God in daily life, was formerly located around 1700. That was a suspiciously round number. It can now be argued that it should be shifted to the middle of the eighteenth century – just a little *less* round.

Enlightened thinkers had to be careful what they wrote, especially about religion. Most of them lived in confessional states where freedom of the press was not accepted. Consequently their public pronouncements cannot automatically be equated with their private beliefs. Nor was the Enlightenment ever an organized movement. It was a climate of opinion. It began in the 1720s when the French *philosophes* (as they called themselves) took up the ideas of the natural philosophers of the later seventeenth century, namely the old forbidden ambition to control nature and the search for a rational order as a means to understand it. Enlightened writers repackaged these intellectual innovations for a wider audience, but never a popular one. Their impact on the masses remained negligible. But by the 1750s they were converting the crucial elites, whose support they needed to get a hearing and make an impact.[81] Enlightened discussion took place round elegant dining tables: this was a champagne-and-oysters readership. Montesquieu cut up *De l'Esprit des Lois* into bite-sized chapters spiced with epigrams in order to flavour it for salon society.[82] Enlightened writers skilfully targeted those who mattered. Symbolically, it was in July 1750 that Voltaire arrived in Berlin to spend three years advising Frederick II of Prussia. Frederick, being the man he was, spent equal time advising Voltaire.

Enlightened thinkers were innovative in two other crucial respects. Firstly, they applied the intellectual innovations of the previous century to a broader agenda. Their enquiry was extended from the physical world (or God's handiwork in nature, as the previous generation preferred to call it) to human society. Secondly, they severed the various spheres of human knowledge from the religious framework which had always contained and controlled them. Religion was deposed as the supreme authority which dictated the terms of debate about everything else. The publicly stated aim of these thinkers was to restrict the sphere of the Christian religion rather than destroy it. Religion became one area of human experience instead of the context from which all other areas derived their meaning and significance. The combination of these initiatives enabled the modern secular disciplines of the natural, social and political sciences to emerge around the middle of the eighteenth century.

The Enlightenment also weakened, though it did not everywhere abandon, the key alliance between religion and reason which had sustained the success of the natural philosophers. Reason was redefined in an exclusively secular manner, in France especially, so as to became an enemy of the Christian religion rather than its ally. Instead reason was identified exclusively with the sciences and philosophy, thereby making them also seem increasingly incompatible with religion. The Enlightenment's termination of the alliance between religion and the physical sciences ended an ancient partnership inherited from ancient Egypt four thousand years before. The sciences were intended for a key progressive role. To fulfil it Enlightened thinkers decided they must be free to follow boldly wherever reason and experiment led them, and not merely tiptoe round parameters defined by the churches. Economic thinking also finally distanced itself from Christian morality and increasingly based itself on market mechanisms. Religion was sidelined in every intellectual sphere except theology, and human knowledge was increasingly placed centre-stage.

This applied also to historical writing. Before the later eighteenth century history was merely the record of God's providence. Cardinal Bossuet's *Histoire Universelle* of 1681 was, like other standard texts of the time, a narrative told through the eyes of God. It began with God's creation of the universe, charted the unfolding of the divine plan for mankind and climaxed in the sunburst of early-modern Christian civilization. Theophilus Gale, a contemporary English historian, aimed to demonstrate that all the arts and sciences arose from the Jewish people – from Moses (history and law), Noah (navigation), Solomon (architecture) and Job (moral philosophy).

Around the middle of the eighteenth century this Bible-centred history was abandoned by historians like Hume, Gibbon and Voltaire. Instead of invoking divine agency as an explanatory tool, they analysed the historical process in terms of cultural, social and economic evolution, as well as of human ambition and drive for improvement. Even the triumph of Christianity itself in the fourth century AD was attributed to human motive and emotion rather than to the purposes of divine Providence. For Gibbon a key explanation was Christ's promise to his followers of immortality, hitherto reserved for the gods. The Almighty's personal supervision of the infinite sum of human affairs was deemed a less probable explanation.[83]

Above all, Enlightened thinkers considered the established fusion of religion and politics to be highly dangerous, and advocated their divorce.[84] They disliked state-sponsored faiths and built on Locke's attempt (which they exaggerated for their own purposes) to provide the state with a secular and rational justification. They also rejected the concept of original sin (inherited from Adam), from which rulers needed to ensure their subjects' salvation. They thus undermined the old argument that religion and politics were by definition inseparable and that religious disunity therefore led inevitably to civil strife. As long as it was the acknowledged business of rulers to promote true religion, their subjects would never agree. But removing religion from politics and making it a private matter would enable people to co-operate peacefully to achieve more attainable goals. As Diderot commented, 'Throne and altar can never be too far apart.' In particular, Montesquieu insisted that religion should be excluded from politics and the criminal law – if God disapproved of heretics he would presumably punish them himself.[85]

The French Enlightenment was more secular and materialistic than elsewhere – and also the most influential. A few thinkers, like Diderot and d'Holbach, were atheists. Most Enlightened thinkers believed the universe displayed evidence of a Creator but considered Christian and other attempts at further definition to be futile and superstitious. Like Voltaire, they were deists. They subscribed to a minimalist religion shorn of ritual and sacred books, merely requiring belief in a supreme intelligent Being who now had little business other than existing. A letter from Voltaire to Frederick II of Brandenburg–Prussia makes it clear that he detested Christianity and disliked all organized religions:

You are absolutely right, Sire: a courageous and wise ruler, with money, troops, laws, may rule men very well without the aid of religion, which is only designed to deceive them; but the stupid masses will soon invent one for themselves; and as long as there are knaves and fools, there will be religions. Ours is without doubt the most ridiculous, absurd and bloody that has ever infected the world. Your Majesty will do mankind an everlasting service by destroying this infamous superstition – I do not mean among the riffraff, who do not deserve to be enlightened and who require every kind of control – I mean among honest, thinking men, men who wish to reason.[86]

Frederick was scarcely a believer in anything and even more sarcastic than Voltaire. He habitually wrote to the local clergy in his lands that 'The Holy Ghost and I have decided that ____ ____ shall be the bishop of ____ ____.' With men like Voltaire and Frederick the Great calling the shots, it is clear that by the mid-eighteenth century the age of baroque piety was officially over.

Enlightened thinkers borrowed an abundance of scientific metaphors from the natural philosophers, but removed them from their religious context. Descartes, Leibnitz and Newton had supplied mechanical metaphors for the cosmos. These were now applied to human beings. As in La Mettrie's *L'Homme machine* of 1747, everything is matter in motion. Even if many Enlightened thinkers believed human beings to have a more spiritual capacity, they were increasingly depicted as machines driven by the pleasure principle. In 1748 appeared the anonymous *Thérèse philosophique* and in 1749 the better known *Fanny Hill*. Sexual activity is reduced to fluids, pumps and hydraulic pressure; sexual organs are pounding engines and thrusting machines. Both titles are apparently pornography for engineers.

The *philosophes* identified earthly happiness as the goal. Their focus was life in the present world and not salvation in the next. The Augustinian Christian belief was that human life was merely a trial and preparation for heaven and that attempts to improve it were ungodly, since human misery was the inevitable result of original sin. All this was rejected. Human welfare, education and economic growth could be transformed by re-ordering government and society.[87] The aim was not original. It derived from the Cameralists of the late seventeenth and early eighteenth centuries who believed that state action could promote the progress of the community. Most Enlightened projects addressed problems which had long exercised political elites. A welfare agenda was mapped out for the French crown in the 1690s. Implementation began only in the 1750s, as government responded increasingly to secular concerns with society's well-being.[88]

The means to this end was reason, which Enlightened thinkers inherited from the natural philosophers of the seventeenth century. Newton had by observation, measurement and calculation discovered the laws which governed the physical world. Scientific method was therefore the only reliable guide to human government and society. Reason was to be extended to the human world of economics, politics, education and morals. Discovery of the laws which governed them would bestow the power to improve them. In Newton's name,

Voltaire offered mankind a new, verifiable test for truth: 'We must take for true what is demonstrated by our eyes and by mathematics. As for all the rest, we should say, I do not know.'[89] For Hume, reason's potential was even more devastating:

> If we take in our hand any volume, of divinity or school metaphysics for instance, let us ask, Does it contain any abstract reasoning concerning quantity or number? No. Does it contain any experimental reasoning concerning matter of fact and existence? No. Commit it then to the flames, for it can contain nothing but sophistry and illusion.[90]

Enlightened thinkers demanded rational grounds for belief and were sceptical about knowledge claimed without evidence. Reason was deployed as a critical and corrective tool against unsubstantiated faith, supposedly divine revelation and unchallenged custom, tradition, prejudice, bigotry and superstition. Innovation was preferred to the *status quo*. The Enlightenment rejected the authority of the past and the alleged lessons of history. It wished to eradicate the old obligation to leave the world as God had allegedly established it. Only radical change would ensure that human beings progressed towards happiness.

The *philosophes* believed that reason (and, what amounted to the same thing, natural law and natural rights) was universally applicable – in every country, every period, every circumstance. But reason was not occupying empty territory. It inevitably collided with a disorderly jumble of traditions inherited from the past. Anomalies and exceptions negated the rational order which should have underpinned them. Untidy local customs, laws, liberties and privileges could therefore be discredited by appealing to scientific thinking.[91]

Enlightened thinkers argued that liberty and equality were essential preconditions of progress. The claim to liberty was nothing new, but it had previously been associated mainly with corporate bodies such as nobles, clergy, judges, guilds and chartered companies. They equated it with their own privileges: 'liberties' and 'privileges' were interchangeable words. Inspired by Locke, Enlightened thinkers argued that liberty was an equal natural right for all and not a privileged corporate right for the few (thereby risking offending their own elite audience). But they confined equality to the realm of human rights and did not extend it to economic and social levelling: their attitude was meritocratic.[92] Aware that the media and education were controlled in most countries by governments and churches, they added Locke's demand for freedom of speech, opinion and the press.

They also championed economic freedom, free markets and the scrapping of guild regulations – a major reversal of the current belief in state regulation of the economy. This derived ultimately from de Mandeville's doctrine (1705) that private vice and greed bring public benefits, especially economic ones. Individual self-interest had always been seen as an impulse of sinful human nature. But it was also perceived as an anti-social force which needed to be checked by government in order to preserve the economic interests of the whole community. In the 1750s the Physiocrats rejected this as unscientific. They argued that self-interest was a powerful motivator and wealth-generator, which governments should not oppose but should utilize for the benefit of the community. Individuals should be left alone to pursue their economic interests unfettered (*laissez-faire, laissez-passer*). As Adam Smith and finally Margaret Thatcher were later to argue, competitive market forces would ensure, far better than muddled intervention by governments, that the whole of society profited.[93] A natural law of social economics, written by the hand of nature, would thus enable the economic greed of individuals to generate the good of the community. The resulting economic growth would increase human happiness.

The thrust of the Enlightenment can thus be written in four words – happiness, reason, liberty and equality. In France its main target was the Catholic Church, which offended against all four of these fine abstractions. Its stress on the afterlife denied earthly happiness, its emphasis on faith denied reason, its privileges denied equality and its persecution, censorship and educational stranglehold denied liberty (until the later eighteenth century the clergy controlled education in every state in Europe, as well as the press in Catholic states). Elsewhere the Enlightenment was less anti-Christian and anti-clerical, though in Italy, Germany and Austria it bitterly criticized the wealth and power of what it considered useless orders of monks and Jesuits.[94] To some extent religion was able to continue its own creative alliance with reason.[95] One result was mystic/scientific secret societies like the Rosicrucians and the Freemasons. Some champions of the Enlightenment were sincere Christians, even Catholic priests, especially in central Europe where the Catholic Enlightenment stressed the need for a religion with fewer rituals, relics and feast days and more social responsibility. In Scotland by the mid-eighteenth century most leading Enlightened figures were Protestant clergymen.[96]

But the general trend from the 1750s is clear, as religion was increasingly separated from other areas of rational enquiry. In that decade the *Encyclopédie* appeared, the French Enlightenment's real breakthrough. It was the first deliberate attempt by an organized group of laymen to break the churches' monopoly of knowledge and education. The *Encyclopédie* was intended as a summary of known fact as opposed to irrational error spawned by the clergy. Its aim was to substitute science for religion as a source of authority and thus exchange faith, fantasy and superstition for verifiable knowledge. Enlightened attitudes were broadcast on everything from the uselessness of priests to the efficiency of scientific manufacturing techniques. The *Encyclopédie* demanded a scientific experimental approach to social problems rather than reliance on Biblical or classical authorities. This would improve human life and happiness on earth.

The *Encyclopédie* was also the Enlightenment's manifesto, as all the *philosophes*, including Montesquieu, Voltaire and Rousseau, contributed to it. It owed most to the determination of its editor Diderot, who recruited 200 other writers to produce 72,000 articles. His publisher originally wanted a summary in one set of books of all knowledge possessed at the time. Diderot converted this into a vehicle of propaganda for Enlightened attitudes. The *Encyclopédie* was published in 28 volumes between 1751 and 1772. By 1789 about 25,000 sets had been sold. Just over half were bought outside France, thus spreading Enlightenment across Europe. It was bought by intellectual, professional and political elites. Its readers were therefore mainly upper class, though later and cheaper editions widened its appeal. Print culture expanded rapidly after 1750 and the publisher Panckoucke, who published the second edition of the *Encyclopédie*, was to have more cultural influence than any noble patron and become one of the first press barons.[97] The *Encyclopédie* helped to create a public sphere and benefited from it.

The *Encyclopédie* was a bestseller in spite of its high price and the inconsistent attitude of the authorities. Its editors were daring to deploy reason, not as before to buttress religion but to undermine it. Europeans were still being hanged, burned alive and sent to the galleys for much less.[98] The *parlement*, Catholic Church and Jesuits were permanently hostile. In 1749, Diderot had been imprisoned for 100 days in Vincennes for subverting religion and morality. In 1759, the Paris *parlement* outlawed the *Encyclopédie* and it was placed on the Papal Index of forbidden books. But Louis XV's government made no serious attempt to suppress it. Malesherbes, the government's censor, considered himself Enlightened, while Mme de Pompadour, the royal mistress, owned a set of the *Encyclopédie* herself and contributed an article on face rouge. When the French government proved unco-operative, Diderot secured sponsorship from foreign rulers like Catherine II of Russia. This support in high places enabled the *Encyclopédie* to convert much of educated French opinion to Enlightened attitudes.

The *Encyclopédie* developed a repertoire of tricks for getting past the censor. It needed to be devious. The whole idea of an encyclopaedia was tacitly subversive in the context of the mid-eighteenth century, as it demolished the ancient hierarchy of subjects. Instead of beginning with reverential articles on God, monarchs, nobles and bishops, it kicked off with a 5,000-word entry on the letter 'A'. Subtle points were also made by the amount of space allocated to subject entries. There was far more about humble artisans and their trades than about cardinals and kings. A final cunning plan of the editorial team was to assign religious topics to the Abbé Mallet – the most boring writer in Paris.[99]

Enlightened thinkers made little impact on elites before the middle of the eighteenth century, with most key texts appearing in western Europe after 1745. As they criticized church, nobility and (to a lesser extent) monarchy, their agenda clearly depended for a hearing on the establishment of an independent public sphere. Luckily for Enlightened thinkers, the explosion of print culture occurred at roughly the same time and offered a rival platform to the pulpit (though sermons and religious tracts accounted for much of the increased printed output). The churches' monopoly role in defining the relationship of religion to all human thought and activity was broken by the expanding media.[100]

A simple example is the reconceptualization of suicide. According to traditional church teaching, it was both sin and crime. Well into the eighteenth century suicides were denied Christian burial and interred at a crossroads with a stake through their heart. But in 1737 Eustace Budgell, a journalist, loaded his pockets with rocks and drowned himself in the Thames. He was found to have left a suicide note justifying himself in terms of the ancient Roman code of honour. Fashionable society and Enlightened opinion promptly condoned the deed. Newspapers and magazines were turning suicides into stories of 'human interest'. Pity was substituted for punitiveness. Like the academic subdivisions of knowledge, which were increasingly being separated from religion and theology, suicide was secularized.[101]

Enlightened thinkers drew different political conclusions from their ideas.[102] Some were in favour of absolute monarchy, some of despotic monarchy and some of republicanism. The crux was the concept of liberty, of which all Enlightened thinkers approved. Liberty was associated traditionally with privileged rights and more recently with equal rights. These were incompatible and the Enlightened had to choose. Montesquieu, one of the earliest Enlightened writers, defended liberty in his *De l'Esprit des Lois* of 1748 in the old privileged sense as a barrier against royal despotism. He insisted that Enlightened liberty was the ally of privilege – it was not for equal individuals but privileged corporate bodies, as they alone could stand up to royal despotism. He thus supported liberty but not equality. Voltaire supported both. He insisted that Enlightened liberty was for equal individuals and therefore the enemy of privileged corporate bodies. The crown must be prepared to take despotic measures against them. For Rousseau also, but on different grounds, Enlightened liberty was the enemy of privilege. People were free only if they made their own laws, as in a republic. The General Will representing the common good of all could therefore despotically overrule the privileged corporate rights of the few.

After the 1750s the Enlightenment thus heralded several departures from traditional ideas of absolute monarchy – and therefore also from established concepts of the composite state. The latter had survived virtually unchanged in the period 1650 to 1750. The French monarch still had to negotiate with each of the thirteen regional *parlements* separately, only to find that they often modified his legislation in accordance with local custom.[103] At the other side of Europe the Habsburg ruler was still obliged to send his agents on a tour of central and eastern Europe in order to secure financial deals with local bosses in the innumerable provincial Estates of his sprawling empire. General legislation for Bourbon or Habsburg territories was consequently impossible.

The first impact of the Enlightenment in this respect was that the concept of equal natural rights began to weaken respect for the corporate rights and privileges of elites. Privileged *parlements* and Estates began to look like selfish interest groups rather than valid consultative and representative bodies. Later eighteenth-century monarchs encouraged these resentments when their drive for equal and uniform tax clashed with privileged non-payers and untidy regional exemptions.

Second, the Enlightenment changed the way despotism was viewed. It was previously considered unacceptably despotic for even absolute monarchs to touch the rights and liberties of their subjects without their consent. But what if possessors of unequal rights and privileges would not consent to give them up? Some rulers now reckoned that use of despotic force (royal interference with rights without consent) might be justified as it would be advancing equal natural rights. Hence 'Enlightened despotism' – despotism employed for Enlightened purposes. This would enable rulers to bypass obstructive bodies (Estates, Diets or *parlements*) without reclassifying themselves as tyrants. The point was to eliminate the element of consent inherent in absolute monarchies in areas traditionally beyond the scope of royal prerogatives. When put into practice this ended the crown's partnership with the nobility, who regarded absolute monarchy as obliged to respect their interests in consultation with themselves. Austrian nobles were unappreciative when Joseph II informed them that he did not need their consent to do good.

Third, the Enlightenment proclaimed reason as an abrasive solvent of traditional political beliefs. Reason supported equal natural rights and tradition upheld privileged corporate rights. The issue of equality versus privilege therefore also became a struggle between reason and tradition, two principles which had formerly lived together and now polarized into opposites. The rapid spread of Enlightened ideas after the 1750s pitched an aggressively rationalist ideology against the traditional diversity of the composite state – a rationalist's nightmare. Only now did rulers launch a sustained drive for unified legal, administrative and financial systems. Monarchs had always viewed disrespect for traditional rights as incompatible with their coronation oaths and their moral duty as God's anointed. Reason was little help since, before the 1750s, it was inseparable from religion. But once reason had been separated from religion, it could be used to counter this ancient mindset. Tradition was an old and powerful argument, but reason trumped it.

In 1788 a King of France officially embraced the cause of rational reform and proposed making a clean sweep of ancient clutter.[104] He declared for the first time that he wished 'to impart to all parts of the monarchy that unity of direction, that ensemble without which a great kingdom is weakened by the very number and extent of its provinces'. He announced that a great state needed one king, one law and one system of registration.[105] Both inside and outside government circles the sanction of the past was losing its power to persuade. The Breton lawyer Volney wrote in his journal:

What does it matter to us what our fathers have done or how and why they have done it ... ? The essential rights of man, his natural relations to his fellows in the state of society – these are the eternal bases of every form of government.[106]

Three years earlier, at the other end of Europe, Joseph II was attempting rational unification of the Habsburg empire by assaulting the separate constitution of Hungary. He had the crown of Hungary brought to Vienna, issued a despotic decree ordering the Estates not to meet, and dismissed their baroque ceremonial as 'peasant dances on an operatic stage'. The Hungarian Chancellor, Count Esterhazy, informed Joseph that no people could relinquish a constitution which they regarded as guaranteeing their liberty and property and which had been confirmed in perpetuity by solemn treaties and traditions. The Emperor explained to an unconvinced Chancellor that liberty should be equated with equal rights for all rather than privileges for an elite. He declared that equality was 'the first article of natural and social law' and that reason was superior to all the customs, treaties and traditions of the ages. His words heralded a new world.[107]

# Conclusion

It will now be obvious that two mental worlds existed side by side in this period. They were, roughly, the medieval and the modern, the traditional and the rational. One culture deferred to the authority of ideas and institutions inherited from generations of ancestors. The other challenged them on the basis of the reasoning power of contemporaries. All ages are ages of transition, since change is continuous and the heritage of the past is necessarily modified to adapt to present circumstances. But between 1650 and 1750 the ideas which were to characterize the next three hundred years were maturing alongside attitudes which had dominated the previous fifteen hundred.

It has been argued here that old and new were rarely in glaring confrontation in the period. Concepts of throne and altar alliance, religious, monarchical and aristocratic values, the weighty authority of the past – all these held firm until the 1750s. The full rigours of the new rational approach were contained, fortunately for ruling elites. They managed to combine innovation with tradition and benefit from new thinking without destroying old certainties. Pressure for stronger and more uniform administration somehow bedded down with basic acceptance of traditionally privileged provinces, institutions and power groups. Innovations were introduced cautiously and selectively – and, Russia apart, rarely to the point where potential for destabilization outweighed maintenance of stability. Few monarchs pushed rational ideas to their logical conclusion. Before the 1750s elites were able to have, literally, the best of both worlds.

The aim of absolute monarchy was to maintain a balance of political power corresponding to the prevailing political culture and to socio-political realities. That balance had been challenged by a century of religious and political civil wars which reached a bloody climax during the 'General Crisis' of the mid-seventeenth century. Elites had rejected rulers' attempts to attack the diversity of composite states and sometimes challenged the basic powers of monarchy. Between the 1650s and the 1750s most rulers retrieved the absolute prerogatives of kingship. But, crucially, they resisted the despotic temptations of taking too literally their own claims to a transcendent sovereignty or *raison d'état* which trumped the legitimate rights of everyone else. Balance was preserved by a political culture that stressed monarchs' duty to consult appropriate institutions on issues of subjects' rights and to embrace elite groups within the nexus of power.

How did this apparently cast-iron social and political system buckle and collapse so swiftly after the mid-eighteenth century? From the 1750s the Enlightenment sharply focused and widely projected the 'scientific' thinking of the 1650–1750 period. Reason now came increasingly into its own. The inheritance of the past, formerly bedfellow of reason, was downgraded. Antiquity, chief glory of the elite brand, ceased to impress. Once tradition was devalued, so also was the triumvirate of monarchs, nobles and clergy whose credibility depended upon it. Monarchs lost their swagger, became almost apologetic and slashed court ceremonial. To give government a sharper cutting edge, total concentration of power was demanded – either despotically in the crown or, finally, democratically in the nation. The baroque state's privileged power groups and corporations, intermediate between crown and people, were seen less as guardians of subjects' rights than as obstacles to the people's improvement. They were also at loggerheads with monarchs over their own despotically infringed rights. To complete a dismal survey of undermined foundations, influential Enlightened thinkers adopted a critical and meritocratic attitude towards elite privilege.[2]

Elite culture had reigned supreme until the 1750s because elites controlled, sponsored or funded most of the existing cultural media. But with the rise of an independent public sphere from the mid-eighteenth century, elites discovered that undesirable material was appearing faster than they could repress it. By 1782 the author Louis-Sébastien Mercier was recording the demise of the court's cultural leadership:

The word 'court' no longer inspires awe among us as at the time of Louis XIV. Reigning opinions are no longer received from the court; it no longer decides on reputations of any sort; no one says now, with ridiculous pomposity, 'The court has pronounced thus'. The court's judgements are countermanded; one says openly that it understands nothing; it has no ideas on the subject [and] could have none; it is not in the know. ... The court has thus lost the ascendancy that it had regarding the fine arts, letters, and everything pertaining to them today.[3]

Courtly values now had to compete in a free media market which was not geared to elite requirements. The empirical theme that ran through from 1650 to 1750 now emerged insistently. What had been implicit now arguably became explicit. Until the religious reaction and revival after 1815, rational, utilitarian, mechanical and contractual conceptions of government triumphed.

Whether the 1750s witnessed the birth of a new political culture is hotly debated.[4] If there was one, as seems plausible, it by no means made revolution inevitable. Rational initiatives could come from above or below. The French Revolution embodied one mode of attack and the Enlightened Despots another. In many respects the results were similar, both before and after 1789. In the second half of the eighteenth century the baroque confessional state was dismantled.[5] Religion as a main inspiration of culture and statecraft evaporated. So did the glorification of monarchs and aristocrats. Though they were destined to survive relatively unscathed into the 1780s, they lost control of the cultural agenda from the 1750s. The new agenda was the improvement of the people, and the jury was out on kings and nobles.

The sumptuous baroque style had expressed and supported to perfection the basically self-interested and self-promoting purposes of elites. This was all the more obvious in contrast to the austere style which followed it after 1750, as the moral earnestness of the Enlightenment demanded something more severely public-spirited. From the mid-eighteenth century many monarchs and aristocrats were reluctant to 'represent' or act out their status in grandiose semi-public ceremonial. They saw themselves as professional commanders-in-chief, heads of the civil service or 'first servants of the state' rather than sacred icons.[6]

Informality therefore challenged ceremony and etiquette. Frederick II and Joseph II were bored by courtly ritual. Louis XVI and Marie Antoinette cultivated a few favourites among the nobility and excluded most of the rest from the royal presence, except for a brief period on Sundays. They discharged their courtly duties in such a perfunctory manner that paying court to them was regarded as a waste of time.[7] The consequences were cataclysmic. Elite opposition grew and the court ceased to contain it – one of its most essential functions. By the 1780s the courts of Prussia, Austria and France were shadows of their former selves. On the accession of Joseph II to the Habsburg empire in 1780 the palace of Schönbrunn was closed down and mothballed, the Hofburg in Vienna was converted to office use and the Emperor moved into a house reminiscent of a Victorian suburban villa.[8] The Emperor travelled ceaselessly round his dominions and informed subjects seeking royal favours that kneeling was 'not a fitting form of behaviour from one human being to another'.[9] George III of Great Britain strolled in the streets of Windsor without his guards and chatted to booksellers; or he rode furiously through the countryside pausing briefly, if he spotted fine specimens, to congratulate farmers on their pigs. Even Catherine the Great of Russia, who was more comfortable with court etiquette than some of her contemporary monarchs, arose early to light her own fire.

From Stockholm to Naples, baroque had been a truly international style. But its palaces and rococo boudoirs were inappropriate venues for working monarchs and conscience-stricken nobles. Along with the abbeys and churches of the 1680–1750 building boom, they represented the climax of the power of monarchs, nobles and clergy before all were submerged under the rising tide of rationalism and nationalism.[10] Baroque celebration of royal, aristocratic and ecclesiastical dominance and god-like status was now deplored. The Enlightenment's stress on merit rather than birth and its devaluation of traditional religion made the baroque project seem overblown and ridiculous. It was an eye-wateringly expensive style and the wars of the mid-eighteenth century drained royal and aristocratic resources. From the 1750s elites refused to fund it. Partly because of the baroque's socio-political associations, its overthrow was one of the most rapid, brutal and decisive in cultural history. The baroque style was universally rejected and some of its greatest exponents were deleted from public memory. Rastrelli, court architect to the Empress Elizabeth of Russia, had enjoyed twenty years of uninterrupted commissions. His establishment of full-blown baroque in Russia was crowned in the 1750s by the building of two monumental royal residences – the Winter Palace and Tsarskoe Selo (now known as Pushkin). But in 1761 his dominance was abruptly terminated when one of his key designs was rejected in favour of a neo-classical Market Hall for St Petersburg. He spent the last decade of his life consumed by bitterness and searching for work.[11]

The fashion which destroyed him was a cult of classical simplicity based on strict adherence to ancient Greek models. In the 1750s the Prussian archaeologist Johann Winckelmann denounced baroque architecture and reintroduced the Greek ideal to Europe. It clearly met a need for something less bombastic. In the second half of the eighteenth century it even overran North America.[12] Baroque building totally ceased, to be replaced by an austere classicism pared down to its essentials – dome, column, portico and pediment. This neo-classical style was used to glorify the rising nation-states of Europe rather than the lords and princes who had ruled the dynastic states. Few royal and aristocratic palaces were built after the early 1760s, though the lesser nobility continued to erect country houses. The main fashion was now for neo-classical public buildings like hospitals, libraries, museums, art galleries and concert halls. In the baroque era most of these were integral to elite palaces, but facilities once for the few now began to be offered to the many. The British Museum was founded by Act of Parliament in 1753, though not in its present building. Perhaps in imitation, in 1769 the Landgrave of Hesse built the Kassel Museum as a public institution.[13] Neo-classicism embraced the severe moral spirit if not the political content of ancient Greek and Roman democracy and republicanism. It was the architecture of public responsibility and the priority was improvement of the people – not the deification of rulers.

In painting and literature after 1750 the Grand Manner gradually went out and informality came in. A demand for sincerity, spontaneity and a kind heart confronted an aristocratic rococo court culture insistent on presenting a flawless appearance with wit, elegance and style. Greuze painted scenes of peasant life and raw emotion, in which tears were the symbolic enemy of expensive cosmetics and saboteur of polite disguise. Yet his paintings became highly acceptable to an aristocracy which was losing confidence in its own values.[14] As established elite conventions faded, Rousseau's cult of natural simplicity tightened its grip. Music reverted to a less complex and sophisticated style. Baroque compositions had sometimes required as many as six different melodies to be played simultaneously. This 'learned' style was now shunned in favour of the 'galant' style, which embraced Enlightened ideals of natural simplicity as opposed to its predecessor's brainy sophistication. The height of good taste was now a clear melody accompanied by simple chords. Bach died neatly with the baroque in 1750. He thus avoided the anguish of seeing his sons, two of whom were also celebrated composers, neglect his music and betray his genius.[15]

The Enlightened and Revolutionary eras ended in 1815 and European elites mounted a recovery of sorts. But there was no revival of the baroque culture which had borne them to unprecedented heights a century before. That had died in the middle of the eighteenth century when one of the strongest winds of change in the history of taste straightened out rococo curves, blew away the rose buds, shells and cupids of Bavarian churches and pleasure-pavilions, and substituted the straight and sober lines of neo-classical public theatres, museums and hospitals.[16] The clear light of reason and the cause of humanity had won permanent victories. The gods and goddesses who had floated on painted ceilings and doubled as royal personages vanished from late eighteenth-century consciousness like ghosts at cockcrow.

# Notes

## Introduction

1. B. Coward, *The Stuart Age* (London: Longman, 1980), pp. 201–2.
2. L. Ettlinger, 'The Role of the Artist in Society', in A. Cobban (ed.), *The Eighteenth Century: Europe in the Age of Enlightenment* (London: Thames & Hudson, 1969), p. 245.
3. K. Baker, *Inventing the French Revolution* (Cambridge: Cambridge University Press, 1990); D. Beales, 'Religion and Culture', in T. Blanning (ed.), *The Eighteenth Century, 1688–1815* (Oxford: Oxford University Press, 2000), pp. 131–77.
4. T. Rabb, *The Struggle for Stability in Early Modern Europe* (Oxford: Oxford University Press, 1975).
5. P. Campbell, *Power and Politics in Old Regime France, 1720–1745* (London: Routledge, 1996), pp. 306–7.
6. T. Aston (ed.), *Crisis in Europe, 1560–1660* (London: Routledge & Kegan Paul, 1965), p. 59.
7. R. Merriman, *Six Contemporaneous Revolutions* (Oxford: Oxford University Press, 1938), p. 89.
8. T. Blanning, *The Pursuit of Glory: Europe, 1648–1815* (London: Allen Lane, 2007), pp. 198–9.
9. C. Hill, *The World Turned Upside Down: Radical Ideas during the English Revolution* (Harmondsworth: Penguin, 1975), pp. 13–18.
10. N. Steensgaard, 'The Seventeenth-Century Crisis', in G. Parker and L. Smith (eds), *The General Crisis of the Seventeenth Century* (London: Routledge, 1997), pp. 45–7; P. Laslett, *The World we have Lost* (London: Methuen, 1965), p. 23; J. Adamson, *The Noble Revolt: The Overthrow of Charles I* (London: Weidenfeld & Nicolson, 2007).

11. J. Hardman, *French Politics, 1774–1789* (London: Longman, 1995), p. 7.

12. D. Cannadine, *The Decline and Fall of the British Aristocracy* (New Haven, CT: Yale University Press, 1990), p. 8.

13. H. Perkin, *The Origins of Modern English Society, 1780–1880* (London: Routledge, 1969), pp. 24, 37–9; H. Scott, *The European Nobilities in the Seventeenth and Eighteenth Centuries*, vol. 1: *Western Europe* (London: Longman, 1995), pp. 21–2, 30–5.

14. M. Bush, *The English Aristocracy: A Comparative Synthesis* (Manchester: Manchester University Press, 1984), pp. 1–4.

15. Scott, *European Nobilities*, vol. 1, pp. 10–13.

16. D. Beales, *Enlightenment and Reform in Eighteenth-Century Europe* (London: Tauris, 2005), p. 270.

17. M. Broers, *Europe under Napoleon, 1799–1815* (London: Edward Arnold, 1996), pp. 86–93, 193–5.

18. J. Sharpe, *Early Modern England: A Social History, 1550–1760* (London: Edward Arnold, 1987), pp. 176–97.

19. M. Bush, *Rich Noble, Poor Noble* (Manchester: Manchester University Press, 1988), pp. 70–1.

20. J. Bergin, *Crown, Church and Episcopate under Louis XIV* (New Haven, CT: Yale University Press, 2004), pp. 58–70.

21. Bush, *Rich Noble, Poor Noble*, pp. 105–6.

22. J. Cannon, 'The British Nobility, 1660–1800', in Scott, *European Nobilities*, vol. 1, p. 54.

23. J. Daly, 'The Idea of Absolute Monarchy in Seventeenth-century England', *Historical Journal*, XXI (1978), pp. 247–50.

24. R. Mettam, *Government and Society in Louis XIV's France* (London: Macmillan, 1977), p. xv.

25. Beales, *Enlightenment and Reform*, pp. 268–70.

26. W. Church, *The Greatness of Louis XIV*, 2nd edn (London: Heath, 1972), pp. 12–13.

27. J. Hurt, *Louis XIV and the Parlements: The Assertion of Royal Authority* (Manchester: Manchester University Press, 2002).

28. H. Koenigsberger, 'Composite States, Representative Institutions and the American Revolution', *British Institute of Historical Research* (1989), p. 135.

29. W. Doyle, *The Old European Order, 1660–1800*, 2nd edn (Oxford: Oxford University Press, 1992), p. 224.

30. W. Blackstone, *Commentaries on the Laws of England* (Oxford: Oxford University Press, 1765), pp. 284, 292–4.

31. R. Asch and H. Duchhardt (eds), *Der Absolutismus – ein Mythos? Strukturwandel monarchischer Herrschaft in West- und Mitteleuropa (ca. 1550–1700)* (Cologne: Böhlau Verlag, 1996).

32. Beales, *Enlightenment and Reform*, pp. 268–71; N. Henshall, *The Myth of Absolutism: Change and Continuity in Early Modern European Monarchy* (London: Longman, 1992), pp. 199–213; F. Hartung, *Enlightened Despotism* (Historical Association Pamphlet, 157), pp. 6–7.

33. L. Colley, *Britons: Forging the Nation, 1707–1837* (New Haven, CT: Yale University Press, 1992), pp. 5–7; J. Black, *Convergence or Divergence? Britain and the Continent* (Basingstoke: Macmillan, 1994), pp. 1–5.

34. Bush, *English Aristocracy*, pp. 1–13.

35. Henshall, *Myth of Absolutism*, p. 132.

36. J. Clark, *Revolution and Rebellion: State and Society in England in the Seventeenth and Eighteenth Centuries* (Cambridge: Cambridge University Press, 1986), pp. 68–91.

37. J. Elliott, 'A Europe of Composite Monarchies', *Past and Present*, 137 (1992), pp. 48–71.

38. D. Armitage, 'Making the Empire British: Scotland in the Atlantic World, 1542–1707', in D. Armitage, *Greater Britain, 1516–1776* (Aldershot: Ashgate, 2004), pp. 37–8.

39. R. Bonney, *Political Change in France under Richelieu and Mazarin, 1624–1661* (Oxford: Oxford University Press, 1978), p. 442.

40. Rabb, *Struggle for Stability*, pp. 60–73.

41. Hurt, *Louis XIV and the Parlements*.

42. J. Black, *Kings, Nobles and Commoners: States and Societies in Early Modern Europe, a Revisionist History* (London: Tauris, 2004); R. Mettam, *Power and Faction in Louis XIV's France* (Oxford: Blackwell, 1988); J. Collins, *The State in Early Modern France* (Cambridge: Cambridge University Press, 1995); Henshall, *Myth of Absolutism*, pp. 35–60; J. Duindam, *Myths of Power* (Amsterdam: Amsterdam University Press, 1994), pp. 193–4.

43. C. Russell, 'Composite Monarchies in Early-modern Europe: the British and Irish example', in A. Grant and K. Stringer (eds), *Uniting the Kingdom? The Making of British History* (London: Routledge, 1995), p. 143.

44. J. Rosenheim, *The Emergence of a Ruling Order: English Landed Society, 1650–1750* (London: Longman, 1998), p. 253.

45. Campbell, *Power and Politics*, p. 306.

46. T. Thornton, 'Local Equity Jurisdictions in the Territories of the English Crown: the Palatinate of Chester, 1450–1540', in D. Dunn (ed.), *Courts, Counties and the Capital in the Later Middle Ages* (Stroud: Sutton, 1996).

47. R. Oresko, G. Gibbs and H. Scott (eds), *Royal and Republican Sovereignty in Early Modern Europe* (Cambridge: Cambridge University Press, 1997), p. 5.

48. Broers, *Europe under Napoleon*, p. 99; H. Trevor-Roper, *The Invention of Scotland: Myth and History* (New Haven, CT: Yale University Press, 2008), p. 2.

49. M. Braddick, *State Formation in Early Modern England, c.1550–1700* (Cambridge: Cambridge University Press, 2000); B. Porter, *War and the Rise of the State: The Military Foundations of Modern Politics* (New York: Free Press, 1994); L. Stone (ed.), *An Imperial State at War* (London: Routledge, 1994).

50. Collins, *State in Early Modern France*, pp. 79–124.

51. Porter, *War and the Rise of the State*, pp. 105–18.

52. A. Johnson, *Europe in the Sixteenth Century, 1494–1598* (London: Rivingtons, 1900), pp. 15, 25.

53. Elliott, 'Europe of Composite Monarchies', pp. 51–2; D. Parrott, 'War and International Relations', in J. Bergin (ed.), *The Seventeenth Century* (Oxford: Oxford University Press, 2001), p. 141.

54. M. Jasanoff, *Edge of Empire: Conquest and Collecting in the East, 1750–1850* (London: Fourth Estate, 2005).

55. J. Meyer, *L'Education des princes en Europe du XVe au XIXe siècle* (Paris: Perrin, 2004).

56. W. Schevill, *The Great Elector* (Hamden, CT: Archon, 1947), pp. 394–9.

57. S. Schama, *Landscape and Memory* (London: Harper Collins, 1995), pp. 75–91.

58. P. Heather, *The Fall of the Roman Empire* (London: Macmillan, 2005), pp. 46–8, 55–8.

59. D. Hume, *The History of England from the Invasion of Julius Caesar to the Revolution in 1688* (London: C. Corral, 1809 edition), vol. 1, p. 8.

60. Society for Promoting Christian Knowledge (author unnamed), *The History of England* (London: Gilbert & Rivington, 1851), pp. 4–5.

61. J. Adamson, *The Princely Courts of Europe, 1500–1750* (London: Weidenfeld & Nicolson, 1998), p. 40; J. Shennan, *The Origins of the Modern European State, 1450–1725* (London: Hutchinson, 1974).

62. J. Swann, *Provincial Power and Absolute Monarchy: The Estates of Burgundy, 1661–1790* (Cambridge: Cambridge University Press, 2003), pp. 1–6.

63. T. Ertman, *The Birth of the Leviathan* (Cambridge: Cambridge University Press, 1997).

64. R. Dawkins, *The Ancestor's Tale: A Pilgrimage to the Dawn of Life* (London: Weidenfeld & Nicolson, 2004), p. 1.

65. Doyle, *Old European Order*, p. 224.

66. T. Harris, *Restoration: Charles II and his Kingdoms, 1660–1685* (Harmondsworth: Penguin, 2005), pp. 14–15.

67. J. Black, *The Hanoverians* (Hambledon and London: Palgrave Macmillan, 2004), p. 22.

68. T. Kjaergaard, *The Danish Revolution, 1500–1800* (Cambridge: Cambridge University Press, 1994), pp. 4–5, 91, 94, 242.

69. M. Roberts, *Gustavus Adolphus: A History of Sweden, 1611–1632*, 2 vols (Harlow: Longman, 1953 and 1958).

70. Ertman, *Birth of the Leviathan*, pp. 312–13.

71. A. Rao and S. Supphellen, 'Power Elites and Dependent Territories', in W. Reinhard (ed.), *Power Elites and State Building* (Oxford: Oxford University Press, 1996), pp. 84–8.

72. R. Hatton, *George I, Elector and King* (London: Thames & Hudson, 1978), p. 128; J. Walters, *The Royal Griffin: Frederick Prince of Wales, 1707–51* (London: Jarrolds, 1973), pp. 21–2.

73. Koenigsberger, 'Composite States, Representative Institutions and the American Revolution', pp. 135–53.

74. M. Graves, *The Parliaments of Early Modern Europe* (London: Longman, 2001), pp. 45, 127.

75. K. Kruger, 'Regional Representation in Schleswig and Holstein', *Parliaments, Estates and Representation*, 7, no. 1 (1987), pp. 33–37.

76. Blanning, *Eighteenth Century*, p. 13.

77. Koenigsberger, 'Composite States, Representative Institutions and the American Revolution', p. 139.

78. J. Elliott, *Richelieu and Olivares* (Cambridge: Cambridge University Press, 1984), p. 45.

79. Scott, *European Nobilities*, vol. 1, pp. 38–9.

80. E. Melton, 'The Prussian Junkers, 1600–1786', in H. Scott, *The European Nobilities in the Seventeenth and Eighteenth Centuries*, vol. 2: *Northern, Central and Eastern Europe* (London: Longman, 1994), p. 92.

81. Ertman, *Birth of the Leviathan*, pp. 224–63.

82. Mettam, *Power and Faction*, pp. 100–1.

83. A. James, *The Origins of French Absolutism, 1598–1661* (Harlow: Pearson, 2006), p. 80.

84. J. Black, *A Military Revolution? Military Change and European Society, 1550–1800* (Basingstoke: Macmillan, 1991), pp. 67–82; James, *Origins of French Absolutism*, p. 81; G. Rowlands, *The Dynastic State and the Army under Louis XIV* (Cambridge: Cambridge University Press, 2002), p. 335.

85. F. Tallett, *War and Society in Early Modern Europe* (London: Routledge, 1992), pp. 188–93.

86.  D. Bell, *The Cult of the Nation in France: Inventing Nationalism, 1680–1800* (Cambridge, MA: Harvard University Press, 2003), pp. 8, 165–8; M. Ozouf, *La fête révolutionnaire, 1789–1799* (Paris: Gallimard, 1976), pp. 441–74.

87.  L. Hunt, *Politics, Culture and Class in the French Revolution* (Berkeley, CA: University of California Press, 1986).

88.  Campbell, *Power and Politics*, pp. 4–5.

89.  W. Beik, *Absolutism and Society in Seventeenth-Century France: State Power and Provincial Aristocracy in Languedoc* (Cambridge: Cambridge University Press, 1985), pp. 324–7.

90.  H. Kamen, *European Society, 1500–1700* (London: Hutchinson, 1984), pp. 296–305.

91.  P. Wilson, *Absolutism in Central Europe* (London: Routledge, 2000), p. 120.

92.  Porter, *War and the Rise of the State*, p. 2.

93.  C. Ingrao, *The Habsburg Monarchy, 1618–1815* (Cambridge: Cambridge University Press, 1994), pp. 96, 127–8.

94.  W. Beik, 'The Absolutism of Louis XIV as Social Collaboration', *Past and Present*, 188 (2005), p. 201.

95.  Hurt, *Louis XIV and the Parlements*.

96.  C. Clark, *Iron Kingdom: The Rise and Downfall of Prussia, 1600–1947* (London: Allen Lane, 2006), pp. 113–14; J. Bergin (ed.), *The Seventeenth Century* (Oxford: Oxford University Press, 2001), p. 224; Beik, *Absolutism and Society*.

97.  A. Upton, 'Politics', in J. Bergin (ed.), *The Seventeenth Century* (Oxford: Oxford University Press, 2001), pp. 81–2; R. Nash, 'The Economy', in Bergin (ed.), *The Seventeenth Century*, p. 28; D. Sella, *Italy in the Seventeenth Century* (London: Longman, 1997), pp. 53–5; J. Plumb, *The Growth of Political Stability in England, 1675–1725* (London: Macmillan, 1967), pp. 21–4; Duindam, *Myths of Power*, p. 194.

98.  G. Symcox, *Victor Amadeus II: Absolutism in the Savoyard State, 1675–1730* (London: Thames & Hudson, 1983), pp. 217–22.

99.  C. Donati, 'The Italian Nobilities in the Seventeenth and Eighteenth Centuries', in Scott, *European Nobilities*, vol. 1, pp. 261–2.

100.  Campbell, *Power and Politics*, pp. 8–9, 42.

101.  Bergin, *Crown, Church and Episcopate*, p. 93.

102.  M. Anderson, *Europe in the Eighteenth Century, 1713–1789*, 4th edn (London: Longman, 2000), p. 119.

103.  James, *Origins of French Absolutism*, pp. 61, 91.

104.  F. Bluche, *Louis XIV* (Oxford: Blackwell, 1990), pp. 133–56.

105. Scott, *European Nobilities*, vol. 1, p. 24; D. Parker, *Class and State in Ancien Régime France: The Road to Modernity?* (London: Routledge, 1996), pp. 26–7.
106. N. Rodger, *The Wooden World: An Anatomy of the Georgian Navy* (London: Collins, 1986), p. 303.
107. James, *Origins of French Absolutism*, p. 79.
108. D. Bohanan, *Old and New Nobility in Aix-en-Provence, 1600–1695: Portrait of an Urban Elite* (Baton Rouge, LA: Louisiana State University Press, 1992), pp. 133–4.
109. Upton, 'Politics', pp. 81–2.
110. Scott, *European Nobilities*, vol. 1, pp. 35–46.
111. J. Salmon, 'Storm over the Noblesse', *Journal of Modern History*, 53 (June 1981), pp. 242–57.
112. James, *Origins of French Absolutism*, pp. 33, 68.
113. J. Smith, *The Culture of Merit: Nobility, Royal Service and the Making of Absolute Monarchy in France, 1600–1789* (Ann Arbor, MI: University of Michigan Press, 1996); M. Motley, *Becoming a French Aristocrat: The Education of the Court Nobility, 1580–1715* (Princeton, NJ: Princeton University Press, 1990).
114. H. Scott, *European Nobilities*, vol. 2, p. 9.
115. Sharpe, *Early Modern England*, p. 193.
116. L. Hughes, *Russia in the Age of Peter the Great* (New Haven, CT: Yale University Press, 1998), pp. 172–3.
117. Black, *Military Revolution*, pp. 77–8.
118. J. Black, *European Warfare, 1660–1815* (London: UCL Press, 1994), pp. 87–92.
119. E. Melton, 'Prussian Junkers, 1600–1786', in H. Scott, *European Nobilities*, vol. 2, pp. 98–9.
120. Rowlands, *Dynastic State and the Army under Louis XIV*, pp. 361–2.
121. D. Dessert and J. Journet, 'Le lobby Colbert: un royaume ou une affaire de famille?', *Annales*, ESC, xxx (1975), pp. 1303–36; D. Bien, 'Offices, Corps and a System of State Credit: the Uses of Privilege under the Ancien Régime', in K. Baker (ed.), *The Political Culture of the Old Régime* (Oxford: Pergamon, 1987), pp. 89–112; Mettam, *Power and Faction*, pp. 109–10; Campbell, *Power and Politics*, pp. 15–16; Beik, 'The Absolutism of Louis XIV as Social Collaboration', p. 203.
122. P. Mansel, *Pillars of Monarchy* (New York: Quartet, 1984), pp. 9–25, 159.
123. Hughes, *Russia in the Age of Peter the Great*, pp. 181–4.
124. M. Anderson, *War and Society in Europe of the Old Regime, 1618–1789* (London: Fontana, 1988), pp. 132–3.

125. H. Scott, 'Diplomatic Culture in Old Regime Europe', in H. Scott and B. Simms (eds), *Cultures of Power in Europe during the Long Eighteenth Century* (Cambridge: Cambridge University Press, 2007), pp. 58–85.

126. Bergin, *Crown, Church and Episcopate*, pp. 58–64.

127. Scott, *European Nobilities*, vol. 1, pp. 44–6.

128. Rosenheim, *Emergence of a Ruling Order*, p. 257.

129. Campbell, *Power and Politics*, pp. 22, 183–4; Rowlands, *Dynastic State and the Army under Louis XIV*.

130. F. Carsten, *The Origins of Prussia* (Oxford: Oxford University Press, 1954), p. 167.

131. Clark, *Revolution and Rebellion*, p. 80.

132. Campbell, *Power and Politics*, p. 306; P. Burke, *The Fabrication of Louis XIV* (New Haven, CT: Yale University Press, 1992), pp. 15–37.

133. H. Smith, *Georgian Monarchy: Politics and Culture, 1714–1760* (Cambridge: Cambridge University Press, 2006), p. 193.

134. Adamson, *Princely Courts of Europe*.

135. *The Court Historian* (1996– ), edited by P. Mansel.

136. Rosenheim, *Emergence of a Ruling Order*, p. 198.

137. Rosenheim, *Emergence of a Ruling Order*, p. 180.

138. J. Dewald, *The European Nobility, 1400–1800* (Cambridge: Cambridge University Press, 1996), pp. 149–62.

139. A. Goldgar, *Impolite Learning: Conduct and Community in the Republic of Letters, 1680–1750* (New Haven, CT: Yale University Press, 1995), pp. 5–6.

140. D. Bell, 'Culture and Religion', in W. Doyle (ed.), *Old Regime France, 1648–1788* (Oxford: Oxford University Press, 2001), pp. 82–5.

141. J. Maravall, *Culture of the Baroque: Analysis of a Historical Structure* (Minneapolis, MN: Minnesota University Press, 1986), pp. 90–1.

142. T. Munck, *Seventeenth Century Europe, 1598–1700* (Basingstoke: Macmillan, 1990), p. 306.

143. L. Hollis, *The Phoenix: St Paul's Cathedral and the Men Who Made Modern London* (London: Weidenfeld & Nicolson, 2008), pp. 11–24.

144. Burke, *Fabrication of Louis XIV*, p. 19.

145. Burke, *Fabrication of Louis XIV*, p. 19.

146. Upton, 'Politics', pp. 81–2.

147. D. Posner, *Antoine Watteau* (London: Weidenfeld & Nicolson, 1984), p. 117; T. Blanning, *The Culture of Power and the Power of Culture: Old Regime Europe, 1660–1789* (Oxford: Oxford University Press, 2002), pp. 104–5.

148. M. Levey, *Painting and Sculpture in France, 1700–1789* (New Haven, CT: Yale University Press, 1993), pp. 29–43; Posner, *Watteau*, pp. 7–9.

149. J. Clark, *English Society, 1660–1832*, 2nd edn (Cambridge: Cambridge University Press, 2000).
150. Beales, 'Religion and Culture', pp. 135–7.
151. Bergin, *Crown, Church and Episcopate*, p. 348.
152. Black, *Military Revolution*, pp. 67–77.
153. Adamson, *Princely Courts of Europe*, p. 40.
154. Collins, *State in Early Modern France*, p. 121.
155. M. Fantoni, 'Work in Progress: "Europe of the Courts" and Court Studies', *Court Historian*, vol. II, 2 (June 1997), pp. 21–3.
156. Campbell, *Power and Politics*, pp. 16–20.
157. Adamson, *Princely Courts of Europe*, p. 10.
158. S. Klingensmith, *The Utility of Splendour: Ceremony, Social Life and Architecture at the Court of Bavaria, 1600–1800* (Chicago, IL: University of Chicago Press, 1993), p. 11.
159. Campbell, *Power and Politics*, pp. 9, 20–4, 183.
160. J. Duindam, *Vienna and Versailles: The Courts of Europe's Dynastic Rivals, 1550–1780* (Cambridge: Cambridge University Press, 2003), p. 253.
161. Campbell, *Power and Politics*, pp. 170, 184.
162. N. Elias, *The Court Society* (Oxford: Oxford University Press, 1983).
163. H. Smith, *Georgian Monarchy: Politics and Culture, 1714–1760* (Cambridge: Cambridge University Press, 2006), p. 227.
164. R. Smuts, 'The Structure of the Court and the Roles of the Artist and Poet under Charles I', *Court Historian*, vol. 9, 2 (December 2004), p. 104.
165. M. Antoine, *Louis XV* (Paris: Fayard, 1989), pp. 157–8.
166. Adamson, *Princely Courts of Europe*, pp. 24–33, 40–1.
167. Adamson, *Princely Courts of Europe*, p. 12.
168. J. Duindam, 'The Courts of the Austrian Habsburgs, c.1500–1750', in Adamson, *Princely Courts of Europe*, pp. 168–71, 177.
169. Klingensmith, *The Utility of Splendour*, pp. 11–12.
170. Scott, *European Nobilities*, vol, 1, pp. 49–52.
171. R. Bucholz, *The Augustan Court: Queen Anne and the Decline of Court Culture* (Stanford, CA: Stanford University Press, 1993), pp. 228–42.
172. Colley, *Britons*, pp. 196–8.
173. Colley, *Britons*, pp. 199–200.
174. Black, *Military Revolution*, pp. 71–4.
175. D. Lieven, *The Aristocracy in Europe, 1815–1914* (Basingstoke: Macmillan, 1992), p. 3.
176. Munck, *Seventeenth Century Europe*, pp. 235–6; Clark, *English Society, 1660–1832*, pp. 23–4.

177. D. Outram, *The Enlightenment* (Cambridge: Cambridge University Press, 1997), pp. 102–3.
178. Ingrao, *Habsburg Monarchy*, pp. 94–5, 127.
179. James, *Origins of French Absolutism*, pp. xviii–xix, 78.
180. Scott, *European Nobilities*, vol. 1, pp. 35, 52, 267–8; vol. II, pp. 277–9.

## Chapter 1: Key Themes of Elite Culture

1. C. Hill, *The World Turned Upside Down: Radical Ideas during the English Revolution* (Harmondsworth: Penguin, 1975), pp. 288–9, 296–7.
2. F. Yates, *The Rosicrucian Enlightenment*, 2nd edn (St Albans: Paladin, 1975), pp. 217–22; R. Strong, *The Spirit of Britain: A Narrative History of the Arts* (London: Pimlico, 2000), pp. 273–4.
3. N. Cohn, *The Pursuit of the Millennium: Revolutionary Millenarians and Mystical Anarchists of the Middle Ages*, 3rd edn (St Albans: Paladin, 1970); M. Burleigh, *Sacred Causes: Religion and Politics from the European Dictators to Al Qaeda* (New York: HarperPress, 2006), p. xi.
4. Strong, *Spirit of Britain*, p. 273.
5. F. Fernandez-Armesto, *Columbus* (Oxford: Oxford University Press, 1991), pp. 34, 39–40, 49–50, 118–19.
6. M. Beloff, *The Age of Absolutism, 1660–1815* (London: Hutchinson, 1954), p. 14.
7. J. Redwood, *Reason, Ridicule and Religion: The Age of Enlightenment in England, 1660–1750* (London: Thames & Hudson, 1976), pp. 10–11.
8. P. Wilson, *Absolutism in Central Europe* (London: Routledge, 2000), pp. 95–6.
9. D. Beales, 'Religion and Culture', in T. Blanning (ed.), *The Eighteenth Century* (Oxford: Oxford University Press, 2000), pp. 131–2.
10. T. Rabb, *The Struggle for Stability in Early Modern Europe* (Oxford: Oxford University Press, 1975), p. 103; R. Morrice, *Stuart and Baroque* (London: Barrie & Jenkins, 1982), pp. 17–18.
11. D. Armitage, 'Literature and Empire', in N. Canny (ed.), *The Origins of Empire: British Overseas Enterprise to the Close of the Seventeenth Century* (Oxford: Oxford University Press, 1998), pp. 103–4; M. Anderson, *Europe in the Eighteenth Century, 1713–1789*, 4th edn (London: Longman, 2000), pp. 326–7.
12. Rabb, *Struggle for Stability*, p. 118.
13. D. Maland, *Culture and Society in Seventeenth-Century France* (London: Batsford, 1970), pp. 202–26.

14. P. Burke, *Tradition and Innovation in Renaissance Italy* (London: Fontana edn, 1974), p. 322.

15. D. Hay, *The Italian Renaissance in its Historical Background* (Cambridge: Cambridge University Press, 1961), pp. 88–9.

16. Anderson, *Europe in the Eighteenth Century*, pp. 325–6.

17. Rabb, *Struggle for Stability*, pp. 112–15; L. Hollis, *The Phoenix: St Paul's Cathedral and the Men Who Made Modern London* (London: Weidenfeld & Nicolson, 2008), pp. 11–24, 36–41.

18. *The Shorter Oxford English Dictionary on Historical Principles*, 3rd edn, reprinted with corrections (Oxford: Oxford University Press, 1959), vol. 1, p. 401.

19. C. Hibbert, *The Grand Tour* (London: Thames Methuen, 1987), pp. 16–18.

20. H. Scott, *The European Nobilities in the Seventeenth and Eighteenth Centuries*, vol. 1: *Western Europe* (London: Longman, 1995), pp. 266–7.

21. V. Kiernan, *The Duel in European History: Honour and the Reign of Aristocracy* (Oxford: Oxford University Press, 1989), p. 113.

22. Kiernan, *Duel in European History*, pp. 153, 64–5.

23. A. Steinmetz, *The Romance of Duelling in all Times and Countries* (London: Chapman & Hall, 1868), pp. 32–6.

24. C. Storrs and H. Scott, 'The Military Revolution and the European Nobility, c. 1600–1800', *War in History*, 3 (1996), pp. 1–41.

25. H. Scott, 'Diplomatic Culture in Old Regime Europe', in H. Scott and B. Simms (eds), *Cultures of Power in Europe during the Long Eighteenth Century* (Cambridge: Cambridge University Press, 2007), pp. 58–85.

26. T. Blanning, *The Triumph of Music: Composers, Musicians and their Audiences, 1700 to the Present* (London: Allen Lane, 2008), pp. 235–6.

27. T. Blanning, 'The Commercialization and Sacralization of European Culture in the Nineteenth Century', in T. Blanning (ed.), *The Oxford Illustrated History of Modern Europe* (Oxford: Oxford University Press, 1996), p. 141.

28. J. Rosenheim, *The Emergence of a Ruling Order: English Landed Society, 1650–1750* (London: Longman, 1998), p. 202.

29. T. Blanning, *The Culture of Power and the Power of Culture: Old Regime Europe, 1660–1789* (Oxford: Oxford University Press, 2002), pp. 15–25; P. Burke, review of *Culture and Power*, *History Today*, vol. 52 (June 2002), p. 60; A. Smith, 'Dating the Nation', *History Today*, vol. 58 (March 2008), pp. 32–4.

30. A. Hastings, *The Construction of Nationhood: Ethnicity, Religion and Nationalism* (Cambridge: Cambridge University Press, 1997), p. 120.

31. J. Sharpe, *Early Modern England: A Social History, 1550–1760* (London: Edward Arnold, 1987), p. 119.

32. E. Hobsbawm, *Nations and Nationalism since 1780: Programme, Myth, Reality* (Cambridge: Cambridge University Press, 1990), p. 14.
33. H. Kamen, *Spain in the Later Seventeenth Century, 1665–1700* (London: Longman, 1980), pp. 3, 6–7.
34. T. Blanning, *Joseph II* (London: Longman, 1994), pp. 18–19.
35. P. Mansel, *Louis VIII* (London: John Murray, 1981), p. 6; D. Bohanan, *Crown and Nobility in Early Modern France* (Basingstoke: Macmillan 2001), pp. 68–9.
36. T. Blanning, *The Pursuit of Glory: Europe, 1648–1815* (London: Allen Lane, 2007), p. 371.
37. G. Robb, *The Discovery of France* (London: Picador, 2007), pp. 19–35; E. Weber, *Peasants into Frenchmen: The Modernization of Rural France* (Stanford, CA: Stanford University Press, 1976); R. Tombs, *France, 1814–1914* (London: Longman, 1996), pp. 302–25.
38. Robb, *Discovery of France*, pp. 50–3.
39. Robb, *Discovery of France*, pp. 306–7
40. D. Robertson, *The Penguin Dictionary of Politics*, 2nd edn (Harmondsworth: Penguin, 1993), pp. 160–70, 331.
41. M. Clark, *Modern Italy, 1871–1995*, 2nd edn (London: Longman, 1996), p. 30.
42. Tombs, *France, 1814–1914*, pp. 1–2; D. Bell, *The Cult of the Nation in France: Inventing Nationalism, 1680–1800* (Cambridge, MA: Harvard University Press, 2001), p. 8.
43. Hastings, *Construction of Nationhood*, pp. 96–147.
44. Tombs, *France, 1814–1914*, p. 306; N. Ferguson, *The War of the World* (London: Allen Lane, 2006), pp. 74–5.
45. Kamen, *Spain in the Later Seventeenth Century*, p. 3.
46. A. Johnson, *Europe in the Sixteenth Century, 1494–1598* (London: Rivingtons, 1894), pp. 2–3; P. Rietbergen, *Europe: A Cultural History* (London: Routledge, 1998), p. 195; D. Potter, *A History of France, 1460–1560: The Emergence of a Nation State* (Basingstoke: Macmillan, 1995); A. Smith, *The Emergence of a Nation State: The Commonwealth of England, 1529–1660* (London: Longman, 1984).
47. A. Upton, 'Politics', in J. Bergin (ed.), *The Seventeenth Century* (Oxford: Oxford University Press, 2001), pp. 99–101.
48. A. Pagden, 'Europe and the Wider World', in J. Bergin (ed.), *The Seventeenth Century* (Oxford: Oxford University Press, 2001), pp. 215.
49. J. Elliott, 'A Europe of Composite Monarchies', *Past and Present*, no. 137 (1992), pp. 59–60.
50. D. Armitage, *The Ideological Origins of the British Empire* (Cambridge: Cambridge University Press, 2000), pp. 14–15.

51. J. Hoppit (ed.), *Parliaments, Nations and Identities in Britain and Ireland, 1660–1850* (Manchester: Manchester University Press, 2003), pp. 1–3; G. Newman, *The Rise of English Nationalism: A Cultural History, 1740–1830*, rev. edn (Basingstoke: Macmillan, 1997); Bell, *Cult of the Nation in France*; L. Colley, *Britons: Forging the Nation, 1707–1837* (New Haven, CT: Yale University Press, 1992).

52. J. Elliott, *Imperial Spain, 1469–1716* (London: Edward Arnold, 1963), p. 7; J. Elliott, *Richelieu and Olivares* (Cambridge: Cambridge University Press, 1984), pp. 72–4.

53. Bell, *Cult of the Nation in France*, pp. 5–6.

54. A. Taylor, *The Habsburg Monarchy, 1809–1918* (Harmondsworth: Penguin edition, 1990), p. 11.

55. C. Ingrao, *The Habsburg Monarchy, 1618–1815* (Cambridge: Cambridge University Press, 1994), pp. 95–101.

56. R. Evans, *The Making of the Habsburg Monarchy, 1550–1700* (Oxford: Oxford University Press, 1979), pp. 444–6.

57. Colley, *Britons*.

58. Colley, *Britons*, pp. 5–6.

59. Armitage, *Ideological Origins*, pp. 170–3.

60. Bell, *Cult of the Nation in France*.

61. J. Elliott, 'Europe of Composite Monarchies', pp. 51–2, 65–6.

62. B. Porter, *War and the Rise of the State: The Military Foundations of Modern Politics* (New York: Free Press, 1994); T. Ertman, *Birth of the Leviathan: Building States and Regimes in Medieval and Early Modern Europe* (Cambridge: Cambridge University Press, 1997).

63. M. Greengrass, *Conquest and Coalescence: The Shaping of the State in Early Modern Europe* (London: Edward Arnold, 1991); J. Adamson, *The Princely Courts of Europe, 1500–1750: Ritual, Politics and Culture under the* Ancien Régime, *1500–1750* (London: Weidenfeld & Nicolson, 1999), p. 40; J. Duindam, *Myths of Power* (Amsterdam: Amsterdam University Press, 1994), pp. 1–5.

64. D. Parrott, 'War and International Relations', in J. Bergin (ed.), *The Seventeenth Century* (Oxford: Oxford University Press, 2001), pp. 141–3.

65. Elliott, 'Europe of Composite Monarchies', pp. 51–2, 57–8.

66. Colley, *Britons*, pp. 5, 374–5.

67. K. Baker, *Inventing the French Revolution* (Cambridge: Cambridge University Press, 1990), pp. 21–2.

68. Bell, *Cult of the Nation*, pp. 12, 56–7.

69. J. Black, *George III: America's Last King* (New Haven, CT: Yale University Press, 2007), pp. 426–7; Bell, *Cult of the Nation in France*.

70. J. Black, *George II: Puppet of the Politicians?* (Exeter: University of Exeter Press, 2007), pp. 183–4.

71. Blanning, *Triumph of Music*, pp. 260–1.

72. Blanning, *Culture of Power*, pp. 354–406.

73. Blanning, *Triumph of Music*, pp. 248–9.

74. Bell, *Cult of the Nation in France*, pp. 46–7; J. Black, *A Subject for Taste: Culture in Eighteenth-Century England* (Hambledon and London: Palgrave Macmillan, 2005), pp. 218–19; Newman, *Rise of English Nationalism*, p. 112.

75. Colley, *Britons*, pp. 85–6.

76. W. Mann, *The Operas of Mozart* (London: Cassell, 1977), pp. 57, 291.

77. Bell, *Cult of the Nation in France*, p. 11.

78. *The Shorter Oxford English Dictionary on Historical Principles*, 3rd edn, reprinted with corrections (Oxford: Oxford University Press, 1959), vol. II, p. 1331.

79. T. Kaufmann, *Court, Cloister and City: The Art and Culture of Central Europe, 1450–1800* (London: Weidenfeld & Nicolson, 1995), pp. 403–4.

80. T. Blanning, *The French Revolution: Class War or Culture Clash?*, 2nd edn (Basingstoke: Macmillan, 1998), p. 21.

## Chapter 2: The Formation of Elite Cultural Hegemony

1. T. Rabb, *The Struggle for Stability in Early Modern Europe* (Oxford: Oxford University Press, 1975), p. 118.

2. H. Scott, *The European Nobilities in the Seventeenth and Eighteenth Centuries*, vol. 1: *Western Europe* (London: Longman, 1995), pp. 21–2.

3. L. Stone and J. Stone, *An Open Elite? England, 1540–1880* (Oxford: Oxford University Press, 1986 edition), pp. 3–6, 283–9.

4. J. Rosenheim, *The Emergence of a Ruling Order: English Landed Society, 1650–1750* (London: Longman, 1998), p. 180.

5. T. Munck, 'Society', in J. Bergin (ed.), *The Seventeenth Century* (Oxford: Oxford University Press, 2001), pp. 52–7.

6. B. Last, *Politics and Letters in the Age of Walpole* (Newcastle: Avero, 1987), p. 8.

7. Rosenheim, *Emergence of a Ruling Order*, pp. 178, 184, 193, 212–4.

8. J. Dewald, *The European Nobility, 1400–1800* (Cambridge: Cambridge University Press, 1996), pp. 157–8.

9. D. Bell, 'Culture and Religion', in W. Doyle (ed.), *Old Regime France* (Oxford: Oxford University Press, 2001), p. 83.

10. A. Dickens, *Reformation and Society in Sixteenth Century Europe* (London: Thames & Hudson, 1966), pp. 84–5.

11. Beales, 'Religion and Culture', pp. 141–2; T. Blanning, *The Culture of Power and the Power of Culture* (Oxford: Oxford University Press, 2002), pp. 234–45.

12. A. Hauser, *The Social History of Art: Rococo, Classicism and Romanticism*, 2nd edn (London: Routledge, 1962), pp. 1–2, 77–8.

13. Dewald, *European Nobility*, pp. 157–8.

14. S. Jenkins, *England's Thousand Best Houses* (London: Allen Lane, 2003), p. 705.

15. D. Maland, *Culture and Society in Seventeenth-Century France* (London: Batsford, 1970), p. 140.

16. R. Holmes, *The Age of Wonder: How the Romantic Generation Discovered the Beauty and Terror of Science* (New York: HarperPress, 2008), p. xix.

17. M. Umbach, 'Culture and *Bürgerlichkeit* in Eighteenth-century Germany', in H. Scott and B. Simms (eds), *Cultures of Power in Europe during the Long Eighteenth Century* (Cambridge: Cambridge University Press, 2007), pp. 185–8.

18. A. Upton, 'Politics', in J. Bergin (ed.), *The Seventeenth Century* (Oxford: Oxford University Press, 2001), pp. 81–2.

19. J. Duindam, *Myths of Power* (Amsterdam: Amsterdam University Press, 1994), pp. 193–5.

20. A. Sisman, *Wordsworth and Coleridge: The Friendship* (London: Harper, 2006), pp. 33–5.

21. Rosenheim, *Emergence of a Ruling Order*, p. 2.

22. J. Dewald, *Aristocratic Experience and the Origins of Modern Culture: France, 1570–1715* (Berkeley, CA: University of California Press, 1993),pp. 137–45.

23. J. Black, *The Politics of Britain, 1688–1800* (Manchester: Manchester University Press, 1993), pp. 14–29.

24. G. Robb, *The Discovery of France* (London: Picador, 2007), pp. 50–70.

25. R. Evans, *The Making of the Habsburg Monarchy, 1550–1700* (Oxford: Oxford University Press, 1979), p. 311.

26. H. Scott, 'Diplomatic Culture in Old Regime Europe', in H. Scott and B. Simms (eds), *Cultures of Power in Europe during the Long Eighteenth Century* (Cambridge: Cambridge University Press, 2007), pp. 58–85.

27. S. Fischer, *A History of Reading* (London: Reaktion Books, 2003), p. 1.

28. Dewald, *European Nobility*, p. 152.

29. D. Bohanan, *Old and New Nobility in Aix-en-Provence, 1600–1695: Portrait of an Urban Elite* (Baton Rouge, LA: Louisiana State University Press, 1992), p. 121.

30. J. Lough, *An Introduction to Seventeenth-Century France* (London: Longman, 1954), pp. 221–2.

31. W. Beik, 'The Absolutism of Louis XIV as Social Collaboration', *Past and Present*, 188 (2005), p. 203; Campbell, *Power and Politics*, pp. 20, 183.

32. Rabb, *Struggle for Stability*, pp. 64–5; A. James, *The Origins of French Absolutism, 1598–1661* (Harlow: Pearson, 2006), p. 80; M. Bannister, *Condé in Context: Ideological Change in Seventeenth Century France* (Oxford: Oxford University Press, 2000).

33. E. Schalk, *From Valor to Pedigree: Ideas of Nobility in France in the Sixteenth and Seventeenth Centuries* (Princeton, NJ: Princeton University Press, 1986).

34. A. Beer, *Milton: Poet, Pamphleteer and Patriot* (London: Bloomsbury, 2008), p. 26.

35. K. Wrightson, *English Society, 1580–1680* (London: Hutchinson, 1982), pp. 189–93.

36. Dewald, *European Nobility*, pp. 151–4.

37. Wrightson, *English Society*, p. 189.

38. J. Smith, *The Culture of Merit: Nobility, Royal Service and the Making of Absolute Monarchy in France, 1600–1789* (Ann Arbor, MI: University of Michigan Press, 1996).

39. L. Hughes, *Russia in the Age of Peter the Great* (New Haven, CT: Yale University Press, 1998), p. 174.

40. J. Black and R. Porter (eds), *A Dictionary of Eighteenth-Century World History* (Oxford: Blackwell, 1994), pp. 312, 754.

41. Bohanan, *Old and New Nobility*, pp. 1–4, 125–6.

42. Wrightson, *English Society*, pp. 191–2; H. de Ridder-Symoens, 'Training and Professionalization', in W. Reinhard, *Power Elites and State Building* (Oxford: Oxford University Press, 1996), pp. 159–60.

43. Rosenheim, *Emergence of a Ruling Order*, pp. 195–8.

44. Rosenheim, *Emergence of a Ruling Order*, p. 202.

45. J. Black, *The British Abroad: The Grand Tour in the Eighteenth Century* (Stroud: Alan Sutton, 1992), pp. 213–14, 235.

46. D. Shawe-Taylor, *The Georgians: Eighteenth-Century Portraiture and Society* (London: Barrie & Jenkins, 1990), p. 40.

47. R. Strong, *Feast: A History of Grand Eating* (London: Jonathan Cape, 2002), pp. 160–2, 246; Rosenheim, *Emergence of a Ruling Order*, pp. 180–1; Lough, *Introduction to Seventeenth-Century France*, pp. 225–6.

48. L. Brockliss, 'The Age of Curiosity', in J. Bergin (ed.), *The Seventeenth Century* (Oxford: Oxford University Press, 2001), pp. 182–3.

49. T. Munck, *Seventeenth Century Europe, 1598–1700* (Basingstoke: Macmillan, 1990), pp. 270–2.

50. V. Gattrell, *City of Laughter: Sex and Satire in Eighteenth-Century London* (London: Atlantic Books, 2006), pp. 18–19; 110–11, 196; J. Black, *A Subject*

*for Taste: Culture in Eighteenth-Century England* (Hambledon and London: Palgrave Macmillan, 2005), pp. 130–1.

51. P. Burke, *Popular Culture in Early-modern Europe* (Aldershot: Wildwood House, 1988), pp. 270–81.

52. G. Parker, *Europe in Crisis, 1598–1648*, 2nd edn (Oxford: Blackwell, 2001), pp. 234–5.

53. P. Ackroyd, *Shakespeare: The Biography* (London: Chatto & Windus, 2005), p. 347.

54. Rosenheim, *Emergence of a Ruling Order*, p. 174.

55. Lord Chesterfield, *Letters to His Son* (London: Everyman's Library, 1929), pp. 122–3.

56. J. Brewer, *The Pleasures of the Imagination: English Culture in the Eighteenth Century* (London: HarperCollins, 1997), p. xvi.

57. J. Sharpe, *Early Modern England: A Social History, 1550–1760* (London: Edward Arnold, 1987), p. 300.

58. D. Mortlock, *Aristocratic Splendour: Money and the World of Thomas Coke, Earl of Leicester* (Stroud: Sutton, 2007), p. 147.

59. Lough, *Seventeenth Century France*, pp. 208–14.

60. R. Muchembled, *Popular Culture and Elite Culture in France, 1400–1750* (Baton Rouge, LA: Louisiana State University Press, 1985), pp. 279–84.

61. R. Hutton, *The Rise and Fall of Merry England: The Ritual Year, 1400–1700* (Oxford: Oxford University Press, 1994), pp. 111–12, 143–4.

62. Rosenheim, *Emergence of a Ruling Order*, p. 207.

63. Rosenheim, *Emergence of a Ruling Order*, pp. 177–8; Sharpe, *Early Modern England*, pp. 285–6.

64. W. Hague, *William Wilberforce: The Life of the Great Anti-Slave Trade Campaigner* (London: HarperCollins, 2008), pp. 103–4.

65. Burke, *Popular Culture*, pp. 234–43.

66. Rosenheim, *Emergence of a Ruling Order*, p. 211; K. Thomas, *Man and the Natural World: Changing Attitudes in England, 1500–1800* (Harmondsworth: Penguin, 1984), pp. 51–87.

67. Burke, *Popular Culture*, p. 272; S. Tillyard, *A Royal Affair: George III and his Troublesome Siblings* (London: Chatto & Windus, 2006), p. 7.

68. M. Bragg, *The Adventure of English: The Biography of a Language* (London: Hodder & Stoughton, 2003), pp. 94–9.

69. A. Bennett, *The History Boys* (London: Faber & Faber, 2004), p. 55.

70. Burke, *Popular Culture*, pp. 272–9.

71. R. Strong, *The Spirit of Britain: A Narrative History of the Arts* (London: Pimlico, 2000), p. 426.

72. Dewald, *European Nobility*, pp. 159–60.

73. C. Clark, *Iron Kingdom: The Rise and Downfall of Prussia, 1600–1947* (London: Allen Lane, 2006), p. 71.

74. P. Langford, *A Polite and Commercial People: England, 1727–1783* (Oxford: Oxford University Press, 1989), pp. 652–5.

75. H. Perkin, *The Origins of Modern English Society, 1780–1880* (London: Routledge, 1969), p. 61.

76. P. Laslett, *The World We Have Lost* (London: Methuen, 1965), pp. 23–4; Perkin, *The Origins of Modern English Society*, pp. 37–8.

77. Langford, *Polite and Commercial People*, pp. 653–4.

78. Molière, *The Miser and Other Plays* (Harmondsworth: Penguin, 1962), pp. 17–19.

79. T. Blanning, *The Pursuit of Glory: Europe, 1648–1815* (London: Allen Lane, 2007), p. 336.

## Chapter 3: Basic Agendas: 'Science', Political Culture and Religion

1. D. Cupitt, *The Sea of Faith* (London: BBC, 1984), pp. 114–18.

2. L. Brockliss, 'The Age of Curiosity', in J. Bergin (ed.), *The Seventeenth Century* (Oxford: Oxford University Press, 2001), pp. 145–6.

3. Brockliss, 'The Age of Curiosity', pp. 145–51.

4. Brockliss, 'The Age of Curiosity', pp. 181–2.

5. J. Black, *A Military Revolution? Military Change and European Society, 1550–1800* (Basingstoke: Macmillan, 1991), pp. 71–7.

6. Brockliss, 'The Age of Curiosity', p. 224, pp. 152–60.

7. P. Fara, *Newton: The Making of a Genius* (London: Picador, 2003), pp. 234–5.

8. A. Hall, *The Revolution in Science, 1500–1750*, 3rd edn (London: Longman, 1983), p. 120.

9. Fara, *Newton*, pp. 70–1.

10. L. Hollis, *The Phoenix: St Paul's Cathedral and the Men Who Made Modern London* (London: Weidenfeld & Nicolson, 2008), p. 24.

11. L. Jardine, *On a Grander Scale: The Outstanding Career of Sir Christopher Wren* (London: HarperCollins, 2002), pp. 414–24.

12. Fara, *Newton*, p. 60.

13. F. Yates, *The Rosicrucian Enlightenment* (St Albans: Paladin, 1975), pp. 229–30.

14. J. Bergin (ed.), *The Seventeenth Century* (Oxford: Oxford University Press, 2001), p. 227.

15. P. Palmer and R. More, *The Sources of the Faust Tradition from Simon Magus to Lessing* (Oxford: Oxford University Press, 1936), p. 241.

16. R. Strong, *The Spirit of Britain: A Narrative History of the Arts* (London: Pimlico, 2000), pp. 273–87.

17. B. Coward, *The Stuart Age* (London: Longman, 1980), p. 429.

18. S. Shapin, 'A Scholar and a Gentleman: the Problematic Identity of the Scientific Practitioner in Early-modern England', *History of Science*, 29, part 3, no. 85 (Sept. 1991), pp. 279–327; A. Goldgar, *Impolite Learning: Conduct and Community in the Republic of Letters, 1680–1750* (New Haven, CT: Yale University Press, 1995), p. 7.

19. Hall, *Revolution in Science*, pp. 210–12.

20. Hall, *Revolution in Science*, pp. 200, 228–9.

21. J. Shennan, *Philippe Duke of Orleans: Regent of France, 1715–1723* (London: Thames & Hudson, 1979), pp. 103–10.

22. J. Shennan, *The Parlement of Paris*, revised edn (Stroud: Sutton, 1998), pp. xxxvi–xxxvii.

23. C. Jones, *The Great Nation: France from Louis XV to Napoleon* (London: Allen Lane, Penguin Press, 2002), pp. 61–73; M. Balen, *A Very English Deceit: The Secret History of the South Sea Bubble and First Great Financial Scandal* (London: Fourth Estate, 2002), pp. 55–77.

24. J. Black, *Kings, Nobles and Commoners: States and Societies in Early-modern Europe, a Revisionist History* (London: Tauris, 2004), p. 93.

25. T. Munck, *Seventeenth Century Europe, 1598–1700* (Basingstoke: Macmillan, 1990), p. 346.

26. J. Plumb, *The Growth of Political Stability in England, 1675–1725* (London: Macmillan, 1967), pp. 24–6.

27. R. Bonney, *The European Dynastic States, 1494–1660* (Oxford: Oxford University Press, 1991), pp. 330–1.

28. D. Robertson, *The Penguin Dictionary of Politics* (Harmondsworth: Penguin, 1993), pp. 44–5.

29. P. Campbell, *Power and Politics in Old Regime France, 1720–1745* (London: Routledge, 1996), pp. 21–4.

30. G. Rowlands, *The Dynastic State and the Army under Louis XIV* (Cambridge: Cambridge University Press, 2002).

31. M. Keynes, 'Newton the Man', in Royal Society, *Newton Tercentenary Celebrations* (Cambridge: Cambridge University Press, 1947), pp. 27–34; Fara, *Newton*, pp. 1–2.

32. S. Barnett, 'The Prophetic Thought of Sir Isaac Newton, its Origin and Context', in B. Taithe and T. Thornton, *Prophecy* (Stroud: Sutton, 1997), p. 101.

33. S. Hawking (ed.), *On the Shoulders of Giants: The Great Works of Physics and Astronomy* (Philadelphia, PA: Running Press, 2002), p. 726.

34. Fara, *Newton*, pp. 13, 59–60, 77.
35. Hawking, *On the Shoulders of Giants*, p. 1160.
36. Hawking, *On the Shoulders of Giants*, p. 1157.
37. Fara, *Newton*, pp. 68–74.
38. M. White, *Newton: The Last Sorcerer* (London: Fourth Estate, 1997), pp. 87, 190–221.
39. White, *Isaac Newton*, pp. 360–1.
40. R. Porter, *The Greatest Benefit to Mankind: A Medical History of Humanity from Antiquity to the Present* (London: HarperCollins, 1997), pp. 281–2; J. Clifford, *Young Samuel Johnson* (London: Heinemann, 1955), pp. 10–13.
41. M. Stafford (ed.), *Private Vices, Public Benefits? The Contemporary Reception of Bernard Mandeville* (Solihull: Ismeron, 1997), pp. xi–xvi.
42. P. Hazard, *The European Mind, 1680–1715* (London: Pelican, 1964), pp. 333–4.
43. H. Koenigsberger, 'Republicanism, Monarchism and Liberty', in R. Oresko, G. Gibbs and H. Scott, *Royal and Republican Sovereignty in Early-modern Europe* (Cambridge: Cambridge University Press, 1997), pp. 64–5.
44. J. Clark, *English Society, 1660–1832*, 2nd edn (Cambridge: Cambridge University Press, 2000), pp. 13, 17.
45. D. Parrott, 'War and International Relations', in J. Bergin (ed.), *The Seventeenth Century* (Oxford: Oxford University Press, 2001), p. 141.
46. A. James, *The Origins of French Absolutism, 1598–1661* (Harlow: Pearson, 2006), pp. xviii–xix, 17, 33, 67.
47. A. Upton, 'Politics', in J. Bergin (ed.), *The Seventeenth Century* (Oxford: Oxford University Press, 2001), pp. 80–1; J. Adamson, *The Princely Courts of Europe, 1500–1750* (London: Weidenfeld & Nicolson, 1998), p. 40.
48. D. Sturdy, *Louis XIV* (Basingstoke: Macmillan, 1998), pp. 12–13.
49. R. Mettam, *Government and Society in Louis XIV's France* (London: Macmillan, 1977), p. xv.
50. Bergin, *The Seventeenth Century*, p. 222; J. Swann, 'Politics and the State in Eighteenth-century Europe', in T. Blanning, *The Eighteenth Century: Europe, 1688–1815* (Oxford: Oxford University Press, 2000), pp. 12–13.
51. S. Chrimes, *English Constitutional Ideas in the Fifteenth Century* (Cambridge: Cambridge University Press, 1936), p. 339, note 68; D. Beales, *Enlightenment and Reform in Eighteenth-Century Europe* (London: Tauris, 2005), pp. 268–71; D. Beales, *Joseph II: Against the World, 1780–1790* (Cambridge: Cambridge University Press, 2009), pp. 356–8, 647–56; N. Henshall, *The Myth of Absolutism: Change and Continuity in early Modern European Monarchy* (London: Longman, 1992), pp. 120–98.
52. Swann, 'Politics and the State', p. 35.

53. Munck, *Seventeenth Century Europe*, p. 35.
54. Koenigsberger, 'Republicanism, Monarchism and Liberty', pp. 64–5; H. Blom, J. Laursen and L. Simonutti, *Monarchisms in the Age of Enlightenment: Liberty, Patriotism and the Common Good* (Toronto: University of Toronto Press, 2007), pp. 3–15.
55. J. Clark, *The Language of Liberty, 1660–1832: Political Discourse and Social Dynamics in the Anglo-American World* (Cambridge: Cambridge University Press, 1994), pp. 76–7; D. Smith, 'The Idea of the Rule of Law in England and France in the Seventeenth Century', in R. Asch and H. Duchhardt, *Der Absolutismus – ein Mythos? Strukturwandel monarchischer Herrschaft in West- und Mitteleuropa (ca. 1550–1700)* (Cologne: Böhlau Verlag, 1996), p. 171.
56. B. Porter, 'My Country Right or Wrong?', *History Today*, July 2006, pp. 32–3.
57. D. MacCulloch, 'Putting the English Reformation on the Map', *Transactions of the Royal Historical Society*, xv (2005), pp. 76–7.
58. D. Cannadine, 'British History as "New Subject": Politics, Perspectives and Prospects', in A. Grant and K. Stringer (eds), *Uniting the Kingdom? The Making of British History* (London: Routledge, 1995), pp. 14–16; Henshall, *Myth of Absolutism*, pp. 199–213.
59. J. Riley, *The Seven Years War and the Old Regime in France: The Financial and Economic Toll* (Princeton, NJ: Princeton University Press, 1986), p. 217; T. Banning, *The Culture of Power and the Power of Culture: Old Regime Europe, 1660–1789* (Oxford: Oxford University Press, 2002), p. 371.
60. J. Shklar, *Montesquieu* (Oxford: Oxford University Press, 1987), pp. 82–3.
61. F. Yates, *Astraea: The Imperial Theme in the Sixteenth Century* (Harmondsworth: Peregrine, 1977), pp. xi–xii.
62. P. Bobbitt, *The Shield of Achilles: War, Peace and the Course of History* (London: Allen Lane, 2002), pp. 518–19.
63. P. Fara, *Newton: The Making of a Genius* (London: Picador, 2003), pp. 113–16.
64. P. Wilson, *Absolutism in Central Europe* (London: Routledge, 2000), pp. 114–15.
65. C. Behrens, *Society, Government and the Enlightenment: The Experiences of Eighteenth-century France and Prussia* (London: Thames & Hudson, 1985), pp. 26–7.
66. L. Hughes, *Russia in the Age of Peter the Great* (New Haven, CT: Yale University Press, 1998), p. 107.
67. Hughes, *Russia in the Age of Peter the Great*, pp. 384–9.
68. Hughes, *Russia in the Age of Peter the Great*, pp. 379–80.
69. J. Henry, *The Scientific Revolution and the Origins of Modern Science* (London: Macmillan, 1997), p. 91.

70. Hughes, *Russia in the Age of Peter the Great*, p. 93.

71. T. Lentin (ed.), *Frederick the Great: Letters and Documents* (Milton Keynes: Open University, 1979), p. 19.

72. P. Burke, *The Fabrication of Louis XIV* (New Haven, CT: Yale University Press, 1992), pp. 127–30.

73. Burke, *Fabrication of Louis XIV*, p. 126.

74. Burke, *Fabrication of Louis XIV*, pp. 127–33.

75. H. Watanabe-O'Kelly, *Court Culture in Dresden: From Renaissance to Baroque* (Basingstoke: Palgrave Macmillan, 2002), pp. 174, 235.

76. D. Parker, *Class and State in Ancien Régime France: The Road to Modernity?* (London: Routledge, 1996), pp. 164–5, 194.

77. P. Zagorin, *Rebels and Rulers, 1500–1660*, vol. 1: *Society, States and Early-modern Revolution* (Cambridge: Cambridge University Press, 1982), p. 93, n. 17.

78. G. Sabine, *A History of Political Theory*, 3rd edn (London: Harrap, 1963), pp. 107–11.

79. Beales, *Enlightenment and Reform*, p. 268.

80. D. Armitage, *The Ideological Origins of the British Empire* (Cambridge: Cambridge University Press, 2000), p. 14.

81. Sabine, *History of Political Theory*, p. 684.

82. W. Doyle, *The Old European Order, 1660–1800*, 2nd edn (Oxford: Oxford University Press, 1992), p. 224.

83. J. Franklin, 'Sovereignty and the Mixed Constitution: Bodin and his Critics', in J. Burns (ed.), *The Cambridge History of Political Thought, 1450–1700* (Cambridge: Cambridge University Press, 1991), p. 298; Oresko, Gibbs and Scott, *Royal and Republican Sovereignty*, pp. 1–11; J. Elliott, 'A Europe of Composite Monarchies', *Past and Present*, no. 137 (1992), p. 50; J. Robertson, *A Union for Empire: Political Thought and the Union of 1707* (Cambridge: Cambridge University Press, 1995), pp. 4–5; C. Russell, 'Composite Monarchies in Early-modern Europe: the British and Irish Example', in A. Grant and K. Stringer (eds), *Uniting the Kingdom? The Making of British History* (London: Routledge, 1995), p. 43; Parker, *Class and State*, pp. 8–9.

84. Beales, *Enlightenment and Reform*, p. 270.

85. Parker, *Class and State*, pp. 170–3.

86. Oresko, Gibbs and Scott, *Royal and Republican Sovereignty*, pp. 2–4.

87. Bergin, *Seventeenth Century*, p. 221.

88. S. Ravenet, after P. Morier (Print, *c.*1745).

89. Russell, 'Composite Monarchies', p. 133.

90. E. Weber, *Peasants into Frenchmen: The Modernization of Rural France, 1870–1914* (Stanford, CA: Stanford University Press, 1976).

91. Doyle, *Old European Order*, p. 224.
92. R. Bonney, *The European Dynastic States, 1494–1660* (Oxford: Oxford University Press, 1994), p. 323.
93. J. Hardman, Lecture to the Manchester branch of the Historical Association, 1996.
94. I. Green, 'The Development of Monarchies in Western Europe, *c.* 1500–1800', in R. Butterwick (ed.), *The Polish–Lithuanian Monarchy, c. 1500–1795* (Basingstoke: Macmillan, 2001), pp. 47–8; M. Greengrass, *Conquest and Coalescence: The Shaping of the State in Early Modern Europe* (London: Edward Arnold, 1991).
95. J. Hurt, *Louis XIV and the Parlements: The Assertion of Royal Authority* (Manchester: Manchester University Press, 2002).
96. N. Ferguson, *Colossus: The Rise and Fall of the American Empire* (Harmondsworth: Penguin, 2005), p. xviii.
97. D. Robertson, *The Penguin Dictionary of Politics* (Harmondsworth: Penguin, 1993), p. 184.
98. G. Parker, *Europe in Crisis, 1598–1648*, 2nd edn (Oxford: Blackwell, 2001), p. 30.
99. Oresko, Gibbs and Scott, *Royal and Republican Sovereignty*, pp. 10–11.
100. D. Parrott, 'A *prince souverain* and the French Crown: Charles of Nevers, 1580–1637', in Oresko, Gibbs and Scott, *Royal and Republican Sovereignty*, pp. 149–87.
101. Oresko, Gibbs and Scott, *Royal and Republican Sovereignty*, pp. 5–6; Greengrass, *Conquest and Coalescence*, p. 3.
102. D. Armitage, *The Declaration of Independence: A Global History* (Cambridge, MA: Harvard University Press, 2007), pp. 22–3.
103. Robertson, *Union for Empire*, pp. 177–8.
104. Sturdy, *Louis XIV*, pp. 12–13.
105. Munck, *Seventeenth Century Europe*, p. 340.
106. T. Kjaergaard, *The Danish Revolution, 1500–1800* (Cambridge: Cambridge University Press, 1994), p. 208.
107. Kjaergaard, *Danish Revolution*, p. 205.
108. Bergin, *Seventeenth Century*, p. 224.
109. S. Tillyard, *A Royal Affair: George III and his Troublesome Siblings* (London: Chatto & Windus, 2006), p. 146.
110. T. Munck, 'The Danish Reformers', in H. M. Scott, *Enlightened Absolutism: Reform and Reformers in Later Eighteenth-Century Europe* (Basingstoke: Macmillan, 1990), pp. 250–2.
111. Bergin, *Seventeenth Century*, p. 221.
112. Elliott, 'Europe of Composite Monarchies', pp. 62–5.

113. J. Cannon and R. Griffiths, *The Oxford Illustrated History of the British Monarchy* (Oxford: Oxford University Press, 1988), p. 389.

114. J. Elliott, *Imperial Spain, 1469–1716* (London: Edward Arnold, 1963), p. 375.

115. Elliott, 'Europe of Composite Monarchies', p. 65.

116. R. Mettam, *Power and Faction in Louis XIV's France* (Oxford: Blackwell, 1988), pp. 29–30; R. Mettam, *Government and Society in Louis XIV's France* (London: Macmillan, 1977).

117. Hurt, *Louis XIV and the Parlements*.

118. J. Swann, *Provincial Power and Absolute Monarchy: The Estates of Burgundy, 1661–1790* (Cambridge: Cambridge University Press, 2003), p. 13; Hurt, *Louis XIV and the Parlements*, pp. 17–66.

119. R. Mettam, Review of Hurt, *Louis XIV and the Parlements*, in *English History Review*, CXVIII, 478 (Sept. 2003), p. 1004; J. Swann, 'Silence, Respect, Obedience: Political Culture in Louis XV's France', in H. Scott and B. Simms (eds), *Cultures of Power in Europe during the Long Eighteenth Century* (Cambridge: Cambridge University Press, 2007), p. 242, note 66.

120. Hurt, *Louis XIV and the Parlements*, pp. 116–17.

121. Mettam, Review of Hurt, *Louis XIV*, p. 1005.

122. W. Hargreaves-Mawdsley, *Spain under the Bourbons, 1700–1833* (London: Macmillan, 1973), pp. 35–6.

123. J. Shennan, *Liberty and Order in Early Modern Europe: The Subject and the State, 1650–1800* (London: Longman, 1986), pp. 59–60, 62.

124. Elliott, 'Europe of Composite Monarchies', pp. 67–8.

125. Shennan, *Liberty and Order*, p. 58.

126. J. Vann, *The Making of a State: Württemberg, 1593–1793* (Ithaca, NY: Cornell University Press, 1984), p. 161.

127. H. Scott, *The European Nobilities in the Seventeenth and Eighteenth Centuries*, vol. 1: *Western Europe* (London: Longman, 1995), p. 38; Doyle, *Old European Order*, p. 224.

128. Oresko, Gibbs and Scott, *Royal and Republican Sovereignty*, pp. 3–6.

129. Mettam, *Power and Faction*, pp. 30–4.

130. Wilson, *Absolutism in Central Europe*, pp. 52–3.

131. Sabine, *History of Political Theory*, p. 467.

132. P. Hazard, *The European Mind, 1680–1715* (Harmondsworth: Pelican edition, 1964); J. Israel, *Radical Enlightenment: Philosophy and the Making of Modernity, 1650–1750* (Oxford: Oxford University Press, 2001).

133. T. Besterman, *Voltaire* (London: Longman, 1969), p. 298.

134. G. Cragg, *The Church and the Age of Reason, 1648–1789* (Harmondsworth: Penguin, 1960), p. 13.

135. W. Spellman, *John Locke* (Basingstoke: Macmillan, 1997), pp. 4, 98, 124–6, 129–30.

136. Henshall, *Myth of Absolutism*, p. 130.

137. Munck, *Seventeenth Century Europe*, p. 35.

138. Henshall, *Myth of Absolutism*, pp. 120–47.

139. J. Black, *Eighteenth Century Europe, 1700–1789* (Basingstoke: Macmillan, 1990), pp. 12–18.

140. B. Behrens, *Society, Government and the Enlightenment: The Experiences of Eighteenth-Century France and Prussia* (London: Thames & Hudson, 1985), p. 26.

141. R. Okey, *Eastern Europe, 1740–1980* (London: Hutchinson, 1982), p. 33.

142. M. Anderson, *Eighteenth Century Europe, 1713–1789* (Oxford: Oxford University Press, 1966), p. 120.

143. T. Blanning, *The Pursuit of Glory: Europe, 1648–1815* (London: Allen Lane, 2007), p. 446.

144. L. Picard, *Dr Johnson's London* (London: Phoenix, 2000), pp. 269–70.

145. S. Schama, *A History of Britain: The British Wars, 1603–1776* (London: BBC, 2001), pp. 262–6.

146. Fara, *Newton*, p. 126.

147. L. Brockliss, 'The Age of Curiosity', in J. Bergin (ed.), *The Seventeenth Century* (Oxford: Oxford University Press, 2001), pp. 159–60.

148. J. Israel, *Radical Enlightenment: Philosophy and the Making of Modernity, 1650–1750* (Oxford: Oxford University Press, 2001).

149. Brockliss, 'The Age of Curiosity', p. 182.

150. W. Reinhard, *Power Elites and State Building* (Oxford: Oxford University Press, 1996), pp. 11–12.

151. A. Thompson, 'The Confessional Dimension', in B. Simms and T. Riotte (eds), *The Hanoverian Dimension in British History, 1714–1837* (Cambridge: Cambridge University Press, 2007), p. 167.

152. Thompson, 'The Confessional Dimension', pp. 161–73.

153. J. Black, *George II: Puppet of the Politicians?* (Exeter: University of Exeter Press, 2007), p. 123.

154. Thompson, 'The Confessional Dimension', pp. 177–8.

155. Blanning, *Pursuit of Glory*, p. 492; F. O'Gorman, *The Long Eighteenth Century: British Political and Social History, 1688–1832* (London: Edward Arnold, 1997), pp. 163–4.

156. Blanning, *Pursuit of Glory*, pp. 198–9.

157. S. Finer, *Comparative Government* (Harmondsworth: Pelican Books, 1974), p. 65.

158. D. Outram, *The Enlightenment* (Cambridge: Cambridge University Press, 1995), pp. 36–7.

159. J. Black, *A Military Revolution? Military Change and European Society, 1550–1800* (Basingstoke: Macmillan, 1991), pp. 71–7.

160. Parker, *Europe in Crisis, 1598–1648*, 2nd edn (Oxford: Blackwell, 2001), pp. 219–20.

161. Tillyard, *A Royal Affair: George III and his Troublesome Siblings*, p. 198.

162. D. MacCulloch, *Reformation: Europe's House Divided, 1490–1700* (Harmondsworth: Penguin, 2003), pp. 677–9, 692.

163. Fara, *Newton*, p. 126.

164. Israel, *Radical Enlightenment*, p. 39.

165. Blanning, *Pursuit of Glory*, p. 492.

166. K. Maxwell, *Pombal: Paradox of the Enlightenment* (Cambridge: Cambridge University Press, 1995), p. 17.

167. D. Beales, 'Religion and Culture', in T. Blanning (ed.), *The Eighteenth Century* (Oxford: Oxford University Press, 2000), pp. 136–7.

168. D. Beales, *Prosperity and Plunder: European Catholic Monasteries in the Age of Revolution, 1650–1815* (Cambridge: Cambridge University Press, 2003), p. 42.

169. Beales, 'Religion and Culture', pp. 135–9.

170. R. Evans, *The Making of the Habsburg Monarchy, 1550–1700* (Oxford: Oxford University Press, 1979), pp. 403–5.

171. B. Levack, *The Witch-Hunt in Early Modern Europe*, 2nd edn (London: Longman, 1995), pp. 238–9.

172. A. Somerset, *The Affair of the Poisons: Murder, Infanticide and Satanism at the Court of Louis XIV* (London: Weidenfeld & Nicolson, 2003), pp. 306, 323, 339.

173. Israel, *Radical Enlightenment*, pp. 103–4.

174. MacCulloch, *Reformation*, pp. 485, 500.

175. J. Mason, *The Indispensable Rousseau* (New York: Quartet, 1979), pp. 241–2.

176. Israel, *Radical Enlightenment*, p. 103.

177. Israel, *Radical Enlightenment*, pp. 104, 275–94.

178. Israel, *Radical Enlightenment*, p. 97.

179. MacCulloch, *Reformation*, p. 679.

180. L. Hughes, *Russia in the Age of Peter the Great* (New Haven, CT: Yale University Press, 1998), p. 109.

181. Hughes, *Peter the Great*, pp. 132–4.

182. J. Black, *Kings, Nobles and Commoners: States and Societies in Early Modern Europe, a Revisionist History* (London: Tauris, 2004), pp. 42–4.

183. J. Cléry, *A Journal of Occurrences at the Temple during the Confinement of Louis XVI, King of France* (London: Folio Society, 1955, under the title *A Journal of the Terror*).

## Chapter 4: Media and Messages: the Arts

1. J. Maravell, *Culture of the Baroque: Analysis of a Historical Structure* (Minneapolis, MN: Minnesota University Press, 1986), pp. 132–3.
2. Maravell, *Culture of the Baroque*, pp. 132–3.
3. T. Blanning, *The French Revolution: Aristocrats Versus Bourgeois?* (Basingstoke: Macmillan, 1987), pp. 27–8.
4. B. Roeck, *Das Historische Auge: Kunstwerke als Zeugen ihrer Zeit* (Göttingen: Vandenhoeck und Ruprecht, 2004).
5. G. Trevelyan, *Illustrated English Social History* (Harmondsworth: Penguin edition, 1964), pp. 17–18; R. Scribner, *For the Sake of Simple Folk: Popular Propaganda for the German Reformation* (Oxford: Oxford University Press, 1981), pp. xiii–xxix.
6. R. Evans, *The Making of the Habsburg Monarchy, 1550–1700* (Oxford: Oxford University Press, 1979), pp. 444–6.
7. R. Mettam, *Power and Faction in Louis XIV's France* (Oxford: Blackwell, 1988); P. Burke, *The Fabrication of Louis XIV* (New Haven, CT: Yale University Press, 1992); N. Henshall, *The Myth of Absolutism: Change and Continuity in Early Modern European Monarchy* (London: Longman, 1992).
8. R. Bonney, *The European Dynastic States, 1494–1660* (Oxford: Oxford University Press, 1994), p. 486.
9. Henshall, *Myth of Absolutism*, pp. 199–213.
10. P. Campbell, *Power and Politics in Old Regime France, 1720–1745* (London: Routledge, 1996), pp. 24–6, 306–7, 313–14.
11. J. Elliott, 'Power and Propaganda in the Spain of Philip IV', in *Spain and its World, 1500–1700* (London: Yale University Press, 1989), pp. 148–9; J. Elliott, 'Philip IV: Prisoner of Ceremony', in A. Dickens (ed.), *The Courts of Europe: Politics, Patronage and Royalty, 1400–1800* (London: Thames & Hudson, 1977), p. 175.
12. M. Levey, *Painting in Eighteenth-Century Venice*, 2nd edn (London: Phaidon, 1980), pp. 225–8.
13. Burke, *Fabrication of Louis XIV*, pp. 58–9.
14. Elliott, 'Power and Propaganda', pp. 146–7.
15. R. Oresko, 'The House of Savoy in Search for a Royal Crown in the Seventeenth Century', in R. Oresko, G. Gibbs and H. Scott, *Royal and*

*Republican Sovereignty in Early Modern Europe* (Cambridge: Cambridge University Press, 1997), pp. 272–350.

16. N. Zaslaw, *The Classical Era: From the 1740s to the End of the Eighteenth Century* (Englewood Cliffs, NJ: Prentice Hall, 1989), pp. 6–7, 113.

17. T. Blanning, *The Culture of Power and the Power of Culture: Old Regime Europe, 1660–1789* (Oxford: Oxford University Press, 2002), p. 44.

18. L. Ettlinger, 'The Role of the Artist in Society', in A. Cobban (ed.), *The Eighteenth Century: Europe in the Age of Enlightenment* (London: Thames & Hudson, 1969), p. 248.

19. T. Blanning, 'Commercialization and Sacralization of European Culture in the Nineteenth Century', in T. Blanning (ed.), *Oxford Illustrated History of Modern Europe* (Oxford: Oxford University Press, 1996), pp. 128–33.

20. T. Blanning, *The Triumph of Music: Composers, Musicians and their Audiences, 1700 to the Present* (London: Allen Lane, 2008), pp. 134–9.

21. Blanning, 'Commercialization and Sacralization of European Culture', pp. 128, 142.

22. Burke, *Fabrication of Louis XIV*, pp. 8–9.

23. D. Beales, 'Religion and Culture', in T. Blanning (ed.), *The Eighteenth Century, 1688–1815* (Oxford: Oxford University Press, 2000), pp. 140–1.

24. Burke, *Fabrication of Louis XIV*, pp. 1–3.

25. J. Collins, *The State in Early Modern France* (Cambridge: Cambridge University Press, 1995), p. 75.

26. R. Evans, *Rituals of Retribution: Capital Punishment in Germany, 1600–1987* (Oxford: Oxford University Press, 1996), p. 50.

27. T. Munck, *Seventeenth Century Europe, 1598–1700* (Basingstoke: Macmillan, 1990), pp. 306, 368.

28. D. Watkin, *A History of Western Architecture* (London: Barrie & Jenkins, 1986), p. 240.

29. N. Llewellyn, 'The World of the Baroque Artist', in *Baroque, 1620–1800: Style in the Age of Magnificence*, Exhibition Catalogue (London: Victoria and Albert Museum, 2009), p. 21.

30. Munck, *Seventeenth Century Europe*, pp. 307–9, 338.

31. J. Adamson (ed.), *The Princely Courts of Europe, 1500–1750* (London: Weidenfeld & Nicolson, 1998), pp. 33–6.

32. Munck, *Seventeenth Century Europe*, p. 326.

33. A. Blunt, *Art and Architecture in France, 1500–1700* (Harmondsworth: Penguin, 1973), p. 325.

34. S. Klingensmith, *The Utility of Splendour: Ceremony, Social Life and Architecture at the Court of Bavaria, 1600–1800* (Chicago, IL: University of Chicago, 1993), p. i.

35. I am indebted for this paragraph to Roger Mettam, who kindly allowed me a sight of his unpublished MS, 'Images of Power: Social and Political Propaganda in Louis XIV's France'.
36. J. Dewald, *The European Nobility, 1400–1800* (Cambridge: Cambridge University Press, 1996), p. 159.
37. D. Sturdy, *Louis XIV* (Basingstoke: Macmillan, 1998), pp. 121–2.
38. Burke, *Fabrication of Louis XIV*, pp. 23–5; O. Ranum, *Paris in the Age of Absolutism* (Bloomington, IN: Indiana University Press, 1968), pp. 132–66.
39. Blunt, *Art and Architecture in France*, pp. 283–97, 345–6.
40. P. Burke, *Tradition and Innovation in Renaissance Italy* (London: Fontana edn, 1974), pp. 166–8, 333–4.
41. Burke, *Tradition and Innovation*, pp. 333–4.
42. Ranum, *Paris in the Age of Absolutism*, pp. 134–5.
43. D. Watkin, *Morality and Architecture Revisited* (London: John Murray, 2001), pp. 70–7.
44. K. Marx, *Manifesto of the Communist Party* (Peking: Foreign Languages Press, 1973), p. 57.
45. Karal Marx and F. Engels, *Selected Works* (Moscow: Foreign Languages Publishing House, 1962), p. 363.
46. Marx, *Manifesto*, p. 32.
47. P. Laslett, *The World We Have Lost* (London: Methuen, 1965), pp. 23–4, 176–7; H. Perkin, *The Origins of Modern English Society, 1780–1880* (London: Routledge, 1969), pp. 37–8.
48. T. Blanning, *The Culture of Power and the Power of Culture* (Oxford: Oxford University Press, 2001), pp. 234–5.
49. C. Duggan, *A Concise History of Italy* (Cambridge: Cambridge University Press, 1994), p. 85.
50. R. Okey, *Eastern Europe, 1740–1980: Feudalism to Communism* (London: Hutchinson, 1982), p. 15.
51. J. Black, *Eighteenth Century Europe, 1700–1789* (Basingstoke: Macmillan, 1990), pp. 254–6.
52. T. Blanning, *Joseph II* (London: Longman, 1994), pp. 70–1.
53. A. Goldgar, *Impolite Learning: Conduct and Community in the Republic of Letters, 1680–1750* (New Haven, CT: Yale University Press, 1995), pp. 1–11; N. Elias, *The History of Manners* (New York: Pantheon Books, 1978); S. Shapin and S. Schaffer, *Leviathan and the Air Pump: Hobbes, Boyle and the Experimental Life* (Princeton, NJ: Princeton University Press, 1985); S. Shapin, 'A Scholar and a Gentleman: the Problematic Identity of the Scientific Practitioner in Early-modern England', *History of Science*, 29, part 3, no. 85 (Sept. 1991), pp. 279–327.

54. O. Field, *The Kit-Cat Club: Friends who Imagined a Nation* (London: Harper Press, 2008), p. 256.

55. J. Lough, *An Introduction to Seventeenth Century France* (London: Longman, 1954), pp. 253–5.

56. D. Crystal, *The Stories of English* (London: Allen Lane, 2004), pp. 377–9.

57. H. Hitchings, *Dr Johnson's Dictionary* (London: John Murray, 2006), pp. 1–6.

58. J. Cannon, *Samuel Johnson and the Politics of Hanoverian England* (Oxford: Oxford University Press, 1994), pp. 237–38; M. Bragg, *The Adventure of English* (London: Hodder & Stoughton, 2003), pp. 210–12; D. Maland, *Culture and Society in Seventeenth-Century France* (London: Batsford, 1970), pp. 99–100; J. Black, *A Subject for Taste: Culture in Eighteenth-Century England* (Hambledon and London: Palgrave Macmillan, 2005), p. 161.

59. F. Bluche, *Louis XIV* (Oxford: Blackwell, 1990), p. 269.

60. Lough, *Seventeenth Century France*, pp. 241–7.

61. D. Nokes, *Raillery and Rage: A Study of Eighteenth Century Satire* (Brighton: Harvester Press, 1987), pp. 92–3.

62. T. Rabb, *The Struggle for Stability in Early Modern Europe* (Oxford: Oxford University Press, 1975), pp. 101–2.

63. H. Bloom, *Shakespeare: The Invention of the Human* (London: Fourth Estate, 1999), p. 423.

64. Lough, *Seventeenth Century France*, pp. 221–6.

65. Maland, *Culture and Society*, pp. 49–50.

66. A. Beer, *Milton: Poet, Pamphleteer and Patriot* (London: Bloomsbury, 2008), pp. 201, 285–7.

67. C. Ricks, *Milton's Grand Style* (Oxford: Oxford University Press, 1963), pp. 23–4, 28, 63.

68. Beer, *Milton*, pp. 338–9, 401.

69. Ricks, *Milton's Grand Style*, pp. 23–4.

70. A. Dyson and J. Lovelock (eds), *Milton: Paradise Lost* (London: Macmillan, 1973), pp. 12–14, 29, 32.

71. Ricks, *Milton's Grand Style*, p. 62.

72. R. Fargher, *Life and Letters in France in the 18th Century* (London: Thomas Nelson, 1970), p. 184.

73. Virgil, *The Aeneid* (Ware: Wordsworth, 1997), Introduction by J. Morwood, p. xxii.

74. I. Bywater (translator), *Aristotle on the Art of Poetry* (Oxford: Oxford University Press, 1920), p. 34.

75. Lough, *Seventeenth Century France*, pp. 213–14, 259; J. Lough, *An Introduction to Eighteenth Century France* (London: Longman, 1960), pp. 264–70, 287–300.

76. J. Cairncross (ed.), Introduction to Racine, *Andromache and Other Plays* (Harmondsworth: Penguin, 1967), pp. 23–4.

77. G. Brereton, *A Short History of French Literature*, 2nd edn (Harmondsworth: Penguin, 1976), pp. 137, 307.

78. S. Wells, *Shakespeare: For All Time* (Basingstoke: Palgrave Macmillan, 2002), p. 145.

79. M. Dobson and S. Wells (eds), *The Oxford Companion to Shakespeare* (Oxford: Oxford University Press, 2001), p. 29.

80. T. Redpath, *The Songs and Sonnets of John Donne* (London: Methuen, 1956), p. xv.

81. R. Muchembled, *Popular Culture and Elite Culture in France, 1400–1750* (Baton Rouge, LA: Louisiana State University Press, 1985), pp. 280–1.

82. P. Collins, 'Restoration Comedy', in B. Ford (ed.), *The Pelican Guide to English Literature: From Dryden to Johnson* (Harmondsworth: Penguin, 1957), p. 157.

83. J. Winn, *John Dryden and his World* (New Haven, CT: Yale University Press, 1987), pp. 167, 570.

84. G. Hunter (ed.), Introduction to Shakespeare, *King Lear* (Harmondsworth: Penguin, 1972), pp. 47, 51.

85. H. Erskine-Hill, 'John Dryden: the Poet and Critic', in R. Lonsdale (ed.), *Dryden to Johnson* (London: Sphere, 1971), pp. 25–6.

86. Maland, *Culture and Society*, pp. 67–8, 215.

87. Erskine-Hill, 'John Dryden', p. 26.

88. Winn, *John Dryden*, pp. 10–11.

89. J. Dryden, *Works* (Ware: Wordsworth, 1995), Introduction by D. Marriott, p. xi.

90. I. Watt, *The Rise of the Novel*, 2nd edn (Berkeley, CA: University of California, 2001).

91. W. Speck, *Literature and Society in Eighteenth-Century England: Ideology, Politics and Culture, 1680–1820* (London: Longman, 1998), pp. 107–12.

92. Speck, *Literature and Society*, pp. 104–5.

93. Speck, *Literature and Society*, pp. 9–10; J. Clark, *English Society, 1660–1832*, 2nd edn (Cambridge: Cambridge University Press, 2000).

94. Black, *A Subject for Taste*, p. 152.

95. M. Butler, *Romantics, Rebels and Reactionaries: English Literature and its Background, 1760–1830* (Oxford: Oxford University Press, 1981), pp. 94–112.

96. Speck, *Literature and Society*, p. 106.

97. D. Sassoon, *The Culture of the Europeans from 1800 to the Present* (London: HarperCollins, 2006), pp. 234, 239.

98. K. Knight, 'Grimmelshausen's *Simplicissimus* – a Popular Baroque Novel', in J. Ritchie (ed.), *Periods in German Literature*, vol. 2 (London: Wolff, 1969), pp. 3–6.

99. J. Bate, *The Genius of Shakespeare* (London: Picador, 1997), pp. 180–4.

100. J. Yolton (ed.), *The Blackwell Companion to the Enlightenment* (Oxford: Blackwell, 1991), pp. 281–2.

101. J. Ritchie, 'The Anacreontic Poets: Gleim, Uz and Götz', in A. Natan (ed.), *German Men of Letters*, vol. 6 (London: Wolff, 1963), p. 139.

102. Blanning, *Culture of Power*, pp. 218, 235.

103. W. Mann, *The Operas of Mozart* (London: Cassell, 1977), p. 57.

104. T. Blanning, *The Pursuit of Glory: Europe, 1648–1815* (London: Allen Lane, 2007), pp. 518–19.

105. P. Burke, *Popular Culture in Early Modern Europe* (Aldershot: Wildwood House, 1988), p. 4.

106. L. Mitchell, *Charles James Fox* (Oxford: Oxford University Press, 1992), pp. 187–8.

107. A. Motion, *Keats* (London: Faber & Faber, 1997), p. 300.

108. S. Coote, *John Keats: A Life* (London: Hodder & Stoughton, 1995), p. 102.

109. Bate, *Genius of Shakespeare*, p. 176.

110. M. Meyer, *Ibsen* (Harmondsworth: Penguin, 1974), p. 516.

111. A. Blunt, *Borromini* (Harmondsworth: Penguin, 1979), p. 13.

112. J. Rosenheim, *The Emergence of a Ruling Order: English Landed Society, 1650–1750* (London: Longman, 1998), pp. 186–92.

113. J. Black, *A Subject for Taste: Culture in Eighteenth-Century England* (Hambledon and London: Palgrave Macmillan, 2005), pp. 44–5.

114. T. Kaufmann, *Court, Cloister and City: The Art and Culture of Central Europe, 1450–1800* (London: Weidenfeld & Nicolson, 1995), pp. 308–9; P. Wilson, *Absolutism in Central Europe* (London: Routledge, 2000), pp. 69–70.

115. Wilson, *Absolutism in Central Europe*, pp. 77–8.

116. J. Brown and J. Elliott, *A Palace for a King: The Buen Retiro and the Court of Philip IV*, 2nd edn (New Haven, CT: Yale University Press, 2004); A. Ubeda de los Cobos, *Paintings for the Planet King: Philip IV and the Buen Retiro Palace* (London: Paul Holberton, 2005).

117. R. Mandrou, 'Le Baroque européen: mentalité pathétique et révolution sociale', *Annales*, xv (1960), pp. 895–914.

118. H. Hibbard, *Bernini* (Harmondsworth: Pelican, 1965), pp. 19–20.

119. A. Blunt, *Art and Architecture in France, 1500–1700* (Harmondsworth: Penguin paperback edition, 1973), pp. 230–3, 325–6; Hibbard, *Bernini*, pp. 178–83.

120. S. Jenkins, *England's Thousand Best Houses* (Harmondsworth: Penguin, 2003), p. 839.

121. T. Mowl and B. Earnshaw, *An Insular Rococo: Architecture, Politics and Society in Ireland and England, 1710–1770* (London: Reaktion Books, 1999), pp. 1–2.

122. Mowl and Earnshaw, *Insular Rococo*, pp. 13–16.

123. Andrea Palladio, *The Four Books of Architecture* (New York: Dover edition, 1965), p. 57.

124. R. Morrice, *Stuart and Baroque* (London: Barrie & Jenkins, 1982), pp. 11–20.

125. T. Mowl and B. Earnshaw, *John Wood: Architect of Obsession* (Bath: Millstream, 1988), pp. 22–6, 95–6, 183–94.

126. B. Hempel, *Baroque Art and Architecture in Central Europe* (Harmondsworth: Penguin, 1965), p. 1.

127. R. Gutman, *Mozart: A Cultural Biography* (London: Secker & Warburg, 2000), pp. 93–4.

128. *Schönbrunn*: Official Guidebook (Vienna: Schlosshauptmannschaft Schönbrunn, 1985), p. 29.

129. J. Maravall, *The Culture of the Baroque: Analysis of an Historical Structure* (Minneapolis, MN: Minnesota University Press, 1986).

130. Wilson, *Absolutism in Central Europe*, p. 69; R. Strong, *The Spirit of Britain: A Narrative History of the Arts* (London: Pimlico, 2000), p. 308.

131. Blunt, *Borromini*, pp. 114–16.

132. R. Adam, *Classical Architecture* (London: Viking paperback, 1992), pp. 34–5.

133. H. Hitchcock, *Rococo Architecture in Southern Germany* (London: Phaidon, 1968), p. 15.

134. N. Pevsner, *An Outline of European Architecture*, 7th edn (Harmondsworth: Penguin paperback, 1963), p. 270.

135. Hitchcock, *Rococo Architecture*, pp. 217–18.

136. M. Girouard, *Life in the English Country House: A Social and Architectural History* (New Haven, CT: Yale University Press, 1978), pp. 136–43.

137. Girouard, *Life in the English Country House*, p. 147.

138. Blunt, *Art and Architecture in France*, pp. 230–3.

139. P. Burke, *The Fabrication of Louis XIV* (New Haven, CT: Yale University Press, 1992), p. 188.

140. D. Watkin, *A History of Western Architecture* (London: Barrie & Jenkins, 1986), pp. 266–8.

141. T. Blanning, *The Triumph of Music: Composers, Musicians and their Audiences, 1700 to the Present* (London: Allen Lane, 2008), p. 74.

142. Watkin, *Western Architecture*, p. 268.

143. P. Campbell, *Louis XIV* (London: Longman, 1993), p. 54.

144. Watkin, *Western Architecture*, pp. 270–2.

145. C. Mukerji, *Territorial Ambitions and the Gardens of Versailles* (Cambridge: Cambridge University Press, 1997), pp. 1–8, 253–63.

146. J. Black, *Maps and Politics* (London: Reaktion Books, 1997), pp. 11–28; P. Barber (ed.), *The Map Book* (London: Weidenfeld & Nicolson, 2005), pp. 174–5.

147. T. Richardson, *The Arcadian Friends: Inventing the English Landscape Garden* (London: Bantam Press, 2007); Rosenheim, *Emergence of a Ruling Order*, pp. 189–90.

148. J. Norwich, 'A Sense of Proportion', in *Spirit of the Age* (London: BBC Publications, 1975), pp. 124–5.

149. Wilson, *Absolutism in Central Europe*, pp. 74–5.

150. J. Summerson, *The Architecture of the Eighteenth Century* (London: Thames & Hudson, 1986), pp. 17–23.

151. G. Symcox, *Victor Amadeus II: Absolutism in the Savoyard State, 1675–1730* (London: Thames & Hudson, 1983), pp. 77–8; Watkin, *Western Architecture*, p. 257.

152. G. Symcox, 'From Commune to Capital: the Transformation of Turin, Sixteenth to Eighteenth Centuries', in R. Oresko, G. Gibbs and H. Scott (eds), *Royal and Republican Sovereignty in Early Modern Europe* (Cambridge: Cambridge University Press, 1997), pp. 251–4.

153. D. Yarwood, *The Architecture of Europe* (London: Batsford, 1974), p. 418.

154. Summerson, *Architecture of the Eighteenth Century*, pp. 23–9.

155. R. Frost, 'Poland–Lithuania, Russia and Peter the Great', *History Review*, no. 38 (March 1998), p. 13.

156. R. Toman (ed.), *Baroque: Architecture, Sculpture, Painting* (Cologne: Könemann, 1998), pp. 210–11.

157. R. Evans, *The Making of the Habsburg Monarchy, 1550–1700* (Oxford: Oxford University Press, 1979), p. 445.

158. R. Furneaux-Jordan, *A Concise History of Western Architecture* (London: Thames & Hudson, 1969), p. 250.

159. Hempel, *Baroque Art and Architecture*, p. 92.

160. Kaufmann, *Court, Cloister and City*, pp. 300–2; Watkin, *History of Western Architecture*, pp. 275–7.

161. Blanning, *Triumph of Music*, p. 122.

162. T. Blanning, *The Pursuit of Glory: Europe, 1648–1815* (London: Allen Lane, 2007), pp. 449–51.

163. Blanning, *Pursuit of Glory*, p. 449.

164. Girouard, *Life in the English Country House*, pp. 126–44.
165. Kaufmann, *Court, Cloister and City*, pp. 294–5.
166. D. Cruickshank, *A Guide to the Georgian Buildings of England and Ireland* (London: Weidenfeld & Nicolson, 1985), pp. 32–4.
167. Mowl and Earnshaw, *John Wood*, pp. 65–6.
168. Summerson, *Architecture of the Eighteenth Century*, pp. 152–4.
169. L. Mumford, *The City in History* (London: Secker & Warburg, 1961), pp. 398–403.
170. Mumford, *City in History*, p. 400.
171. M. Girouard, *Cities and People* (New Haven, CT: Yale University Press, 1985), pp. 115–16.
172. H. Koenigsberger, G. Mosse and G. Bowler, *Europe in the Sixteenth Century*, 2nd edn (London: Longman, 1989), pp. 121–3.
173. L. Picard, *Restoration London* (London: Phoenix paperback, 1998), pp. 30–1.
174. L. Hollis, *The Phoenix: St Paul's Cathedral and the Men Who Made Modern London* (London: Weidenfeld & Nicolson, 2008), pp. 4–6, 11–55.
175. J. Summerson, *Architecture in Britain, 1530–1830*, 6th edn (Harmondsworth: Pelican, 1977), pp. 239–50.
176. M. Anderson, *Peter the Great* (London: Thames & Hudson, 1978), p. 122.
177. Symcox, 'From Commune to Capital: the Transformation of Turin, Sixteenth to Eighteenth Centuries', in Oresko, Gibbs and Scott, *Royal and Republican Sovereignty*, pp. 260–2.
178. Girouard, *Cities and People*, p. 223.
179. Summerson, *Architecture of the Eighteenth Century*, p. 32.
180. J. Black, *George II: Puppet of the Politicians?* (Exeter: University of Exeter Press, 2007), pp. 124–5.
181. Blunt, *Art and Architecture in France*, p. 325.
182. Blunt, *Art and Architecture in France*, p. 321.
183. D. Sturdy, *Louis XIV* (Basingstoke: Macmillan, 1998), p. 17.
184. I am indebted for the whole of this final section to Roger Mettam, who kindly allowed me a sight of his unpublished MS, 'Images of Power: Social and Political Propaganda in Louis XIV's France'.
185. H. Osborne (ed.), *The Oxford Companion to Art* (Oxford: Oxford University Press, 1970), pp. 125, 499, 555–6.
186. P. Burke, *The Fabrication of Louis XIV* (New Haven, CT: Yale University Press, 1992), pp. 23–5; O. Ranum, *Paris in the Age of Absolutism* (Bloomington, IN: Indiana University Press, 1968), pp. 132–66.
187. A. Blunt, *Art and Architecture in France, 1500–1700* (Harmondsworth: Penguin paperback edition, 1973), pp. 283–97, 345–6.

188. P. Conisbee, *Painting in Eighteenth-Century France* (London: Phaidon, 1981).

189. Samuel Johnson, *Selected Writings*, ed. Simon Cruttwell (Harmondsworth: Penguin, 1968), p. 393.

190. L. Brockliss, 'The Age of Curiosity', in J. Bergin (ed.), *The Seventeenth Century* (Oxford: Oxford University Press, 2001), pp. 150–1.

191. N. Penny, *Reynolds*, exhibition catalogue (London: Royal Academy of Arts, 1986), p. 25.

192. M. Levey, *Painting and Sculpture in France, 1700–1789* (New Haven, CT: Yale University Press, 1993), p. 61.

193. Conisbee, *Painting in Eighteenth-Century France*, p. 171.

194. S. Schama, *The Embarrassment of Riches: An Interpretation of Dutch Culture in the Golden Age* (London: Collins, 1987), pp. 4, 375–86.

195. Burke, *Fabrication of Louis XIV*, p. 33.

196. D. Shawe-Taylor, *The Georgians: Eighteenth-Century Portraiture and Society* (London: Barrie & Jenkins, 1990), p. 57.

197. M. Falomir, 'The Court Portrait', in *Renaisssance Faces: Van Eyck to Titian*, exhibition catalogue (London: National Gallery, 2008), p. 70.

198. Falomir, 'The Court Portrait', pp. 72–8.

199. N. Henshall, *The Myth of Absolutism: Change and Continuity in Early Modern European Monarchy* (London: Longman, 1992), p. 166.

200. Burke, *Fabrication of Louis XIV*, pp. 33.

201. R. Wilkinson, *Louis XIV* (London: Routledge, 2007), pp. 96–7.

202. J. Elliott, 'Appearance and Reality in the Spain of Velazquez', in *Velazquez*, exhibition catalogue (London: National Gallery, 2006), pp. 16–17; G. Mancini, catalogue entry, in *Velazquez*, p. 234.

203. Burke, *Fabrication of Louis XIV*, p. 9.

204. J. Boswell, *Life of Johnson* (Oxford: Oxford World's Classics, 1980), p. 26.

205. D. Bindman, *Hogarth* (London: Thames & Hudson, 1981), pp. 131–3.

206. J. Uglow, *Hogarth: A Life and a World* (London: Faber & Faber, 1997), pp. 333–4; Shawe-Taylor, *The Georgians*, pp. 83–5.

207. J. Black, *A Subject for Taste: Culture in Eighteenth-Century England* (Hambledon and London: Palgrave Macmillan, 2005), p. 80.

208. J. Laver, *A Concise History of Costume* (London: Thames & Hudson, 1969), pp. 112–16; A. Ribeiro, *Dress in Eighteenth Century Europe, 1715–1789* (London: Batsford, 1984), p. 20; D. de Marly, *Fashion for Men* (London: Batsford paperback, 1989), pp. 56–7.

209. Ribeiro, *Dress in Eighteenth Century Europe*, pp. 58–9, 202; A. Buck, *Dress in Eighteenth-Century England* (London: Batsford, 1979) p. 21.

210. Ribeiro, *Dress in Eighteenth Century Europe*, p. 14.

211. J. Styles, *The Dress of the People: Everyday Fashion in 18th-Century England* (New Haven, CT: Yale University Press, 2008).

212. L. Colley, *Britons: Forging the Nation, 1707–1837* (New Haven, CT: Yale University Press, 1992), pp. 187–8.

213. M. Pointon, *Hanging the Head: Portraiture and Social Formation in Eighteenth-Century England* (New Haven, CT: Yale University Press, 1993), pp. 117–23.

214. C. Hibbert, *Nelson: A Personal History* (London: Viking, 1994), p. 202.

215. A. Scott, *The Royal Naval College, Greenwich* (West Yorkshire: Larkfield Printing, 2003), pp. 4–5.

216. S. Schama, *A History of Britain: The British Wars, 1603–1776* (London: BBC, 2001), pp. 341, 346–7.

217. C. Wortmann, Frontispiece to Matthäus Pöppelmann's *L'Orangerie de Dresden avec ses pavillons et embellissements. Bâtie en 1711* (Dresden, 1729).

218. R. Chartier, *The Cultural Origins of the French Revolution* (Durham, NC: Duke University Press, 1991), p. 36.

219. D. Bindman, *Hogarth and his Times* (London: British Museum Press, 1997), pp. 29–30.

220. X. Bray, *Velasquez,* exhibition catalogue (London: National Gallery, 2006), catalogue entry, p. 120.

221. G. Parker, *Europe in Crisis, 1598–1648,* 2nd edn (Oxford: Blackwell, 2001), p. 237.

222. Schama, *Embarrassment of Riches,* pp. 4–6, 316–19; Parker, *Europe in Crisis,* pp. 237–8.

223. J. Clark, *English Society, 1660–1832,* 2nd edn (Cambridge: Cambridge University Press, 2000), pp. 19–26; J. Black, *Convergence or Divergence? Britain and the Continent* (Basingstoke: Macmillan, 1994), pp. 1–5.

224. Schama, *Embarrassment of Riches,* p. 8.

225. S. Schama, *Rembrandt's Eyes* (Harmondsworth: Penguin Press, 1999), p. 490–1.

226. Schama, *Rembrandt's Eyes,* pp. 487, 496.

227. Schama, *Rembrandt's Eyes,* pp. 270–1.

228. J. Boomgaard and R. Scheller, 'A Delicate Balance: a Brief Survey of Rembrandt Criticism', in C. Brown, J. Kelch and P. van Thiel, *Rembrandt: The Master and his Workshop* (New Haven, CT, and London: Yale University Press & National Gallery Publications, 1991), pp. 106–7.

229. Parker, *Europe in Crisis,* pp. 238–9.

230. G. Bazin, *Baroque and Rococo* (London: Thames & Hudson, 1964), pp. 23–6; E. Gombrich, *The Story of Art,* 11th edn (London: Phaidon, 1966), p. 328.

231. A. Graham-Dixon, *A History of British Art* (London: BBC Books, 1996), p. 34.

232. C. Lloyd, 'Portraits of Sovereigns and Heads of State', in *Citizens and Kings*, exhibition catalogue (London: Royal Academy of Arts, 2007), pp. 60–2.

233. R. Rosenblum, 'Portraiture: Facts versus Fiction', in *Citizens and Kings*, p. 18.

234. M. Levey, *Rococo to Revolution: Major Trends in Eighteenth-Century Painting* (London: Thames & Hudson, 1967), pp. 15–16.

235. R. Babel, 'The Courts of the Wittelsbachs, c. 1500–1750', in J. Adamson, *The Princely Courts of Europe, 1500–1750* (London: Weidenfeld & Nicolson, 1998), p. 203.

236. Rosenblum, 'Portraiture', p. 17.

237. Lloyd, 'Portraits of Sovereigns', pp. 60–2.

238. Graham-Dixon, *History of British Art*, p. 104.

239. S. Allard, 'The Status Portrait', in *Citizens and Kings*, p. 83.

240. J. Reynolds, *Discourses on Art* (New Haven, CT: Yale University Press, 1975), pp. 59–60.

241. Graham-Dixon, *History of British Art*, p. 106; Shawe-Taylor, *The Georgians*, p. 65.

242. H. Osborne (ed.), *The Oxford Companion to Art* (Oxford: Oxford University Press, 1970), p. 286.

243. M. Umbach, 'Culture and *Bürgerlichkeit* in Eighteenth-century Germany', in H. Scott and B. Simms (eds), *Cultures of Power in Europe during the Long Eighteenth Century* (Cambridge: Cambridge University Press, 2007), pp. 180–99.

244. G. Lammel (ed.), *Daniel Chodowiecki* (Berlin: Eulenspiegel Verlag, 1987), p. 48.

245. M. Levey, *Giambattista Tiepolo: His Life and Work* (New Haven, CT: Yale University Press, 1986), pp. 287–9.

246. W. Newman, *The Sonata in the Baroque Era* (Wilmington, NC: University of North Carolina Press, 1966), pp. 34–6.

247. R. Fiske, 'The Viennese Classical Period', in A. Jacobs (ed.), *Choral Music* (Harmondsworth: Penguin, 1963), p. 164.

248. P. Burke, *Popular Culture in Early Modern Europe* (Aldershot: Wildwood House, 1988), p. 100.

249. H. Schonberg, *The Lives of the Great Composers*, 3rd edn (London: Abacus, 1998), p. 39.

250. J. Brotton, *The Sale of the Late King's Goods* (Basingstoke: Palgrave Macmillan, 2006), p. 107.

251. P. Burke, *The Renaissance* (London: Longman, 1964), p. 77.

252. A. Kendall, *Vivaldi: His Music, Life and Times* (New York: Granada, 1979), pp. 184–94.

253. W. Mann, *The Operas of Mozart* (London: Cassell, 1977), p. 633.

254. M. Phillips-Matz, *Verdi: A Biography* (Oxford: Oxford University Press, 1993), p. 607.

255. D. Maland, *Culture and Society in Seventeenth-Century France* (London: Batsford, 1970), pp. 255.

256. T. Blanning, *The Pursuit of Glory: Europe, 1648–1815* (London: Allen Lane, 2007), p. 454.

257. Blanning, *Pursuit of Glory*, p. 393.

258. R. Oresko, 'The Duchy of Savoy and the Kingdom of Sardinia: the Sabaudian Court, 1563–c.1750', in J. Adamson, *The Princely Courts of Europe, 1500–1750: Ritual, Politics and Culture under the* Ancien Régime, *1500–1750* (London: Weidenfeld & Nicolson, 1999), pp. 243, 248.

259. P. Salvadori, *La chasse sous l'ancien régime* (Paris: Fayard, 1997); S. Sitwell, *The Hunters and the Hunted* (London: Macmillan, 1947), pp. 79–87.

260. M. Solomon, *Mozart* (London: Hutchinson, 1995), p. 127.

261. Blanning, *The Pursuit of Glory*, p. 462.

262. Schonberg, *Lives of the Great Composers*, p. 25.

263. T. Blanning, *The Triumph of Music: Composers, Musicians and their Audiences, 1700 to the Present* (London: Allen Lane, 2008), pp. 7–72.

264. J. S. Bach, *The Six Brandenburg Concertos* (New York: Dover Publications, reprint of Bach-Gesellschaft edition, 1976), p. vii.

265. Blanning, *Triumph of Music*, p. 15.

266. D. Beales, *Enlightenment and Reform in Eighteenth-Century Europe* (London: Tauris, 2005), p. 90; H. Robbins Landon (ed.), *Haydn: Chronicle and Works*, 5 vols, vol. 1: *The Early Years, 1732–65* (Bloomington, IN: Indiana University Press, 1976–80), pp. 350–2.

267. Blanning, *Triumph of Music*, p. 15.

268. Blanning, *Triumph of Music*, p. 16.

269. H. Robbins Landon, *Vivaldi: Voice of the Baroque* (London: Thames & Hudson, 1993), p. 16.

270. Blanning, *Pursuit of Glory*, p. 460.

271. J. Gaines, *Evening in the Palace of Reason: Bach meets Frederick the Great in the Age of Enlightenment* (London: Fourth Estate, 1995), pp. 116–22.

272. Newman, *Sonata in the Baroque Era*, p. 21.

273. J. Glover, *Mozart's Women* (London: Macmillan, 2005), p. 264.

274. V. Lederer, *Bach's St Matthew Passion* (London: Continuum, 2008), pp. 9–10, 54–5.

275. S. Sadie (ed.), *The Grove Concise Dictionary of Music* (London: Macmillan, 1988), pp. 789–90.

276. M. Bawtree, 'No Opera Please – We're British', in C. Ricks and L. Michaels (eds), *The State of the Language* (London: Faber & Faber, 1991), pp. 381–91.

277. P. Wilson, *Absolutism in Central Europe* (London: Routledge, 2000), pp. 71–2.

278. Blanning, *Triumph of Music*, p. 81.

279. Blanning, *Triumph of Music*, pp. 125–31.

280. M. Anderson, *Europe in the Eighteenth Century, 1713–1789*, 4th edn (London: Longman, 2000), pp. 331–2.

281. T. Blanning, *The Culture of Power and the Power of Culture: Old Regime Europe, 1660–1789* (Oxford: Oxford University Press, 2002), pp. 43–6, 63–9; Blanning, *Triumph of Music*, pp. 78–9.

282. A. Holden, *The Penguin Opera Guide* (Harmondsworth: Penguin, 1995), pp. xxii–xxiii; D. Beales, 'Religion and Culture', in T. Blanning (ed.), *The Eighteenth Century, 1688–1815* (Oxford: Oxford University Press, 2000), pp. 146–7.

283. D. Neville, 'Metastasio and Court Studies', *Court Historian*, vol. 1, no. 3 (October 1996), p. 16.

284. Blanning, *Culture of Power*, p. 68.

285. Neville, 'Metastasio', p. 17.

286. G. Buelow, *The Late Baroque Era from the 1680s to 1740* (Englewood Cliffs, NJ: Prentice Hall, 1993), p. 106.

287. Blanning, *Culture of Power*, pp. 64–6.

288. H. Koegler, *The Concise Oxford Dictionary of Ballet*, 2nd edn (Oxford: Oxford University Press, 1982), p. 32.

289. F. Bluche, *Louis XIV* (Oxford: Blackwell, 1990), pp. 183–5.

290. W. Mann, *Operas of Mozart* (London: Cassell, 1977), p. 211.

291. Adamson, *Princely Courts of Europe*, pp. 34–6.

292. Mann, *Operas of Mozart*, pp. 427–48.

293. Blanning, *Culture of Power*, pp. 363–4.

294. M. Cranston, *The Romantic Movement* (Oxford: Blackwell, 1994), pp. 1–2; Mann, *Operas of Mozart*, pp. 427–8; J. Rousseau, *The Confessions* (Harmondsworth: Penguin edition, 1953), pp. 358–9.

295. Blanning, *Culture of Power*, pp. 365–72.

296. R. Gutman, *Mozart: A Cultural Biography* (London: Secker & Warburg, 2000), pp. 130–59.

297. Blanning, *Culture of Power*, p. 360.

298. E. Anderson (ed.), *The Letters of Mozart and his Family*, 3rd edn (New York: W. W. Norton, 1985), p. 630.

299. D. Sassoon, *The Culture of the Europeans from 1800 to the Present* (London: HarperCollins, 2006), pp. 237–8.

300. Anderson, *Europe in the Eighteenth Century*, p. 330.
301. Blanning, *Culture of Power*, pp. 110–11.


## Chapter 5: The End of an Age: the Mid-eighteenth Century

1. G. Buelow, *The Late Baroque Era from the 1680s to 1740* (Englewood Cliffs, NJ: Prentice Hall, 1993), p. 6.
2. Buelow, *Late Baroque Era*, p. 13.
3. T. Blanning, *The Triumph of Music: Composers, Musicians and their Audiences, 1700 to the Present* (London: Allen Lane, 2008), pp. 13, 88.
4. D. Beales, 'Religion and Culture', in T. Blanning (ed.), *The Eighteenth Century, 1688–1815* (Oxford: Oxford University Press, 2000), pp. 141–2; T. Blanning, *The Culture of Power and the Power of Culture: Old Regime Europe, 1660–1789* (Oxford: Oxford University Press, 2002), p. 234.
5. J. Habermas, *The Structural Transformation of the Public Sphere: An Enquiry into a Category of Bourgeois Society* (Cambridge, MA: MIT Press, 1989).
6. M. Anderson, *Europe in the Eighteenth Century, 1713–1789*, 4th edn (London: Longman, 2000), pp. 326–7.
7. J. Collins, *The State in Early Modern France* (Cambridge: Cambridge University Press, 1995), pp. 193–4.
8. R. Muchembled, *Popular Culture and Elite Culture in France, 1400–1750* (Baton Rouge, LA: Louisiana State University Press, 1985), p. 11.
9. Muchembled, *Popular Culture and Elite Culture*, p. 283.
10. S. Fischer, *A History of Reading* (London: Reaktion Books, 2005), p. 256; Blanning, *Culture of Power*, pp. 112–14.
11. T. Blanning, *The Eighteenth Century* (Oxford: Oxford University Press, 2000), p. 4.
12. Blanning, *Triumph of Music*, pp. 18–19.
13. J. Black, *Eighteenth Century Europe, 1700–1789* (Basingstoke: Macmillan, 1990), pp. 254–5.
14. T. Blanning, *The Pursuit of Glory: Europe, 1648–1815* (London: Allen Lane, 2007), p. 476.
15. Black, *Eighteenth Century Europe*, p. 255.
16. Blanning, *Eighteenth Century*, pp. 3–5.
17. Habermas, *Structural Transformation of the Public Sphere*.
18. J. Brewer, *The Pleasures of the Imagination: English Culture in the Eighteenth Century* (London: HarperCollins, 1997), p. xvii; P. Campbell, *Power and Politics in Old Regime France, 1720–45* (London: Routledge, 1996), p. 28; Black, *Eighteenth Century Europe*, pp. 234–9.

19. Brewer, *Pleasures of the Imagination*, pp. xvi–xvii, p. 3.

20. Brewer, *Pleasures of the Imagination*, pp. 34–8.

21. Brewer, *Pleasures of the Imagination*; R. Porter, *Enlightenment: Britain and the Creation of the Modern World* (London: Allen Lane, 2000), pp. 268–70.

22. J. Black, *A Subject for Taste: Culture in Eighteenth-Century England* (Hambledon and London: Palgrave Macmillan, 2005), p. 114.

23. Blanning, *Culture of Power*, p. 12.

24. Black, *Subject for Taste*, p. 114.

25. H. Honour, *Neo-Classicism* (Harmondsworth: Penguin, 1968), pp. 69–72; Black, *Eighteenth Century Europe*, p. 238; M. Levey, *Rococo to Revolution* (London: Thames & Hudson, 1966) p. 141.

26. P. Langford, *A Polite and Commercial People: England, 1727–1783* (Oxford: Oxford University Press, 1989), p. 96.

27. C. Jones, *The Great Nation: France from Louis XV to Napoleon* (London: Allen Lane, 2002), p. xxv.

28. H. Kamen, *European Society, 1500–1700* (London: Hutchinson, 1984), pp. 215–18.

29. R. Darnton, *The Forbidden Best-Sellers of Pre-Revolutionary France* (London: HarperCollins, 1996), pp. 209–10.

30. Fischer, *History of Reading*, pp. 253–4.

31. Beales, 'Religion and Culture', pp. 147–50.

32. J. Black, *Kings, Nobles and Commoners: States and Societies in Early Modern Europe, a Revisionist History* (London: Tauris, 2004), p. 1.

33. B. Harris, *Politics and the Rise of the Press: Britain and France, 1620–1800* (London: Routledge, 1996), p. 106.

34. F. O'Gorman, *The Long Eighteenth Century: British Political and Social History, 1688–1832* (London: Edward Arnold, 1997), p. 128.

35. Jones, *Great Nation*, pp. 180–1.

36. Harris, *Politics and the Rise of the Press*, pp. 53–4.

37. Jones, *Great Nation*, p. xxv, p. 223; J. Black, *The English Press, 1621–1861* (Stroud: Sutton, 2001), pp. 127–40.

38. Harris, *Politics and the Rise of the Press*, pp. 31–4.

39. Jones, *Great Nation*, pp. 181–2.

40. Brewer, *Pleasures of the Imagination*, pp. 92–3.

41. E. Buch, *Beethoven's Ninth* (Chicago, IL: University of Chicago Press, 2003), p. 13.

42. Brewer, *Pleasures of the Imagination*.

43. Blanning, *Triumph of Music*, pp. 30–2.

44. J. Rosenheim, *The Emergence of a Ruling Order: English Landed Society, 1650–1750* (London: Longman, 1998), pp. 200–1.

45. Blanning, *Culture of Power*, pp. 161–82; E. Anderson, *The Letters of Mozart and his Family*, 3rd edn (New York: W. W. Norton, 1985), pp. 870–2.

46. Brewer, *Pleasures of the Imagination*, pp. 92–3.

47. D. Burrows, 'London: Commercial Wealth and Cultural Expansion', in Buelow, *Late Baroque Era*, pp. 355–6.

48. Brewer, *Pleasures of the Imagination*, p. 382.

49. J. Israel, *Radical Enlightenment: Philosophy and the Making of Modernity, 1650–1750* (Oxford: Oxford University Press, 2001), pp. 97–118.

50. Darnton, *Forbidden Best-Sellers*, p. 225.

51. Buelow, *Late Baroque Era*, pp. 11–13.

52. R. Hatton, *George I* (London: Thames & Hudson, 1978), pp. 265–6.

53. Blanning, *Culture of Power*, pp. 179–80.

54. Buelow, *Late Baroque Era*, pp. 14–15.

55. Rosenheim, *Emergence of a Ruling Order*, pp. 200–1.

56. H. Schonberg, *The Lives of the Great Composers*, 3rd edn (London: Abacus, 1998), p. 39.

57. Buelow, *Late Baroque Era*, p.13.

58. Beales, 'Religion and Culture', pp. 141–2.

59. P. Burke, *Popular Culture in Early Modern Europe* (Aldershot: Wildwood House, 1988), pp. 226–7.

60. Blanning, *Culture of Power*, p. 243.

61. J. Lough, *An Introduction to Eighteenth Century France* (London: Longman, 1960), pp. 231–44.

62. W. Speck, *Literature and Society in Eighteenth-Century England: Ideology, Politics and Culture, 1680–1820* (London: Longman, 1998), p. 11.

63. Porter, *Enlightenment*, pp. 276–7; O. Field, *The Kit-Cat Club: Friends Who Imagined a Nation* (London: HarperPress, 2008).

64. Fischer, *History of Reading*, p. 260.

65. Speck, *Literature and Society*, p. 12.

66. W. St Clair, *The Reading Nation in the Romantic Period* (Cambridge: Cambridge University Press, 2004).

67. St Clair, *Reading Nation*, pp. 103–21.

68. St Clair, *Reading Nation*, pp. 88–9.

69. St Clair, *Reading Nation*, pp. 66–73.

70. St Clair, *Reading Nation*, pp. 109–10.

71. St Clair, *Reading Nation*, p. 109.

72. St Clair, *Reading Nation*, pp. 10–11.

73. St Clair, *Reading Nation*, pp. 118–19.

74. Blanning, *Pursuit of Glory*, p. 486.

75. J. Sharpe, *Early Modern England: A Social History, 1550–1760* (London: Edward Arnold, 1987), p. 300.

76. J. Brewer, *Party Ideology and Popular Politics at the Accession of George III* (Cambridge: Cambridge University Press, 1976), pp. 163–200, 267–9; L. Stone (ed.), *An Imperial State at War* (London: Routledge, 1994), p. 3.

77. D. Beales, 'Religion and Culture', in T. Blanning (ed.), *The Eighteenth Century, 1688–1815* (Oxford: Oxford University Press, 2000), pp. 150–1.

78. Darnton, *Forbidden Best-Sellers*, pp. 232–46.

79. D. Jarrett, *Begetters of Revolution* (London: Longman, 1973), pp. 1–2.

80. R. Chartier, *The Cultural Origins of the French Revolution* (Durham, NC: Duke University Press, 1991), pp. 92–135; T. Blanning, *The French Revolution: Aristocrats versus Bourgeois?* (Basingstoke: Macmillan, 1987), p. 28.

81. Beales, 'Religion and Culture', in Blanning, *Eighteenth Century*, p. 154; C. Jones, *The Great Nation: France from Louis XV to Napoleon* (London: Allen Lane, 2002), p. 212.

82. Darnton, *Forbidden Best-Sellers*, p. 107.

83. R. Porter, *Enlightenment: Britain and the Creation of the Modern World* (London: Allen Lane, 2000), pp. 230–1.

84. T. Blanning, *The Pursuit of Glory: Europe, 1648–1815* (London: Allen Lane, 2007), p. 493.

85. J. Shklar, *Montesquieu* (Oxford: Oxford University Press, 1987), pp. 89–90.

86. T. Besterman (ed.), Voltaire to Frederick II, January 1767, in *Voltaire's Correspondence*, ed. T. Besterman, vol. XLIV (Geneva: Institut et Musée Voltaire, 1961), p. 19.

87. D. Lieven, *The Aristocracy in Europe, 1815–1914* (Basingstoke: Macmillan, 1992), p. 1.

88. Jones, *The Great Nation*, pp. 215, 218–19.

89. T. Besterman, *Voltaire* (London: Longman, 1969), p. 236.

90. D. Hume, *Enquiries concerning Human Understanding and concerning the Principles of Morals*, 3rd edn (Oxford: Oxford University Press, 1975),p. 165.

91. J. Clark, *The Language of Liberty, 1660–1832: Political Discourse and Social Dynamics in the Anglo-American World* (Cambridge: Cambridge University Press, 1994), p. 65.

92. T. Blanning, *The French Revolution: Class War or Culture Clash?* 2nd edn (Basingstoke: Macmillan, 1998), p. 21.

93. D. Graham and P. Clarke, *The New Enlightenment: The Rebirth of Liberalism* (Basingstoke: Macmillan, 1986).

94. R. Porter and M. Teich (eds), *The Enlightenment in National Context* (Cambridge: Cambridge University Press, 1981).

95. P. Rietbergen, *Europe: A Cultural History* (London: Routledge, 1998), p. 319.
96. A. Herman, *The Scottish Enlightenment: The Scots' Invention of the Modern World* (London: Fourth Estate, 2001), pp. 184–6.
97. R. Darnton, *The Business of Enlightenment: A Publishing History of the* Encyclopédie (Cambridge, MA: Harvard University Press, 1979), p. 537.
98. P. Blom, *Encyclopédie: The Triumph of Reason in an Unreasonable Age* (London: Fourth Estate, 2004), pp. xiii–xiv.
99. Blom, *Encyclopédie,* pp. 95–8.
100. R. Porter, *Flesh in the Age of Reason* (Harmondsworth: Penguin, 2003), p. 226.
101. Porter, *Flesh in the Age of Reason,* pp. 225–6.
102. M. Cranston, *Philosophers and Pamphleteers* (Oxford: Oxford University Press, 1986).
103. J. Hardman, *The French Revolution: The Fall of the Ancien Régime to the Thermidorian Reaction, 1785–1795* (London: Edward Arnold, 1981), p. 51; W. Doyle, *The Oxford History of the French Revolution* (Oxford: Oxford University Press, 1989), p. 4.
104. Hardman, *The French Revolution,* p. 51.
105. Hardman, *The French Revolution,* p. 59.
106. S. Schama, *Citizens* (London: Viking, 1989), pp. 299–300.
107. T. Blanning, *Joseph II* (London: Longman, 1994), pp. 65, 115–16.

## Conclusion

1. P. Campbell, *Power and Politics in Old Regime France, 1720–1745* (London: Routledge, 1996), pp. 183, 305–14.
2. T. Blanning, *The French Revolution: Class War or Culture Clash?* 2nd edn (Basingstoke: Macmillan, 1998), p. 21.
3. R. Chartier, *The Cultural Origins of the French Revolution* (Durham, NC: Duke University Press, 1991), p. 179.
4. Campbell, *Power and Politics,* pp. 4–5, 302–5.
5. J. Black, *Kings, Nobles and Commoners: States and Societies in Early Modern Europe, a Revisionist History* (London: Tauris, 2004), pp. 42–4.
6. D. Beales, 'Religion and Culture', in T. Blanning (ed.), *The Eighteenth Century, 1688–1815* (Oxford: Oxford University Press, 2000), pp. 156–7.
7. P. Mansel, *The Court of France* (Cambridge: Cambridge University Press, 1988), pp. 3–15; T. Blanning, *The Culture of Power and the Power of Culture* (Oxford: Oxford University Press, 2002), pp. 416–17.

8. D. Beales, *Joseph II: In the Shadow of Maria Theresa, 1741–1780* (Cambridge: Cambridge University Press, 1987), pp. 196–7; T. Blanning, *Joseph II* (London: Longman, 1994), pp. 63–4.

9. Blanning, *Culture of Power*, p. 431.

10. D. Watkin, *A History of Western Architecture* (London: Barrie & Jenkins, 1986), p. 240.

11. J. Fleming, H. Honour and N. Pevsner, *The Penguin Dictionary of Architecture*, 3rd edn (Harmondsworth: Penguin, 1980), pp. 258–9.

12. R. Adam, *Classical Architecture* (London: Viking paperback, 1992), p. 36.

13. J. Summerson, *The Architecture of the Eighteenth Century* (London: Thames & Hudson, 1986), pp. 124–5.

14. S. Schama, *Citizens: A Chronicle of the French Revolution* (London: Viking, 1989), pp. 147–55.

15. R. Gutman, *Mozart: A Cultural Biography* (London: Secker & Warburg, 2000), p. 116.

16. H. Honour, *Neoclassicism* (Harmondsworth: Penguin, 1968), p. 17.

# Bibliography

Ackroyd, P., *Shakespeare: The Biography* (London: Chatto & Windus, 2005).

Adam, R., *Classical Architecture* (London: Viking, 1992).

Adamson, J., *The Noble Revolt: The Overthrow of Charles I* (London: Weidenfeld & Nicolson, 2007).

Adamson, J. (ed.), *The Princely Courts of Europe, 1500–1750* (London: Weidenfeld & Nicolson, 1998).

Anderson, E. (ed.), *The Letters of Mozart and his Family*, 3rd edition (New York: W. W. Norton, 1985).

Anderson, M., *Europe in the Eighteenth Century, 1713–1789*, 4th edition (London: Longman, 2000).

Anderson, M., *Peter the Great* (London: Thames & Hudson, 1978).

Anderson, M., *War and Society in Europe of the Old Regime, 1618–1789* (London: Fontana, 1988).

Antoine, M., *Louis XV* (Paris: Fayard, 1989).

Armitage, D., *The Declaration of Independence: A Global History* (Cambridge, MA: Harvard University Press, 2007).

Armitage, D., 'Greater Britain: a Useful Category of Historical Analysis?' in *Greater Britain, 1516–1776* (Aldershot: Ashgate, 2004).

Armitage, D., *The Ideological Origins of the British Empire* (Cambridge: Cambridge University Press, 2000).

Armitage, D., 'Literature and Empire', in N. Canny (ed.), *The Origins of Empire: British Overseas Enterprise to the Close of the Seventeenth Century* (Oxford: Oxford University Press, 1998).

Armitage, D., 'Making the Empire British: Scotland in the Atlantic World, 1542–1707', in D. Armitage, *Greater Britain, 1516–1776* (Aldershot: Ashgate, 2004).

Asch, R. and H. Duchhardt (eds), *Der Absolutismus – ein Mythos? Strukturwandel monarchischer Herrschaft in West- und Mitteleuropa (ca. 1550–1700)* (Cologne: Böhlau Verlag, 1996).

Aston, T. (ed.), *Crisis in Europe, 1560–1660* (London: Routledge & Kegan Paul, 1965).

Babel, R., 'The Courts of the Wittelsbachs, c. 1500–1750', in J. Adamson, *The Princely Courts of Europe, 1500–1750* (London: Weidenfeld & Nicolson, 1998).

Baker, K., *Inventing the French Revolution* (Cambridge: Cambridge University Press, 1990).

Balen, M., *A Very English Deceit: The Secret History of the South Sea Bubble and First Great Financial Scandal* (London: Fourth Estate, 2002).

Bannister, M., *Condé in Context: Ideological Change in Seventeenth Century France* (Oxford: Oxford University Press, 2000).

Barber, P. (ed.), *The Map Book* (London: Weidenfeld & Nicolson, 2005).

Barnett, S., 'The Prophetic Thought of Sir Isaac Newton, its Origin and Context', in B. Taithe and T. Thornton, *Prophecy* (Stroud: Sutton, 1997).

Bate, J., *The Genius of Shakespeare* (London: Picador, 1997).

Bazin, G., *Baroque and Rococo* (London: Thames & Hudson, 1964).

Beales, D., *Enlightenment and Reform in Eighteenth-Century Europe* (London: Tauris, 2005).

Beales, D., *Joseph II: In the Shadow of Maria Theresa, 1741–1780* (Cambridge: Cambridge University Press, 1987).

Beales, D., *Joseph II: Against the World, 1780–1790* (Cambridge: Cambridge University Press, 2009).

Beales, D., *Prosperity and Plunder: European Catholic Monasteries in the Age of Revolution, 1650–1815* (Cambridge: Cambridge University Press, 2003).

Beales, D., 'Religion and Culture', in T. Blanning (ed.), *The Eighteenth Century, 1688–1815* (Oxford: Oxford University Press, 2000).

Beer, A., *Milton: Poet, Pamphleteer and Patriot* (London: Bloomsbury, 2008).

Behrens, B., *Society, Government and the Enlightenment: The Experiences of Eighteenth-Century France and Prussia* (London: Thames & Hudson, 1985).

Beik, W., *Absolutism and Society in Seventeenth-Century France: State Power and Provincial Aristocracy in Languedoc* (Cambridge: Cambridge University Press, 1985).

Beik, W., 'The Absolutism of Louis XIV as Social Collaboration', *Past and Present*, 188 (2005).

Bell, D., *The Cult of the Nation in France: Inventing Nationalism, 1680–1800* (Cambridge, MA: Harvard University Press, 2003).

Bell, D., 'Culture and Religion', in W. Doyle (ed.), *Old Regime France, 1648–1788* (Oxford: Oxford University Press, 2001).

Beloff, M., *The Age of Absolutism, 1660–1815* (London: Hutchinson, 1954).

Bergin, J., *Crown, Church and Episcopate under Louis XIV* (New Haven, CT: Yale University Press, 2004).

Bergin, J. (ed.), *The Seventeenth Century* (Oxford: Oxford University Press, 2001).

Besterman, T., *Voltaire* (London: Longman, 1969).

Bien, D., 'Offices, Corps and a System of State Credit: the Uses of Privilege under the Ancien Régime', in K. Baker (ed.), *The Political Culture of the Old Régime* (Oxford: Pergamon, 1987).

Bindman, D., *Hogarth* (London: Thames & Hudson, 1981).

Black, J., *The British Abroad: The Grand Tour in the Eighteenth Century* (Stroud: Alan Sutton, 1992).

Black, J., *Convergence or Divergence? Britain and the Continent* (Basingstoke: Macmillan, 1994).

Black, J., *Eighteenth-Century Europe, 1700–1789* (Basingstoke: Macmillan, 1990).

Black, J., *The English Press, 1621–1861* (Stroud: Sutton, 2001).

Black, J., *European Warfare, 1660–1815* (London: UCL Press, 1994).

Black, J., *George II: Puppet of the Politicians?* (Exeter: University of Exeter Press, 2007).

Black, J., *George III: America's Last King* (New Haven, CT: Yale University Press, 2007).

Black, J., *The Hanoverians* (Hambledon and London: Palgrave Macmillan, 2004).

Black, J., *Kings, Nobles and Commoners: States and Societies in Early Modern Europe, a Revisionist History* (London: Tauris, 2004).

Black, J., *Maps and Politics* (London: Reaktion Books, 1997).

Black, J., *A Military Revolution? Military Change and European Society, 1550–1800* (Basingstoke: Macmillan, 1991).

Black, J., *The Politics of Britain, 1688–1800* (Manchester: Manchester University Press, 1993).

Black, J., *A Subject for Taste: Culture in Eighteenth-Century England* (Hambledon and London: Palgrave Macmillan, 2005).

Black, J., and R. Porter (eds), *A Dictionary of Eighteenth-Century World History* (Oxford: Blackwell, 1994).

Blackstone, W., *Commentaries on the Laws of England* (Oxford: Oxford University Press, 1765).

Blanning, T., 'The Commercialization and Sacralization of European Culture in the Nineteenth Century', in Blanning (ed.), *Oxford Illustrated History of Modern Europe* (Oxford: Oxford University Press, 1996).

Blanning, T., *The Culture of Power and the Power of Culture: Old Regime Europe, 1660–1789* (Oxford: Oxford University Press, 2002).

Blanning, T. (ed.), *The Eighteenth Century, 1688–1815* (Oxford: Oxford University Press, 2000).

Blanning, T., *The French Revolution: Aristocrats versus Bourgeois?*, 1st edition (Basingstoke: Macmillan, 1987).

Blanning, T., *The French Revolution: Class War or Culture Clash?*, 2nd edition (Basingstoke: Macmillan, 1998).

Blanning, T., *Joseph II* (London: Longman, 1994).

Blanning, T., *The Pursuit of Glory: Europe, 1648–1815* (London: Allen Lane, 2007).

Blanning, T., *The Triumph of Music: Composers, Musicians and their Audiences, 1700 to the Present* (London: Allen Lane, 2008).

Blom, H., J. Laursen and L. Simonutti, *Monarchisms in the Age of Enlightenment: Liberty, Patriotism and the Common Good* (Toronto: University of Toronto Press, 2007).

Blom, P., *Encyclopédie: The Triumph of Reason in an Unreasonable Age* (London: Fourth Estate, 2004).

Bloom, H., *Shakespeare: The Invention of the Human* (London: Fourth Estate, 1999).

Bluche, F., *Louis XIV* (Oxford: Blackwell, 1990).

Blunt, A., *Art and Architecture in France, 1500–1700* (Harmondsworth: Penguin, 1973).

Blunt, A., *Borromini* (Harmondsworth: Penguin, 1979).

Bobbitt, P., *The Shield of Achilles: War, Peace and the Course of History* (London: Allen Lane, 2002).

Bohanan, D., *Crown and Nobility in Early Modern France* (Basingstoke: Macmillan, 2001).

Bohanan, D., *Old and New Nobility in Aix-en-Provence, 1600–1695: Portrait of an Urban Elite* (Baton Rouge, LA: Louisiana State University Press, 1992).

Bonney, R., *The European Dynastic States, 1494–1660* (Oxford: Oxford University Press, 1991).

Bonney, R., *Political Change in France under Richelieu and Mazarin, 1624–1661* (Oxford: Oxford University Press, 1978).

Braddick, M., *State Formation in Early Modern England, c. 1550–1700* (Cambridge: Cambridge University Press, 2000).

Bragg, M., *The Adventure of English: The Biography of a Language* (London: Hodder & Stoughton, 2003).

Brereton, G., *A Short History of French Literature*, 2nd edition (Harmondsworth: Penguin, 1976).

Brewer, J., *The Pleasures of the Imagination: English Culture in the Eighteenth Century* (London: HarperCollins, 1997).

Brockliss, L., 'The Age of Curiosity', in J. Bergin (ed.), *The Seventeenth Century* (Oxford: Oxford University Press, 2001).

Broers, M., *Europe under Napoleon, 1799–1815* (London: Edward Arnold, 1996).

Brotton, J., *The Sale of the Late King's Goods* (Basingstoke: Palgrave Macmillan, 2006).

Brown, J., and J. Elliott, *A Palace for a King: The Buen Retiro and the Court of Philip IV,* 2nd edition (New Haven, CT: Yale University Press, 2004).

Bucholz, R., *The Augustan Court: Queen Anne and the Decline of Court Culture* (Stanford, CA: Stanford University Press, 1993).

Buck, A., *Dress in Eighteenth-Century England* (London: Batsford, 1979).

Buelow, G., *Music and Society: the Late Baroque Era from the 1680s to 1740* (Englewood Cliffs, NJ: Prentice Hall, 1993).

Burke, P., *The Fabrication of Louis XIV* (New Haven, CT: Yale University Press, 1992).

Burke, P., *Popular Culture in Early Modern Europe* (Aldershot: Wildwood House, 1988).

Burke, P., *The Renaissance* (London: Longman, 1964).

Burke, P., *Tradition and Innovation in Renaissance Italy* (London: Fontana edition, 1974).

Burleigh, M., *Sacred Causes: Religion and Politics from the European Dictators to Al Qaeda* (New York: HarperPress 2006).

Bush, M., *Rich Noble, Poor Noble* (Manchester: Manchester University Press, 1988).

Bush, M., *The English Aristocracy: A Comparative Synthesis* (Manchester: Manchester University Press, 1984).

Bywater, I. (trans.), *Aristotle on the Art of Poetry* (Oxford: Oxford University Press, 1920).

Cairncross, J. (ed.), Introduction to *Racine, Andromache and Other Plays* (Harmondsworth: Penguin, 1967).

Campbell, P., *Louis XIV* (London: Longman, 1993).

Campbell, P., *Power and Politics in Old Regime France, 1720–1745* (London: Routledge, 1996).

Cannadine, D., *The Decline and Fall of the British Aristocracy* (New Haven, CT: Yale University Press, 1990).

Cannon, J., *Samuel Johnson and the Politics of Hanoverian England* (Oxford: Oxford University Press, 1994).

Carsten, F., *The Origins of Prussia* (Oxford: Oxford University Press, 1954).

Chartier, R., *The Cultural Origins of the French Revolution* (Durham, NC: Duke University Press, 1991).

Chesterfield, Lord, *Letters to His Son* (London: Everyman's Library, 1929).

Chrimes, S., *English Constitutional Ideas in the Fifteenth Century* (Cambridge: Cambridge University Press, 1936).

Church, W., *The Greatness of Louis XIV*, 2nd edition (London: Heath, 1972).

Clark, C., *Iron Kingdom: The Rise and Downfall of Prussia, 1600–1947* (London: Allen Lane, 2006).

Clark, J., *English Society, 1660–1832*, 2nd edition (Cambridge: Cambridge University Press, 2000).

Clark, J., *The Language of Liberty, 1660–1832: Political Discourse and Social Dynamics in the Anglo-American World* (Cambridge: Cambridge University Press, 1994).

Clark, J., *Revolution and Rebellion: State and Society in England in the Seventeenth and Eighteenth Centuries* (Cambridge: Cambridge University Press, 1986).

Clark, M., *Modern Italy 1871–1995*, 2nd edition (London: Longman, 1996).

Clifford, J., *Young Samuel Johnson* (London: Heinemann, 1955).

Cohn, N., *The Pursuit of the Millennium: Revolutionary Millenarians and Mystical Anarchists of the Middle Ages*, 3rd edition (St Albans: Paladin, 1970).

Colley, L., *Britons: Forging the Nation, 1707–1837* (New Haven, CT: Yale University Press, 1992).

Collins, J., *The State in Early Modern France* (Cambridge: Cambridge University Press, 1995).

Collins, P., 'Restoration Comedy', in B. Ford (ed.), *The Pelican Guide to English Literature: From Dryden to Johnson* (Harmondsworth: Penguin, 1957).

Conisbee, P., *Painting in Eighteenth-Century France* (London: Phaidon, 1981).

Coward, B., *The Stuart Age* (London: Longman, 1980).

Cragg, G., *The Church and the Age of Reason, 1648–1789* (Harmondsworth: Penguin, 1960).

Cranston, M., *Philosophers and Pamphleteers* (Oxford: Oxford University Press, 1986).

Cruickshank, D., *A Guide to the Georgian Buildings of England and Ireland* (London: Weidenfeld & Nicolson, 1985).

Crystal, D., *The Stories of English* (London: Allen Lane, 2004).

Darnton, R., *The Business of Enlightenment: A Publishing History of the Encyclopédie* (Cambridge, MA: Harvard University Press, 1979).

Darnton, R., *The Forbidden Best-Sellers of Pre-Revolutionary France* (London: HarperCollins, 1996).

Dessert, D., and J. Journet, 'Le lobby Colbert: un royaume ou une affaire de famille?' *Annales, ESC* xxx (1975).

Dewald, J., *Aristocratic Experience and the Origins of Modern Culture: France, 1570–1715* (Berkeley, CA: University of California Press, 1993).

Dewald, J., *The European Nobility, 1400–1800* (Cambridge: Cambridge University Press, 1996).

Dobson, M., and S. Wells (eds), *The Oxford Companion to Shakespeare* (Oxford: Oxford University Press, 2001).

Doyle, W., *The Old European Order, 1660–1800*, 2nd edition (Oxford: Oxford University Press, 1992).

Doyle, W., *The Oxford History of the French Revolution* (Oxford: Oxford University Press, 1989).

Duggan, C., *A Concise History of Italy* (Cambridge: Cambridge University Press, 1994).

Duindam, J., *Myths of Power* (Amsterdam: Amsterdam University Press, 1994).

Duindam, J., *Vienna and Versailles: The Courts of Europe's Dynastic Rivals, 1550–1780* (Cambridge: Cambridge University Press, 2003).

Dyson, A., and J. Lovelock (eds), *Milton: Paradise Lost* (London: Macmillan, 1973).

Elias, N., *The Court Society* (Oxford: Oxford University Press, 1983).

Elias, N., *The History of Manners* (New York: Pantheon Books, 1978).

Elliott, J., 'A Europe of Composite Monarchies', *Past and Present*, 137 (1992).

Elliott, J., *Imperial Spain, 1469–1716* (London: Edward Arnold, 1963).

Elliott, J., 'Philip IV: Prisoner of Ceremony', in A. Dickens (ed.), *The Courts of Europe: Politics, Patronage and Royalty, 1400–1800* (London: Thames & Hudson, 1977).

Elliott, J., 'Power and Propaganda in the Spain of Philip IV', in *Spain and its World, 1500–1700* (London: Yale University Press, 1989).

Elliott, J., *Richelieu and Olivares* (Cambridge: Cambridge University Press, 1984).

Ertman, T., *Birth of the Leviathan: Building States and Regimes in Medieval and Early Modern Europe* (Cambridge: Cambridge University Press, 1997).

Ettlinger, L., 'The Role of the Artist in Society', in A. Cobban (ed.), *The Eighteenth Century: Europe in the Age of Enlightenment* (London: Thames & Hudson, 1969).

Evans, R., *The Making of the Habsburg Monarchy, 1550–1700* (Oxford: Oxford University Press, 1979).

Fara, P., *Newton: The Making of a Genius* (London: Picador, 2003).

Fargher, R., *Life and Letters in France in the 18th Century* (London: Thomas Nelson, 1970).

Ferguson, N., *The War of the World* (London: Allen Lane, 2006).

Field, O., *The Kit-Cat Club: Friends Who Imagined a Nation* (London: HarperPress, 2008).

Finer, S., *Comparative Government* (Harmondsworth: Pelican Books, 1974).

Fischer, S., *A History of Reading* (London: Reaktion Books, 2005).

Fiske, R., 'The Viennese Classical Period', in A. Jacobs (ed.), *Choral Music* (Harmondsworth: Penguin, 1963).

Fleming, J., H. Honour and N. Pevsner, *The Penguin Dictionary of Architecture*, 3rd edition (Harmondsworth: Penguin, 1980).

Franklin, J., 'Sovereignty and the Mixed Constitution: Bodin and his Critics', in J. Burns (ed.), *The Cambridge History of Political Thought, 1450–1700* (Cambridge: Cambridge University Press, 1991).

Furneaux-Jordan, R., *A Concise History of Western Architecture* (London: Thames & Hudson, 1969).

Gaines, J., *Evening in the Palace of Reason: Bach meets Frederick the Great in the Age of Enlightenment* (London: Fourth Estate, 1995).

Gattrell, V., *City of Laughter: Sex and Satire in Eighteenth-Century London* (London: Atlantic Books, 2006).

Girouard, M., *Cities and People* (New Haven, CT: Yale University Press, 1985).

Girouard, M., *Life in the English Country House: A Social and Architectural History* (New Haven, CT: Yale University Press, 1978).

Glover, J., *Mozart's Women* (London: Macmillan, 2005).

Goldgar, A., *Impolite Learning: Conduct and Community in the Republic of Letters, 1680–1750* (New Haven, CT: Yale University Press, 1995).

Gombrich, E., *The Story of Art*, 11th edn (London: Phaidon, 1966).

Graham, D., and P. Clarke, *The New Enlightenment: The Rebirth of Liberalism* (Basingstoke: Macmillan, 1986).

Graham-Dixon, A., *A History of British Art* (London: BBC Books, 1996).

Graves, M., *The Parliaments of Early Modern Europe* (London: Longman, 2001).

Green, I., 'The Development of Monarchies in Western Europe, c. 1500–1800', in R. Butterwick (ed.), *The Polish–Lithuanian Monarchy, c. 1500–1795* (Basingstoke: Macmillan, 2001).

Greengrass, M., (ed.), *Conquest and Coalescence: The Shaping of the State in Early Modern Europe* (London: Edward Arnold, 1991).

Gutman, R., *Mozart: A Cultural Biography* (London: Secker & Warburg, 2000).

Habermas, J., *The Structural Transformation of the Public Sphere: An Enquiry into a Category of Bourgeois Society* (Cambridge, MA: MIT Press, 1989).

Hall, A., *The Revolution in Science, 1500–1750*, 3rd edition (London: Longman, 1983).

Hardman, J., *French Politics, 1774–1789* (London: Longman, 1995).

Hardman, J., *The French Revolution: The Fall of the Ancien Régime to the Thermidorian Reaction, 1785–1795* (London: Edward Arnold, 1981).

Hargreaves-Mawdsley, W., *Spain under the Bourbons, 1700–1833* (London: Macmillan, 1973).

Harris, B., *Politics and the Rise of the Press: Britain and France, 1620–1800* (London: Routledge, 1996).

Harris, T., *Restoration: Charles II and his Kingdoms, 1660–1685* (Harmondsworth: Penguin, 2005).

Hartung, F., *Enlightened Despotism* (London: Historical Association, 1957).

Hastings, A., *The Construction of Nationhood: Ethnicity, Religion and Nationalism* (Cambridge: Cambridge University Press, 1997).

Hatton, R., *George I, Elector and King* (London: Thames & Hudson, 1978).

Hauser, A., *The Social History of Art: Rococo, Classicism and Romanticism*, 2nd edition (London: Routledge, 1962).

Hawking, S. (ed.), *On the Shoulders of Giants: The Great Works of Physics and Astronomy* (Philadelphia, PA: Running Press, 2002).

Hay, D., *The Italian Renaissance in its Historical Background* (Cambridge: Cambridge University Press, 1961).

Hazard, P., *The European Mind, 1680–1715* (Harmondsworth: Pelican, 1964).

Heather, P., *The Fall of the Roman Empire* (London: Macmillan, 2005).

Hempel, B., *Baroque Art and Architecture in Central Europe* (Harmondsworth: Penguin, 1965).

Henry, J., *The Scientific Revolution and the Origins of Modern Science* (London: Macmillan, 1997).

Henshall, N., *The Myth of Absolutism: Change and Continuity in Early Modern European Monarchy* (London: Longman, 1992).

Herman, A., *The Scottish Enlightenment: The Scots' Invention of the Modern World* (London: Fourth Estate, 2001).

Hibbard, H., *Bernini* (Harmondsworth: Pelican, 1965).

Hibbert, C., *The Grand Tour* (London: Thames Methuen, 1987).

Hill, C., *The World Turned Upside Down: Radical Ideas during the English Revolution* (Harmondsworth: Penguin, 1975).

Hitchcock, H., *Rococo Architecture in Southern Germany* (London: Phaidon, 1968).

Hitchings, H., *Dr Johnson's Dictionary* (London: John Murray, 2006).

Hobsbawm, E., *Nations and Nationalism since 1780: Programme, Myth, Reality* (Cambridge: Cambridge University Press, 1990).

Holden, A., *The Penguin Opera Guide* (Harmondsworth: Penguin, 1995).

Hollis, L., *The Phoenix: St Paul's Cathedral and the Men Who Made Modern London* (London: Weidenfeld & Nicolson, 2008).

Holmes, R., *The Age of Wonder: How the Romantic Generation Discovered the Beauty and Terror of Science* (New York: HarperPress, 2008).

Honour, H., *Neo-Classicism* (Harmondsworth: Penguin, 1968).

Hoppit, J. (ed.), *Parliaments, Nations and Identities in Britain and Ireland, 1660–1850* (Manchester: Manchester University Press, 2003).

Howe, S., *Empire: A Very Short Introduction* (Oxford: Oxford University Press, 2002).

Hughes, L., *Russia in the Age of Peter the Great* (New Haven, CT: Yale University Press, 1998).

Hume, D., *Enquiries Concerning Human Understanding and Concerning the Principles of Morals*, 3rd edition (Oxford: Oxford University Press, 1975).

Hume, D., *The History of England from the Invasion of Julius Caesar to the Revolution in 1688* (London: C. Corral, 1809 edition).

Hunt, L., *Politics, Culture and Class in the French Revolution* (Berkeley, CA: University of California Press, 1986).

Hurt, J., *Louis XIV and the Parlements: The Assertion of Royal Authority* (Manchester: Manchester University Press, 2002).

Hutton, R., *The Rise and Fall of Merry England: The Ritual Year, 1400–1700* (Oxford: Oxford University Press, 1994).

Ingrao, C., *The Habsburg Monarchy, 1618–1815* (Cambridge: Cambridge University Press, 1994).

Israel, J., *Radical Enlightenment: Philosophy and the Making of Modernity, 1650–1750* (Oxford: Oxford University Press, 2001).

James, A., *The Origins of French Absolutism, 1598–1661* (Harlow: Pearson, 2006).

Jardine, L., *On a Grander Scale: The Outstanding Career of Sir Christopher Wren* (London: HarperCollins, 2002).

Jarrett, D., *The Begetters of Revolution* (London: Longman, 1973).

Jasanoff, M., *Edge of Empire: Conquest and Collecting in the East, 1750–1850* (London: Fourth Estate, 2005).

Jenkins, S., *England's Thousand Best Houses* (Harmondsworth: Penguin, 2003).

Johnson, A., *Europe in the Sixteenth Century, 1494–1598* (London: Rivingtons, 1900).

Jones, C., *The Great Nation: France from Louis XV to Napoleon* (London: Allen Lane, 2002).

Kamen, H., *European Society, 1500–1700* (London: Hutchinson, 1984).

Kamen, H., *Spain in the Later Seventeenth Century, 1665–1700* (London: Longman, 1980).

Kaufmann, T., *Court, Cloister and City: The Art and Culture of Central Europe, 1450–1800* (London: Weidenfeld & Nicolson, 1995).

Kendall, A., *Vivaldi: His Music, Life and Times* (New York: Granada, 1979).

Kiernan, V., *The Duel in European History: Honour and the Reign of Aristocracy* (Oxford: Oxford University Press, 1989).

Kjaergaard, T., *The Danish Revolution, 1500–1800* (Cambridge: Cambridge University Press, 1994).

Klingensmith, S., *The Utility of Splendour: Ceremony, Social Life and Architecture at the Court of Bavaria, 1600–1800* (Chicago, IL: University of Chicago Press, 1993).

Koegler, H., *The Concise Oxford Dictionary of Ballet,* 2nd edition (Oxford: Oxford University Press, 1982).

Koenigsberger, H., 'Composite States, Representative Institutions and the American Revolution', *British Institute of Historical Research,* 1989.

Koenigsberger, H., 'Republicanism, Monarchism and Liberty', in R. Oresko, G. Gibbs and H. Scott, *Royal and Republican Sovereignty in Early Modern Europe* (Cambridge: Cambridge University Press, 1997).

Kruger, K., 'Regional Representation in Schleswig and Holstein', *Parliaments, Estates and Representation,* 7, no. 1 (1987).

Lammel, G. (ed.), *Daniel Chodowiecki* (Berlin: Eulenspiegel Verlag, 1987).

Langford, P., *A Polite and Commercial People: England, 1727–1783* (Oxford: Oxford University Press, 1989).

Laslett, P., *The World We Have Lost* (London: Methuen, 1965).

Last, B., *Politics and Letters in the Age of Walpole* (Newcastle: Avero, 1987).

Laver, J., *A Concise History of Costume* (London: Thames & Hudson, 1969).

Lederer, V., *Bach's St Matthew Passion* (London: Continuum, 2008).

Lentin, T. (ed.), *Frederick the Great: Letters and Documents* (Milton Keynes: Open University, 1979).

Levack, B., *The Witch-Hunt in Early Modern Europe,* 2nd edition (London: Longman, 1995).

Levey, M., *Giambattista Tiepolo: His Life and Work* (New Haven, CT: Yale University Press, 1986).

Levey, M., *Painting and Sculpture in France, 1700–1789* (New Haven, CT: Yale University Press, 1993).

Levey, M., *Painting in Eighteenth-Century Venice,* 2nd edition (London: Phaidon, 1980).

Levey, M., *Rococo to Revolution: Major Trends in Eighteenth-Century Painting* (London: Thames & Hudson, 1967).

Lieven, D., *The Aristocracy in Europe, 1815–1914* (Basingstoke: Macmillan, 1992).

Lord Chesterfield, *Letters to His Son* (London: Everyman's Library, 1929).

Llewellyn, N., 'The World of the Baroque Artist', in *Baroque, 1620–1800: Style in the Age of Magnificence,* Exhibition Catalogue (London: Victoria and Albert Museum, 2009).

Lonsdale, R. (ed.), *Dryden to Johnson* (London: Sphere, 1971).

Lough, J., *An Introduction to Seventeenth-Century France* (London: Longman, 1954).

Lough, J., *An Introduction to Eighteenth-Century France* (London: Longman, 1960).

MacCulloch, D., *Reformation: Europe's House Divided, 1490–1700* (Harmondsworth: Penguin, 2003).

Maland, D., *Culture and Society in Seventeenth-Century France* (London: Batsford, 1970).

Mandrou, R., 'Le Baroque européen: mentalité pathétique et révolution sociale', *Annales*, xv (1960).

Mann, W., *The Operas of Mozart* (London: Cassell, 1977).

Mansel, P., *The Court of France* (Cambridge: Cambridge University Press, 1988).

Mansel, P., *Louis VIII* (London: John Murray, 1981).

Mansel, P., *Pillars of Monarchy* (New York: Quartet, 1984).

Maravall, J., *Culture of the Baroque: Analysis of a Historical Structure* (Minneapolis: Minnesota University Press, 1986).

Marly, D. de, *Fashion for Men* (London: Batsford, 1989).

Mason, J., *The Indispensable Rousseau* (New York: Quartet, 1979).

Maxwell, K., *Pombal: Paradox of the Enlightenment* (Cambridge: Cambridge University Press, 1995).

Merriman, R., *Six Contemporaneous Revolutions* (Oxford: Oxford University Press, 1938).

Mettam, R., *Government and Society in Louis XIV's France* (London: Macmillan, 1977).

Mettam, R., *Power and Faction in Louis XIV's France* (Oxford: Blackwell, 1988).

Meyer, J., *L'Éducation des princes en Europe du XVe au XIXe siècle* (Paris: Perrin, 2004).

Miller, J., *Absolutism in Seventeenth-Century Europe* (Basingstoke: Macmillan, 1990).

Morrice, R., *Stuart and Baroque* (London: Barrie & Jenkins, 1982).

Mortlock, D., *Aristocratic Splendour: Money and the World of Thomas Coke, Earl of Leicester* (Stroud: Sutton, 2007).

Motley, M., *Becoming a French Aristocrat: The Education of the Court Nobility, 1580–1715* (Princeton, NJ: Princeton University Press, 1990).

Mowl, T., and B. Earnshaw, *An Insular Rococo: Architecture, Politics and Society in Ireland and England, 1710–1770* (London: Reaktion Books, 1999).

Mowl, T., and B. Earnshaw, *John Wood: Architect of Obsession* (Bath: Millstream, 1988).

Muchembled, R., *Popular Culture and Elite Culture in France, 1400–1750* (Baton Rouge, LA: Louisiana State University Press, 1985).

Mukerji, C., *Territorial Ambitions and the Gardens of Versailles* (Cambridge: Cambridge University Press, 1997).

Mumford, L., *The City in History* (London: Secker & Warburg, 1961).

Munck, T., 'The Danish Reformers', in H. Scott, *Enlightened Absolutism: Reform and Reformers in Later Eighteenth-Century Europe* (Basingstoke: Macmillan, 1990).

Munck, T., *Seventeenth Century Europe, 1598–1700* (Basingstoke: Macmillan, 1990).

Nash, R., 'The Economy', in J. Bergin (ed.), *The Seventeenth Century* (Oxford: Oxford University Press, 2001).

Neville, D., 'Metastasio and Court Studies', *The Court Historian*, vol. 1, no. 3 (October 1996).

Newman, G., *The Rise of English Nationalism: A Cultural History, 1740–1830*, revised edition (Basingstoke: Macmillan, 1997).

Newman, W., *The Sonata in the Baroque Era* (Wilmington, NC: University of North Carolina Press, 1966).

Nokes, D., *Raillery and Rage: A Study of Eighteenth Century Satire* (Brighton: Harvester Press, 1987).

O'Gorman, F., *The Long Eighteenth Century: British Political and Social History, 1688–1832* (London: Edward Arnold, 1997).

Okey, R., *Eastern Europe, 1740–1980: Feudalism to Communism* (London: Hutchinson, 1982).

Oresko, R., G. Gibbs and H. Scott (eds), *Royal and Republican Sovereignty in Early Modern Europe* (Cambridge: Cambridge University Press, 1997).

Osborne, H. (ed.), *The Oxford Companion to Art* (Oxford: Oxford University Press, 1970).

Outram, D., *The Enlightenment* (Cambridge: Cambridge University Press, 1995).

Ozouf, M., *La fête révolutionnaire, 1789–1799* (Paris: Gallimard, 1976).

Pagden, A., 'Europe and the Wider World', in J. Bergin (ed.), *The Seventeenth Century* (Oxford: Oxford University Press, 2001).

Palladio, A., *The Four Books of Architecture* (New York: Dover edition, 1965).

Palmer, P. and R. More, *The Sources of the Faust Tradition from Simon Magus to Lessing* (Oxford: Oxford University Press, 1936).

Parker, D., *Class and State in Ancien Régime France: The Road to Modernity?* (London: Routledge, 1996).

Parker, G., *Europe in Crisis, 1598–1648*, 2nd edition (Oxford: Blackwell, 2001).

Parrott, D., 'War and International Relations', in J. Bergin (ed.), *The Seventeenth Century* (Oxford: Oxford University Press, 2001).

Penny, N., *Reynolds*, Exhibition Catalogue (London: Royal Academy of Arts, 1986).

Perkin, H., *The Origins of Modern English Society, 1780–1880* (London: Routledge, 1969).

Pevsner, N., *An Outline of European Architecture*, 7th edition (Harmondsworth: Penguin, 1963).

Picard, L., *Dr Johnson's London* (London: Phoenix, 2000).

Picard, L., *Restoration London* (London: Phoenix, 1998).

Plumb, J., *The Growth of Political Stability in England, 1675–1725* (London: Macmillan, 1967).

Pointon, M., *Hanging the Head: Portraiture and Social Formation in Eighteenth-Century England* (New Haven, CT: Yale University Press, 1993).

Porter, B., *War and the Rise of the State: The Military Foundations of Modern Politics* (New York: Free Press, 1994).

Porter, R., *The Greatest Benefit to Mankind: A Medical History of Humanity from Antiquity to the Present* (London: HarperCollins, 1997).

Porter, R., *Enlightenment: Britain and the Creation of the Modern World* (London: Allen Lane, 2000).

Porter, R., *Flesh in the Age of Reason* (Harmondsworth: Penguin, 2003).

Porter, R. and M. Teich (eds), *The Enlightenment in National Context* (Cambridge: Cambridge University Press, 1981).

Posner, D., *Antoine Watteau* (London: Weidenfeld & Nicolson, 1984).

Potter, D., *A History of France, 1460–1560: The Emergence of a Nation State* (Basingstoke: Macmillan, 1995).

Rabb, T., *The Struggle for Stability in Early Modern Europe* (Oxford: Oxford University Press, 1975).

Ranum, O., *Paris in the Age of Absolutism* (Bloomington, IN: Indiana University Press, 1968).

Redwood, J., *Reason, Ridicule and Religion: The Age of Enlightenment in England, 1660–1750* (London: Thames & Hudson, 1976).

Reinhard, W. (ed.), *Power Elites and State Building* (Oxford: Oxford University Press, 1996).

Reynolds, J., *Discourses on Art* (New Haven, CT: Yale University Press, 1975).

Ribeiro, A., *Dress in Eighteenth Century Europe, 1715–1789* (London: Batsford, 1984).

Richardson, T., *The Arcadian Friends: Inventing the English Landscape Garden* (London: Bantam Press, 2007).

Ricks, C., *Milton's Grand Style* (Oxford: Oxford University Press, 1963).

Ridder-Symoens, H. de, 'Training and Professionalization', in W. Reinhard, *Power Elites and State Building* (Oxford: Oxford University Press, 1996).

Rietbergen, P., *Europe: A Cultural History* (London: Routledge, 1998).

Riley, J., *The Seven Years War and the Old Regime in France: The Financial and Economic Toll* (Princeton, NJ: Princeton University Press, 1986).

Robb, G., *The Discovery of France* (London: Picador, 2007).

Robbins Landon, H. (ed.), *Haydn: Chronicle and Works*, 5 vols, vol. 1: *The Early Years, 1732–65* (Bloomington, IN: Indiana University Press, 1976–80).

Robbins Landon, H., *Vivaldi: Voice of the Baroque* (London: Thames & Hudson, 1993).

Roberts, M., *Gustavus Adolphus: A History of Sweden, 1611–1632*, 2 vols (Harlow: Longman, 1953 and 1958).

Robertson, J., *A Union for Empire: Political Thought and the Union of 1707* (Cambridge: Cambridge University Press, 1995).

Rodger, N., *The Wooden World: An Anatomy of the Georgian Navy* (London: Collins, 1986).

Rosenheim, J., *The Emergence of a Ruling Order: English Landed Society, 1650–1750* (London: Longman, 1998).

Rowlands, G., *The Dynastic State and the Army under Louis XIV* (Cambridge: Cambridge University Press, 2002).

Russell, C., 'Composite Monarchies in Early-modern Europe: the British and Irish Example', in A. Grant and K. Stringer (eds), *Uniting the Kingdom? The Making of British History* (London: Routledge, 1995).

Sabine, G., *A History of Political Theory*, 3rd edition (London: Harrap, 1963).

Sadie, S. (ed.), *The Grove Concise Dictionary of Music* (London: Macmillan, 1988).

Salvadori, P., *La chasse sous l'ancien régime* (Paris: Fayard, 1997).

Sassoon, D., *The Culture of the Europeans from 1800 to the Present* (London: HarperCollins, 2006).

Schalk, E., *From Valor to Pedigree: Ideas of Nobility in France in the Sixteenth and Seventeenth Centuries* (Princeton, NJ: Princeton University Press, 1986).

Schama, S., *The Embarrassment of Riches: An Interpretation of Dutch Culture in the Golden Age* (London: Collins, 1987).

Schama, S., *Citizens: A Chronicle of the French Revolution* (London: Viking, 1989).

Schama, S., *Landscape and Memory* (London: HarperCollins, 1995).

Schama, S., *Rembrandt's Eyes* (Harmondsworth: Penguin Press, 1999).

Schevill, W., *The Great Elector* (Hamden, CT: Archon, 1947).

Schonberg, H., *The Lives of the Great Composers*, 3rd edition (London: Abacus, 1998).

Scott, H., 'Diplomatic Culture in Old Regime Europe', in H. Scott and B. Simms (eds), *Cultures of Power in Europe during the Long Eighteenth Century* (Cambridge: Cambridge University Press, 2007).

Scott, H., *The European Nobilities in the Seventeenth and Eighteenth Centuries*, vol. 1: *Western Europe* (London: Longman, 1995).

Scott, H., *The European Nobilities in the Seventeenth and Eighteenth Centuries*, vol. 2: *Northern, Central and Eastern Europe* (London: Longman, 1995).

Scott, H., and B. Simms (eds), *Cultures of Power in Europe during the Long Eighteenth Century* (Cambridge: Cambridge University Press, 2007).

Scribner, R., *For the Sake of Simple Folk: Popular Propaganda for the German Reformation* (Oxford: Oxford University Press, 1981).

Sella, D., *Italy in the Seventeenth Century* (London: Longman, 1997).

Shapin, S., 'A Scholar and a Gentleman: the Problematic Identity of the Scientific Practitioner in Early-modern England', *History of Science*, 29, part 3, no. 85 (Sept. 1991).

Shapin, S. and S. Schaffer, *Leviathan and the Air Pump: Hobbes, Boyle and the Experimental Life* (Princeton, NJ: Princeton University Press, 1985).

Sharpe, J., *Early Modern England: A Social History, 1550–1760* (London: Edward Arnold, 1987).

Shawe-Taylor, D., *The Georgians: Eighteenth-Century Portraiture and Society* (London: Barrie & Jenkins, 1990).

Shennan, J., *Liberty and Order in Early Modern Europe: The Subject and the State, 1650–1800* (London: Longman, 1986).

Shennan, J., *The Origins of the Modern European State, 1450–1725* (London: Hutchinson, 1974).

Shennan, J., *The Parlement of Paris*, revised edition (Stroud: Sutton, 1998).

Shennan, J., *Philippe Duke of Orleans: Regent of France, 1715–1723* (London: Thames & Hudson, 1979).

Shklar, J., *Montesquieu* (Oxford: Oxford University Press, 1987).

Sisman, A., *Wordsworth and Coleridge: The Friendship* (London: Harper, 2006).

Sitwell, S., *The Hunters and the Hunted* (London: Macmillan, 1947).

Smith, D., 'The Idea of the Rule of Law in England and France in the Seventeenth Century', in R. Asch and H. Duchhardt, *Der Absolutismus – ein Mythos? Strukturwandel monarchischer Herrschaft in West- und Mitteleuropa (ca. 1550–1700)* (Cologne: Böhlau Verlag, 1996).

Smith, H., *Georgian Monarchy: Politics and Culture, 1714–1760* (Cambridge: Cambridge University Press, 2006).

Smith, J., *The Culture of Merit: Nobility, Royal Service and the Making of Absolute Monarchy in France, 1600–1789* (Ann Arbor, MI: University of Michigan Press, 1996).

Solomon, M., *Mozart* (London: Hutchinson, 1995).

Somerset, A., *The Affair of the Poisons: Murder, Infanticide and Satanism at the Court of Louis XIV* (London: Weidenfeld & Nicolson 2003).

Speck, W., *Literature and Society in Eighteenth-Century England: Ideology, Politics and Culture, 1680–1820* (London: Longman, 1998).

Spellman, W., *John Locke* (Basingstoke: Macmillan, 1997).

St Clair, W., *The Reading Nation in the Romantic Period* (Cambridge: Cambridge University Press, 2004).

Stafford, M. (ed.), *Private Vices, Public Benefits? The Contemporary Reception of Bernard Mandeville* (Solihull: Ismeron, 1997).

Steensgaard, N., 'The Seventeenth-Century Crisis', in G. Parker and L. Smith (eds), *The General Crisis of the Seventeenth Century* (London: Routledge, 1997).

Steinmetz, A., *The Romance of Duelling in All Times and Countries* (London: Chapman & Hall, 1868).

Stone, L. (ed.), *An Imperial State at War* (London: Routledge, 1994).

Stone, L. and J. Stone, *An Open Elite? England, 1540–1880* (Oxford: Oxford University Press, 1986 edition).

Storrs, C. and H. Scott, 'The Military Revolution and the European Nobility, c. 1600–1800', *War in History* (1996).

Strong, R., *The Spirit of Britain: A Narrative History of the Arts* (London: Pimlico, 2000).

Strong, R., *Feast: A History of Grand Eating* (London: Jonathan Cape, 2002).

Sturdy, D., *Louis XIV* (Basingstoke: Macmillan, 1998).

Styles, J., *The Dress of the People: Everyday Fashion in 18th-Century England* (New Haven, CT: Yale University Press, 2008).

Summerson, J., *Architecture in Britain, 1530–1830*, 6th edition (Harmondsworth: Pelican, 1977).

Summerson, J., *The Architecture of the Eighteenth Century* (London: Thames & Hudson, 1986).

Swann, J., 'Politics and the State in Eighteenth-century Europe', in T. Blanning, *The Eighteenth Century: Europe, 1688–1815* (Oxford: Oxford University Press, 2000).

Swann, J., *Provincial Power and Absolute Monarchy: The Estates of Burgundy, 1661–1790* (Cambridge: Cambridge University Press, 2003).

Swann, J., 'Silence, Respect, Obedience: Political Culture in Louis XV's France', in H. Scott and B. Simms (eds), *Cultures of Power in Europe during the Long Eighteenth Century* (Cambridge: Cambridge University Press, 2007).

Symcox, G., 'From Commune to Capital: the Transformation of Turin, Sixteenth to Eighteenth Centuries', in R. Oresko, G. Gibbs and H. Scott (eds), *Royal and Republican Sovereignty in Early Modern Europe* (Cambridge: Cambridge University Press, 1997).

Symcox, G., *Victor Amadeus II: Absolutism in the Savoyard State, 1675–1730* (London: Thames & Hudson, 1983).

Tallett, F., *War and Society in Early Modern Europe* (London: Routledge, 1992).

Thomas, K., *Man and the Natural World: Changing Attitudes in England, 1500–1800* (Harmondsworth: Penguin, 1984).

Thompson, A., 'The Confessional Dimension', in B. Simms and T. Riotte (eds), *The Hanoverian Dimension in British History, 1714–1837* (Cambridge: Cambridge University Press, 2007).

Thornton, T., 'Local Equity Jurisdictions in the Territories of the English Crown: the Palatinate of Chester, 1450–1540', in D. Dunn (ed.), *Courts, Counties and the Capital in the Later Middle Ages* (Stroud: Sutton, 1996).

Tillyard, S., *A Royal Affair: George III and his Troublesome Siblings* (London: Chatto & Windus, 2006).

Toman, R. (ed.), *Baroque: Architecture, Sculpture, Painting* (Cologne: Könemann, 1998).

Tombs, R., *France 1814–1914* (London: Longman, 1996).

Trevor-Roper, H., *The Invention of Scotland: Myth and History* (New Haven, CT: Yale University Press, 2008).

Ubeda de los Cobos, A., *Paintings for the Planet King: Philip IV and the Buen Retiro Palace* (London: Paul Holberton, 2005).

Uglow, J., *Hogarth: A Life and a World* (London: Faber & Faber, 1997).

Umbach, M., 'Culture and *Bürgerlichkeit* in Eighteenth-century Germany', in H. Scott and B. Simms (eds), *Cultures of Power in Europe during the Long Eighteenth Century* (Cambridge: Cambridge University Press, 2007).

Upton, A., 'Politics', in J. Bergin (ed.), *The Seventeenth Century* (Oxford: Oxford University Press, 2001).

Vann, J., *The Making of a State: Württemberg, 1593–1793* (Ithaca, NY: Cornell University Press, 1984).

Walters, J., *The Royal Griffin: Frederick Prince of Wales, 1707–51* (London: Jarrolds, 1973).

Watanabe-O'Kelly, H., *Court Culture in Dresden: From Renaissance to Baroque* (Basingstoke: Palgrave Macmillan, 2002).

Watkin, D., *A History of Western Architecture* (London: Barrie & Jenkins, 1986).

Watt, I., *The Rise of the Novel*, 2nd edition (Berkeley, CA: University of California Press, 2001).

Weber, E., *Peasants into Frenchmen: The Modernization of Rural France* (Stanford, CA: Stanford University Press, 1976).

Wells, S., *Shakespeare: For All Time* (Basingstoke: Palgrave Macmillan, 2002).

White, M., *Newton: The Last Sorcerer* (London: Fourth Estate, 1997).

Wilkinson, R., *Louis XIV* (London: Routledge, 2007).

Wilson, P., *Absolutism in Central Europe* (London: Routledge, 2000).

Winn, J., *John Dryden and his World* (New Haven, CT: Yale University Press, 1987).

Wrightson, K., *English Society, 1580–1680* (London: Hutchinson, 1982).

Yarwood, D., *The Architecture of Europe* (London: Batsford, 1974).

Yates, F., *Astraea: The Imperial Theme in the Sixteenth Century* (Harmondsworth: Peregrine, 1977).

Yates, F., *The Rosicrucian Enlightenment*, 2nd edition (St Albans: Paladin, 1975).

Yolton, J., (ed.), *The Blackwell Companion to the Enlightenment* (Oxford: Blackwell, 1991).

Zagorin, P., *Rebels and Rulers, 1500–1660*, vol. 1: *Society, States and Early-modern Revolution* (Cambridge: Cambridge University Press, 1982).

Zaslaw, N., *The Classical Era: From the 1740s to the End of the Eighteenth Century* (Englewood Cliffs, NJ: Prentice Hall, 1989).

# Index

abbeys 113, 158–9
absolute monarchy/monarchs 8–9,
  16, 23, 44, 87–8, 89, 96, 98,
  107–8
  achievements 98
  aim of 216
  attempt to control opinion 115–16
  and consent 10, 107–8, 214
  consulting by 5, 6–7, 12, 15, 16,
    18, 85, 87–9, 214, 217
  definition and characteristics
    6, 87
  distinction between despotic
    monarchy and 6–7, 87
  and Enlightenment 214
  and executions 126
  reasons for increased grip of 98
  zenith of 26–7
'absolutism' 7, 18, 96, 100–1,
  107, 121, 164 *see also* despotic
  'absolutism'
*Académie Française* 54, 133
*Académie Royale des Sciences
  et Belles-Lettres* 131
academies 77–8, 134
Academy of Dancing 189
Academy of Experiments
  (Florence) 77
Academy of Sciences 77, 93
Act of Succession (1701) 163
Addison, Joseph 132
adultery 112

afterlife 211
Aikenhead, Thomas 115
Aix-en-Provence University 64
Albinoni 179
alchemy 75, 80
Algarotti
  *Newton for the Ladies* 109, 112
  *Allgemeine Musikalische Zeitung*
    (periodical) 192
Amadeus, Victor 122
Anne, Queen 76, 82, 83
anti-revisionism 97–8
architects 74–5
architecture 59, 144–65
  and arts 2
  baroque 127, 130, 146–8,
    149–50, 151
  church building 157–9
  classical 147–8, 220
  Gothic 148
  neo-classical 43, 147,
    150, 220
  order in 146–7, 161
  palace-building *see* palaces
  Palladian 123, 147, 148
  as a political player 156–7,
    164–5
  rococo 150–1
aristocracy 4, 28, 56–7, 58, 61, 130,
  142
Aristotle 76, 81, 83
  *Poetics* 137

287